Dedicated to

William Tyndale

The Father of the English Bible
The Ultimate Rebel

c. 1494 – 1536

For there is one God, one mediator also between God and men, the man Christ Jesus.

1 Timothy 2:5
REVISED VERSION (1901)

THE UNREDACTED TYNDALE BIBLE
// THE TYNDALE RECOVERY COLLECTION

The Case for the Sacred Record
A systematic recovery of the 83.7% Source Code

Volume I: THE PRIMEVAL RECORD
Old Testament: The Torah

Volume II: THE COVENANT HISTORY
Old Testament: The Histories

Volume III-A: THE PROPHETIC TESTIMONY
Old Testament: The Major Prophets

Volume III-B: THE PROPHETIC TESTIMONY
Old Testament: The Minor Prophets

Volume IV-A: ONE MEDIATOR
The Unredacted Tyndale Gospels
New Testament: Matthew – John

Volume IV-B: THE APOSTOLIC WITNESS
New Testament: Acts – Revelation

Restoring 500 Years of Suppressed Truth

A Declaration of Independence of Conscience

Reclaiming the Sovereign Jurisdiction of the Individual Soul

WHEREAS, in 380 AD, Roman Emperor *Theodosius I* seized control of the human mind, criminalized Apostolic Monotheism, and established a State-Mandated Monopoly on Truth;

AND WHEREAS, for sixteen centuries, this *Imperial Filter* has obscured the Sacred Record and silenced the dissenting voice through the machinery of ecclesiastical power;

AND WHEREAS, the American Restoration of 1776 provided the first Constitutional Shield capable of protecting the individual search for the Creator;

NOW, THEREFORE, be it known that *The Unredacted Tyndale Bible* is published as a formal act of **FORENSIC RESTORATION**.

WE HEREBY DECLARE the Imperial Filter is broken. We return the definition of God to the words of Jesus Christ and the interpretation of the Record to the jurisdiction of the individual seeker.

UNDER THE SHIELD of the First Amendment, and in the Quincentenary Year of the Tyndale Legacy, we present this recovery to the Free People of the World.

Study Bible

THE UNREDACTED TYNDALE BIBLE

(Formerly known as the "Authorized Version")

The Unredacted Tyndale Bible is based on William Tyndale's English translation, with revisions from the American Revision Committee's 1901 Revised Version (RV) 'Standard American Edition'. 2026 Updates replace 'Jehovah' with 'Yahweh' only.

CASE STATUS: RESTORED
CORRECTING 490 YEARS OF ROYAL PLAGIARISM

A FORENSIC RECOVERY OF THE SACRED RECORD
Restoring the 83.7% Source Code to the Public Record
and the Name YAHWEH to 6,837 Original Coordinates

ONE MEDIATOR
New Testament Gospels
Matthew – John

VOL. IV-A

A NOTE ON THE TEXT AND TITLE

THE TITLE: The present volume bears the title *The Unredacted Tyndale Bible* to honor the primary architect of the English Bible and the true author of the majority of this text. Computer analysis by scholars (Jon Nielson and Royal Skousen) has confirmed that **83.7%** of the New Testament in the King James Version—and by extension, the literal successor, the 1901 Revised Version—is the work of William Tyndale.

THE TEXT: The Scripture text contained herein is the **Revised Version (Standard American Edition), 1901**. The Editors selected the 1901 text for three forensic reasons:

1. **The Crown's Admission**: In the Revised Version (1881/1885) Preface to the work, the Committee finally admitted what the Crown had hidden for centuries: *"The foundation was laid by William Tyndale. His translation of the New Testament was the true primary version."*
2. **The Pronouns**: The Revised Version (1901) by the American Revision Committee, the volume you're holding, is the final revision of the "Authorized" legacy to retain the grammatical precision of the Second Person Pronouns (*Thou, Thee, Ye, You*).
3. **The Literal Standard**: The 1901 text remains the most literal word-for-word revision of the Tyndale–King James tradition, prioritizing accuracy over modern paraphrasing.

The Monarchy seized William Tyndale's work, adopted his structure, and retained the martyr's words—while erasing Tyndale's name. The Unredacted Tyndale Bible corrects the 490-year omission by putting Tyndale back, *front and center*.

THE UNREDACTED TYNDALE BIBLE
Translation:
William Tyndale
American Revision Committee
General Editor:
John W.T. Rogers
Published by **One God Publishing**
Klamath Falls, Oregon
johnwtrogers@gmail.com

Translation Credit: The Scripture text contained herein is the *Revised Version, Standard American Edition* (1901), originally translated by William Tyndale (1526) and revised by the American Revision Committee (1901). The text resides in the public domain in the United States.

Copyright © 2026 by One God Publishing.
General Editor: John W.T. Rogers.
All rights reserved regarding the study notes, cross-references, intro/outro essays, and additional original content. No part of the copyrighted material in this publication may be reproduced, distributed, or transmitted in any form or by any means, including photocopying, recording, or other electronic or mechanical methods, without the prior written permission of the publisher, except in the case of brief quotations embodied in critical reviews and certain other noncommercial uses permitted by copyright law.

ISBN 978-1-971691-03-9 (Hardcover – Giant Print Edition)
ISBN 978-1-971691-02-2 (Paperback – Large Print Edition)
Cover design by One God Publishing
Interior design by One God Publishing
Printed in the United States of America
First Edition: February 2026
10 9 8 7 6 5 4 3 2 1
1526–2026 · 500th Anniversary Tyndale Restoration

This study Bible is intended for educational and inspirational purposes. The interpretations and notes are the opinions of the General Editor and do not represent any official doctrinal position unless otherwise stated.

FORENSIC MISSION STATEMENT

[CLASSIFIED: FOR JUROR EYES ONLY]
INVESTIGATIVE PROTOCOL: RECOVERY

SUBJECT: EXPECTATION MANAGEMENT

Most Bibles comfort. This volume empowers you with the RAW TRUTH.

Treat this as an INVESTIGATIVE DOSSIER. Treat the text as a COLD CASE.

BACKGROUND: For 1,600 years, State Clergy tampered with the "Chain of Custody"—adding words, erasing names, and enforcing doctrine by the sword.

CASE STATUS: REOPENED.

The History Restoring edition operates on three protocols:

EXH 1: THE UNREDACTED AUTHOR
<u>William Tyndale</u> returns to the title deed. He bought 83.7% of this text with his blood.

EXH 2: THE UNREDACTED NAME
Generic titles vanish. The Father's personal name, <u>YAHWEH</u>, returns to its 6,837 original coordinates.

EXH 3: THE UNREDACTED THEOLOGY
4th Century "Legislated Theology" is removed. The <u>One God</u> stands exactly as the Apostles left Him.

SUBJECT: JUROR RESPONSIBILITY

Standard Bibles: Editor = Teacher. Reader = Student.

HERE: EDITOR = PROSECUTOR. READER = JURY.

We present primary evidence. We demand verification.

- ☐ Question the notes.
- ☐ Check the references.
- ☐ Follow the money.

*"History records not merely what happened.
History records what survived the burning."*

Translator's Preface to
The Unredacted Tyndale Bible

> ### THE FORENSIC MANDATE
>
> **fo-ren-sic** (*adj.*) From Latin *forensis*, "in open court."
>
> - **The Opposite of Tyranny:** Dictators dictate truth in secret; free men debate truth in the open forum.
> - **The Method of Liberty:** The application of rigorous investigation to uncover tampering and restore the "Chain of Custody."
>
> *This Edition is a Forensic Study, rejecting the Decrees of 380 AD in favor of the Testimony of the Apostles.*

So WHO is the *one and only true* **God** of our *Bible*?

The argument has been debated since Early Christianity.

1600 years of human history reveals a dark and sobering story behind the *meaning of God* and the interpretation of God's Holy Word:

- Imperial Mandates by Emperors
- Forced conformity to the State and Church
- Suppression of individual conscience and choice
- Years of pre-study to get a license, issued by a bishop, to read the Bible
- **Execution** for "heresy" from *wrong belief*, even for printing an **English Bible!**

The Apostle John explained the root of this tyranny:

"We know that we are of God, and the whole world *lieth in* the evil one." — **1 John 5:19** (*RV - Greek keimai (κεῖμαι) G2749*)

Inside these pages, you'll discover a shocking history of the church and the Bible—the raw truth hidden from you during your years in the pews.

Knowing the history told in *The Unredacted Tyndale Bible* will enlighten you.

PROMISE.

Your new knowledge will make studying your Bible an adventure.

Prepare yourself. You're encouraged to wrestle with what you read.

Hang in there. **Keep wrestling!**

Any unease will eventually transition to the joy of "owning" your own theology (not others) with a fresh understanding, never realized ever before.

Let's start with a bit of Bible translation history...

The Blood on the Page

It was an outlawed book. A text so dangerous "it could only be countered by the most vicious burnings, of books and men and women."

But what book could incite such violence and bloodshed?

The year is 1526—the age of the tyrannical reign of King Henry VIII (1509-1547), who brutally executed 57,000-72,000 of his own English "subjects" (citizens) for "heresy", "treason", and denying his supremacy as head of the Church of England. The times are treacherous. The Church controls every aspect of English life, including access to the very Word of God. The hierarchy will stop at nothing to keep it that way.

Into this darkness steps William Tyndale.

A gifted, courageous "heretic" who dared translate the Word of God into English. He worked in secret, in exile, in peril, always on the move. Neither England nor the English language would ever be the same again.

History hands King James I the credit for the "majesty" of *the English Bible*. **But history is wrong.**

Scholarly analysis proves the vast majority of the classic New Testament—**at least 83.7% of every word**—is the direct work of William Tyndale. But Tyndale did not write in a palace; he wrote in the hollows of the earth, his ink thinned by tears and his parchment stained by the sweat of a hunted animal.

83.7% of the New Testament was bought with his heartbeat.

Imagine the crushing silence of 1523. A young scholar kneels before Bishop Tunstall, his heart a furnace of hope, pleading only to translate the Word so that a plowboy might finally understand

God's voice. He was met not with grace, but with a snarl. Under the weight of laws that transformed the Holy Scriptures into a death warrant, Tyndale became a man without a country—an exile for the sake of the Light.

He fled into the winter of Germany, a ghost in the shadows.

In 1525, as the first pages finally breathed life in Cologne, the Judas-whisper of a spy named Cochlaeus brought the authorities crashing down. Picture Tyndale in the frantic dark, grabbing ten ink-wet sheets and vanishing into the night, clutching those fragments of Gospel like a father desperately pulling his only child from a house on fire.

The sheer, suffocating ache of the flight: holding the hope of a nation in trembling hands while the world hunts you for it.

By 1526, his words reached England, only to be met by a spectacle of hatred. At St. Paul's Cross, Bishop Tunstall cast the New Testaments into a towering pyre. Can you hear the roar of the flames? Can you see the ashes of the Word of God drifting over the weeping poor?

The Church sought to drown the truth in smoke, unwittingly using their gold to fund Tyndale's next edition. It is a hollow, bitter irony: the oppressors' silver sharpened the very sword that would eventually cut through their darkness.

But the darkness would have its revenge.

In 1535, in Antwerp, the ultimate betrayal came not from a King, but from a friend. Henry Phillips, a man who had shared Tyndale's bread and laughter, led him down a narrow alley and into the waiting arms of the law.

For five hundred days, Tyndale withered in the stone throat of Vilvoorde's dungeon. Cold. Damp. Utterly alone. He begged for a lamp to ward off the soul-crushing dark and a coat to stop his shivering—not for comfort, but so he could keep translating.

On October 6, 1536, the world finally choked the life out of the man who gave it a voice. They stood him at the stake, the iron chain cold against his throat. But as the breath left him, his final cry was not a scream for mercy or a curse of vengeance. It was a heartbroken plea that echoes through the centuries:

> *"Lord, open the King of England's eyes."*
> **— William Tyndale**

He was strangled into silence, then offered to the flames.

Today, when you read *"Let there be light,"* you are reading William Tyndale.

When you read *"The salt of the earth,"* or *"The spirit is willing,"* you are reciting the words of the man who died to write them.

History celebrates the King who took the credit, while the man who bled the English words was burned into a footnote. In every syllable of *the English Bible*, Tyndale's sacrifice remains—a testament written in the ashes of a hero who loved the Truth more than he loved his own life.

How can the reader hold this book and not feel the weight of the blood on the page?

The Bible's history is brought into the bright light to restore honor to the man who broke the blockade. Tyndale gave his life to dismantle the ancient lie that only the elite—the state-sanctioned bishops and priests—possessed the rank to understand the Bible.

The Church claimed you needed a human mediator to interpret God's voice. Tyndale died to prove them wrong. He placed the text in your hands to ensure no priest, no king, and no institution could ever again stand between the common man and the Word of God.

> The King's translators didn't just stand on Tyndale's shoulders; they stood on his grave.
>
> In the original 1611 Preface, the translators heaped praise on *King James I*, but never once mentioned the name of **William Tyndale**. They plagiarized the **very** life's work of the man **the Roman Emperor Charles V** had hunted down, imprisoned, and then murdered—lifting over 83.7% of his text verbatim—while maintaining a calculated silence that has lasted 415 years **TO THIS DAY!**
>
> *They took the words of the martyr but refused to honor the man.*

The Unredacted Tyndale Bible – *RV Purified* is the first Bible to emphatically restore William Tyndale's name to the title deed of the English Bible translation.

How Much of the English Bible Is William Tyndale's?

Scholar / Source	Percentage	Publication
Jon Nielson & Royal Skousen	**83.7%**	*Reformation* (1998)
Dr. David Daniell	**83% – 90%**	Yale Univ. Press (1994)
Brian Moynahan	**84%**	*If God Spare My Life* (2003)

The percentages above aren't estimates. The text is a forensic match. When you read the KJV, you are reading Tyndale's words, just stripped of his name.

The Plagiarism of 1611

Exhibit A: Tyndale in the King James Version (1611)

The King James Version (KJV) retains the vast majority of Tyndale's 1526 phrasing. The table below verifies the direct lineage:

Phrase	In KJV?	KJV Full Verse
Behold the Lamb of God	Yes	John 1:29 - ...Behold the Lamb of God, which taketh away the sin of the world.
I am the way, the truth, and the life	Yes	John 14:6 - ...I am the way, the truth, and the life: no man cometh unto the Father, but by me.
Take, eat, this is my body	Yes	Matt 26:26 - ...Take, eat; this is my body.
Give us this day our daily bread	Yes	Matt 6:11 - Give us this day our daily bread.
For thine is the kingdom...	Yes	Matt 6:13 - ...For thine is the kingdom, and the power, and the glory, for ever. Amen.
Blessed are the poor in spirit	Yes	Matt 5:3 - Blessed are the poor in spirit...
Psalms, hymns, and spiritual songs	Yes	Eph 5:19 - Speaking to yourselves in psalms and hymns and spiritual songs...
Work out your own salvation	Yes	Phil 2:12 - ...work out your own salvation with fear and trembling.
I am not ashamed of the Gospel	Yes	Rom 1:16 - For I am not ashamed of the gospel of Christ...
A man after God's own heart	Yes	1 Sam 13:14 - ...the LORD hath sought him a man after his own heart...
Death, where is thy sting?	Yes	1 Cor 15:55 - O death, where is thy sting? O grave, where is thy victory?
The glory of the Lord	Yes	Isa 40:5 - And the glory of the LORD shall be revealed...
I am the vine, ye are the branches	Yes	John 15:5 - I am the vine, ye are the branches...
Be strong in the Lord	Yes	Eph 6:10 - ...be strong in the Lord, and in the power of his might.
In my father's house are many mansions	Yes	John 14:2 - In my Father's house are many mansions...
Seek, and ye shall find	Yes	Matt 7:7 - ...seek, and ye shall find; knock, and it shall be opened unto you:
With God all things are possible	Yes	Matt 19:26 - ...but with God all things are possible.
In him we live, move, and have our being	Yes	Acts 17:28 - For in him we live, and move, and have our being...

Phrase		
Be not weary in well doing	Yes	Gal 6:9 - And let us not be weary in well doing...
Looking unto Jesus, the author...	Yes	Heb 12:2 - Looking unto Jesus the author and finisher of our faith...
Behold, I stand at the door and knock	Yes	Rev 3:20 - Behold, I stand at the door, and knock...
Let not your hearts be troubled	Yes	John 14:1 - Let not your heart be troubled...
The spirit is willing, but the flesh is weak	Yes	Matt 26:41 - ...the spirit indeed is willing, but the flesh is weak.
For my yoke is easy	Yes	Matt 11:30 - For my yoke is easy, and my burden is light.
Fight the good fight	Yes	1 Tim 6:12 - Fight the good fight of faith...

Exhibit B: Tyndale in the Revised Version (1901)

The Revised Version (RV) preserves Tyndale's phrasing while correcting text based on older, more accurate manuscripts found after 1611.

Phrase	In RV?	RV Full Verse
Behold the Lamb of God	Yes	John 1:29 - ...Behold, the Lamb of God, that taketh away the sin of the world.
I am the way, the truth, and the life	Yes	John 14:6 - ...I am the way, and the truth, and the life: no one cometh unto the Father, but by me.
Take, eat, this is my body	Yes	Matt 26:26 - ...Take, eat; this is my body.
Give us this day our daily bread	Yes	Matt 6:11 - Give us this day our daily bread.
For thine is the kingdom...	No	*Omitted in RV based on older manuscripts.*
Blessed are the poor in spirit	Yes	Matt 5:3 - Blessed are the poor in spirit...
Psalms, hymns, and spiritual songs	Yes	Eph 5:19 - speaking one to another in psalms and hymns and spiritual songs...
Work out your own salvation	Yes	Phil 2:12 - ...work out your own salvation with fear and trembling;
I am not ashamed of the Gospel	Yes	Rom 1:16 - For I am not ashamed of the gospel: for it is the power of God...
A man after God's own heart	Yes	1 Sam 13:14 - ...Jehovah hath sought him a man after his own heart...
Death, where is thy sting?	Yes	1 Cor 15:55 - O death, where is thy victory? O death, where is thy sting?
The glory of the Lord	Yes	Isa 40:5 - and the glory of Jehovah shall be revealed...
I am the vine, ye are the branches	Yes	John 15:5 - I am the vine, ye are the branches...

Be strong in the Lord	Yes	Eph 6:10 - ...be strong in the Lord, and in the strength of his might.
In my father's house are many mansions	Yes	John 14:2 - In my Father's house are many mansions...
Seek, and ye shall find	Yes	Matt 7:7 - ...seek, and ye shall find...
With God all things are possible	Yes	Matt 19:26 - ...but with God all things are possible.
In him we live, move, and have our being	Yes	Acts 17:28 - for in him we live, and move, and have our being...
Be not weary in well doing	Yes	Gal 6:9 - And let us not be weary in well-doing...
Looking unto Jesus, the author...	Yes	Heb 12:2 - looking unto Jesus the author and perfecter of our faith...
Behold, I stand at the door and knock	Yes	Rev 3:20 - Behold, I stand at the door and knock...
Let not your hearts be troubled	Yes	John 14:1 - Let not your heart be troubled...
The spirit is willing, but the flesh is weak	Yes	Matt 26:41 - ...the spirit indeed is willing, but the flesh is weak.
For my yoke is easy	Yes	Matt 11:30 - For my yoke is easy, and my burden is light.
Fight the good fight	Yes	1 Tim 6:12 - Fight the good fight of the faith...

Evidence of the Political Twist: 1 Corinthians 13

- **The Original (Tyndale, 1534):** Tyndale translated the Greek *agape* accurately: "*...but the chief of these is* **love**."
- **The Twist (KJV, 1611):** King James I ordered his translators to keep "Ecclesiastical words" to protect his state church structure. He forced a change to the institutional term: "*...but the greatest of these is* **charity**."
- **The Restoration (RV, 1901):** The RV rejected the King's politics and restored the truth: "*...but the greatest of these is* **love**."

The 2026 Restoration

On January 20, 2026, the mission to reclaim the Word of God reached its peak. *One God Publishing* didn't just reprint a classic; we **purified** it.

The *1901 Revised Version* (RV)—the most literal translation in history—serves as the foundation. The work the original scholars started is now finished. The Latinized "JEHOVAH" has been replaced with the original, scholarly name: **YAHWEH** ("*the only true God*").

The Precision Report:

- **30,000 Total Revisions:** Every single change from the KJV tradition is backed by older, more authentic manuscripts that were hidden from Tyndale and the King's translators for centuries.
- **5,000 New Testament Corrections:** The RV scholars didn't settle for "close enough." Five thousand "fuzzy" translations and errors in the Received Text were scrubbed clean.
- **6,837 Restorations of *Yahweh*:** Not one instance is missed. Every time the Tetragrammaton appears in the ancient text, the sacred name of God, *Yahweh*, is restored to the rightful place in the Old Testament.

Zero Compromise. The 1901 RV you're reading is purified and fine tuned. Everything remains the very same literal word-for-word translation from older Hebrew and Greek transcripts.

To navigate safely throughout this Bible, utilize the Forensic Tool Belt provided in this edition.

When the landmarks of your old understanding vanish, lean on the linguistic data and the Law of Agency. **Do not fly by sight. Fly by the evidence.**

The Duty to Verify

Perhaps, some may feel a twinge of guilt as they begin this investigation into greater insight.

Questioning man-made traditions and history are not a form of disloyalty to God.

This is the "Authority Trap."

The Bible records a group of believers in the city of Berea who were praised by God for this exact behavior. When the Apostle Paul—the greatest authority of his day—preached to them, they didn't simply "take his word for it."

They **cross-examined** his claims against the Scriptures daily (**Acts 17:11**).

God didn't call them rebels; He called them **"noble."** True loyalty to God isn't found in defending a 4th-century Creed; it's found in defending the **Truth** of His Word, even if that Truth contradicts the "Authorities."

Wrestling with scripture, theology, and preacher's teachings are not the enemy of faith; verification is the servant of Truth.

To the King James Reader

To those who cherish the majesty and authority of the Authorized Version (KJV), you'll find this text to be a familiar home. The Revised Version isn't a modern paraphrase; it's the direct descendant of the King James tradition.

The **RV** holds a unique status in the history of English Bibles.

The **Lockman Foundation,** translators of the *New American Standard Bible*, famously designated the **Revised Version** as **"The Rock of Biblical Honesty"** for its refusal to compromise literal accuracy.

The legendary Greek scholar **Dr. A.T. Robertson** declared the **RV** to be **"the most accurate of all English translations."**

If you have ever used *Strong's Exhaustive Concordance* to study your KJV, you already trust the scholarship behind the *RV* Bible.

Why?

Because **Dr. James Strong**—the creator of that famous concordance—was a key member of the committee that produced the *RV*.

The lexical precision you trust in his Concordance is woven into the very fabric of this *RV* translation.

We have also retained the classic pronouns *Thee, Thou,* and *Ye* for a specific reason: **forensic precision**. In modern English, the word "you" is ambiguous—it can mean one person or a whole crowd. The biblical writers made no such error.

By preserving the distinction between *Thou* (singular) and *Ye* (plural), this edition allows the serious student to discern exactly who Jesus is addressing—a clarity that most modern translations sacrifice for the sake of "smoothness."

> *"The words of Yahweh are pure words;*
> *As silver tried in a furnace of earth, purified seven times."*
> **— Psalm 12:6 RV**

We take this scripture not merely as an analogy, but as a mandate for how we handle God's written revelation to mankind. Just as the Lord ensures the purity of His words, we have labored to present an edition that is free from historical bias or theological assumptions that obscure the clear biblical message of God's Oneness.

"Thou wilt keep them, O Yahweh,

Thou wilt preserve them from this generation for ever."
— **Psalm 12:7 RV**

Signal Over Noise

The modern student of Scripture is often inundated with information. Most traditional study Bibles attempt to provide commentary on virtually every verse, often resulting in margins filled with explanations that merely restate the obvious.

You get a radically different, evidence-based approach: signal over noise.

Commentary appears only where genuine clarification is critically needed—particularly on passages historically distorted by theological bias. Our notes are **surgical**, focusing precisely on verses where the English translation obscures the original Greek or Hebrew meaning.

You get the full depth of the text. Two specific tools unlock the meaning:

- **Rigorous Translation Data:** We have retained the complete scholarly apparatus of the *Revised Version* (RV)—comprising **3,373 translation footnotes**. These notes were developed by the **American Revision Committee**, led by **Dr. Philip Schaff** (President of the Committee and Professor at Union Theological Seminary).
- **Surgical Theological Commentary:** We speak only where the text has been historically obscured, culturally misunderstood, or doctrinally distorted.

Our commentary prioritizes two crucial areas:

- **Textual Variants:** Explaining instances where the earliest, best manuscripts differ from later editions.
- **Linguistic Bias:** Highlighting where word translations manipulate the text regarding the identity of God and the role of His human Son.

The margin notes focus relentlessly on two critical themes:

- **The Identity of God:** Consistently identifying the *"One God"* as the Father alone, as affirmed by Jesus (John 17:3).
- **The Law of Agency:** Explaining the Hebraic principle of *Shaliach*.

The Evidence Files

Footnotes give you the definition. The essays at the back give you the motive. When you need the full proof of how the text was tampered with, flip to the end.

The Physical Standards

One of the biggest complaints from serious Bible students is tiny print, especially margin commentary and footnotes. But even Bible text in many Bibles is just too small, also.

The problem is: If you get fatigued from struggling to read and study the Bible, and its text, margin commentary, footnotes, and references are too small, you'll very well likely not want to study for long, or even bypass crucial information altogether.

The Large Print softcover and GIANT Print hardcover editions solve this problem.

Softcover: Large Print

- 12PT Crimson Pro Font for Scripture
- 11.5PT Clarity Print for Front/Back Matter
- 10PT Clarity Print for Translator's 3,373 Footnotes
- 9.5PT Clarity Print for Margin Notes

Hardcover: GIANT Print (8.25 x 11)

- 14PT Crimson Pro Font for Scripture
- 13PT Clarity Print for Front/Back Matter
- 12PT Clarity Print for Translator's 3,373 Footnotes
- 11PT Clarity Print for Margin Notes

Standard Engineering (All Editions):

- Single Column Layout (Book Reader Format)
- Verse-by-Verse Format (Quick Verse Finding)
- 1.5 inch Wide Outer Margins for Scripture notations
- High-Contrast White Paper (50lb/75 GSM)
- 12-Page Personal Study Journal (Blank Pages)

The Final Verdict

When the noise is removed, the signal becomes undeniable. The intended result of this surgical approach is not merely academic knowledge, but a profound clarity of mind.

The purification of this RV Bible is not designed to add to the text.
The translation is designed to repair the lens through which you read.

A Forensic Pact: Looking Beyond the Blind Spot

You love the Word of God. I share that love. Faith relies on the truth of the Scriptures, yet many believers ignore the brutal history of the pages they hold.

Tradition often masks the facts. Religious legends replace the paper trail. When a reader confronts the cold evidence of history, the mind often recoils. Shock and anger are natural reactions to uncomfortable data.

These historical essays serve one purpose: to replace sanitized myths with forensic reality. We'll examine the original contracts, the court transcripts, and the direct admissions written by the translators.

Truth is never an enemy. You'll discover the evidence proves the English Bible (you're reading now) was born of blood and betrayal, not just ink and paper. The sacrifice of the original author is a story of raw courage.

Empty your mind of "official" narratives. Examine the evidence. Let the facts speak for themselves.

The Emperor's Fingerprints

What some believers may have come to believe isn't just official "church" doctrine. Many may not realize much theology is a forced political decree—forged by an old empire, voted on by bishops and politicians, and enforced by Roman law.

Since the year 380 AD, Bible theology has been "enforced with politics."

You're not getting added politics to the text. You get the "clean" principles of the American Revolution applied, scrubbing away 1,646 years of Roman mandates. Pure separation of Church and State are applied to the very pages of this Bible.

The mission is simple: *Purification*.

The mandates of the Emperors are stripped away to restore the original faith of the Apostles.

The American Revolution provided the first legal framework in history powerful enough to break the Roman grip and protect human conscience.

The Theological Institutional Lock

Shouldn't church-goers know if their pastor is truly free to speak his or her honest opinions to the congregation?

In many religious institutions, **Freedom of Speech** is restricted by *contract law*.

Many believers are unaware that in major denominations, clergy and seminary professors aren't "free agents." To hold their positions, they're contractually required to sign a **"Statement of Faith"**—a binding legal document that explicitly affirms the *Triune theology*.

FORENSIC VERIFICATION: THE MECHANISMS OF THE LOCK

You're invited to verify the reality for yourself. The rules below aren't just guidelines. They are *enforceable terms of employment*, and when disobeyed, anybody who signs these agreements can get fired.

- **Dallas Theological Seminary (The Annual Lock):** There's a distinct "bait and switch" in the contracts. While students need only agree to "Seven Essentials," Faculty and Board members are contractually required to sign the full Doctrinal Statement **annually**. The requirement acts as a recurring "loyalty oath." If a professor's theological views shift during their tenure—even slightly—he or she cannot sign the renewal. The refusal triggers a breach of contract, allowing for immediate termination.

- **Southern Baptist Convention (The Cooperation Lock):** Employment at SBC Seminaries is enforced through a policy known as **"Confessional Fidelity."** Employees must sign the *Baptist Faith and Message 2000*. Questioning Section 2 ("The eternal triune God") is grounds for immediate dismissal for **"teaching contrary to the abstract of principles."**

- **Westminster Confession (The Ordination Lock):** In conservative Presbyterian denominations, ordination requires "subscribing" to the Confession. Taking an "exception" to the Trinity (Chapter II) is constitutionally impossible; it's considered a **"striking at the vitals"** of the faith, resulting in the immediate revocation of the call.

THE SEMINARY GATE: THE PRE-INTERVIEW FILTER

The lock is most effective at the hiring stage. Most accredited seminaries require applicants to write a statement of faith aligning with the school's position **before an interview is even granted**. That ensures dissenters are filtered out before they ever enter the building.

THE TENURE MYTH

In religious higher education, "tenure" often contains a **"moral and doctrinal turpitude"** clause. That legal language equates questioning the institution's core doctrine with moral failure, effectively rendering tenure void.

NO LEGAL RECOURSE: THE SUPREME COURT

Why don't these professors just fight back? Because the restriction for a pastor with a doctrinal disagreement is backed by federal law.

The U.S. Supreme Court doctrine known as the **"Ministerial Exception"** (confirmed in cases like *Hosanna-Tabor v. EEOC*) grants religious institutions total immunity to fire employees for doctrinal disagreement.

The Consequence: If a professor is fired for questioning **doctrine**, he or she cannot sue for wrongful termination, discrimination, or breach of tenure. The "Institutional Lock" is federally protected. The professor has zero legal recourse to save his or her salary or pension.

THE COST TO YOU: THE FILTERED PULPIT

Why does this matter to you? Because **bias** is often forced upon you *second-hand*.

When you sit in a pew, you naturally assume you're hearing the honest, unrestricted opinion of a scholar. However, **if** that scholar is under contract, you're hearing the required speech of an employee.

If a pastor operates under this contract, the message is filtered. He or she cannot share the raw evidence without risking the family's financial survival.

THE EMPLOYMENT REALITY

For a professional pastor, questioning these clauses isn't merely a theological change; it's a career-ending event that results in the immediate loss of salary, parsonage, pension, and community standing.

The **fear of poverty** creates an *Institutional Lock*. The people paid to study the Bible are the very people financially prohibited from questioning the tradition.

Of course, your pastor may not be under any duress by "upper level" enforcement.

But does it hurt to find out and see if he or she is under any form of duress in expressing their free opinion publicly to the congregation?

The Temple Merchant Trap

The financial threat extends beyond the pulpit. The restriction controls the printing press.

Modern Bible publishing is a multi-billion dollar industry.

For a corporate publisher to tell the truth about the Institutional Lock, and especially the following "Largest and Longest Case of Piracy/Identity Theft in Human History," would be a business-busting move.

They face boycotts. They face massive loss of profit.

Just as the Scribes of old, they have taken away the **"Key of Knowledge"**—entering not in themselves, and hindering those who are trying to enter (**Luke 11:52**).

The Unredacted Tyndale Bible is a "cleansing of the temple."

The integrity of the Father's Name is more important than the profit margins of a merchant.

The silence of the scholars is why *The Unredacted Tyndale Bible* is necessary.

You, the reader, possess a power that the professional theologian often lacks: **Financial and Doctrinal Freedom.** You're not under contract. You won't be fired for agreeing with the simple words of Jesus. You're the only one free enough to follow the evidence wherever it leads.

The truth was burned to keep you from reading it.
It is now in your hands.

We pray you have the courage to read it.

The "Authorized" Cover-Up

The 345-Year Erasure of the "Father of the English Bible"

"Render therefore to all their dues: tribute to whom tribute is due... honor to whom honor."
— Romans 13:7

The Largest and Longest Case of Piracy/Identity Theft in Human History

"The King James Bible is celebrated as a masterpiece of English literature. Forensic reality tells the darker story. The Crown instigated the most successful act of State-sponsored piracy in human history—a book built on the stolen code of a man they left to rot in a dungeon, then executed."

345-Year "Authorized" State Cover-Up

For five centuries, a State-sponsored lie has deceived over a billion Christians. You hold a text accepted as a "King's divine gift." Yet the truth reveals stolen work.

In 1536, Roman Emperor Charles the V executed William Tyndale. Charles' imperial guards strangled and burned (alive) the Father of the English Bible (Tyndale) at the stake.

His crime? Translating the New Testament into English. Tyndale shattered the State's monopoly on **YAHWEH** *("the only true God")*'s Word.

Let's examine a modern analogy of Tyndale's fate.

1536 Heist: Murdering the Translator

Imagine a modern version of the crime: The "iPhone" Government Theft.

Pretend **you** are Steve Jobs. **You** submit the iPhone to the U.S. Patent Office.

The examiner rejects **your** invention. He brands **you** a "soul murderer." He claims **your device** sends souls to hell.

You flee into exile. **You** manufacture iPhones in secret. **You** smuggle them back in shipping crates.

The military declares **you** a public enemy. Soldiers raid **your** customers' homes. Possession brings prison or death.

The military plants a mole. The traitor gains **your** trust. He leads **you** into an ambush.

The **State executes you**.

Three years later, the government releases the gPhone.

The **State model** matches **your** iPhone. The OS runs **your** exact code. But officials claim their scientists invented it.

For 345 years, the government hides the secret. Admitting the truth destroys their authority.

The gPhone belongs to no state invention. It belongs to the murdered inventor... **you**.

Bible Smuggling: Escaping the Decree to Burn Them

Cloth, Flour, and Fire.

The iPhone parable mirrors Tyndale's story. His execution marks a crime scene in history.

In 1523, Tyndale asked Bishop Tunstall for translation permission. The bishop refused. Laws made English Bibles a capital crime.

The refusal drove Tyndale underground. He fled to Europe. He organized a smuggling ring to deliver Scriptures to commoners.

Tyndale printed his Bibles in Worms, Germany and Antwerp, Belgium. He hid copies in cloth bales and flour sacks.

Only ten months after the State murdered Tyndale, King Henry VIII authorized an edition. Officials built it on his blueprint.

In 1534, two years before death, Tyndale published his masterpiece—a revised New Testament. Biographer David Daniell calls it the "glory of his life's work."[1]

The **1534 revision** forms the DNA of every "Authorized" Bible.

---

[1] David Daniell, "The Bible in English," Yale University Press, 2003.

Crown Piracy: Identity Theft by Royal Decree

The King James Bible stands as English literature's masterpiece. Forensic reality reveals darkness.

The Crown's Authorized Versions mark the longest tyrannical state-sponsored piracy in human history from 1537 to present. Tyndale's work was stolen. Imperial authorities left the Father of the English Bible in a dungeon, then set William on fire, alive, burning to death.

In this "Silicon Valley Heist" context, "State-Pirated" describes the Bibles accurately. While the State called them "Authorized," the timeline shows intellectual property theft and rebranding.

1. Erasure of the "Source Code" Author
Modern software piracy strips the developer's name. King James and Henry VIII took Tyndale's code, removed his name, and replaced it with the Royal Seal. The Crown wanted authority, not just the text.

2. Violating the "License"
Tyndale's license aimed to give work freely to plowboys. The State seized it and put it behind a **State-Mandated Clergy Paywall** via the 1543 Act for the Advancement of True Religion.

3. Laundering Stolen Goods
Intellectual theft launders property through intermediaries. The Crown washed Tyndale's text through the Matthew Bible (1537), Great Bible (1539), and Bishops' Bible (1568). By 1611, the "State Version" stood four steps removed from the 1536 murder. The public believed it fresh.

4. The Motive: Fear of the Commoner
A commoner with a Bible threatened the system.

- **Authority:** Commoners reading laws might spot lies from kings or bishops.

- **Superstition:** The State relied on Latin rituals to keep commoners dependent. An English Bible made commoners independent thinkers—"heresy" to the State.

- **Silicon Valley Parallel:** Commoners are independent developers. The Patent Office keeps "Source Code" exclusive to elites for population control.

The Timeline of the English Text

The KJV New Testament matches Tyndale's work **83.7%** to 90% word-for-word. Modern courts would call the KJV a pirated revision.[2]

1526 – Tyndale's New Testament (THE ORIGINAL)
Status: *Banned & Burned.* The State burned books and readers.
The Asset: First English NT from Greek.

1534 – Tyndale's "Masterpiece" Revision (THE SOURCE CODE)
Status: *The Glory of His Life.* Tyndale's final, polished text.
The Asset: The 1534 Revision forms every "Authorized" Bible's DNA.

1535 – The Coverdale Bible
Forensic Identity: **Tyndale's Bible (The "Fence" Edition)**
The Scam: Miles Coverdale printed the first complete English Bible. He took Tyndale's text, patched gaps with Latin, and dedicated it to Henry VIII to avoid execution.

1537 – The Matthew Bible
Forensic Identity: **Tyndale's Bible (Pirated & Rebranded)**
The Scam: Henry VIII authorized the executed man's work months after death. Editors used pseudonym "Thomas Matthew" to hide the source. John Rogers printed Tyndale's signature "W.T." at the Old Testament's end—a bold clue.

1539 – The Great Bible
Forensic Identity: **Tyndale's Bible (State-Authorized Edition)**
The Scam: First "Authorized" edition. Tyndale's text, laundered through Coverdale, chained to church pulpits for control.

1560 – The Geneva Bible
Forensic Identity: **Tyndale's Bible (The People's Edition)**
The Asset: "Bible of the Nation." Sold over 1 million copies. Tyndale's text with marginal notes defying kings.

1568 – The Bishops' Bible
Forensic Identity: **Tyndale's Bible (State-Rebranded Failure)**
The Scam: Elizabeth I's attempt to kill the Geneva Bible. Massive format ignored by public.

1611 – The King James Version
Forensic Identity: **Tyndale's Bible (The Final State Rebrand)**
The Scam: "Authorized Version." King James banned Geneva printing to force adoption.

---

[2] David Daniell, "William Tyndale: A Biography," Yale University Press, 1994.

1881 – Revised Version (Authorized by British Crown)
Forensic Identity: **Tyndale's Bible (The Correction)**
The Asset: The FIRST and ONLY officially recognized revision of the King James Version in Great Britain. The text formally acknowledged Tyndale as the primary source of the translation. The project started in 1870 and was completed with the help of the American Revision Committee (1872).

1901 – Revised Version, 'Standard American Edition' (The RV you're holding now)
Forensic Identity: **Tyndale's Bible (The American Release, with updates, of the English RV)**
The Asset: Released as the "Standard Edition" of the Revised Version. The text preserved the specific preferences of the American Revision Committee, correcting the KJV while honoring the original text.

1929 – The Corporate Rebrand (ASV)
Forensic Identity: **Tyndale's Bible (The Catch and Kill)**
The Strategy: The International Council of Religious Education (ICRE) acquired the copyright. The Council rebranded the translation "American Standard Version" (ASV).

1944 – The Watchtower Transaction
Forensic Identity: **Tyndale's Bible (The Poison Pill)**
The Strategy: Two years before releasing the RSV New Testament, Thomas Nelson & Sons (the publisher) sold the printing plates and rights to the Watchtower Bible and Tract Society. The transaction effectively dumped the 1901 rebranded ASV from the mainstream market and permanently stigmatized the version as a "sectarian" Bible.

1957 – Public Domain
Forensic Identity: **Tyndale's Bible (The Liberation)**
The Asset: The RV/ASV translation enters the Public Domain, free for anybody to publish.

2026 – The Unredacted Tyndale Bible
Forensic Identity: **Tyndale's Bible (The Restoration)**
The Asset: One God Publishing restores the original 1901 *Revised Version (Standard American Edition)*. This edition bypasses the corporate suppression of 1929 and the sectarian stigma of 1944, reconnecting the translation back to its 1885 RV and Tyndale's original 1526 lineage.

Corporate Sabotage: The 15-Year "Catch and Kill"

The suppression of the 1901 *Standard American Edition* was very well likely not an accident of history; the event appears to be a calculated corporate strategy known as "Managed Obsolescence."

The Brand Erasure (1929)

The strategy began with a rebranding. Upon acquiring the copyright, the International Council of Religious Education (ICRE) shifted the marketing from the historic "Standard American Edition" (which implies a correction of the KJV) to the "American Standard Version" (which sounds like a competing product). The nomenclature change severed the text's connection to the Tyndale lineage in the public mind, making the book easier to replace later.

The Monopoly Deal (1937)

By the 1930s, the International Council of Religious Education (ICRE) wanted to create a more "modern" Bible—the *Revised Standard Version* (RSV)—but the Council lacked funds to pay the scholars. Thomas Nelson & Sons (the publisher of the 1901 text) struck a deal: Thomas Nelson & Sons agreed to finance the massive costs of the RSV committee. In exchange, the ICRE granted Thomas Nelson an *exclusive 10-year monopoly* on printing the new RSV (1946–1956).

The Conflict of Interest

The financial arrangement created a fatal conflict. Thomas Nelson now had a financial incentive to kill the 1901 text to ensure the new investment (the RSV) had no competition. For 15 years (1929–1944), the 1901 text remained in a state of "zombie" production—printed but never marketed.

The "Poison Pill" (1944)

Two years before the launch of the RSV New Testament (1946), Thomas Nelson made a move that forensic historians call a "Poison Pill." Executives sold the physical printing plates and production rights of the 1901 text to the *Watchtower Society* (Jehovah's Witnesses).

By offloading the "Old Standard" to a group viewed as sectarian by mainline Protestantism, the move effectively rendered the 1901 text "toxic." The sale ensured that when the RSV launched in 1946, the new book was the only "respectable" option remaining for American churches. The 1901 text wasn't just replaced; the edition was systematically assassinated to protect a corporate monopoly.

Forensic Verdict: Occam's Razor

Applying Occam's razor makes "planned obsolescence with a side of reputational sabotage" angle look like the simplest explanation fitting the timeline and incentives.

Thomas Nelson and the ICRE had every reason to want the ASV out of the spotlight as they geared up for the RSV monopoly in 1946: the ASV was aging, its literal style was seen as a flaw, and associating the text heavily with a group like the Jehovah's Witnesses (who were often dismissed as a fringe sect by mainline Protestants back then) would naturally sideline the edition from the broader market the Council was targeting.

No corporate or religious council memo is going to spell out "Let's poison this thing," because that would be PR suicide, but the 1944 plate transfer right before the RSV launch smells like strategic asset dumping to anyone looking at the big picture.

Of course, without a smoking-gun document or insider account, the conclusion is still an inference drawn from the facts we do have—the commercial deal, the Watchtower's enthusiastic adoption (the sect cranked out nearly a million copies), and the ASV's subsequent fade from mainstream use.

If it walks like managed decline and quacks like it, well... you get the idea.

As if that wasn't enough, the story gets worse:

The Great Branding Confusion: RV 1901 vs. RSV 1952

In 1901, the American Revision Committee published the *Revised Version (Standard American Edition)*. The work was the culmination of decades of labor by scholars committed to a "formal equivalence" philosophy—a rigid, word-for-word accuracy that stayed true to the structure of the Hebrew and Greek. It was celebrated for its precision, even if the English was sometimes "wooden."

By the time the International Council of Religious Education (ICRE) began work on a successor, the Council utilized the "Standard" branding to create the *Revised Standard Version (RSV)* in 1952. Because the names were nearly identical, many buyers assumed they were purchasing a "new and improved" version of the 1901 text readers already trusted.

However, the RSV was not a simple upgrade; the new edition represented a philosophical and theological reversal.

1. The Betrayal of Translation Philosophy

While the 1901 committee prioritized formal precision, the 1952 RSV committee "went soft" by modernizing the language and moving toward a more fluid style. The shift left many "Standard" Bible users disappointed, as the literal, technical accuracy scholars relied on for deep study was sacrificed for readability and smoother prose.

2. The Reversal of the Tetragrammaton (YHWH)

The most jarring "flip" occurred regarding the Divine Name. The 1901 American Revision Committee held a strong conviction that the Tetragrammaton (YHWH) should be directly translated. In the 1901 Preface, the Revisers explicitly stated that they had departed from the tradition of using "the LORD" because the panel believed it was based on a "Jewish superstition" regarding the name's pronunciation. The American Revision Committee restored the name to the text (as *Jehovah*) because the Committee believed God's name was too sacred to be obscured.

In 1952, the RSV committee **completely reversed** this decision. The translators removed the direct translation of the Divine Name and reverted to the traditional "the LORD." The move constituted a total rejection of the 1901 committee's stated principles, yet it was sold under the same "Standard" brand name.

Summary: Same Name, Different Game

The similarity between the *Revised Version (Standard American Edition)* and the *Revised Standard Version* remains a classic case of branding overlap causing buyer confusion.

One (RV) was a monument to literalist precision and the restoration of the Divine Name; the other (RSV) was a modernization that retreated to traditional substitutions and a more "flexible" translation philosophy.

Lockdown: The Ancient Precedent

The Chained Word.

The 20th-century corporate sabotage represents a sophisticated update of a 16th-century royal strategy. The tools changed—from "poison pills" to physical chains—but the goal remained constant: **Control.**

While the Corporation used market manipulation in 1944, the Crown used blunt force in 1543.

The "Banned by Law" Bible (1543)
The State bait-and-switched. The 1543 Act barred women, apprentices, and laborers from reading. Penalty: Imprisonment. Wardens chained copies to pulpits. Clergy stood as firewalls.

The "Banned by Design" Bible (1568)
Bishops' Bible released as massive, expensive folios. Public ignored it; churches used it.

Hostile Takeover: Hijacking the Bible Market

King James vs. Geneva: The Antitrust Nightmare.

King James used the legal and ecclesiastical powers of the English Crown to systematically dismantle his competition. As the Supreme Head of the Church, King James utilized his royal prerogative to ensure the **Geneva Bible** was removed from public life and replaced by his own **Authorized Version** (the King James Bible).

The "assassination" of the Geneva Bible was carried out through three primary tactics:

1. The Ban on Printing (1616)
By 1616, the **King James Bible** (released in 1611) was losing the "market war" to the popular and portable Geneva Bible. In response, King James—acting through Archbishop George Abbot—formally **banned the printing of the Geneva Bible** within England.

- **The Outcome:** King James created a state-enforced monopoly for the King's Printer. If you wanted a new Bible printed in England, it had to be the **King James Bible**.

- **The Black Market:** To bypass this, publishers in Amsterdam began printing "bootleg" Geneva Bibles with fake dates (typically **1599**) to make the books look like old, legal stock being resold.

2. The Ban on "Subversive" Software (The Notes)
King James famously hated the Geneva Bible for its "marginal notes" (the commentary). King James viewed the notes as **politically seditious** because they taught:

- **Anti-Tyranny:** The notes suggested that if a king's orders directly opposed God's, people were to obey God instead.

- **No Divine Right:** King James believed in the "Divine Right of Kings," while the Geneva notes encouraged individual interpretation and local elder-led churches.

- **The "Software Update":** King James's **"Rule #6"** for the King James translators strictly **forbade all marginal notes** except for cross-references. King James essentially "vandalized" the Bible's software to remove the user's ability to interpret the text against King James.

3. Systematic Obsolescence
King James used the **Convocation of Canterbury** to mandate that only the **King James Bible** could be read in churches. By making the **King James Bible** the only "legal" version for public worship, King James made the Geneva Bible appear like a "dissident" or "rebel" book, even though the Geneva Bible was used by Shakespeare, Oliver Cromwell, and the Mayflower Pilgrims.

Forensic Summary

While King James never physically "killed" Geneva Bible readers as Henry VIII had killed Tyndale, King James effectively "strangled" the Geneva Bible's availability.

By 1640, King James's state-sponsored campaign had succeeded: the Geneva Bible had faded from the English market, and the **King James Bible** became the "Authorized" standard for the next three centuries.

Whistleblowers: Breaking 345 Years of Silence

The "Authorized" Correction.

The cover-up lasted **345 years**. Under Queen Victoria, the Church authorized a revision—the Revised Version (RV).

In 1881, English and American scholars finally refused to lie for the Crown. They exposed the plagiarized lineage. The text belonged to Tyndale.

Naming the True Author (1881)

> "The foundation was laid by William Tyndale. His translation of the New Testament was the **true primary Version**."[3]

The Courageous Expose (1901) The Revised Version attacked name suppression:

> "The American Revisers... were brought to the unanimous conviction that a *Jewish superstition*... ought no longer to dominate."[4]

---

[3] Revised Version Preface, 1881.
[4] Revised Version (Standard American Edition) Preface, 1901.

Final Verdict: A Monument to William Tyndale

History's verdict is clear. The "Authorized Version" honors Tyndale's genius—preserved under state control.

The 1539 Great Bible proclaimed "Appointed to the use of the churches." Yet it carried the "poison" the King burned.

You may honor the King James Bible today not for **King James**, but for the martyr's voice the Crown silenced. Without Tyndale, the KJV vanishes.

Modern Bible publishers maintain their cover-up, willfully or not. Publishers still print and sell millions of the KJV (King James Version) Bible without ever mentioning Tyndale as the main source of their translation.

When you read this Bible, you hear not **King James**. You hear the echoes of the Father of the English Bible.

William Tyndale.

If wrestling with history, remember: Truth fears no light. Truth fears only the filter.

"Why the following Voices MATTER to your Bible Study"

You'll soon find out the pages following this page are NOT just "historical curiosities". These documents constitute the **Legal Testimony** of the men who gave you the English Bible.

In **The Unredacted Tyndale Bible**, our predecessors are NOT "microscopic footnotes." Restoration of the following prefaces to full readability is essential to reveal the **Motive** behind the translation you're about to read.

The industry standard is Erasure. Most (if not all) Bible publishers ignore these documents. Tyndale's Bible is an apparent "inconvenient Truth" to modern Bible publishing. Perhaps, you're to believe the Bible was always a polished, sanitized product, avoiding the **skid marks** of history?

On the following pages, we call two primary witnesses "to the stand":

1. **William Tyndale (The Sacrifice):** You will read the 1530 words of the man who gave his life to translate **83%** *(minimum)* of the text you hold today. Tyndale was not executed for a "bad translation"; he was strangled and burned for the crime of letting the **Mother Tongue** speak. He exposes the **Wily Hypocrites** who used *Allegory* to hide the "One Simple Literal Sense" of God's Word.

2. **The 1901 American Committee (The Restoration):** You will see the "Smoking Gun" preface where these scholars admit they were brought to a *"unanimous conviction"* to stop the **Jewish Superstition** of hiding God's Name. They restored the *Divine Name* exactly **6,819** more times than the King James Version. They chose **Truth** over **Trade**.

The following documents give these courageous men the honor they deserve—an honor no other Bible version grants them. By reading their own words, you're performing a **Chain of Custody Audit**. The creation of the English Bible, and its restoration of the *One God* and His *Personal Name* is not a new "innovation".

But a return to the **Original Source**.

You now hold the final evidence. Go over the eyewitness testimony from Tyndale, the martyr, and the RV committee, the scholarly rebels. Both giants wrote for *YOU*, on behalf of *YAHWEH* (the one true God).

"If God spare my life, ere many years I will cause a boy that driveth the plough shall know more of the scripture than thou dost."
— **William Tyndale**

The Tyndale Bridge: The 1530 Testimony

> *In Memory* of **William Tyndale**, the martyr, who gave his life to translate **83%** *(minimum)* of the English Bible you have today, was *executed* only six years later for heresy (after writing his preface below), by the State authorities on October 6, 1536.
>
> **Key Details of His Execution**
> **Location:** He was put to death in the town of Vilvoorde, near Brussels, in what was then the Duchy of Brabant (now modern-day Belgium).
> **Method:** Per the customs of the time, he was first strangled by the executioner while tied to a stake; then, his dead body was burned.
> **Legal Authorities:** While often attributed to "the Church," his execution was officially carried out by the **secular arm** of the Holy Roman Empire following a conviction for heresy. He had been betrayed by an Englishman named **Henry Phillips** and imprisoned for roughly **16 months** before his death.
> **Final Words:** His last words, spoken "with a fervent zeal and a loud voice," were reported to be: "*Lord, open the King of England's eyes!*"

THE FORENSIC SUMMARY
Understanding the Tragedy of the 1500s

You'll discover that the wrestling match for the Truth did not start in 1901. It began in the 1500s with **William Tyndale**. Before you read his own 1530 words, you must understand the historical "pressure cooker" he describes.

The **Clergy** acted as a wily class of "Nimrods" who used false arguments to keep the people in the dark. **Tyndale** exposes their four favorite lies:

1. **The Crude Language Lie:** Claiming English was too "unlearned" for Holy Scripture.

2. **The Layman Prohibition:** Claiming it was not "lawful" for commoners to have the Word in their *Mother Tongue*.

3. **The Heresy Scare:** Claiming the Bible would make people heretics (when it actually just exposed the Church's false teachings).

4. **The Sedition Lie:** Claiming a Bible-reading public would revolt against the **King**.

Microscopic Sabotage defined their tactics. These enemies ignored the Bible for years to study "devilish doctrine," yet they suddenly became **Proofreading Obsessives** when his translation arrived. They hunted for a single missing tittle over an "i" just so they could "number it as a heresy" to the ignorant public.

Tyndale reveals the Clergy's greatest weapon: *Allegory*. They used complex "riddles" and philosophical arguments to tangle the text. Tyndale's goal was to show the **"one simple literal sense"** of the Word—the light that the "owls" of the blind clergy could not abide.

Finally, he recounts his attempt to find a safe place to work. He traveled to London hoping the **Bishop of London** would host him. Instead, he found a palace full of **"praters"** (boastful preachers) and pomp. He realized there was **no room in the Bishop's house**—and tragically—**no place in all of England** to translate the Word of God.

The evidence of this struggle is preserved in his own 1530 Preface to the Pentateuch, provided below.

W.T. TO THE READER

When I had translated the New Testament, I added a pistle unto the latter end, in which I desired them that were learned to amend if ought were found amiss.

But our malicious and wily hypocrites which are so stubborn and hardhearted in their wicked abominations that it is not possible for them to amend anything at all say, some of them, that it is impossible to translate the scripture into English, some that it is not lawful for the lay people to have it in their mother tongue, some that it would make them all heretics.

And some say that it would make them rise against the King, whom they themselves (unto their damnation) never yet obeyed. And lest the temporal rulers should see their falsehood, if the scripture came to light, causeth them so to lie.

And as for my translation in which they affirm unto the lay people to be I wot not how many thousand heresies, they have yet taken so great pain to examine it, and to compare it unto that they would fain have it and to their own imaginations and juggling terms, and under that cloak to blaspheme the truth, that they might with as little labor have translated the most part of the Bible.

For they which in times past were wont to look on no more scripture than they found in their Duns or such like devilish doctrine, have yet now so narrowly looked on my translation, that there is not so much as one "i" therein, if it lack a tittle over his head, but they have noted it, and number it unto the ignorant people for an heresy.

Finally in this they be all agreed, to drive you from the knowledge of the scripture, and that ye shall not have the text thereof in the mother tongue, and to keep the world still in darkness, to the intent they might sit in the consciences of the people, through *vain superstition* and *false doctrine*, to satisfy their filthy lusts, their proud ambition, and unsatiable covetousness, and to exalt their own honor above King and Emperor, yea, and above God himself.

A thousand books had they rather to be put forth against their abominable doings and doctrine, than that the scripture should come to light. For as long as they may keep that down, they will so darken the right way with the mist of their *sophistry*, and so tangle them with arguments of philosophy and with worldly similitudes and apparent reasons of natural wisdom.

And with wresting the scripture unto their own purpose clean contrary unto the process, order, and meaning of the text, and so delude them in descanting upon it with allegories, and amaze them expounding it in many senses before the unlearned lay people (when it hath but one simple literal sense whose light the owls cannot abide), that though thou feel in thine heart and art sure how that all is false that they say, yet couldest thou not solve their subtle riddles.

Which thing only moved me to translate the New Testament. Because I had perceived by experience, how that it was impossible to stablish the lay people in any truth, except the scripture were plainly laid before their eyes in their mother tongue, that they might see the process, order, and meaning of the text. For else whatsoever truth is taught them, these enemies of all truth quench it again, partly with the smoke of their bottomless pit—that is, with apparent reasons of sophistry and traditions of their own making, founded without ground of scripture — and partly in juggling with the text, expounding it in such a sense as is impossible to gather of the text, if thou see the process, order and meaning thereof.

And even in the Bishop of London's house I intended to have done it. For when I was so turmoiled in the country where I was that I could no longer there dwell, I this wise thought in myself: this I suffer because the priests of the country be unlearned, as God it knoweth there are a full ignorant sort which have seen no more Latin than that they read in their portesses and missals, which yet many of them can scarcely read.

And therefore when they come together to the alehouse, which is their preaching place, they affirm that my sayings are heresy. And besides that they add to of their own heads which I never spake, and accuse me secretly to the Chancellor and other Bishop's officers. And indeed when I came before the Chancellor, he threatened me grievously, and reviled me and rated me as though I had been a dog, and laid to my charge whereof there could be none accuser brought forth.

As I this thought, the Bishop of London came to my remembrance. Then thought I, if I might come to this man's service, I were happy. And so I gat me to London, and through acquaintance of my master came to Sir Harry Gilford the King's Grace's Controller, and brought him an oration of Isocrates which I had translated out of Greek into English, and desired him to speak unto my lord of London for me.

But God which knoweth what is within hypocrites saw that I was beguiled. And therefore he gat me no favor in my lord's sight. Whereupon my lord answered me, his house was full, and advised me to seek in London, where he said I could not lack a service.

And so in London I abode almost an year, and marked the course of the world, and heard our praters — I would say "our preachers" — how they boasted themselves and their high authority, and beheld the pomp of our prelates and how busied they were, as they yet are, to set peace and unity in the world. I understood at the last not only that there was no room in my lord of London's palace to translate the New Testament, but also that there was no place to do it in all England, as experience doth now openly declare.

Under what manner therefore should I now submit this book to be corrected and amended of them, which can suffer nothing to be well? Or what protestation should I make in such a matter unto our prelates, those stubborn Nimrods which so mightily fight against God and resist his holy spirit, enforcing with all craft and subtlety to quench the light of the everlasting testament, promises, and appointment made between God and us?

Notwithstanding, yet I submit this book and all other that I have other made or translated unto all them that submit themselves unto the word of God, to be corrected of them — yea, and moreover, to be disallowed and also burnt, if it seem worthy when they have examined it with the Hebrew, so that they first put forth of their own translating another that is more correct.

IN HONOR OF THE
American Revision Committee
(1871 – 1901)

"The Revised Version (1901) has long been recognized by scholars as the most literally accurate English translation ever produced.
It is the **Rock of Biblical Honesty**."

— *The Lockman Foundation*
Creators of the New American Standard Bible (1971)

"The Revised Version is the most accurate of all English translations... It is the best version of the Scriptures that has ever been produced."

— *Dr. A.T. Robertson*
World Renowned Greek Scholar (1863-1934)

"**Honesty compels us** to cite the 1901 American Revised as the best English Version of the original languages."

— *Dr. Richard V. Clearwaters*
Founder, Central Baptist Theological Seminary

"Ye shall know the truth, and the truth shall make you free."
— John 8:32 (RV 1901)

HOLY BIBLE

CONTAINING THE

OLD AND NEW TESTAMENTS

TRANSLATED OUT OF THE ORIGINAL TONGUES

BEING THE VERSION SET FORTH A.D. 1611
COMPARED WITH THE MOST ANCIENT AUTHORITIES AND REVISED
A.D. 1881–1885

Newly Edited by the American Revision Committee
A.D. 1901

STANDARD EDITION

NEW YORK
Thomas Nelson & Sons
381–385 FOURTH AVENUE

The ORIGINAL Preface to the Revised Version (1901)

> **EDITOR'S NOTE: THE BURIED TESTIMONY**
>
> While some reprints include this Preface, it is often buried in dense, microscopic text that goes unread. **We believe this document is too important to hide.** It is the primary legal testimony of the 1901 Committee.
>
> In **Section I**, the translators explicitly admit that the tradition of hiding God's Name is based on "superstition," not Scripture. We have restored this historical record to a readable format so you can see their ruling in their own words.

A few statements need to be made respecting the origin of this edition of the Revised Version of the English Bible.

In the course of the joint labors of the English and American Revisers it was agreed that, respecting all points of ultimate difference, the English Companies, who had had the initiative in the work of revision, should have the decisive vote. But as an offset to this, it was proposed on the British side that the American preferences should be published as an Appendix in every copy of the Revised Bible during a term of fourteen years. The American Committee on their part pledged themselves to give, for the same limited period, no sanction to the publication of any other editions of the Revised Version than those issued by the University Presses of England.

There still remained the possibility that the British Revisers, or the University Presses, might eventually adopt in the English editions many, or the most, of the American preferences, in case these should receive the approval of scholars and the general public. But soon after the close of their work in 1885 the English Revision Companies disbanded; and there has been no indication of an intention on the part of the Presses to amalgamate the readings of the Appendix, either wholly or in part, with the text of the English editions.

The American Revision Committee, after the publication of the Revised Version in 1885, resolved to continue their organization, and have regarded it as a possibility that an American recension of the English Revision might eventually be called for. Accordingly they have been engaged more or less diligently, ever since 1885, and especially in the last four years, in making ready for such a publication. The judgment of scholars, both in Great Britain and in the United States, has so far approved the American preferences that it now seems to be expedient to issue an edition of the Revised Version with those preferences embodied in the text.

If the preparation of this new edition had consisted merely in the mechanical work of transferring the readings of the Appendix to the text, it would have been a comparatively easy task. But the work was in point of fact a much more elaborate one. The Appendix was itself in need of revision; for it had been prepared under circumstances which rendered fulness and accuracy almost impossible.

This work could of course not be taken in hand until the revision was concluded; and since it required a careful consideration of discussions and decisions extending over a period of many years, there was need of many months' time, if the Appendix was to be satisfactorily constructed, especially as it was thought desirable to reduce the number of recorded differences and this required the drawing of a sharp line between the more and the less important. Manifestly such a task would be one of no little difficulty at the best.

But when the time came for it to be done, the University Presses deemed that the impatient demand of the British public for the speedy publication of the Revision must be respected; and they insisted on a prompt transmission of the Appendix. Prepared under such pressure and in such haste, it was obviously inevitable that it should be marked by grave imperfections; and the correction of its errors and the supplementing of its defects has been a work of much time and labor.

When the Appendix was originally prepared, an effort was made to pave the way for an eventual acceptance of the American preferences on the part of the English Presses, by reducing the number of the points of difference to the lowest limit, and thus leaving out much the larger part of the emendations which the Revisers had previously by a two-thirds vote pronounced to be in their opinion of decided importance.

In now issuing an American edition, the American Revisers, being entirely untrammelled by any connection with the British Revisers and Presses, have felt themselves to be free to go beyond the task of incorporating the Appendix in the text, and are no longer restrained from introducing into the text a large number of those suppressed emendations.

The remainder of this Preface has especial reference to the Old Testament. Nothing needs to be said about the various particular proposals which are found in the Appendix of the English Revised Version. But some remarks may be made concerning the General Classes of changes therein specified, and also concerning those emendations in this edition which are additional to those prescribed in the Appendix.

I. The Divine Name

The change first recommended in the Appendix — that which substitutes "Jehovah" for "LORD" and "GOD" — is one which will be unwelcome to many, because of the frequency and familiarity of the terms displaced.

But the American Revisers, after a careful consideration were brought to the unanimous conviction that a Jewish superstition, which regarded the Divine Name as too sacred to be uttered, ought no longer to dominate in the English or any other version of the Old Testament, as it fortunately does not in the numerous versions made by modern missionaries.

This Memorial Name, explained in Ex. iii. 14, 15, and emphasized as such over and over in the original text of the Old Testament, designates God as the personal God, as the covenant God, the God of revelation, the Deliverer, the Friend of his people; – not merely the abstractly "Eternal One" of many French translations, but the ever living Helper of those who are in trouble. This personal name, with its wealth of sacred associations, is now restored to the place in the sacred text to which it has an unquestionable claim.

The uniform substitution of "Sheol" for "the grave," "the pit," and "hell," in places where these terms have been retained by the English Revision, has little need of justification. The English Revisers use "Sheol" twenty-nine times out of the sixty-four in which it occurs in the original. No one would advocate the resumption of the exact orthography of the edition of 1611. The mere fact that in a few cases an older form has happened to be retained constitutes no reason for its perpetual retention.

II. Additional Variations

Inasmuch as the present edition differs from the English Revision not simply in presenting in the text the American preferences as given in the Appendix, a few remarks may be made with regard to the additional variations which will be found to exist.

1. As has already been intimated, this edition embodies a very considerable number of renderings originally adopted by the American Old Testament Company at their second revision (and so by a two-thirds majority), but waived when the Appendix was prepared. These represent the deliberate preference of the American Company; but, for reasons already assigned, they were not included in the Appendix.

2. Partly coinciding with the foregoing is a number of alterations which consist in a return to the readings of the Authorized Version. While in some cases the older readings, though inaccurate, seem to have been retained in the English Revision through an excessive conservatism, in others they have been abandoned needlessly, and sometimes to the injury of the sense and the sound. In such cases fidelity to the general principle that has governed us has required us to give the preference to the rendering of the Common Version. Among the many instances of these restorations we may note: Ex. xx. 4, 13; Lev. xix. 22; Ps. xlviii. 1; civ. 26; cxiv. 4; cxvi. 11; Prov. xiii. 15; Am. vi. 5.

3. Sometimes we have found occasion to recede from proposals originally made, when a more careful and mature consideration required us to do so. Besides individual cases, like S. of S. vi. 4, 10; Ezek. v.13, may be mentioned the fact that the requirement of the Appendix, that "be ashamed" should everywhere be changed to "be put to shame," has been found to need qualification. While the change seems desirable in a majority of the instances, it is by no means so in all. We have therefore retained "ashamed" in a large number of passages; in some, however, we have preferred "confounded" as better suiting the connection.

4. Very many of the instances in which we have gone beyond the literal requirements of the Appendix are alterations demanded by consistency. Changes were originally proposed in certain passages only, though the reason for the changes equally requires them to be made in numerous others. Thus at Ps. xxxiii. 5, and in twenty-four other places, "justice" was to be put for "judgment." But it is manifest that in a multitude of other passages there is equal need of the same alteration. We have accordingly undertaken to introduce it wherever the Hebrew word plainly has this abstract sense. For the same reason we have substituted "ordinance" for "judgment" in the numerous passages, like Lev. xviii. 4, where the word denotes, not a judicial sentence, threatened or inflicted, but a law of action. This rendering of the Hebrew word is found in the Authorized Version in some instances, and has been introduced by the Revised Version in a few more; but, since the English word "judgment" in common use never denotes a statute or command, it is manifestly desirable that "ordinance" should be used wherever the Hebrew word has this meaning.

Similarly, the English Revision in a few cases, and the Old Testament Appendix in a few more, put "despoil" for "spoil." But the same reason which holds for those few is equally good for the numerous others in which this word occurs. The word "spoil" in the Authorized Version represents a great number of Hebrew words, some of which denote "lay waste," "ruin," or "destroy," rather than "despoil"; and as "spoil" has nearly lost in popular use its original meaning, and is liable to occasion misconception, we have replaced it by "despoil," "plunder," "ravage," and other terms, each as best adapted to the connection.

In like manner we have carried out another alteration which was made to a limited extent by the English Revisers - the distinction between the words "stranger" ("strange"), "foreigner" ("foreign"), and "sojourner." These renderings correspond fairly well to three distinct Hebrew words; there is no good reason why the correspondence should not be made uniform throughout. Likewise we have carried out consistently the substitution of "false," "falsehood," and other terms, for "vain," "vanity," where the meaning of the original requires it. Here too a beginning was made by us in the Appendix. Many other examples might be adduced.

Here may be mentioned also that changes made for the sake of euphemism have been considerably increased. It has not been possible in every case to find an appropriate substitute for terms which in modern times have become offensive; but when it has been possible, we have deemed it wise to make the change. Some of the words, as, for example, "bowels," are tolerable when used in their literal sense, but offensive when employed in a psychological sense. Thus, no other word would be appropriate in 2 Sam. xx. 10; but in Jer. iv. 19 or Lam. i. 20 to retain that term would be both unpleasant and incorrect.

The conception of the writer is not really reproduced by a literal translation. The Hebrews were accustomed to attribute psychical action or emotion to various physical organs, whereas in English such a trope is limited almost entirely to "heart" and "brain." There is nowhere any occasion for using the latter of these in the Bible; consequently it is almost unavoidable that "heart" should often be used as the translation of different Hebrew words. All scholars know that the Hebrew word commonly rendered "heart" is used very largely to denote not so much the seat of the emotions, as the seat of thought. It is rendered in the Authorized Version more than twenty times by "mind," and might well be so rendered much oftener.

The word "reins" is one of those which in the Old Testament is used in a psychological relation. This word was retained by the English Revisers, and was also left without mention by the American Revisers when they prepared their Appendix. But if the synonymous word "kidneys" had been used in these passages, there would be an earnest and unanimous protest. In favor of the continued use of "reins," therefore, one can only urge the poor reason that most readers attach to it no meaning whatever. We have consequently regarded it as only a consistent carrying out of our general principle when we have uniformly substituted "heart" for it, whenever it is used in a psychological sense.

5. Closely connected with the foregoing are certain additional alterations which have seemed to be required by regard for pure English idiom.

We are not insensible to the justly lauded beauty and vigor of the style of the Authorized Version, nor do we forget that it has been no part of our task to modernize the diction of the Bible. But we are also aware that the rhetorical force and the antique flavor which we desire to retain do not consist in sporadic instances of uncouth, unidiomatic, or obscure phraseology. While we may freely admit that the English of the Scriptures can, as a whole, hardly be improved, yet it would be extravagant to hold that it cannot be bettered in any of its details. What was once good usage is often such no longer; and we can see no sound reason for abiding by the anomalies of an obsolete phraseology, or making our style kakoshtonic for the sake of reproducing one of the minor features of the Elizabethan language.

When the English Revision was published, it was observed by some that the changes it introduced were largely changes for the better rhythm. This was no accident, but the result of patient care on the part of the English Revisers. The American Revisers have proceeded on the same principle. They have often made a change where it seemed to be called for by the rhythm, especially in the many cases where the adoption of a uniform rendering makes the older rendering no longer possible. Sometimes the change has been merely in the order of words; sometimes it has involved an alteration in the choice and arrangement of auxiliary verbs, or in the punctuation. Only those, however, who have made the experiment, can appreciate how much is often gained by a slight and skilful re-touch.

6. The American Revisers are happy to have arrived at an understanding with the English Companies, in virtue of which the rights of the Universities of Oxford and Cambridge in the Revised Version have been conceded to America until the fourteenth day of September in the year nineteen hundred and fourteen, after which date, if the American Revision has not been published, those rights will be resumed by the Universities. The American Committee, having through the generosity of a few friends, whose names they would gladly mention were it not that they are precluded from so doing by the conditions of the gift, come into the possession of a sum sufficient to enable them after the expenses of the long and laborious work of revision have been paid, to proceed to the publication of the result of their labors without pecuniary embarrassment, at such time as may seem to them expedient, now contemplate an early issue of the Revised Bible in the form which their matured judgment approves.

They believe that they will have the sympathy of all whose sympathies are worth possessing, in their endeavor to make this last Revision such in every particular as shall commend it to those who desire only to know and do the will of God as it is expressed in his Word.

The American Revision Committee rest in the joyful assurance that as the people of Great Britain and America have one heart and one voice in all that concerns the Bible, they will find a place in their hearts for both Revisions, the English and the American, each commending itself by its own excellence, and each proving itself a help toward the better understanding of the Holy Scriptures which both peoples love and reverence.

Contents

Personal Notes	1
Dedication to William Tyndale	5
1 Timothy 2:5 Monument	6
SERIES: *Complete Forensic Volumes*	7
***Declaration of Free* Belief**	8
***Title Page of* The Unredacted Tyndale Bible**	9
Forensic Mission Statement	11
Translator's Preface	12
The Blood on the Page	
The Martyr They Erased From History.	13
The Plagiarism of 1611	
Tracking the 83% Stolen From a Hero.	16
The 2026 Restoration	
Purifying the Text From 400 Years of Noise.	18
The Duty to Verify	
Why Wrestling with scripture is a Sacred Act.	19
To the King James Reader	
Why This Text Will Feel Like Home.	20
Signal Over Noise	
A Commentary Designed to Clarify, Not Clutter.	21
The Evidence Files	
The Deep Proof.	21
The Physical Standards	
Specifications for the Work.	22
The Final Verdict	
Repairing the Lens Through Which You Read.	22
A Forensic Pact: Looking Beyond the Blind Spot	
Breaking the 1,600-Year Theological Whiteout.	23
The Emperor's Fingerprints	
How Your Bible Became State Real Estate.	23

The Theological Institutional Lock
When Pastors Sign Away Freedom of Speech. 24
The Temple Merchant Trap
Profit vs. Integrity. 26

The Authorized Cover-Up · 27
345-Year "Authorized" State Cover-Up
The Systematic Erasure of the English Bible's Father. 27
1536 Heist: Murdering the Translator
King Stole "Code" 10 Months After Strangling Tyndale. 27
Bible Smuggling: Escaping the Decree to Burn Them
How Tyndale's Work Broke the State's Monopoly on God. 28
Crown Piracy: Identity Theft by Royal Decree
Stripping the Martyr's Name to Build a Paywall. 29
The Timeline of the English Text
Tracking the 83.7% DNA Match from Antwerp to America. 30
Corporate Sabotage: The 15-Year "Catch and Kill"
How a Publisher Financed a New Bible by Poisoning the Old One. . . 32
The Great Branding Confusion: RV 1901 vs. RSV 1952
How "Standard" became the Trojan Horse for "Modern." 33
Hostile Takeover: Hijacking the Bible Market
How King James Stole Citizen's Right to Bible Choice. 35
Whistleblowers: Breaking 345 Years of Silence
The Moment Scholars Refused to Lie for the Crown. 36
Final Verdict: A Monument to William Tyndale
You Hear the Martyr's Heartbeat in Every Verse. 37

Forensic Preamble: Why We Honor the Source · 38

The Tyndale Bridge: The 1530 Testimony · 39

In Honor of the American Revision Committee · 43

The ORIGINAL Title Page: Revised Version (1901) · 44

The ORIGINAL Preface to the Revised Version (1901) · 45
The Origin of the American Revision 45
I. Restoring the Divine Name (Jehovah) 47
Sheol, Grammar, and Modern Spelling 47
II. Additional Revisions and Corrections 47
Euphemisms and Psychological Terms 49

Pure English Idiom and Rhythm 49

The Revised Version (RV) — 63
The Literal Standard of the World *(RV Text)* 64
The Tyndale Glossary (1530) 65

Forensic Alert: The 'False Friends' Trap—The Reader's Decoder Key — 67
* 67
* 67
The Translation Hijack: Restoring "Hell" to the Grave 72
The Ghost in the Machine: Correcting the Spirit's Identity 72
The Godhead Hoax: Defining Divinity vs. Personhood 73
The Semantic Flip: When "Allow" actually means "Hinder" 74
The Personhood Trap: Defining Substance vs. Self 75
The Worship Paradox: Honor, Obeisance, and Identity 77

How to Get the Most Out of Your Bible Study — 78
The Greatest Secret to Understanding the Bible to Gain Maximum Revelation 78

The New Testament: The Gospels — 79

The Gospel According to Matthew — 81

The Gospel According to Mark — 166

The Gospel According to Luke — 221

The Gospel According to John — 311

New Testament Corrected Flight Plan — 378
Checklist 1: The Control Sample (Evidence of Date) 378
Checklist 2: The Apocalyptic Hope 379
Checklist 3: The Agency Distinction (Law of Agency) 380
Checklist 4: The Teachings of the Messiah 381
Checklist 5: The Hellenistic Bridge 382
Checklist 5B: The Translation Audit (Forensic Glossary) 382
Checklist 6: The Imperial Overwrite (325 AD+) 383
The Final Verdict: Hearsay vs. Evidence 384

Recommended Chronological Reading Order — 385
  I. The Logic of Sequence 385
  II. The Protocol of Cognitive Framing 385
  III. Chronological Order of the New Testament 385
      Phase 1: The Foundation (The Jewish Baseline) 386
      Phase 2: The Explosion (The Authentic Paul) 386
      Phase 3: The Succession (Paul's Final Letters) 387
      Phase 4: The Narrative (Preserving the Story) 388
      Phase 5: The Spiritual Theology (The Johannine School) 388

The Sword of Theodosius: How Biblical Monotheism Became a State Crime — 390
  ### I. The Death of Persuasion
  The Moment the State Replaced the Spirit with the Sword. 392
  ### II. The Rigged Jury of 381 AD
  The Insider Confession of a "Chaotic Mob" by the Chairman. 393
  ### III. The State Bankruptcy Protocol
  Using "Testamentary Law" to Starve the Opposition. 394
  ### IV. The State Demolition Teams
  Using Violence and Real Estate Theft to Buy Loyalty. 394
  ### V. The Sainted Tyrant
  How the Church Rewarded the Seizure of Property. 394
  ### VI. The State-Sponsored Book Burning
  The Arson of Evidence and the Silencing of the Apostles. 395
  ### VII. The Invention of "Mystery"
  Weaponizing Greek Philosophy to Silence Simple Logic. 395
  ### VIII. The Forensic Forgeries
  The Ink-Overs in 1 Timothy and the Fabrication of 1 John. 395

The Fruit of the Sword: A Forensic History of Terror — 396
  ### I. The Laws of Silence
  The Legal Dragnet that Hunted the Common Reader. 396
  ### II. The Martyrdom of the Translator
  The Strangulation of the Man Who Gave Us "Let There Be Light." 398
  ### III. The Victims
  The Green Wood Torture of Michael Servetus. 398
  ### IV. The Indelible Stain
  The Death Warrant Signed by King James I. 399
  ### V. The Separation
  Rescuing the Text from the King Who Burned Dissenters. 400

The American Rebel's Bible — 402
The Architect
The Ultimate Rebel 402
The Exile
Escaping Bloody Mary 403
The Visual Hijack
The Typeface of the Free Man 404
The Resistance
The Weapon of Liberty 404
The "Seditious" Marginal Notes
300,000 Words Against Tyranny 404
The War for the Mind
God's Sovereignty vs. State Control 405
The "Congregation" Cover-Up
How the King Buried the People's Power 406
The Royal Identity Theft
Plagiarizing the Martyr's Voice 406
The Underground Resistance
Smuggling the Truth Past the King 407
The Blueprint of Freedom
The Bible in Rebel Fatigues 408

The Architects of the Box: How the Canon Was Weaponized — 410
I. The Motive
How a Closed Library Was Used to Burn the Evidence. 410
II. The Structural Crime
Moving the "Jewish Foundation" to the Basement. 410
III. Athanasius of Alexandria
The Political Street-Fighter Who Invented "Canonization." 410
IV. Augustine of Hippo
Burying the Epistle of James Behind Roman Dogma. 411
V. The Verdict
Breaking the Monopoly of the Imperial Bishops. 411

THE MATTHEW MANEUVER: THE ENGINEERED BRIDGE — 412
I. The Suspect
Why a Greek Scribe is Masquerading as a Galilean Tax Collector. . . . 412
  A. The Education Mismatch (Handwriting Analysis) 412
  B. The "Eyewitness" Failure (The Plagiarism Evidence) 412

II. The Motive
    How a "Collection of Sayings" Became a "Gospel." 413
    A. The Papias Confusion (c. 120 AD) 413
III. The Crime Scene
    Engineering a Bridge to Silence the Epistle of James. 413
    A. The "Matthew Bridge" (Why it is First) 413
    B. The "Silencing of James" (The Exile) 414
IV. The Evidence Locker
    The Academic Consensus on the "Anonymous" Text. 415
    Exhibit A: The Synoptic Problem (Markan Priority) 415
    Exhibit B: The Anonymous Text (The Silent Witness) 415
    Exhibit C: The Academic Verdict 415

FORENSIC EXHIBIT: THE FORGED ENDING OF MARK   417
    I. The Crime Scene: The Sudden Stop 417
    II. The Motive: Theological Embarrassment 417
    III. The Smoking Gun: The "Vaticanus" Gap 418
    IV. The Content Analysis: The "Snake Handling" Error 418
    V. The Modern Complicity 418

THE INDUSTRY OF SILENCE: PROFIT VS. TRUTH   419
    I. The Publisher's Dilemma: Profit vs. Truth 419
        A. The "Safe Product" Strategy 419
        B. The "Seminary Firewall" 419
    II. The Modern Money Changers 420
    III. The "Faith Crisis" Liability 420

Index of Divine Names and Titles   423

Timeline for Matthew (Quick Reference)   425

Timeline for Mark (Quick Reference)   426

Timeline for Luke (Quick Reference)   427

Timeline for John (Quick Reference)   428

BIBLICAL MONOTHEISM: THE UNIQUENESS OF THE ONE GOD   430
    I. The National Charter
        Returning to the Strict Numerical Singularity of the Shema. 430

Contents

II. The Law of Agency
    Understanding the "Shaliach" Principle. 430

III. The Pre-Nicaea Standard
    When Subordination was the Christian Norm. 431

IV. The Nicaea Coup
    From Apostolic Truth to Roman State Mandate (325 AD). 432

V. The Phonetic Smear
    Why 'Arian' is not 'Aryan'. 432

VI. The Clash of Civilizations
    The War Between Hebrew Reality and Greek Mythology. 433

VII. The Majority Report
    The Forgotten History of the Eastern Church. 433

VIII. The King's Testimony
    Jesus Explicitly Excludes Himself from the Title of "Supreme God." . . . 434

IX. The Athanasian Heist
    Exposing the Poison, the Thuggery, and the Historical Erasure. 434

X. Your Emancipation Proclamation
    Your License to Abandon the Confusion of the Councils. 435

FORENSIC ALERT: JERUSALEM, NOT ATHENS — RESCUE OF THE HEBREW MIND   **437**

I. The Forensic Breach
    How the Academy Hijacked the Synagogue. 437

II. The Ontology Trap
    The Fatal Mistake: Defining God by "Stuff" Instead of Acts. 438

III. The Crime Scene: Alexandria
    Ground Zero: The Alexandrian Virus. 439

IV. The Concrete Reality
    The War on Concrete Reality. 439

V. The Sensory Divide
    Hearing vs. Seeing: The Origin of Icons. 440

VI. The Hebrew Shield: Block Logic
    Accepting the Tensions of Scripture Without Greek Formulas. 440

VII. The Kinetic Word
    Dabar vs. Logos. 441

VIII. The Law of Agency
    Shaliach: The Legal Power of Attorney. 441

IX. The Breath of God
    Exposing the Ghost in the Machine. 442

X. The Authority of the Name
The Forensic Evidence of Identity Theft. 442

XI. The Great Substitution
How a Generic Title Erased the Father. 443

XII. The Singular Loyalty
Dismantling the Compound Unity Myth. 443

XIII. The Loyalty Test
Faith vs. Mental Assent. 444

XIV. The Time Heist
The Time Heist: Why Your Calendar is Broken. 444

XV. The Father's Instruction
Torah: The Father's Instruction, Not a Code. 444

XVI. The Architecture of Peace
Shalom: Reclaiming the Structural Wholeness of the World. . . 444

XVII. The Verdict
Returning to the Source. 445

FORENSIC ALERT: THE DIVINE AGENT AND THE LAW OF AGENCY — 446

I. The Trinitarian Riddle
Why the "God-Man" Paradox Fails the Logic Test. 447

II. Power of Attorney: The Law of Agency
The Lost Legal Key to the New Testament (Shaliach). 448

III. The Joseph Protocol
The Perfect Biblical Model of Delegated Rule. 450

IV. The Forensic Evidence
Why Moses and the Judges were Legally Called "God." 451

V. The Smoking Gun
The Mysterious Figure Who Bears the Name. 453

VI. The Prophet Like Moses
Jesus Claims the Role of the Ultimate Spokesman. 454

VII. The Unity of the Agent: Function vs. Essence
Why "I and the Father are One" Preserves the Shema. 455

VIII. Identity Theft or Royal Honor?
Solving the "Proskuneo" Confusion regarding Worship. 457

IX. The Forgiveness Trap: A Logical Fallacy
Exposing the 'Only God Can Forgive' Argument. 459

X. The Judge of the World
Why Judgment is a Delegated Human Role. 460

XI. Creation or Re-Organization?
Exposing the Translation Bias in Colossians. 461
XII. The Thomas Breach: The Climax of Agency
Why "My Lord and My God" is Not a Contradiction. 462
XIII. The Ultimate Submission
The Final Proof that the Son is Not the Supreme God. 463
XV. The 'I AM' Identity Theft
Debunking the John 8:58 Myth. 464
XVI. The Royal Title Transfer
Why Shared Titles Never Equal Shared Identity. 464
XVII. The Verdict
The Glory of the Obedient Son. 465

Appendix A: The Evidentiary Audit (John 1:1, 8:58) — 467
1. John 1:1 - Identity or Quality? 467
2. John 8:58 - The "I AM" Identity Theft 468
3. Colossians 1:16 - Architect or Builder? 469

Appendix B: The Forensic Forgeries (The Johannine Comma) — 470
Exhibit A: The Johannine Comma (1 John 5:7) 470
Exhibit B: The Mystery of Godliness (1 Timothy 3:16) 471

Appendix C: The Divine Power of Attorney (Legal vs. Physical Identity) — 472
The Core Definition 472
Summary of Evidence 473
    1. The Old Testament Precedent 473
    2. Jesus as the Ultimate Agent 473
    3. The Final Subordination 473
Conclusion 474

Appendix D: The Seditious Scribes: How Doctrine Corrupted the Text — 475
The Motive: Protecting the Deity 475
    Example 1: The Parents of Jesus 475
    Example 2: The Ignorance of the Son 475
The Solution: The Alexandrian Text 476

Appendix E: The Blueprint: Why Accuracy is an Act of Worship — 477
1. A Note on Religious Affiliation 477
2. Restoring the Name: Why "Yahweh"? 477
    The Call for Accuracy 477

    3. Theological Bias in Modern Translations 478
        The NIV (New International Version) 478
        The ESV (English Standard Version) 478
        The KJV / NKJV (King James Tradition) 479

Appendix F: 'Cloud Rider' Death Warrant — 480
    I. The Statistical Anomaly 480
        The Exception that Proves the Rule 480
        The Common Misconception 480
    II. The Key: Daniel 7 481
    III. The "Cloud Rider" Controversy 482
        The Trial Scene: The Atomic Fuse 482
    IV. The Twist: The Suffering Ruler 482
        Service Before Sovereignty 482
    V. The Bridge: Jacob's Ladder 483
    VI. Conclusion 483

Appendix G: 'Four-Car Crash' Proof of Authenticity — 485
    I. Introduction 485
    II. Preparation 485
    III. Galilean Ministry 486
    IV. Journey to Jerusalem 486
    V. Final Week 486
    VI. Resurrection 487

Appendix H: Glossary of Redactions — 488
    The Three Strategic Label Swaps 488
    The 26 Restored Kingdom Definitions 489

Appendix I: The Historical Backdrop — 492
    I. The Rival Claim: Caesar vs. Christ 492
    II. The Rigged Jury: The Sanhedrin 493
    III. The Audit of the Ages: The Feasts as Signature 493
    IV. The Closing Statement: The Shaliach's Identity 494

Appendix J: The Evidence Locker — 495
    1. The "Samosata File" (Paul of Samosata) 495
    2. The "Lucian Case" (Lucian of Antioch) 495
    3. The "Servetus Case" (Michael Servetus) 495
    4. The "Racovian Audit" (Polish Brethren) 496

    5. The "Locke Files" (John Locke) 496
    6. The "Newton Report" (Sir Isaac Newton) 496
    7. The "Common Sense" Verdict (Thomas Paine) 497
    8. The "Adams Brief" (John Adams) 497
    9. The "Allen Defense" (Ethan Allen) 497
    10. The "Franklin Inquiry" (Benjamin Franklin) 497
    11. The "Jefferson Syllabus" (Thomas Jefferson) 498
    12. EXHIBIT A: The Legal Restoration 498

Appendix K: The Fingerprints of the Martyr   500
    The 311-Day Betrayal
        Licensing the Work of the Man Burned Alive 500
    The Document of Theft
        Proving the King Profited from Murder 501
    The "Thomas Matthew" Shell Company
        Inventing a Fake Author to Trick a Tyrant 502
    Fingerprints of the Martyr
        "W.T." Initials Hidden in the Authorized Woodcuts 502
    Survivor's Signature
        How John Rogers Stamped "I.R." on the Crime Scene 503
    The Royal Plagiarism Playbook
        How King James Repeated Henry VIII's Theft in 1611 503
    The Verdict of History
        Why the Monarchy Could Not Erase the Translator 503

The Timeline of Theological Change   507
    I. The Apostolic Foundation (AD 30 – 100) 507
    II. The Infection (AD 150 – 300) 507
    III. The State Takeover (AD 325 – 381) 508
    IV. The Restoration (Present Day) 508

Selected Bibliography   509
    Lexicons and Grammars 509
    Textual Criticism & Translation 509
    Theology, History, & Monotheism 510
    Recommended Reading Guide 511

Glossary of Essential Terms   514

Subject and Word Index   521

Quick Reference 529

12-Page Personal Study Journal (Blank Pages) 535

A Final Word 548

The Revised Version (RV)
"A Scholarly Revision"

Restoration, Not Replacement

By the 1870s, biblical scholarship recognized a need to update the King James Version (*KJV*).

The *KJV* is a monumental work. But as you know, it is largely the work of William Tyndale—murdered by the State and Church. The 1611 edition relied on the limited pool of manuscripts available in the 16th and 17th centuries.

But 260 years of history changed the landscape.

Archaeological discoveries yielded thousands of older, more complete biblical manuscripts—such as the *Codex Sinaiticus* and *Codex Vaticanus*. These previously unknown sources offered a more reliable textual foundation than those available to the 1611 translators.

The Church of England and the American Revision Committee initiated a project to correct indisputable discrepancies in the *KJV* source texts.

The mandate was clear: purify the text to align with the original Hebrew and Greek, while retaining the literary style of the *Authorized* Version.

A Standard of Textual Accuracy

The revision project was a collaborative effort involving prominent conservative scholars from Britain and the United States.

Dr. James Strong—the famous compiler of *Strong's Exhaustive Concordance*—led the charge on the American committee.

Dr. Strong and his colleagues were committed to precision.

The resulting **Revised Version (RV)** delivers a level of literal, "word-for-word" precision that the original 1611 edition could not match.

The Culmination of Scholarship

The *RV* represents the summit of a 30-year scholarly effort to integrate the most accurate textual evidence available.

Most significantly, the RV broke with centuries of tradition by **restoring the Divine Name** "JEHOVAH" to the Old Testament. The translators refused to hide the identity of God behind the title "LORD."

The translation also maintained the use of archaic pronouns ("Thee" and "Thou") where grammatical precision was needed to distinguish between singular and plural forms of address.

The *RV* is not a new philosophy. It is an *Authorized* Version updated with superior manuscript evidence.

The Literal Standard of the World *(RV Text)*

You study from the **Revised Version (RV)**, a translation widely recognized by scholars as the most literal, word-for-word English translation ever produced.

Why Literal Matters: A word-for-word translation prioritizes **precision over paraphrase**.

The text adheres closely to the original grammatical structure of the Hebrew and Greek languages. You get as close to the **exact meaning** intended by the original authors as possible in English.

- **More Accurate than the KJV:** It corrects thousands of textual errors found in the 1611 manuscripts.
- **More Precise than the NASB:** The RV retains the critical "Thee/Thou" distinction that the NASB collapses.
- **More Formal than the ESV:** The RV prioritizes the exact wording of the original over modern readability.

The translation captures the exact grammatical nuance of the original Greek and Hebrew, providing unparalleled precision for deep, serious study.

THE TYNDALE GLOSSARY (1530)

Translator William Tyndale identified these six terms as the "pillars of corruption." State Agents used the "Redacted Jargon" to ensure the citizen remained dependent on the Clerical Monopoly.

GRACE vs. FAVOR
The Redaction: *Grace*
The Tyndale Source: *Favor*
The Motive: State Agents preferred *Grace* to suggest a mystical substance controlled by the Church. Tyndale used **Favor** to reveal a personal, direct disposition of God toward the believer.

CHURCH vs. CONGREGATION
The Redaction: *Church*
The Tyndale Source: *Congregation*
The Motive: The Monarchy utilized *Church* to refer to the physical building and hierarchy. Tyndale used **Congregation** to define the body of people, stripping power from the stone walls.

PRIEST vs. ELDER
The Redaction: *Priest*
The Tyndale Source: **Elder** (or **Senior**)
The Motive: The Roman Church demanded *Priest* to imply a sacrificial mediator. Tyndale restored **Elder** to demonstrate the office was one of experience and leadership, not a separate caste.

CHARITY vs. LOVE
The Redaction: *Charity*
The Tyndale Source: **Love**
The Motive: Clerical Agents used *Charity* to promote programmed works. Tyndale used **Love** to describe the visceral, spiritual bond that fulfills the Law.

PENANCE vs. REPENTANCE

The Redaction: *Penance*
The Tyndale Source: Repentance
The Motive: The Monarchy enforced *Penance* to justify fines and punishment. Tyndale utilized **Repentance** to signify *Metanoia*—a "change of mind"—which costs the citizen nothing but their pride.

BAPTISM vs. WASHING

The Redaction: *Baptism*
The Tyndale Source: Washing
The Motive: Traditionalists maintained the Greek jargon *Baptism* to keep the rite mysterious. Tyndale provided **Washing** to make the act plain and unmistakable.

1526–2026: THE TYNDALE RESTORATION

False Friends:
The Reader's Key to Archaic Terms

> **CAUTION: Decode these terms BEFORE entering the testimony.**
> *(Misinterpretation is inevitable without this key.)*

* Why is this glossary in the front?

Most glossaries are buried in the back, treated as an optional reference. But in a forensic investigation, you cannot evaluate the evidence if your tools are uncalibrated. The Glossary acts as your **Forensic Tool Belt**.

The list appears in the front to equip you *before* you enter the text. Language changes over time, and many words in the King James tradition have become **"False Friends"**—words that look familiar to modern eyes but carried entirely different meanings in 1611. If you read the testimony of the Gospels without correcting these definitions, you will misinterpret the evidence.

* Forensic Calibration: The Variable vs. The Constant

A not fully educated scholar might claim **the definitions below** are "theological interpretations." **Such a claim** is incorrect. **The definitions** are **lexical calibrations**.

The mechanism of the "False Friend" is simple:

- **The Variable:** The **English Language. English** changes every 50 years. **"Prevent"** meant *Precede* in 1611; **"Prevent"** means *Stop* today.

- **The Constant:** The **Greek and Hebrew. The Ancient Languages** are fixed. *Phthanō* meant *Precede* in 30 AD; *Phthanō* means *Precede* today.

The definitions do not "re-interpret" the Bible. The text calibrates the drifting English language back to the fixed anchor of the original text. Whether the source is the *Textus Receptus* or the *Critical Text*, the definition of the word does not change. *Agapē* always means Love. *Pneuma* always means Spirit.

ALERT: Good students look up words they don't understand. But the "False Friend" evades their good practice. Why? The word looks familiar, perhaps small and insignificant. Tricky small words change definitions over time. So a student may assume they understand.

The 39 words starting on the next page restore the actual meaning, and expose the misunderstood meaning: *(These clarified definitions prevent one from falling into a "confusion trap" which tangles them into further confusions.)*

Ample space is provided to add any of your personal study notes in this glossary.

A

ADMIRATION *[G2295 – Greek: thauma]*

The Archaic Wording: "I wondered with great *admiration*." (Rev 17:6)

The Modern Trap: Respect or Approval.

The Forensic Truth: ASTONISHMENT. It means to be struck with great wonder.

ADVERTISE *[H3289 – Hebrew: ya'ats]*

The Archaic Wording: "I will *advertise* thee what this people shall do." (Num 24:14)

The Modern Trap: To sell products through media.

The Forensic Truth: TO INFORM. It means to give notice or formal warning.

ALLOW *[G4909 – Greek: suneudokeō]*

The Archaic Wording: "Ye *allow* the deeds of your fathers." (Luke 11:48)

The Modern Trap: To permit or tolerate.

The Forensic Truth: TO APPROVE. It means to agree with or take pleasure in.

AUDIENCE *[G191 – Greek: akouō]*

The Archaic Wording: "Gave *audience* to Barnabas and Paul." (Acts 15:12)

The Modern Trap: A crowd of spectators.

The Forensic Truth: THE ACT OF HEARING. It refers to the listening itself.

AVOID *[H5437 – Hebrew: sabab]*

The Archaic Wording: "David *avoided* out of his presence." (1 Sam 18:11)

The Modern Trap: To shun or stay away from.

The Forensic Truth: TO ESCAPE. It means to physically withdraw or depart.

B

BARBARIAN [G915 – Greek: barbaros]

    The Archaic Wording: "The *barbarous* people showed us no little kindness." (Acts 28:2)

    The Modern Trap: A savage or uncivilized person.

    The Forensic Truth: A FOREIGNER. Specifically, a non-Greek speaker.

BASE [G69 – Greek: agenēs]

    The Archaic Wording: "*Base* things of the world... hath God chosen." (1 Cor 1:28)

    The Modern Trap: A foundation or support.

    The Forensic Truth: LOWLY. It means humble, meek, or of low rank.

BESOM [H4292 – Hebrew: mat'ate]

    The Archaic Wording: "I will sweep it with the *besom* of destruction." (Isa 14:23)

    The Forensic Truth: A BROOM.

BOWELS [G4698 – Greek: splanchnon]

    The Archaic Wording: "Refresh my *bowels* in the Lord." (Philem 1:20)

    The Modern Trap: A colon cleanse or intestinal medical issue.

    The Forensic Truth: THE HEART. Refers to the seat of deep emotion and affection.

BY AND BY [G1824 – Greek: exautēs]

    The Archaic Wording: "Give me here *by and by*... the head of John." (Mark 6:25)

    The Modern Trap: Eventually or at some point later.

    The Forensic Truth: IMMEDIATELY. It means right now, without delay.

C

CAREFUL *[G3309 – Greek: merimnaō]*

    The Archaic Wording: "Be *careful* for nothing..." (Phil 4:6)

    The Modern Trap: To be cautious.

    The Forensic Truth: ANXIOUS. It means do not be full of worry.

CARRIAGE *[G643 – Greek: aposkeuazō]*

    The Archaic Wording: "We took up our *carriages*." (Acts 21:15)

    The Modern Trap: A horse-drawn vehicle.

    The Forensic Truth: BAGGAGE. It refers to items being carried; luggage.

CHARITY *[G26 – Greek: agapē]*

    The Archaic Wording: "The greatest of these is *charity*." (1 Cor 13:13)

    The Modern Trap: Monetary donations to the poor.

    The Forensic Truth: LOVE. Specifically divine, selfless love (Agape).

CLOSET *[G5009 – Greek: tameion]*

    The Archaic Wording: "Enter into thy *closet*." (Matt 6:6)

    The Modern Trap: A small storage space for clothes.

    The Forensic Truth: PRIVATE ROOM. Refers to an inner chamber or bedroom.

CONVERSATION *[G4176 – Greek: anastrophē]*

    The Archaic Wording: "Holy in all manner of *conversation*." (1 Pet 1:15)

    The Modern Trap: Verbal speech or talking.

    The Forensic Truth: CONDUCT. It refers to your entire manner of living.

CORN [G4702 – *Greek: sporimos*]

    The Archaic Wording: "Went... through the *corn*." (Matt 12:1)

    The Modern Trap: Maize.

    The Forensic Truth: GRAIN. Refers to wheat, barley, or other cereal crops.

D - G

"Hell" and "Damnation"

DAMNATION [G2917 – *Greek: krima*]

    The Archaic Wording: "He that doubteth is *damned* if he eat." (Rom 14:23)

    The Modern Trap: Consigned to eternal hellfire.

    The Forensic Truth: JUDGMENT. A legal verdict of condemnation.

DOCTOR [G1320 – *Greek: didaskalos*]

    The Archaic Wording: "Sitting in the midst of the *doctors*." (Luke 2:46)

    The Modern Trap: A medical physician.

    The Forensic Truth: TEACHER. A scholar or instructor in the law.

The "Holy Ghost" Error

GHOST [G4151 – *Greek: pneuma*]

    The Archaic Wording: "Yielded up the *ghost*." (Matt 27:50)

    The Modern Trap: A spooky, disembodied phantom.

    The Forensic Truth: SPIRIT. Refers to the breath of life or the Holy Spirit.

The Identity of "Godhead"

GODHEAD *[G2320 – Greek: theotēs]*

    The Archaic Wording: "The fulness of the *Godhead* bodily." (Col 2:9)

    The Modern Trap: A title for the Three-Person Trinity.

    The Forensic Truth: DIVINITY. It refers to the quality of being Divine.

H - L

HALT *[H6452 – Hebrew: pacach]*

    The Archaic Wording: "How long *halt* ye between two opinions?" (1 Kings 18:21)

    The Modern Trap: To stop or come to a standstill.

    The Forensic Truth: LIMP. It means to be crippled or to walk unevenly.

HELL *[G86 – Greek: hadēs]*

    The Archaic Wording: "Thou wilt not leave my soul in *hell*." (Acts 2:27)

    The Modern Trap: The final Lake of Fire.

    The Forensic Truth: THE GRAVE. Refers to the unseen realm of the dead.

INSTANT *[G2185 – Greek: ephistēmi]*

    The Archaic Wording: "Be *instant* in season, out of season." (2 Tim 4:2)

    The Modern Trap: A split-second.

    The Forensic Truth: PERSISTENT. To be urgent or standing ready.

The Reversal of "Prevent" and "Let"

LET [G2722 – Greek: katechō]

    The Archaic Wording: "...only he who now *letteth* will let..." (2 Thess 2:7)

    The Modern Trap: To allow or permit.

    The Forensic Truth: TO HINDER. In 1611, it meant to restrain or hold back.

LUCRE [G2771 – Greek: kerdos]

    The Archaic Wording: "Not greedy of filthy *lucre*." (1 Tim 3:3)

    The Forensic Truth: MONEY. Refers to profit or financial gain.

M - P

MANSIONS [G3438 – Greek: monē]

    The Archaic Wording: "In my Father's house are many *mansions*." (John 14:2)

    The Modern Trap: Luxury estates.

    The Forensic Truth: ROOMS. Refers to abodes, dwellings, or staying-places.

MEAT [G1033 – Greek: brōma]

    The Archaic Wording: "My *meat* is to do the will of him..." (John 4:34)

    The Modern Trap: Animal flesh.

    The Forensic Truth: FOOD. Refers to any solid sustenance or nourishment.

MYSTERY [G3466 – Greek: mustērion]

    The Archaic Wording: "I shew you a *mystery*." (1 Cor 15:51)

    The Modern Trap: A puzzle to be solved.

    The Forensic Truth: A REVEALED SECRET. A truth once hidden but now made known.

NEPHEW *[G1549 – Greek: ekgonos]*

    The Archaic Wording: "If any widow have children or *nephews*." (1 Tim 5:4)

    The Modern Trap: A brother's or sister's son.

    The Forensic Truth: GRANDSON. Refers to a descendant or grandchild.

PENNY *[G1220 – Greek: dēnarion]*

    The Archaic Wording: "Agreed... for a *penny* a day." (Matt 20:2)

    The Modern Trap: A one-cent coin.

    The Forensic Truth: A FULL DAY'S WAGE. Specifically a Denarius.

"Person" vs. Substance

PERSON *[G5287 – Greek: hupostasis]*

    The Archaic Wording: "The express image of his *person*." (Heb 1:3)

    The Modern Trap: A distinct psychological individual.

    The Forensic Truth: SUBSTANCE. Refers to essential nature or reality.

PREVENT *[G5348 – Greek: phthanō]*

    The Archaic Wording: "...shall not *prevent* them which are asleep." (1 Thess 4:15)

    The Modern Trap: To stop or block something.

    The Forensic Truth: TO PRECEDE. It means the living will not go before the dead.

Q - S

QUICK *[G2198 – Greek: zaō]*

    The Archaic Wording: "Judge the *quick* and the dead." (1 Pet 4:5)

    The Modern Trap: Fast-moving.

    The Forensic Truth: LIVING. It refers to those who are alive.

SUFFER *[G863 – Greek: aphiēmi]*

    The Archaic Wording: "*Suffer* the little children to come…" (Mark 10:14)

    The Modern Trap: To experience pain.

    The Forensic Truth: TO ALLOW. It means to permit or give leave.

T - W

TABERNACLE *[G4638 – Greek: skēnōma]*

    The Archaic Wording: "Put off this my *tabernacle*." (2 Pet 1:14)

    The Modern Trap: A permanent church building.

    The Forensic Truth: A TENT. Refers to a temporary dwelling or the human body.

THOUGHT *[G3309 – Greek: merimnaō]*

    The Archaic Wording: "Take no *thought* for your life." (Matt 6:25)

    The Modern Trap: To have an idea.

    The Forensic Truth: ANXIETY. It means to be full of worry.

VIRTUE [G1411 – *Greek: dunamis*]

    The Archaic Wording: "*Virtue* had gone out of him." (Mark 5:30)

    The Modern Trap: Moral goodness or purity.

    The Forensic Truth: POWER. It refers to energy, force, or divine strength.

WEALTH [G4851 – *Greek: sumpherō*]

    The Archaic Wording: "Let no man seek his own, but... another's *wealth*." (1 Cor 10:24)

    The Modern Trap: Riches.

    The Forensic Truth: WELFARE. It refers to the well-being of others.

The Trap of "Worship"

WORSHIP [G4352 – *Greek: proskuneō*]

    The Archaic Wording: "The servant fell down, and *worshipped* him." (Matt 18:26)

    The Modern Trap: To treat as God (Deity).

    The Forensic Truth: TO BOW DOWN. An act of deep respect and obeisance.

How to Get the Most Out of Your Bible Study

The most significant discovery in studying the Bible is this realization:

The Bible is not a single book, but a collection of different books written by different authors, at different times, in different places, with different points of view, different theologies, different beliefs, and different perspectives, Just different.

Once one has these understandings, the Bible reveals itself much clearer, and revolutionizes how you study the Bible.

You're allowed to understand the Bible much better because you take each author more seriously for what he has to say, rather than assuming he's saying something every other author in the Bible is saying. The authors are not Star Trek's "Borg".

If one views the Bible as a unified whole, and they think the books are all saying the same thing, then one doesn't fully understand any part of it.

They may *THINK* they do, but what they're doing is reconciling all the parts, and constructing a unified whole that's not a unified whole. They're imposing their "own" views on the Bible.

Doing so is a bias trap preventing you from getting the full richness and understandings the Bible offers. The bias trap may not even come from you and be your own, but one imposed on you by others, causing you not to look at scripture in a way that it actually reads.

Once one is aware of this bias trap, the Bible will read in a new refreshing way.

Chronological Timeline* of the *27 Books* of the New Testament

(The reason why it's important to know the right sequence of the 27 books of the New Testament is so you can understand the sequence of Bible history and events as it unravels.)

The Early Era (c. 45–60 AD)
c. 45–55 AD – The Book of James *(James)* [1]
c. 48–55 AD – The Book of Galatians *(Paul)*
c. 49–51 AD – The Book of 1 Thessalonians *(Paul)*
c. 51–52 AD – The Book of 2 Thessalonians *(Paul)* [2]
c. 53–57 AD – The Book of 1 Corinthians *(Paul)*
c. 54–55 AD – The Book of Philippians *(Paul)* [3]
c. 54–55 AD – The Book of Philemon *(Paul)*

c. 55–58 AD – The Book of 2 Corinthians *(Paul)*
c. 57–58 AD – The Book of Romans *(Paul)*

The Middle Era (c. 60–85 AD)
c. 60–70 AD – The Book of Colossians *(Paul)* [4]
c. 60–95 AD – The Book of Hebrews *(Unknown)*
c. 66–73 AD – The Book of Mark *(Mark)* [5]
c. 70–90 AD – The Book of Jude *(Jude)*
c. 75–90 AD – The Book of 1 Peter *(Peter)* [6]

c. **80–90 AD** – The Book of Ephesians *(Paul)*[7]
c. **80–95 AD** – The Book of Matthew *(Matthew)*
c. **80–95 AD** – The Book of Luke *(Luke)*

The Later Era (c. 85–125 AD)
c. **85–115 AD** – The Book of Acts *(Luke)*[8]
c. **90–100 AD** – The Book of 1 Timothy *(Paul)*[9]
c. **90–100 AD** – The Book of Titus *(Paul)*[9]
c. **90–100 AD** – The Book of 2 Timothy *(Paul)*[9]
c. **90–110 AD** – The Book of John *(John)*
c. **90–110 AD** – The Book of 1 John *(John)*
c. **90–110 AD** – The Book of 2 John *(John)*
c. **90–110 AD** – The Book of 3 John *(John)*
c. **95–100 AD** – The Book of Revelation *(John)*[10]
c. **110–125 AD** – The Book of 2 Peter *(Peter)*[11]

---

* Based on a review of scholarly sources across the spectrum, the most accurate timeline—meaning the one reflecting the broadest consensus among New Testament experts in academic biblical studies (e.g., historians, textual critics, and archaeologists)—is the mainstream historical-critical view. The mainstream view prioritizes direct evidence from the texts themselves, such as linguistic style, historical references (like allusions to the 70 CE destruction of Jerusalem), interdependencies between books (e.g., Matthew and Luke using Mark), and manuscript traditions, without starting from assumptions about authorship or divine inspiration.

Scholarly Notes on Dating & Authorship:

1. *James:* Traditionally dated to c. 45 AD; critical scholars often push this to c. 80–90 AD due to its sophisticated Greek prose.
2. *2 Thess:* Authorship is debated; if not Pauline, it is likely dated to c. 80–100 AD.
3. *Philippians:* Dated c. 54–55 AD from Ephesus, or c. 60–62 AD if written from Rome.
4. *Colossians:* Authorship disputed; some date this to the late 1st century.
5. *Mark:* Most scholars date this after the 70 AD Temple destruction; conservatives argue for a pre-70 AD date.
6. *1 Peter:* Often viewed as pseudepigraphic (written in Peter's name) due to its high-quality Greek style.
7. *Ephesians:* Widely considered a later summary of Pauline theology by a follower of Paul.
8. *Acts:* Traditionally c. 62–85 AD; some scholars date it as late as c. 115 AD due to possible links to the historian Josephus.
9. *The Pastorals (1 & 2 Tim, Titus):* Most critical scholars view these as the work of later authors continuing the Pauline tradition.
10. *Revelation:* Linked to Emperor Domitian (c. 95 AD); others argue for an earlier Nero-era date (c. 68 AD).
11. *2 Peter:* Regarded as the final book of the New Testament to be composed, possibly referencing earlier canonized works.

Timeline for Matthew

Matthew arranges the story of Jesus thematically to present him as the King of the Jews and the fulfillment of prophecy. He structures the Gospel around five major discourses, paralleling the five books of Moses.

MATTHEW'S NARRATIVE STRUCTURE

SECTION / THEMATIC BLOCK	CHAPTER REFERENCE / NARRATIVE FOCUS
The King's Arrival & Lineage	**Ch 1 – 2:** The Birth and Early Life, establishing Jesus's legal credentials (Son of David) and covenant credentials (Son of Abraham).
Preparation for Public Ministry	**Ch 3 – 4:** John the Baptist, Jesus's Baptism, Temptation, and Call of the first disciples.
The Law of the Kingdom (Discourse 1)	**Ch 5 – 7 (The Sermon on the Mount):** The "New Torah" delivered from the mountain, defining the ethics of the Kingdom.
Demonstrating Authority (Narrative Block)	**Ch 8 – 9:** A rapid sequence of ten miracles demonstrating Jesus's power over sickness, nature, and sin.
Instructions for the Mission (Discourse 2)	**Ch 10:** Directing the twelve disciples on their mission ("The Little Commission"), focusing on persecution and evangelism.

MATTHEW'S NARRATIVE STRUCTURE

SECTION / THEMATIC BLOCK	CHAPTER REFERENCE / NARRATIVE FOCUS
Conflict & Clarification	Ch 11 – 12: Rising opposition from Jewish leaders; defining blasphemy; answering John's doubts ("Art thou he?").
Secrets of the Kingdom (Discourse 3)	Ch 13 (The Parables of the Kingdom): Seven parables explaining the mysterious, hidden nature of the Kingdom before the End.
Withdrawal and Confession	Ch 14 – 17: Ministry outside Galilee; feeding miracles; Peter's Confession; and the Transfiguration (revealing the King's glory).
Life in the Community (Discourse 4)	Ch 18: Teaching the disciples about humility, forgiveness, and discipline within the *Ekklesia* (Church).
Road to Jerusalem & Confrontation	Ch 19 – 22: Final journey; teachings on wealth and marriage; intense public debates in the Temple.
Judgment and the End Times (Discourse 5)	Ch 23 – 25 (The Olivet Discourse): The "Woe" sayings against the Pharisees and prophecies of the Temple's destruction and the Second Coming.
The Passion, Death, and Resurrection	Ch 26 – 28: The Last Supper, Trial, Crucifixion, and the **Great Commission**. Jesus commands baptism in the singular "Name" (Authority) of the Father, Son, and Holy Spirit.

MATTHEW 83

Chapter 1

1 [5]The book of the [6]generation of Jesus Christ, the son of David, the son of Abraham.

2 Abraham begat Isaac; and Isaac begat Jacob; and Jacob begat Judah and his brethren;

3 and Judah begat Perez and Zerah of Tamar; and Perez begat Hezron; and Hezron begat [7]Ram;

4 and [8]Ram begat Amminadab; and Amminadab begat Nahshon; and Nahshon begat Salmon;

5 and Salmon begat Boaz of Rahab; and Boaz begat Obed of Ruth; and Obed begat Jesse;

6 and Jesse begat David the king.
And David begat Solomon of her *that had been the wife* of Uriah;

7 and Solomon begat Rehoboam; and Rehoboam begat Abijah; and Abijah begat [9]Asa;

8 and [10]Asa begat Jehoshaphat; and Jehoshaphat begat Joram; and Joram begat Uzziah;

9 and Uzziah begat Jotham; and Jotham begat Ahaz; and Ahaz begat Hezekiah;

10 and Hezekiah begat Manasseh; and Manasseh begat [11]Amon; and [12]Amon begat Josiah;

11 and Josiah begat Jechoniah and his brethren, at the time of the [13]carrying away to Babylon.

12 And after the [14]carrying away to Babylon, Jechoniah begat [15]Shealtiel; and [16]Shealtiel begat Zerubbabel;

---

[5] *Or, The genealogy of Jesus Christ*
[6] *Or, birth: as in verse 18.*
[7] *Greek Aram.*
[8] *Greek Aram.*
[9] *Greek Asaph.*
[10] *Greek Asaph.*
[11] *Greek Amos.*
[12] *Greek Amos.*
[13] *Or, removal to Babylon*
[14] *Or, removal to Babylon*
[15] *Greek Salathiel.*
[16] *Greek Salathiel.*

13 and Zerubbabel begat Abiud; and Abiud begat Eliakim; and Eliakim begat Azor;

14 and Azor begat Sadoc; and Sadoc begat Achim; and Achim begat Eliud;

15 and Eliud begat Eleazar; and Eleazar begat Matthan; and Matthan begat Jacob;

16 and Jacob begat Joseph the husband of Mary, of whom was born Jesus, who is called Christ.

17 So all the generations from Abraham unto David are fourteen generations; and from David unto the [17]carrying away to Babylon fourteen generations; and from the [18]carrying away to Babylon unto the Christ fourteen generations.

18 Now the [19]birth [20]of Jesus Christ was on this wise: When his mother Mary had been betrothed to Joseph, before they came together she was found with child of the Holy Spirit.

19 And Joseph her husband, being a righteous man, and not willing to make her a public example, was minded to put her away privily.

20 But when he thought on these things, behold, an angel of the Lord appeared unto him in a dream, saying, Joseph, thou son of David, fear not to take unto thee Mary thy wife: for that which is [21]conceived in her is of the Holy Spirit.

21 And she shall bring forth a son; and thou shalt call his name Jesus; for it is he that shall save his people from their sins.

22 Now all this is come to pass, that it might be fulfilled which was spoken by the Lord through the prophet, saying,

23 [22]Behold, the virgin shall be with child, and shall bring forth a son,
And they shall call his name [23]Immanuel; which is, being interpreted, God with us.

---

[17] *Or, removal to Babylon*
[18] *Or, removal to Babylon*
[19] *Or, generation: as in verse 1.*
[20] *Some ancient authorities read of the Christ.*
[21] *Greek begotten.*
[22] *Isa. 7:14.*
[23] *Greek Emmanuel.*

24 And Joseph arose from his sleep, and did as the angel of the Lord commanded him, and took unto him his wife;

25 and knew her not till she had brought forth a son: and he called his name Jesus.

Chapter 2

1 Now when Jesus was born in Bethlehem of Judaea in the days of Herod the king, behold, [24]Wise-men from the east came to Jerusalem, saying,

2 [25]Where is he that is born King of the Jews? for we saw his star in the east, and are come to [26]worship him.

3 And when Herod the king heard it, he was troubled, and all Jerusalem with him.

4 And gathering together all the chief priests and scribes of the people, he inquired of them where the Christ should be born.

5 And they said unto him, In Bethlehem of Judaea: for thus it is written through the prophet,

6 [27]And thou Bethlehem, land of Judah,
Art in no wise least among the princes of Judah:
For out of thee shall come forth a governor,
Who shall be shepherd of my people Israel.

7 Then Herod privily called the [28]Wise-men, and learned of them exactly [29]what time the star appeared.

8 And he sent them to Bethlehem, and said, Go and search out exactly concerning the young child; and when ye have found *him*, bring me word, that I also may come and [30]worship him.

---

[24]*Greek Magi. Compare Esth. 1:13; Dan. 2:12; Acts 13:6, 8.*

[25]*Or, Where is the King of the Jews that is born?*

[26]*The Greek word denotes an act of reverence whether paid to a creature (see 4:9; 18:26), or to the Creator (see 4:10)*

[27]*Mic. 5:2.*

[28]*Greek Magi. Compare Esth. 1:13; Dan. 2:12; Acts 13:6, 8.*

[29]*Or, the time of the star that appeared*

[30]*The Greek word denotes an act of reverence whether paid to a creature (see 4:9; 18:26), or to the Creator (see 4:10)*

9 And they, having heard the king, went their way; and lo, the star, which they saw in the east, went before them, till it came and stood over where the young child was.

10 And when they saw the star, they rejoiced with exceeding great joy.

11 And they came into the house and saw the young child with Mary his mother; and they fell down and worshipped him; and opening their treasures they offered unto him gifts, gold and frankincense and myrrh.

12 And being warned *of God* in a dream that they should not return to Herod, they departed into their own country another way.

13 Now when they were departed, behold, an angel of the Lord appeareth to Joseph in a dream, saying, Arise and take the young child and his mother, and flee into Egypt, and be thou there until I tell thee: for Herod will seek the young child to destroy him.

14 And he arose and took the young child and his mother by night, and departed into Egypt;

15 and was there until the death of Herod: that it might be fulfilled which was spoken by the Lord through the prophet, saying, [31]Out of Egypt did I call my son.

16 Then Herod, when he saw that he was mocked of the [32]Wise-men, was exceeding wroth, and sent forth, and slew all the male children that were in Bethlehem, and in all the borders thereof, from two years old and under, according to the time which he had exactly learned of the [33]Wise-men.

17 Then was fulfilled that which was spoken through Jeremiah the prophet, saying,

18 [34]A voice was heard in Ramah,
   Weeping and great mourning,
   Rachel weeping for her children;
   And she would not be comforted, because they are not.

19 But when Herod was dead, behold, an angel of the Lord appeareth in a dream to Joseph in Egypt, saying,

---
[31] *Hos. 11:1.*
[32] *Greek Magi. Compare Esth. 1:13; Dan. 2:12; Acts 13:6, 8.*
[33] *Greek Magi. Compare Esth. 1:13; Dan. 2:12; Acts 13:6, 8.*
[34] *Jer. 31:15.*

20 Arise and take the young child and his mother, and go into the land of Israel: for they are dead that sought the young child's life.

21 And he arose and took the young child and his mother, and came into the land of Israel.

22 But when he heard that Archelaus was reigning over Judaea in the room of his father Herod, he was afraid to go thither; and being warned *of God* in a dream, he withdrew into the parts of Galilee,

23 and came and dwelt in a city called Nazareth; that it might be fulfilled which was spoken through the prophets, [35]that he should be called a Nazarene.

Chapter 3

1 And in those days cometh John the Baptist, preaching in the wilderness of Judaea, saying,

2 Repent ye; for the kingdom of heaven is at hand.

3 For this is he that was spoken of through Isaiah the prophet, saying,
[36]The voice of one crying in the wilderness,
Make ye ready the way of the Lord,
Make his paths straight.

4 Now John himself had his raiment of camel's hair, and a leathern girdle about his loins; and his food was locusts and wild honey.

5 Then went out unto him Jerusalem, and all Judaea, and all the region round about the Jordan;

6 and they were baptized of him in the river Jordan, confessing their sins.

7 But when he saw many of the Pharisees and Sadducees coming [37]to his baptism, he said unto them, Ye offspring of vipers, who warned you to flee from the wrath to come?

8 Bring forth therefore fruit worthy of [38]repentance:

---

[35] *Isa. 11:1 in the Hebrew?*
[36] *Isa. 40:3.*
[37] *Or, for baptism*
[38] *Or, your repentance*

9 and think not to say within yourselves, We have Abraham to our father: for I say unto you, that God is able of these stones to raise up children unto Abraham.

10 And even now the axe lieth at the root of the trees: every tree therefore that bringeth not forth good fruit is hewn down, and cast into the fire.

11 I indeed baptize you [39]in water unto repentance: but he that cometh after me is mightier than I, whose shoes I am not [40]worthy to bear: he shall baptize you [41]in the Holy Spirit and *in* fire:

12 whose fan is in his hand, and he will thoroughly cleanse his threshing-floor; and he will gather his wheat into the garner, but the chaff he will burn up with unquenchable fire.

13 Then cometh Jesus from Galilee to the Jordan unto John, to be baptized of him.

14 But John would have hindered him, saying, I have need to be baptized of thee, and comest thou to me?

15 But Jesus answering said unto him, Suffer [42]*it* now: for thus it becometh us to fulfil all righteousness. Then he suffereth him.

16 And Jesus, when he was baptized, went up straightway from the water: and lo, the heavens were opened [43]unto him, and he saw the Spirit of God descending as a dove, and coming upon him;

17 and lo, a voice out of the heavens, saying, [44]This is my beloved Son, in whom I am well pleased.

---

[39] *Or, with*
[40] *Greek sufficient.*
[41] *Or, with*
[42] *Or, me*
[43] *Some ancient authorities omit unto him.*
[44] *Or, This is my Son; my beloved in whom I am well pleased. See 12:18.*

Chapter 4

†✓ **Jesus was tempted. God cannot be tempted (James 1:13).** The Scripture (James 1:13) states clearly that "God cannot be tempted with evil." Since Jesus was genuinely tempted here (and "in all points" per Heb 4:15), he cannot be the God described by James. He is the human Messiah, the Second Adam.

1 Then was Jesus led up of the Spirit into the wilderness to be tempted of the devil.

2 And when he had fasted forty days and forty nights, he afterward hungered.

3 And the tempter came and said unto him, If thou art the Son of God, command that these stones become [45]bread.

4 But he answered and said, It is written, [46]Man shall not live by bread alone, but by every word that proceedeth out of the mouth of God.

5 Then the devil taketh him into the holy city; and he set him on the [47]pinnacle of the temple,

6 and saith unto him, If thou art the Son of God, cast thyself down: for it is written,

[48]He shall give his angels charge concerning thee: and,
On their hands they shall bear thee up,
Lest haply thou dash thy foot against a stone.

7 Jesus said unto him, Again it is written, [49]Thou shalt not make trial of the Lord thy God.

8 Again, the devil taketh him unto an exceeding high mountain, and showeth him all the kingdoms of the world, and the glory of them;

9 and he said unto him, All these things will I give thee, if thou wilt fall down and [50]worship me.

10 Then saith Jesus unto him, Get thee hence, Satan: for it is written, [51]Thou shalt worship the Lord thy God, and him only shalt thou serve.

11 Then the devil leaveth him; and behold, angels came and ministered unto him.

12 Now when he heard that John was delivered up, he withdrew into Galilee;

---

[45] *Greek loaves.*
[46] Dt. 8:3.
[47] *Greek wing.*
[48] Ps. 91:11, 12.
[49] Dt. 6:16.
[50] *See marginal note on 2:2.*
[51] Dt. 6:13.

13 and leaving Nazareth, he came and dwelt in Capernaum, which is by the sea, in the borders of Zebulun and Naphtali:

14 that it might be fulfilled which was spoken through Isaiah the prophet, saying,

15 [52]The land of Zebulun and the land of Naphtali,
    [53]Toward the sea, beyond the Jordan,
    Galilee of the [54]Gentiles,

16 The people that sat in darkness
    Saw a great light,
    And to them that sat in the region and shadow of death,
    To them did light spring up.

17 From that time began Jesus to preach, and to say, Repent ye; for the kingdom of heaven is at hand.

18 And walking by the sea of Galilee, he saw two brethren, Simon who is called Peter, and Andrew his brother, casting a net into the sea; for they were fishers.

19 And he saith unto them, Come ye after me, and I will make you fishers of men.

20 And they straightway left the nets, and followed him.

21 And going on from thence he saw two other brethren, [55]James the *son* of Zebedee, and John his brother, in the boat with Zebedee their father, mending their nets; and he called them.

22 And they straightway left the boat and their father, and followed him.

23 And [56]Jesus went about in all Galilee, teaching in their synagogues, and preaching the [57]gospel of the kingdom, and healing all manner of disease and all manner of sickness among the people.

24 And the report of him went forth into all Syria: and they brought unto him all that were sick, holden with divers diseases and torments,

---

[52] *Isa. 9:1, 2.*
[53] *Greek The way of the sea.*
[54] *Greek nations: and so elsewhere.*
[55] *Or, Jacob*
[56] *Some ancient authorities read he.*
[57] *Or, good tidings: and so elsewhere.*

[58]possessed with demons, and epileptic, and palsied; and he healed them.

25 And there followed him great multitudes from Galilee and Decapolis and Jerusalem and Judaea and *from* beyond the Jordan.

Chapter 5

1 And seeing the multitudes, he went up into the mountain: and when he had sat down, his disciples came unto him:

2 and he opened his mouth and taught them, saying,

3 Blessed are the poor in spirit: for theirs is the kingdom of heaven.

4 [59]Blessed are they that mourn: for they shall be comforted.

5 Blessed are the meek: for they shall inherit the earth.

6 Blessed are they that hunger and thirst after righteousness: for they shall be filled.

7 Blessed are the merciful: for they shall obtain mercy.

8 Blessed are the pure in heart: for they shall see God.

9 Blessed are the peacemakers: for they shall be called sons of God.

10 Blessed are they that have been persecuted for righteousness' sake: for theirs is the kingdom of heaven.

11 Blessed are ye when *men* shall reproach you, and persecute you, and say all manner of evil against you falsely, for my sake.

12 Rejoice, and be exceeding glad: for great is your reward in heaven: for so persecuted they the prophets that were before you.

13 Ye are the salt of the earth: but if the salt have lost its savor, wherewith shall it be salted? it is thenceforth good for nothing, but to be cast out and trodden under foot of men.

14 Ye are the light of the world. A city set on a hill cannot be hid.

15 Neither do *men* light a lamp, and put it under the bushel, but on the stand; and it shineth unto all that are in the house.

16 Even so let your light shine before men; that they may see your good works, and glorify your Father who is in heaven.

---

[58] *Or, demoniacs*
[59] *Some ancient authorities transpose verses 4 and 5.*

17 Think not that I came to destroy the law or the prophets: I came not to destroy, but to fulfil.

18 For verily I say unto you, Till heaven and earth pass away, one jot or one tittle shall in no wise pass away from the law, till all things be accomplished.

19 Whosoever therefore shall break one of these least commandments, and shall teach men so, shall be called least in the kingdom of heaven: but whosoever shall do and teach them, he shall be called great in the kingdom of heaven.

20 For I say unto you, that except your righteousness shall exceed *the righteousness* of the scribes and Pharisees, ye shall in no wise enter into the kingdom of heaven.

21 Ye have heard that it was said to them of old time, [60]Thou shalt not kill; and whosoever shall kill shall be in danger of the judgment:

22 but I say unto you, that every one who is angry with his brother [61]shall be in danger of the judgment; and whosoever shall say to his brother, [62]Raca, shall be in danger of the council; and whosoever shall say, [63]Thou fool, shall be in danger [64]of the [65]hell of fire.

23 If therefore thou art offering thy gift at the altar, and there rememberest that thy brother hath aught against thee,

24 leave there thy gift before the altar, and go thy way, first be reconciled to thy brother, and then come and offer thy gift.

25 Agree with thine adversary quickly, while thou art with him in the way; lest haply the adversary [66]deliver thee to the judge, and the judge deliver thee to the officer, and thou be cast into prison.

26 Verily I say unto thee, Thou shalt by no means come out thence, till thou have paid the last farthing.

27 Ye have heard that it was said, [67]Thou shalt not commit adultery:

---

[60] *Ex. 20:13; Dt. 5:17.*
[61] *Many ancient authorities insert without cause.*
[62] *An expression of contempt.*
[63] *Or, Moreh, a Hebrew expression of condemnation.*
[64] *Greek unto or into.*
[65] *Greek Gehenna of fire.*
[66] *Some ancient authorities omit deliver thee.*
[67] *Ex. 20:14; Dt. 5:18.*

28 but I say unto you, that every one that looketh on a woman to lust after her hath committed adultery with her already in his heart.

29 And if thy right eye causeth thee to stumble, pluck it out, and cast it from thee: for it is profitable for thee that one of thy members should perish, and not thy whole body be cast into [68]hell.

30 And if thy right hand causeth thee to stumble, cut it off, and cast it from thee: for it is profitable for thee that one of thy members should perish, and not thy whole body go into [69]hell.

31 It was said also, [70]Whosoever shall put away his wife, let him give her a writing of divorcement:

32 but I say unto you, that every one that putteth away his wife, saving for the cause of fornication, maketh her an adulteress: and whosoever shall marry her when she is put away committeth adultery.

33 Again, ye have heard that it was said to them of old time, [71]Thou shalt not forswear thyself, but shalt perform unto the Lord thine oaths:

34 but I say unto you, Swear not at all; neither by the heaven, for it is the throne of God;

35 nor by the earth, for it is the footstool of his feet; nor [72]by Jerusalem, for it is the city of the great King.

36 Neither shalt thou swear by thy head, for thou canst not make one hair white or black.

37 [73]But let your speech be, Yea, yea; Nay, nay: and whatsoever is more than these is of [74]the evil *one*.

38 Ye have heard that it was said, An [75]eye for an eye, and a tooth for a tooth:

39 but I say unto you, Resist not [76]him that is evil: but whosoever smiteth thee on thy right cheek, turn to him the other also.

---

[68] *Greek Gehenna.*
[69] *Greek Gehenna.*
[70] *Dt. 24:1, 3.*
[71] *Lev. 19:12; Num. 30:2; Dt. 23:21.*
[72] *Or, toward*
[73] *Some ancient authorities read But your speech shall be.*
[74] *Or, evil: as in verse 39; 6:13.*
[75] *Ex. 21:24; Lev. 24:20; Dt. 19:21.*
[76] *Or, evil*

40 And if any man would go to law with thee, and take away thy coat, let him have thy cloak also.

41 And whosoever shall [77]compel thee to go one mile, go with him two.

42 Give to him that asketh thee, and from him that would borrow of thee turn not thou away.

43 Ye have heard that it was said, [78]Thou shalt love thy neighbor, and hate thine enemy:

44 but I say unto you, Love your enemies, and pray for them that persecute you;

45 that ye may be sons of your Father who is in heaven: for he maketh his sun to rise on the evil and the good, and sendeth rain on the just and the unjust.

46 For if ye love them that love you, what reward have ye? do not even the [79]publicans the same?

47 And if ye salute your brethren only, what do ye more *than others*? do not even the Gentiles the same?

48 Ye therefore shall be perfect, as your heavenly Father is perfect.

Chapter 6

1 Take heed that ye do not your righteousness before men, to be seen of them: else ye have no reward with your Father who is in heaven.

2 When therefore thou doest alms, sound not a trumpet before thee, as the hypocrites do in the synagogues and in the streets, that they may have glory of men. Verily I say unto you, They have received their reward.

3 But when thou doest alms, let not thy left hand know what thy right hand doeth:

4 that thine alms may be in secret: and thy Father who seeth in secret shall recompense thee.

5 And when ye pray, ye shall not be as the hypocrites: for they love to stand and pray in the synagogues and in the corners of the streets, that

---

[77] *Greek impress.*
[78] *Lev. 19:18.*
[79] *That is, collectors or renters of Roman taxes.*

they may be seen of men. Verily I say unto you, They have received their reward.

6 But thou, when thou prayest, enter into thine inner chamber, and having shut thy door, pray to thy Father who is in secret, and thy Father who seeth in secret shall recompense thee.

7 And in praying use not vain repetitions, as the Gentiles do: for they think that they shall be heard for their much speaking.

8 Be not therefore like unto them: for [80]your Father knoweth what things ye have need of, before ye ask him.

9 After this manner therefore pray ye: Our Father who art in heaven, Hallowed be thy name.

10 Thy kingdom come. Thy will be done, as in heaven, so on earth.

11 Give us this day [81]our daily bread.

12 And forgive us our debts, as we also have forgiven our debtors.

*⚡ **FORGERY.** The Doxology was added later. The famous ending is absent from the oldest MSS. It was likely a liturgical addition for church services.*

13 And bring us not into temptation, but deliver us from [82]the evil *one*. [83][84]

14 For if ye forgive men their trespasses, your heavenly Father will also forgive you.

15 But if ye forgive not men their trespasses, neither will your Father forgive your trespasses.

16 Moreover when ye fast, be not, as the hypocrites, of a sad countenance: for they disfigure their faces, that they may be seen of men to fast. Verily I say unto you, They have received their reward.

17 But thou, when thou fastest, anoint thy head, and wash thy face;

18 that thou be not seen of men to fast, but of thy Father who is in secret: and thy Father, who seeth in secret, shall recompense thee.

19 Lay not up for yourselves treasures upon the earth, where moth and rust consume, and where thieves break through and steal:

---

[80] *Some ancient authorities read God your Father.*
[81] *Greek our bread for the coming day. Or, our needful bread*
[82] *Or, evil*
[83] *Many authorities, some ancient, but with variations, add For thine is the kingdom, and the power, and the glory, for ever. Amen.*
[84] **Textual Variation:** The famous ending "For thine is the kingdom..." is found in the KJV but is absent from the oldest Greek witnesses (Sinaiticus, Vaticanus). The RV restores the prayer to its authentic, original form.

MATTHEW 6

20 but lay up for yourselves treasures in heaven, where neither moth nor rust doth consume, and where thieves do not [85]break through nor steal:

21 for where thy treasure is, there will thy heart be also.

22 The lamp of the body is the eye: if therefore thine eye be single, thy whole body shall be full of light.

23 But if thine eye be evil, thy whole body shall be full of darkness. If therefore the light that is in thee be darkness, how great is the darkness!

24 No man can serve two masters: for either he will hate the one, and love the other; or else he will hold to one, and despise the other. Ye cannot serve God and mammon.

25 Therefore I say unto you, Be not anxious for your life, what ye shall eat, or what ye shall drink; nor yet for your body, what ye shall put on. Is not the life more than the food, and the body than the raiment?[86]

26 Behold the birds of the heaven, that they sow not, neither do they reap, nor gather into barns; and your heavenly Father feedeth them. Are not ye of much more value than they?

27 And which of you by being anxious can add one cubit unto [87]the measure of his life?

28 And why are ye anxious concerning raiment? Consider the lilies of the field, how they grow; they toil not, neither do they spin:

29 yet I say unto you, that even Solomon in all his glory was not arrayed like one of these.

30 But if God doth so clothe the grass of the field, which to-day is, and to-morrow is cast into the oven, *shall he* not much more *clothe* you, O ye of little faith?

31 Be not therefore anxious, saying, What shall we eat? or, What shall we drink? or, Wherewithal shall we be clothed?

---

[85] *Greek dig through.*

[86] **False Friend:** The KJV reads "Is not the life more than meat?" In 1611, "meat" meant all food. Today, it means animal flesh. The RV "food" accurately reflects the Greek *trophe*, clarifying that God provides *all* sustenance, not just meat.

[87] *Or, his stature*

32 For after all these things do the Gentiles seek; for your heavenly Father knoweth that ye have need of all these things.

33 But seek ye first his kingdom, and his righteousness; and all these things shall be added unto you.

34 Be not therefore anxious for the morrow: for the morrow will be anxious for itself. Sufficient unto the day is the evil thereof.

Chapter 7

1 Judge not, that ye be not judged.

2 For with what judgment ye judge, ye shall be judged: and with what measure ye mete, it shall be measured unto you.[88]

3 And why beholdest thou the mote that is in thy brother's eye, but considerest not the beam that is in thine own eye?

4 Or how wilt thou say to thy brother, Let me cast out the mote out of thine eye; and lo, the beam is in thine own eye?

5 Thou hypocrite, cast out first the beam out of thine own eye; and then shalt thou see clearly to cast out the mote out of thy brother's eye.

6 Give not that which is holy unto the dogs, neither cast your pearls before the swine, lest haply they trample them under their feet, and turn and rend you.

7 Ask, and it shall be given you; seek, and ye shall find; knock, and it shall be opened unto you:

8 for every one that asketh receiveth; and he that seeketh findeth; and to him that knocketh it shall be opened.

9 Or what man is there of you, who, if his son shall ask him for a loaf, will give him a stone;

10 or if he shall ask for a fish, will give him a serpent?

11 If ye then, being evil, know how to give good gifts unto your children, how much more shall your Father who is in heaven give good things to them that ask him?

12 All things therefore whatsoever ye would that men should do unto you, even so do ye also unto them: for this is the law and the prophets.

---

[88]**Textual Restoration:** The KJV adds the word "again" ("measured to you again"). This word is absent from the oldest Greek manuscripts. The RV omits it to strictly follow the original text.

13 Enter ye in by the narrow gate: for wide [89]is the gate, and broad is the way, that leadeth to destruction, and many are they that enter in thereby.

14 [90]For narrow is the gate, and straitened the way, that leadeth unto life, and few are they that find it.

15 Beware of false prophets, who come to you in sheep's clothing, but inwardly are ravening wolves.

16 By their fruits ye shall know them. Do *men* gather grapes of thorns, or figs of thistles?

17 Even so every good tree bringeth forth good fruit; but the corrupt tree bringeth forth evil fruit.

18 A good tree cannot bring forth evil fruit, neither can a corrupt tree bring forth good fruit.

19 Every tree that bringeth not forth good fruit is hewn down, and cast into the fire.

20 Therefore by their fruits ye shall know them.

21 Not every one that saith unto me, Lord, Lord, shall enter into the kingdom of heaven; but he that doeth the will of my Father who is in heaven.

22 Many will say to me in that day, Lord, Lord, did we not prophesy by thy name, and by thy name cast out demons, and by thy name do many [91]mighty works?

23 And then will I profess unto them, I never knew you: depart from me, ye that work iniquity.

24 Every one therefore that heareth these words of mine, and doeth them, shall be likened unto a wise man, who built his house upon the rock:

25 and the rain descended, and the floods came, and the winds blew, and beat upon that house; and it fell not: for it was founded upon the rock.

26 And every one that heareth these words of mine, and doeth them not, shall be likened unto a foolish man, who built his house upon the sand:

---

[89] *Some ancient authorities omit is the gate.*
[90] *Many ancient authorities read How narrow is the gate, etc.*
[91] *Greek powers.*

27 and the rain descended, and the floods came, and the winds blew, and smote upon that house; and it fell: and great was the fall thereof.

28 And it came to pass, when Jesus had finished these words, the multitudes were astonished at his teaching:

29 for he taught them as *one* having authority, and not as their scribes.

Chapter 8

1 And when he was come down from the mountain, great multitudes followed him.

2 And behold, there came to him a leper and [92]worshipped him, saying, Lord, if thou wilt, thou canst make me clean.

3 And he stretched forth his hand, and touched him, saying, I will; be thou made clean. And straightway his leprosy was cleansed.

4 And Jesus saith unto him, [93]See thou tell no man; but go, show thyself to the priest, and offer the gift that Moses commanded, for a testimony unto them.

5 And when he was entered into Capernaum, there came unto him a centurion, beseeching him,

6 and saying, Lord, my [94]servant lieth in the house sick of the palsy, grievously tormented.

7 And he saith unto him, I will come and heal him.

8 And the centurion answered and said, Lord, I am not [95]worthy that thou shouldest come under my roof; but only say [96]the word, and my [97]servant shall be healed.

9 For I also am a man [98]under authority, having under myself soldiers: and I say to this one, Go, and he goeth; and to another, Come, and he cometh; and to my [99]servant, Do this, and he doeth it.

---

[92] *See marginal note on 2:2.*
[93] *Lev. 13:49; 14:2ff.*
[94] *Or, boy*
[95] *Greek sufficient.*
[96] *Greek with a word.*
[97] *Or, boy*
[98] *Some ancient authorities insert set: as in Lk. 7:8.*
[99] *Greek bondservant.*

10 And when Jesus heard it, he marvelled, and said to them that followed, Verily I say unto you, [100]I have not found so great faith, no, not in Israel.

11 And I say unto you, that many shall come from the east and the west, and shall [101]sit down with Abraham, and Isaac, and Jacob, in the kingdom of heaven:

12 but the sons of the kingdom shall be cast forth into the outer darkness: there shall be the weeping and the gnashing of teeth.

13 And Jesus said unto the centurion, Go thy way; as thou hast believed, *so* be it done unto thee. And the [102]servant was healed in that hour.

14 And when Jesus was come into Peter's house, he saw his wife's mother lying sick of a fever.

15 And he touched her hand, and the fever left her; and she arose, and ministered unto him.

16 And when even was come, they brought unto him many [103]possessed with demons: and he cast out the spirits with a word, and healed all that were sick:

17 that it might be fulfilled which was spoken through Isaiah the prophet, saying, [104]Himself took our infirmities, and bare our diseases.

18 Now when Jesus saw great multitudes about him, he gave commandment to depart unto the other side.

19 And there came [105]a scribe, and said unto him, Teacher, I will follow thee whithersoever thou goest.

20 And Jesus saith unto him, The foxes have holes, and the birds of the heaven *have* [106]nests; but the Son of man hath not where to lay his head.

21 And another of the disciples said unto him, Lord, suffer me first to go and bury my father.

22 But Jesus saith unto him, Follow me; and leave the dead to bury their own dead.

23 And when he was entered into a boat, his disciples followed him.

---

[100] *Many ancient authorities read With no man in Israel have I found so great faith.*
[101] *Greek recline.*
[102] *Or, boy*
[103] *Or, demoniacs*
[104] *Isa. 53:4.*
[105] *Greek one scribe.*
[106] *Greek lodging-places.*

24 And behold, there arose a great tempest in the sea, insomuch that the boat was covered with the waves: but he was asleep.

25 And they came to him, and awoke him, saying, Save, Lord; we perish.

26 And he saith unto them, Why are ye fearful, O ye of little faith? Then he arose, and rebuked the winds and the sea; and there was a great calm.

27 And the men marvelled, saying, What manner of man is this, that even the winds and the sea obey him?

28 And when he was come to the other side into the country of the Gadarenes, there met him two [107]possessed with demons, coming forth out of the tombs, exceeding fierce, so that no man could pass by that way.

29 And behold, they cried out, saying, What have we to do with thee, thou Son of God? art thou come hither to torment us before the time?

30 Now there was afar off from them a herd of many swine feeding.

31 And the demons besought him, saying, If thou cast us out, send us away into the herd of swine.

32 And he said unto them, Go. And they came out, and went into the swine: and behold, the whole herd rushed down the steep into the sea, and perished in the waters.

33 And they that fed them fled, and went away into the city, and told everything, and what was befallen to them that were [108]possessed with demons.

34 And behold, all the city came out to meet Jesus: and when they saw him, they besought *him* that he would depart from their borders.

Chapter 9

1 And he entered into a boat, and crossed over, and came into his own city.

2 And behold, they brought to him a man sick of the palsy, lying on a bed: and Jesus seeing their faith said unto the sick of the palsy, [109]Son, be of good cheer; thy sins are forgiven.

---

[107] *Or, demoniacs*
[108] *Or, demoniacs*
[109] *Greek Child.*

3 And behold, certain of the scribes said within themselves, This man blasphemeth.

4 And Jesus [110]knowing their thoughts said, Wherefore think ye evil in your hearts?

5 For which is easier, to say, Thy sins are forgiven; or to say, Arise, and walk?

6 But that ye may know that the Son of man hath authority on earth to forgive sins (then saith he to the sick of the palsy), Arise, and take up thy bed, and go unto thy house.

7 And he arose, and departed to his house.

8 But when the multitudes saw it, they were afraid, and glorified God, who had given such authority unto men.

9 And as Jesus passed by from thence, he saw a man, called Matthew, sitting at the place of toll: and he saith unto him, Follow me. And he arose, and followed him.

10 And it came to pass, as he [111]sat at meat in the house, behold, many [112]publicans and sinners came and sat down with Jesus and his disciples.

11 And when the Pharisees saw it, they said unto his disciples, Why eateth your Teacher with the [113]publicans and sinners?

12 But when he heard it, he said, They that are [114]whole have no need of a physician, but they that are sick.

13 But go ye and learn what *this* meaneth, [115]I desire mercy, and not sacrifice: for I came not to call the righteous, but sinners.

14 Then come to him the disciples of John, saying, Why do we and the Pharisees fast [116]oft, but thy disciples fast not?

---

[110]*Many ancient authorities read seeing.*
[111]*Greek reclined: and so always.*
[112]*See marginal note on 5:46.*
[113]*See marginal note on 5:46.*
[114]*Greek strong.*
[115]*Hos. 6:6.*
[116]*Some ancient authorities omit oft.*

15 And Jesus said unto them, Can the [117]sons of the bridechamber mourn, as long as the bridegroom is with them? but the days will come, when the bridegroom shall be taken away from them, and then will they fast.

16 And no man putteth a piece of undressed cloth upon an old garment; for that which should fill it up taketh from the garment, and a worse rent is made.

17 Neither do *men* put new wine into old [118]wine-skins: else the skins burst, and the wine is spilled, and the skins perish: but they put new wine into fresh wine-skins, and both are preserved.

18 While he spake these things unto them, behold, there came [119]a ruler, and [120]worshipped him, saying, My daughter is even now dead: but come and lay thy hand upon her, and she shall live.

19 And Jesus arose, and followed him, and *so did* his disciples.

20 And behold, a woman, who had an issue of blood twelve years, came behind him, and touched the border of his garment:

21 for she said within herself, If I do but touch his garment, I shall be [121]made whole.

22 But Jesus turning and seeing her said, Daughter, be of good cheer; thy faith hath [122]made thee whole. And the woman was [123]made whole from that hour.

23 And when Jesus came into the ruler's house, and saw the flute-players, and the crowd making a tumult,

24 he said, Give place: for the damsel is not dead, but sleepeth. And they laughed him to scorn.

25 But when the crowd was put forth, he entered in, and took her by the hand; and the damsel arose.

26 And [124]the fame hereof went forth into all that land.

---

[117] *That is, companions of the bridegroom.*
[118] *That is, skins used as bottles.*
[119] *Greek one ruler. Compare Mk. 5:22.*
[120] *See marginal note on 2:2.*
[121] *Or, saved*
[122] *Or, saved thee*
[123] *Or, saved*
[124] *Greek this fame.*

27 And as Jesus passed by from thence, two blind men followed him, crying out, and saying, Have mercy on us, thou son of David.

28 And when he was come into the house, the blind men came to him: and Jesus saith unto them, Believe ye that I am able to do this? They say unto him, Yea, Lord.

29 Then touched he their eyes, saying, According to your faith be it done unto you.

30 And their eyes were opened. And Jesus [125]strictly charged them, saying, See that no man know it.

31 But they went forth, and spread abroad his fame in all that land.

32 And as they went forth, behold, there was brought to him a dumb man possessed with a demon.

33 And when the demon was cast out, the dumb man spake: and the multitudes marvelled, saying, It was never so seen in Israel.

34 But the Pharisees said, [126]By the prince of the demons casteth he out demons.

35 And Jesus went about all the cities and the villages, teaching in their synagogues, and preaching the [127]gospel of the kingdom, and healing all manner of disease and all manner of sickness.

36 But when he saw the multitudes, he was moved with compassion for them, because they were distressed and scattered, as sheep not having a shepherd.

37 Then saith he unto his disciples, The harvest indeed is plenteous, but the laborers are few.

38 Pray ye therefore the Lord of the harvest, that he send forth laborers into his harvest.

---

[125] *Or, sternly*
[126] *Or, In*
[127] *See marginal note on 4:23.*

Chapter 10

1 And he called unto him his twelve disciples, and gave them authority over unclean spirits, to cast them out, and to heal all manner of disease and all manner of sickness.

2 Now the names of the twelve apostles are these: The first, Simon, who is called Peter, and Andrew his brother; [128]James the *son* of Zebedee, and John his brother;

3 Philip, and Bartholomew; Thomas, and Matthew the [129]publican; [130]James the *son* of Alphaeus, and Thaddaeus;

4 Simon the [131]Cananaean, and Judas Iscariot, who also [132]betrayed him.

5 These twelve Jesus sent forth, and charged them, saying, Go not into *any* way of the Gentiles, and enter not into any city of the Samaritans:

6 but go rather to the lost sheep of the house of Israel.

7 And as ye go, preach, saying, The kingdom of heaven is at hand.

8 Heal the sick, raise the dead, cleanse the lepers, cast out demons: freely ye received, freely give.

9 Get you no gold, nor silver, nor brass in your [133]purses;

10 no wallet for *your* journey, neither two coats, nor shoes, nor staff: for the laborer is worthy of his food.

11 And into whatsoever city or village ye shall enter, search out who in it is worthy; and there abide till ye go forth.

12 And as ye enter into the house, salute it.

13 And if the house be worthy, let your peace come upon it: but if it be not worthy, let your peace return to you.

14 And whosoever shall not receive you, nor hear your words, as ye go forth out of that house or that city, shake off the dust of your feet.

15 Verily I say unto you, It shall be more tolerable for the land of Sodom and Gomorrah in the day of judgment, than for that city.

---

[128] *Or, Jacob*
[129] *See marginal note on 5:46.*
[130] *Or, Jacob*
[131] *Or, Zealot. See Lk. 6:15; Acts 1:13.*
[132] *Or, delivered him up*
[133] *Greek girdles.*

16 Behold, I send you forth as sheep in the midst of wolves: be ye therefore wise as serpents, and [134]harmless as doves.

17 But beware of men: for they will deliver you up to councils, and in their synagogues they will scourge you;

18 yea and before governors and kings shall ye be brought for my sake, for a testimony to them and to the Gentiles.

19 But when they deliver you up, be not anxious how or what ye shall speak: for it shall be given you in that hour what ye shall speak.

20 For it is not ye that speak, but the Spirit of your Father that speaketh in you.

21 And brother shall deliver up brother to death, and the father his child: and children shall rise up against parents, and [135]cause them to be put to death.

22 And ye shall be hated of all men for my name's sake: but he that endureth to the end, the same shall be saved.

23 But when they persecute you in this city, flee into the next: for verily I say unto you, Ye shall not have gone through the cities of Israel, till the Son of man be come.

24 A disciple is not above his teacher, nor a [136]servant above his lord.

25 It is enough for the disciple that he be as his teacher, and the [137]servant as his lord. If they have called the master of the house [138]Beelzebub, how much more them of his household!

26 Fear them not therefore: for there is nothing covered, that shall not be revealed; and hid, that shall not be known.

27 What I tell you in the darkness, speak ye in the light; and what ye hear in the ear, proclaim upon the house-tops.

28 And be not afraid of them that kill the body, but are not able to kill the soul: but rather fear him who is able to destroy both soul and body in [139]hell.

---

[134]*Or, simple*
[135]*Or, put them to death*
[136]*Greek bondservant.*
[137]*Greek bondservant.*
[138]*Greek Beelzebul.*
[139]*Greek Gehenna.*

29 Are not two sparrows sold for a penny? and not one of them shall fall on the ground without your Father:

30 but the very hairs of your head are all numbered.

31 Fear not therefore: ye are of more value than many sparrows.

32 Every one therefore who shall confess [140]me before men, [141]him will I also confess before my Father who is in heaven.

33 But whosoever shall deny me before men, him will I also deny before my Father who is in heaven.

34 Think not that I came to [142]send peace on the earth: I came not to [143]send peace, but a sword.

35 For I came to set a man at variance against his father, and the daughter against her mother, and the daughter in law against her mother in law:

36 and a man's foes *shall be* they of his own household.

37 He that loveth father or mother more than me is not worthy of me; and he that loveth son or daughter more than me is not worthy of me.

38 And he that doth not take his cross and follow after me, is not worthy of me.

39 He that [144]findeth his life shall lose it; and he that [145]loseth his life for my sake shall find it.

40 He that receiveth you receiveth me, and he that receiveth me receiveth him that sent me.

41 He that receiveth a prophet in the name of a prophet shall receive a prophet's reward: and he that receiveth a righteous man in the name of a righteous man shall receive a righteous man's reward.

42 And whosoever shall give to drink unto one of these little ones a cup of cold water only, in the name of a disciple, verily I say unto you he shall in no wise lose his reward.

---

[140] *Greek in me.*
[141] *Greek in him.*
[142] *Greek cast.*
[143] *Greek cast.*
[144] *Or, found*
[145] *Or, lost*

Chapter 11

1 And it came to pass when Jesus had finished commanding his twelve disciples, he departed thence to teach and preach in their cities.

2 Now when John heard in the prison the works of the Christ, he sent by his disciples

3 and said unto him, Art thou he that cometh, or look we for another?

4 And Jesus answered and said unto them, Go and tell John the things which ye hear and see:

5 the blind receive their sight, and the lame walk, the lepers are cleansed, and the deaf hear, and the dead are raised up, and the poor have [146]good tidings preached to them.

6 And blessed is he, whosoever shall find no occasion of stumbling in me.

7 And as these went their way, Jesus began to say unto the multitudes concerning John, What went ye out into the wilderness to behold? a reed shaken with the wind?

8 But what went ye out to see? a man clothed in soft *raiment*? Behold, they that wear soft *raiment* are in kings' houses.

9 [147]But wherefore went ye out? to see a prophet? Yea, I say unto you, and much more than a prophet.

10 This is he, of whom it is written,
   [148]Behold, I send my messenger before thy face,
   Who shall prepare thy way before thee.

11 Verily I say unto you, Among them that are born of women there hath not arisen a greater than John the Baptist: yet he that is [149]but little in the kingdom of heaven is greater than he.

12 And from the days of John the Baptist until now the kingdom of heaven suffereth violence, and men of violence take it by force.

13 For all the prophets and the law prophesied until John.

---

[146] *Or, the gospel*
[147] *Many ancient authorities read But what went ye out to see? a prophet?*
[148] *Mal. 3:1.*
[149] *Greek lesser.*

14 And if ye are willing to receive [150]*it*, this is Elijah, that is to come.

15 He that hath ears [151]to hear, let him hear.

16 But whereunto shall I liken this generation? It is like unto children sitting in the marketplaces, who call unto their fellows

17 and say, We piped unto you, and ye did not dance; we wailed, and ye did not [152]mourn.

18 For John came neither eating nor drinking, and they say, He hath a demon.

19 The Son of man came eating and drinking, and they say, Behold, a gluttonous man and a winebibber, a friend of [153]publicans and sinners! And wisdom [154]is justified by her [155]works.

20 Then began he to upbraid the cities wherein most of his [156]mighty works were done, because they repented not.

21 Woe unto thee, Chorazin! woe unto thee, Bethsaida! for if the [157]mighty works had been done in Tyre and Sidon which were done in you, they would have repented long ago in sackcloth and ashes.

22 But I say unto you, it shall be more tolerable for Tyre and Sidon in the day of judgment, than for you.

23 And thou, Capernaum, shalt thou be exalted unto heaven? thou shalt [158]go down unto Hades: for if the [159]mighty works had been done in Sodom which were done in thee, it would have remained until this day.

24 But I say unto you that it shall be more tolerable for the land of Sodom in the day of judgment, than for thee.

---

[150] *Or, him*
[151] *Some ancient authorities omit* to hear.
[152] *Greek* beat the breast.
[153] *See marginal note on* 5:46.
[154] *Or, was*
[155] *Many ancient authorities read* children: *as in Lk.* 7:35.
[156] *Greek* powers.
[157] *Greek* powers.
[158] *Many ancient authorities read* be brought down.
[159] *Greek* powers.

25 At that season Jesus answered and said, I ¹⁶⁰thank thee, O Father, Lord of heaven and earth, that thou didst hide these things from the wise and understanding, and didst reveal them unto babes:

26 yea, Father, ¹⁶¹for so it was well-pleasing in thy sight.

27 All things have been delivered unto me of my Father: and no one knoweth the Son, save the Father; neither doth any know the Father, save the Son, and he to whomsoever the Son willeth to reveal *him*.

28 Come unto me, all ye that labor and are heavy laden, and I will give you rest.

29 Take my yoke upon you, and learn of me; for I am meek and lowly in heart: and ye shall find rest unto your souls.

30 For my yoke is easy, and my burden is light.

Chapter 12

1 At that season Jesus went on the sabbath day through the grainfields; and his disciples were hungry and began to pluck ears and to eat.

2 But the Pharisees, when they saw it, said unto him, Behold, thy disciples do that which it is not lawful to do upon the sabbath.

3 But he said unto them, ¹⁶²Have ye not read what David did, when he was hungry, and they that were with him;

4 how he entered into the house of God, and ¹⁶³ate the showbread, which it was not lawful for him to eat, neither for them that were with him, but only for the priests?

5 Or have ye not read in the law, ¹⁶⁴that on the sabbath day the priests in the temple profane the sabbath, and are guiltless?

6 But I say unto you, that ¹⁶⁵one greater than the temple is here.

7 But if ye had known what this meaneth, ¹⁶⁶I desire mercy, and not sacrifice, ye would not have condemned the guiltless.

---

¹⁶⁰ *Or, praise*
¹⁶¹ *Or, that*
¹⁶² *1 Sam. 21:6.*
¹⁶³ *Some ancient authorities read they ate.*
¹⁶⁴ *Num. 28:9, 10.*
¹⁶⁵ *Greek a greater thing.*
¹⁶⁶ *Hos. 6:6.*

8 For the Son of man is lord of the sabbath.

9 And he departed thence, and went into their synagogue:

10 and behold, a man having a withered hand. And they asked him, saying, Is it lawful to heal on the sabbath day? that they might accuse him.

11 And he said unto them, What man shall there be of you, that shall have one sheep, and if this fall into a pit on the sabbath day, will he not lay hold on it, and lift it out?

12 How much then is a man of more value than a sheep! Wherefore it is lawful to do good on the sabbath day.

13 Then saith he to the man, Stretch forth thy hand. And he stretched it forth; and it was restored whole, as the other.

14 But the Pharisees went out, and took counsel against him, how they might destroy him.

15 And Jesus perceiving *it* withdrew from thence: and many followed him; and he healed them all,

16 and charged them that they should not make him known:

17 that it might be fulfilled which was spoken through Isaiah the prophet, saying,

18 [167]Behold, my [168]servant whom I have chosen;
My beloved in whom my soul is well pleased:
I will put my Spirit upon him,
And he shall declare judgment to the [169]Gentiles.

19 He shall not strive, nor cry aloud;
Neither shall any one hear his voice in the streets.

20 A bruised reed shall he not break,
And smoking flax shall he not quench,
Till he send forth judgment unto victory.

21 And in his name shall the [170]Gentiles hope.

---

[167] *Isa. 42:1ff.*
[168] *See marginal note on Acts 3:13.*
[169] *See marginal note on 4:15.*
[170] *See marginal note on 4:15.*

22 Then was brought unto him [171]one possessed with a demon, blind and dumb: and he healed him, insomuch that the dumb man spake and saw.

23 And all the multitudes were amazed, and said, Can this be the son of David?

24 But when the Pharisees heard it, they said, This man doth not cast out demons, but [172]by [173]Beelzebub the prince of the demons.

25 And knowing their thoughts he said unto them, Every kingdom divided against itself is brought to desolation; and every city or house divided against itself shall not stand:

26 and if Satan casteth out Satan, he is divided against himself; how then shall his kingdom stand?

27 And if I [174]by [175]Beelzebub cast out demons, [176]by whom do your sons cast them out? therefore shall they be your judges.

28 But if I [177]by the Spirit of God cast out demons, then is the kingdom of God come upon you.

29 Or how can one enter into the house of the strong *man*, and spoil his goods, except he first bind the strong *man*? and then he will spoil his house.

30 He that is not with me is against me; and he that gathereth not with me scattereth.

31 Therefore I say unto you, Every sin and blasphemy shall be forgiven unto men; but the blasphemy against the Spirit shall not be forgiven.

32 And whosoever shall speak a word against the Son of man, it shall be forgiven him; but whosoever shall speak against the Holy Spirit, it shall not be forgiven him, neither in this [178]world, nor in that which is to come.

---

[171] *Or, a demoniac*
[172] *Or, in*
[173] *Greek Beelzebul.*
[174] *Or, in*
[175] *Greek Beelzebul.*
[176] *Or, in*
[177] *Or, in*
[178] *Or, age*

33 Either make the tree good, and its fruit good; or make the tree corrupt, and its fruit corrupt: for the tree is known by its fruit.

34 Ye offspring of vipers, how can ye, being evil, speak good things? for out of the abundance of the heart the mouth speaketh.

35 The good man out of his good treasure bringeth forth good things: and the evil man out of his evil treasure bringeth forth evil things.

36 And I say unto you, that every idle word that men shall speak, they shall give account thereof in the day of judgment.

37 For by thy words thou shalt be justified, and by thy words thou shalt be condemned.

38 Then certain of the scribes and Pharisees answered him, saying, Teacher, we would see a sign from thee.

39 But he answered and said unto them, An evil and adulterous generation seeketh after a sign; and there shall no sign be given to it but the sign of Jonah the prophet:

40 for as Jonah was three days and three nights in the belly of the [179]whale; so shall the Son of man be three days and three nights in the heart of the earth.

41 The men of Nineveh shall stand up in the judgment with this generation, and shall condemn it: for they repented at the preaching of Jonah; and behold, [180]a greater than Jonah is here.

42 The queen of the south shall rise up in the judgment with this generation, and shall condemn it: for she came from the ends of the earth to hear the wisdom of Solomon; and behold, [181]a greater than Solomon is here.

43 But the unclean spirit, when [182]he is gone out of the man, passeth through waterless places, seeking rest, and findeth it not.

44 Then [183]he saith, I will return into my house whence I came out; and when [184]he is come, [185]he findeth it empty, swept, and garnished.

---

[179] *Greek sea-monster.*
[180] *Greek more than.*
[181] *Greek more than.*
[182] *Or, it*
[183] *Or, it*
[184] *Or, it*
[185] *Or, it*

45 Then goeth [186]he, and taketh with [187]himself seven other spirits more evil than [188]himself, and they enter in and dwell there: and the last state of that man becometh worse than the first. Even so shall it be also unto this evil generation.

46 While he was yet speaking to the multitudes, behold, his mother and his brethren stood without, seeking to speak to him.

47 [189]And one said unto him, Behold, thy mother and thy brethren stand without, seeking to speak to thee.

48 But he answered and said unto him that told him, Who is my mother? and who are my brethren?

49 And he stretched forth his hand towards his disciples, and said, Behold, my mother and my brethren!

50 For whosoever shall do the will of my Father who is in heaven, he is my brother, and sister, and mother.

Chapter 13

1 On that day went Jesus out of the house, and sat by the sea side.

2 And there were gathered unto him great multitudes, so that he entered into a boat, and sat; and all the multitude stood on the beach.

3 And he spake to them many things in parables, saying, Behold, the sower went forth to sow;

4 and as he sowed, some *seeds* fell by the way side, and the birds came and devoured them:

5 and others fell upon the rocky places, where they had not much earth: and straightway they sprang up, because they had no deepness of earth:

6 and when the sun was risen, they were scorched; and because they had no root, they withered away.

7 And others fell upon the thorns; and the thorns grew up and choked them:

---

[186] *Or, it*
[187] *Or, itself*
[188] *Or, itself*
[189] *Some ancient authorities omit verse 47.*

8 and others fell upon the good ground, and yielded fruit, some a hundredfold, some sixty, some thirty.

9 He that hath ears, [190] let him hear.

10 And the disciples came, and said unto him, Why speakest thou unto them in parables?

11 And he answered and said unto them, Unto you it is given to know the mysteries of the kingdom of heaven, but to them it is not given.

12 For whosoever hath, to him shall be given, and he shall have abundance: but whosoever hath not, from him shall be taken away even that which he hath.

13 Therefore speak I to them in parables; because seeing they see not, and hearing they hear not, neither do they understand.

14 And unto them is fulfilled the prophecy of Isaiah, which saith,
[191] By hearing ye shall hear, and shall in no wise understand;
And seeing ye shall see, and shall in no wise perceive:

15 For this people's heart is waxed gross,
And their ears are dull of hearing,
And their eyes they have closed;
Lest haply they should perceive with their eyes,
And hear with their ears,
And understand with their heart,
And should turn again,
And I should heal them.

16 But blessed are your eyes, for they see; and your ears, for they hear.

17 For verily I say unto you, that many prophets and righteous men desired to see the things which ye see, and saw them not; and to hear the things which ye hear, and heard them not.

18 Hear then ye the parable of the sower.

19 When any one heareth the word of the kingdom, and understandeth it not, *then* cometh the evil *one*, and snatcheth away that which hath been sown in his heart. This is he that was sown by the way side.

20 And he that was sown upon the rocky places, this is he that heareth the word, and straightway with joy receiveth it;

---

[190] *Some ancient authorities add here, and in verse 43, to hear: as in Mk. 4:9; Lk. 8:8.*
[191] *Isa. 6:9, 10.*

21 yet hath he not root in himself, but endureth for a while; and when tribulation or persecution ariseth because of the word, straightway he stumbleth.

22 And he that was sown among the thorns, this is he that heareth the word; and the care of the [192]world, and the deceitfulness of riches, choke the word, and he becometh unfruitful.

23 And he that was sown upon the good ground, this is he that heareth the word, and understandeth it; who verily beareth fruit, and bringeth forth, some a hundredfold, some sixty, some thirty.

24 Another parable set he before them, saying, The kingdom of heaven is likened unto a man that sowed good seed in his field:

25 but while men slept, his enemy came and sowed [193]tares also among the wheat, and went away.

26 But when the blade sprang up and brought forth fruit, then appeared the tares also.

27 And the [194]servants of the householder came and said unto him, Sir, didst thou not sow good seed in thy field? whence then hath it tares?

28 And he said unto them, [195]An enemy hath done this. And the [196]servants say unto him, Wilt thou then that we go and gather them up?

29 But he saith, Nay; lest haply while ye gather up the tares, ye root up the wheat with them.

30 Let both grow together until the harvest: and in the time of the harvest I will say to the reapers, Gather up first the tares, and bind them in bundles to burn them; but gather the wheat into my barn.

31 Another parable set he before them, saying, The kingdom of heaven is like unto a grain of mustard seed, which a man took, and sowed in his field:

32 which indeed is less than all seeds; but when it is grown, it is greater than the herbs, and becometh a tree, so that the birds of the heaven come and lodge in the branches thereof.

---

[192] *Or, age*
[193] *Or, darnel*
[194] *Greek bondservants.*
[195] *Greek A man that is an enemy.*
[196] *Greek bondservants.*

33 Another parable spake he unto them; The kingdom of heaven is like unto leaven, which a woman took, and hid in three [197]measures of meal, till it was all leavened.

34 All these things spake Jesus in parables unto the multitudes; and without a parable spake he nothing unto them:

35 that it might be fulfilled which was spoken through the prophet, saying,
    [198]I will open my mouth in parables;
    I will utter things hidden from the foundation [199]of the world.

36 Then he left the multitudes, and went into the house: and his disciples came unto him, saying, Explain unto us the parable of the tares of the field.

37 And he answered and said, He that soweth the good seed is the Son of man;

38 and the field is the world; and the good seed, these are the sons of the kingdom; and the tares are the sons of the evil *one*;

39 and the enemy that sowed them is the devil: and the harvest is [200]the end of the world; and the reapers are angels.

40 As therefore the tares are gathered up and burned with fire; so shall it be in [201]the end of the world.

41 The Son of man shall send forth his angels, and they shall gather out of his kingdom all things that cause stumbling, and them that do iniquity,

42 and shall cast them into the furnace of fire: there shall be the weeping and the gnashing of teeth.

43 Then shall the righteous shine forth as the sun in the kingdom of their Father. He that hath ears, [202]let him hear.

---

[197]*The word in the Greek denotes the Hebrew seah, a measure containing nearly a peck and a half.*
[198]*Ps. 78:2.*
[199]*Many ancient authorities omit of the world.*
[200]*Or, the consummation of the age*
[201]*Or, the consummation of the age*
[202]*See verse 9.*

44 The kingdom of heaven is like unto a treasure hidden in the field; which a man found, and hid; and [203]in his joy he goeth and selleth all that he hath, and buyeth that field.

45 Again, the kingdom of heaven is like unto a man that is a merchant seeking goodly pearls:

46 and having found one pearl of great price, he went and sold all that he had, and bought it.

47 Again, the kingdom of heaven is like unto a [204]net, that was cast into the sea, and gathered of every kind:

48 which, when it was filled, they drew up on the beach; and they sat down, and gathered the good into vessels, but the bad they cast away.

49 So shall it be in [205]the end of the world: the angels shall come forth, and sever the wicked from among the righteous,

50 and shall cast them into the furnace of fire: there shall be the weeping and the gnashing of teeth.

51 Have ye understood all these things? They say unto him, Yea.

52 And he said unto them, Therefore every scribe who hath been made a disciple to the kingdom of heaven is like unto a man that is a householder, who bringeth forth out of his treasure things new and old.

53 And it came to pass, when Jesus had finished these parables, he departed thence.

54 And coming into his own country he taught them in their synagogue, insomuch that they were astonished, and said, Whence hath this man this wisdom, and these [206]mighty works?

55 Is not this the carpenter's son? is not his mother called Mary? and his brethren, [207]James, and Joseph, and Simon, and Judas?

56 And his sisters, are they not all with us? Whence then hath this man all these things?

57 And they were [208]offended in him. But Jesus said unto them, A prophet is not without honor, save in his own country, and in his own house.

---

[203] *Or, for joy thereof*
[204] *Greek drag-net.*
[205] *Or, the consummation of the age*
[206] *Greek powers.*
[207] *Or, Jacob*
[208] *Greek caused to stumble.*

58 And he did not many [209]mighty works there because of their unbelief.

Chapter 14

1 At that season Herod the tetrarch heard the report concerning Jesus,

2 and said unto his servants, This is John the Baptist; he is risen from the dead; and therefore do these powers work in him.

3 For Herod had laid hold on John, and bound him, and put him in prison for the sake of Herodias, his brother Philip's wife.

4 For John said unto him, It is not lawful for thee to have her.

5 And when he would have put him to death, he feared the multitude, because they counted him as a prophet.

6 But when Herod's birthday came, the daughter of Herodias danced in the midst, and pleased Herod.

7 Whereupon he promised with an oath to give her whatsoever she should ask.

8 And she, being put forward by her mother, saith, Give me here on a platter the head of John the Baptist.

9 And the king was grieved; but for the sake of his oaths, and of them that sat at meat with him, he commanded it to be given;

10 and he sent and beheaded John in the prison.

11 And his head was brought on a platter, and given to the damsel: and she brought it to her mother.

12 And his disciples came, and took up the corpse, and buried him; and they went and told Jesus.

13 Now when Jesus heard *it*, he withdrew from thence in a boat, to a desert place apart: and when the multitudes heard *thereof*, they followed him [210]on foot from the cities.

14 And he came forth, and saw a great multitude, and he had compassion on them, and healed their sick.

15 And when even was come, the disciples came to him, saying, The place is desert, and the time is already past; send the multitudes away, that they may go into the villages, and buy themselves food.

---

[209] *Greek powers.*
[210] *Or, by land*

MATTHEW 14

16 But Jesus said unto them, They have no need to go away; give ye them to eat.

17 And they say unto him, We have here but five loaves, and two fishes.

18 And he said, Bring them hither to me.

19 And he commanded the multitudes to [211]sit down on the grass; and he took the five loaves, and the two fishes, and looking up to heaven, he blessed, and brake and gave the loaves to the disciples, and the disciples to the multitudes.

20 And they all ate, and were filled: and they took up that which remained over of the broken pieces, twelve baskets full.

21 And they that did eat were about five thousand men, besides women and children.

22 And straightway he constrained the disciples to enter into the boat, and to go before him unto the other side, till he should send the multitudes away.

23 And after he had sent the multitudes away, he went up into the mountain apart to pray: and when even was come, he was there alone.

24 But the boat [212]was now in the midst of the sea, distressed by the waves; for the wind was contrary.

25 And in the fourth watch of the night he came unto them, walking upon the sea.

26 And when the disciples saw him walking on the sea, they were troubled, saying, It is a ghost; and they cried out for fear.

27 But straightway Jesus spake unto them, saying, Be of good cheer; it is I; be not afraid.

28 And Peter answered him and said, Lord, if it be thou, bid me come unto thee upon the waters.

29 And he said, Come. And Peter went down from the boat, and walked upon the waters [213]to come to Jesus.

30 But when he saw the [214]wind, he was afraid; and beginning to sink, he cried out, saying, Lord, save me.

---

[211] *Greek recline.*
[212] *Some ancient authorities read was many furlongs distant from the land.*
[213] *Some ancient authorities read and came.*
[214] *Many ancient authorities add strong.*

31 And immediately Jesus stretched forth his hand, and took hold of him, and saith unto him, O thou of little faith, wherefore didst thou doubt?

32 And when they were gone up into the boat, the wind ceased.

33 And they that were in the boat [215]worshipped him, saying, Of a truth thou art the Son of God.

34 And when they had crossed over, they came to the land, unto Gennesaret.

35 And when the men of that place knew him, they sent into all that region round about, and brought unto him all that were sick;

36 and they besought him that they might only touch the border of his garment: and as many as touched were made whole.

Chapter 15

1 Then there come to Jesus from Jerusalem Pharisees and scribes, saying,

2 Why do thy disciples transgress the tradition of the elders? for they wash not their hands when they eat bread.

3 And he answered and said unto them, Why do ye also transgress the commandment of God because of your tradition?

4 For God said, [216]Honor thy father and thy mother: and, [217]He that speaketh evil of father or mother, let him [218]die the death.

5 But ye say, Whosoever shall say to his father or his mother, That wherewith thou mightest have been profited by me is given *to God*;

6 he shall not honor his father. [219]And ye have made void the [220]word of God because of your tradition.

7 Ye hypocrites, well did Isaiah prophesy of you, saying,

8 [221]This people honoreth me with their lips;
   But their heart is far from me.

---

[215] *See marginal note on 2:2.*
[216] *Ex. 20:12; Dt. 5:16.*
[217] *Ex. 21:17; Lev. 20:9.*
[218] *Or, surely die*
[219] *Some ancient authorities add or his mother.*
[220] *Some ancient authorities read law.*
[221] *Isa. 29:13.*

9 But in vain do they worship me,
   Teaching *as their* doctrines the precepts of men.

10 And he called to him the multitude, and said unto them, Hear, and understand:

11 Not that which entereth into the mouth defileth the man; but that which proceedeth out of the mouth, this defileth the man.

12 Then came the disciples, and said unto him, Knowest thou that the Pharisees were [222]offended, when they heard this saying?

13 But he answered and said, Every [223]plant which my heavenly Father planted not, shall be rooted up.

14 Let them alone: they are blind guides. And if the blind guide the blind, both shall fall into a pit.

15 And Peter answered and said unto him, Declare unto us the parable.

16 And he said, Are ye also even yet without understanding?

17 Perceive ye not, that whatsoever goeth into the mouth passeth into the belly, and is cast out into the draught?

18 But the things which proceed out of the mouth come forth out of the heart; and they defile the man.

19 For out of the heart come forth evil thoughts, murders, adulteries, fornications, thefts, false witness, railings:

20 these are the things which defile the man; but to eat with unwashen hands defileth not the man.

21 And Jesus went out thence, and withdrew into the parts of Tyre and Sidon.

22 And behold, a Canaanitish woman came out from those borders, and cried, saying, Have mercy on me, O Lord, thou son of David; my daughter is grievously vexed with a demon.

23 But he answered her not a word. And his disciples came and besought him, saying, Send her away; for she crieth after us.

24 But he answered and said, I was not sent but unto the lost sheep of the house of Israel.

---

[222] *Greek caused to stumble.*
[223] *Greek planting.*

25 But she came and [224]worshipped him, saying, Lord, help me.

26 And he answered and said, It is not meet to take the children's [225]bread and cast it to the dogs.

27 But she said, Yea, Lord: for even the dogs eat of the crumbs which fall from their masters' table.

28 Then Jesus answered and said unto her, O woman, great is thy faith: be it done unto thee even as thou wilt. And her daughter was healed from that hour.

29 And Jesus departed thence, and came nigh unto the sea of Galilee; and he went up into the mountain, and sat there.

30 And there came unto him great multitudes, having with them the lame, blind, dumb, maimed, and many others, and they cast them down at his feet; and he healed them:

31 insomuch that the multitude wondered, when they saw the dumb speaking, the maimed whole, and the lame walking, and the blind seeing: and they glorified the God of Israel.

32 And Jesus called unto him his disciples, and said, I have compassion on the multitude, because they continue with me now three days and have nothing to eat: and I would not send them away fasting, lest haply they faint on the way.

33 And the disciples say unto him, Whence should we have so many loaves in a desert place as to fill so great a multitude?

34 And Jesus said unto them, How many loaves have ye? And they said, Seven, and a few small fishes.

35 And he commanded the multitude to sit down on the ground;

36 and he took the seven loaves and the fishes; and he gave thanks and brake, and gave to the disciples, and the disciples to the multitudes.

37 And they all ate, and were filled: and they took up that which remained over of the broken pieces, seven baskets full.

38 And they that did eat were four thousand men, besides women and children.

---

[224] *See marginal note on 2:2.*
[225] *Or, loaf*

39 And he sent away the multitudes, and entered into the boat, and came into the borders of Magadan.

Chapter 16

1 And the Pharisees and Sadducees came, and trying him asked him to show them a sign from heaven.

2 But he answered and said unto them, [226]When it is evening, ye say, *It will be* fair weather: for the heaven is red.

3 And in the morning, *It will be* foul weather to-day: for the heaven is red and lowering. Ye know how to discern the face of the heaven; but ye cannot *discern* the signs of the times.

4 An evil and adulterous generation seeketh after a sign; and there shall no sign be given unto it, but the sign of Jonah. And he left them, and departed.

5 And the disciples came to the other side and forgot to take [227]bread.

6 And Jesus said unto them, Take heed and beware of the leaven of the Pharisees and Sadducees.

7 And they reasoned among themselves, saying, [228]We took no [229]bread.

8 And Jesus perceiving it said, O ye of little faith, why reason ye among yourselves, because ye have no [230]bread?

9 Do ye not yet perceive, neither remember the five loaves of the five thousand, and how many [231]baskets ye took up?

10 Neither the seven loaves of the four thousand, and how many [232]baskets ye took up?

11 How is it that ye do not perceive that I spake not to you concerning [233]bread? But beware of the leaven of the Pharisees and Sadducees.

---

[226] *The following words, to the end of verse 3, are omitted by some of the most ancient and other important authorities.*
[227] *Greek loaves.*
[228] *Or, It is because we took no bread.*
[229] *Greek loaves.*
[230] *Greek loaves.*
[231] *Basket in verses 9 and 10 represents different Greek words.*
[232] *Basket in verses 9 and 10 represents different Greek words.*
[233] *Greek loaves.*

12 Then understood they that he bade them not beware of the leaven of [234]bread, but of the teaching of the Pharisees and Sadducees.

13 Now when Jesus came into the parts of Caesarea Philippi, he asked his disciples, saying, Who do men say [235]that the Son of man is?

14 And they said, Some *say* John the Baptist; some, Elijah; and others, Jeremiah, or one of the prophets.

15 He saith unto them, But who say ye that I am?

16 And Simon Peter answered and said, Thou art the Christ, the Son of the living God.

17 And Jesus answered and said unto him, Blessed art thou, Simon Bar-Jonah: for flesh and blood hath not revealed it unto thee, but my Father who is in heaven.

18 And I also say unto thee, that thou art [236]Peter, and upon this [237]rock I will build my church; and the gates of Hades shall not prevail against it.

19 I will give unto thee the keys of the kingdom of heaven: and whatsoever thou shalt bind on earth shall be bound in heaven; and whatsoever thou shalt loose on earth shall be loosed in heaven.

20 Then charged he the disciples that they should tell no man that he was the Christ.

21 From that time began [238]Jesus to show unto his disciples, that he must go unto Jerusalem, and suffer many things of the elders and chief priests and scribes, and be killed, and the third day be raised up.

22 And Peter took him, and began to rebuke him, saying, [239]Be it far from thee, Lord: this shall never be unto thee.

23 But he turned, and said unto Peter, Get thee behind me, Satan: thou art a stumbling-block unto me: for thou mindest not the things of God, but the things of men.

24 Then said Jesus unto his disciples, If any man would come after me, let him deny himself, and take up his cross, and follow me.

---

[234] *Greek loaves.*
[235] *Many ancient authorities read that I the Son of man am. See Mk. 8:27; Lk. 9:18.*
[236] *Greek Petros.*
[237] *Greek petra.*
[238] *Some ancient authorities read Jesus Christ.*
[239] *Or, God have mercy on thee*

25 For whosoever would save his life shall lose it: and whosoever shall lose his life for my sake shall find it.

26 For what shall a man be profited, if he shall gain the whole world, and forfeit his life? or what shall a man give in exchange for his life?

27 For the Son of man shall come in the glory of his Father with his angels; and then shall he render unto every man according to his [240]deeds.

28 Verily I say unto you, There are some of them that stand here, who shall in no wise taste of death, till they see the Son of man coming in his kingdom.

Chapter 17

1 And after six days Jesus taketh with him Peter, and [241]James, and John his brother, and bringeth them up into a high mountain apart:

2 and he was transfigured before them; and his face did shine as the sun, and his garments became white as the light.

3 And behold, there appeared unto them Moses and Elijah talking with him.

4 And Peter answered, and said unto Jesus, Lord, it is good for us to be here: if thou wilt, I will make here three [242]tabernacles; one for thee, and one for Moses, and one for Elijah.

5 While he was yet speaking, behold, a bright cloud overshadowed them: and behold, a voice out of the cloud, saying, This is my beloved Son, in whom I am well pleased; hear ye him.

6 And when the disciples heard it, they fell on their face, and were sore afraid.

7 And Jesus came and touched them and said, Arise, and be not afraid.

8 And lifting up their eyes, they saw no one, save Jesus only.

9 And as they were coming down from the mountain, Jesus commanded them, saying, Tell the vision to no man, until the Son of man be risen from the dead.

---

[240] *Greek doing.*
[241] *Or, Jacob*
[242] *Or, booths*

10 And his disciples asked him, saying, Why then say the scribes that Elijah must first come?

11 And he answered and said, Elijah indeed cometh, and shall restore all things:

12 but I say unto you, that Elijah is come already, and they knew him not, but did unto him whatsoever they would. Even so shall the Son of man also suffer of them.

13 Then understood the disciples that he spake unto them of John the Baptist.

14 And when they were come to the multitude, there came to him a man, kneeling to him, and saying,

15 Lord, have mercy on my son: for he is epileptic, and suffereth grievously; for oft-times he falleth into the fire, and oft-times into the water.

16 And I brought him to thy disciples, and they could not cure him.

17 And Jesus answered and said, O faithless and perverse generation, how long shall I be with you? how long shall I bear with you? bring him hither to me.

18 And Jesus rebuked him; and the demon went out of him: and the boy was cured from that hour.

19 Then came the disciples to Jesus apart, and said, Why could not we cast it out?

20 And he saith unto them, Because of your little faith: for verily I say unto you, If ye have faith as a grain of mustard seed, ye shall say unto this mountain, Remove hence to yonder place; and it shall remove; and nothing shall be impossible unto you.[243]

22 And while they [244]abode in Galilee, Jesus said unto them, The Son of man shall be [245]delivered up into the hands of men;

23 and they shall kill him, and the third day he shall be raised up. And they were exceeding sorry.

---

[243] *Many authorities, some ancient, insert verse 21 But this kind goeth not out save by prayer and fasting. See Mk. 9:29.*

[244] *Some ancient authorities read were gathering themselves together.*

[245] *See 10:4.*

24 And when they were come to Capernaum, they that received the [246]half-shekel came to Peter, and said, Doth not your teacher pay the [247]half-shekel?

25 He saith, Yea. And when he came into the house, Jesus spake first to him, saying, What thinkest thou, Simon? the kings of the earth, from whom do they receive toll or tribute? from their sons, or from strangers?

26 And when he said, From strangers, Jesus said unto him, Therefore the sons are free.

27 But, lest we cause them to stumble, go thou to the sea, and cast a hook, and take up the fish that first cometh up; and when thou hast opened his mouth, thou shalt find a [248]shekel: that take, and give unto them for me and thee.

Chapter 18

1 In that hour came the disciples unto Jesus, saying, Who then is [249]greatest in the kingdom of heaven?

2 And he called to him a little child, and set him in the midst of them,

3 and said, Verily I say unto you, Except ye turn, and become as little children, ye shall in no wise enter into the kingdom of heaven.

4 Whosoever therefore shall humble himself as this little child, the same is the [250]greatest in the kingdom of heaven.

5 And whoso shall receive one such little child in my name receiveth me:

6 but whoso shall cause one of these little ones that believe on me to stumble, it is profitable for him that [251]a great millstone should be hanged about his neck, and *that* he should be sunk in the depth of the sea.

7 Woe unto the world because of occasions of stumbling! for it must needs be that the occasions come; but woe to that man through whom the occasion cometh!

---

[246] *Greek didrachma. Compare marginal note on Lk. 15:8.*
[247] *Greek didrachma. Compare marginal note on Lk. 15:8.*
[248] *Greek stater.*
[249] *Greek greater.*
[250] *Greek greater.*
[251] *Greek a millstone turned by an ass.*

8 And if thy hand or thy foot causeth thee to stumble, cut it off, and cast it from thee: it is good for thee to enter into life maimed or halt, rather than having two hands or two feet to be cast into the eternal fire.

9 And if thine eye causeth thee to stumble, pluck it out, and cast it from thee: it is good for thee to enter into life with one eye, rather than having two eyes to be cast into the [252]hell of fire.

10 See that ye despise not one of these little ones: for I say unto you, that in heaven their angels do always behold the face of my Father who is in heaven.[253]

12 How think ye? if any man have a hundred sheep, and one of them be gone astray, doth he not leave the ninety and nine, and go unto the mountains, and seek that which goeth astray?

13 And if so be that he find it, verily I say unto you, he rejoiceth over it more than over the ninety and nine which have not gone astray.

14 Even so it is not [254]the will of [255]your Father who is in heaven, that one of these little ones should perish.

15 And if thy brother sin [256]against thee, go, show him his fault between thee and him alone: if he hear thee, thou hast gained thy brother.

16 But if he hear *thee* not, take with thee one or two more, that at the mouth of two witnesses or three every word may be established.

17 And if he refuse to hear them, tell it unto the [257]church: and if he refuse to hear the [258]church also, let him be unto thee as the Gentile and the [259]publican.

18 Verily I say unto you, What things soever ye shall bind on earth shall be bound in heaven; and what things soever ye shall loose on earth shall be loosed in heaven.

---

[252] *Greek Gehenna of fire.*

[253] *Many authorities, some ancient, insert verse 11 For the Son of man came to save that which was lost. See Lk. 19:10.*

[254] *Greek a thing willed before your Father.*

[255] *Some ancient authorities read my.*

[256] *Some ancient authorities omit against thee.*

[257] *Or, congregation*

[258] *Or, congregation*

[259] *See marginal note on 5:46.*

19 Again I say unto you, that if two of you shall agree on earth as touching anything that they shall ask, it [260]shall be done for them of my Father who is in heaven.

20 For where two or three are gathered together in my name, there am I in the midst of them.

21 Then came Peter and said to him, Lord, how oft shall my brother sin against me, and I forgive him? until seven times?

22 Jesus saith unto him, I say not unto thee, Until seven times; but, Until [261]seventy times seven.

23 Therefore is the kingdom of heaven likened unto a certain king, who would make a reckoning with his [262]servants.

24 And when he had begun to reckon, one was brought unto him, that owed him ten thousand [263]talents.

25 But forasmuch as he had not *wherewith* to pay, his lord commanded him to be sold, and his wife, and children, and all that he had, and payment to be made.

26 The [264]servant therefore fell down and [265]worshipped him, saying, Lord, have patience with me, and I will pay thee all.

27 And the lord of that [266]servant, being moved with compassion, released him, and forgave him the [267]debt.

28 But that [268]servant went out, and found one of his fellow-servants, who owed him a hundred [269]shillings: and he laid hold on him, and took *him* by the throat, saying, Pay what thou owest.

29 So his fellow-servant fell down and besought him, saying, Have patience with me, and I will pay thee.

---

[260] *Greek shall become.*
[261] *Or, seventy times and seven*
[262] *Greek bondservants.*
[263] *This talent was probably worth about £200, or $1000.*
[264] *Greek bondservant.*
[265] *See marginal note on 2:2.*
[266] *Greek bondservant.*
[267] *Greek loan.*
[268] *Greek bondservant.*
[269] *The word in the Greek denotes a coin worth about eight pence half-penny, or nearly seventeen cents.*

30 And he would not: but went and cast him into prison, till he should pay that which was due.

31 So when his fellow-servants saw what was done, they were exceeding sorry, and came and told unto their lord all that was done.

32 Then his lord called him unto him, and saith to him, Thou wicked [270]servant, I forgave thee all that debt, because thou besoughtest me:

33 shouldest not thou also have had mercy on thy fellow-servant, even as I had mercy on thee?

34 And his lord was wroth, and delivered him to the tormentors, till he should pay all that was due.

35 So shall also my heavenly Father do unto you, if ye forgive not every one his brother from your hearts.

Chapter 19

1 And it came to pass when Jesus had finished these words, he departed from Galilee, and came into the borders of Judaea beyond the Jordan;

2 and great multitudes followed him; and he healed them there.

3 And there came unto him [271]Pharisees, trying him, and saying, Is it lawful *for a man* to put away his wife for every cause?

4 And he answered and said, Have ye not read, [272]that he who [273]made *them* from the beginning made them male and female,

5 and said, [274]For this cause shall a man leave his father and mother, and shall cleave to his wife; and the two shall become one flesh?

6 So that they are no more two, but one flesh. What therefore God hath joined together, let not man put asunder.

7 They say unto him, [275]Why then did Moses command to give a bill of divorcement, and to put *her* away?

8 He saith unto them, Moses for your hardness of heart suffered you to put away your wives: but from the beginning it hath not been so.

---

[270] *Greek bondservant.*
[271] *Many authorities, some ancient, insert the.*
[272] Gen. 1:27; 5:2.
[273] *Some ancient authorities read created.*
[274] Gen. 2:24.
[275] Dt. 24:1–4.

9 And I say unto you, Whosoever shall put away his wife, [276]except for fornication, and shall marry another, committeth adultery: [277]and he that marrieth her when she is put away committeth adultery.

10 The disciples say unto him, If the case of the man is so with his wife, it is not expedient to marry.

11 But he said unto them, Not all men can receive this saying, but they to whom it is given.

12 For there are eunuchs, that were so born from their mother's womb: and there are eunuchs, that were made eunuchs by men: and there are eunuchs, that made themselves eunuchs for the kingdom of heaven's sake. He that is able to receive it, let him receive it.

13 Then were there brought unto him little children, that he should lay his hands on them, and pray: and the disciples rebuked them.

14 But Jesus said, Suffer the little children, and forbid them not, to come unto me: for [278]to such belongeth the kingdom of heaven.

15 And he laid his hands on them, and departed thence.

16 And behold, one came to him and said, [279]Teacher, what good thing shall I do, that I may have eternal life?

17 And he said unto him, [280]Why askest thou me concerning that which is good? One there is who is good: but if thou wouldest enter into life, keep the commandments.[281]

18 He saith unto him, Which? And Jesus said, [282]Thou shalt not kill, Thou shalt not commit adultery, Thou shalt not steal, Thou shalt not bear false witness,

†✓ **Jesus distinguishes himself from the Source of Good.** RV restores "Why askest thou me..." contrasting Jesus (the Teacher) with the One God (the Good).

---

[276] *Some ancient authorities read saving for the cause of fornication, maketh her an adulteress: as in 5:32.*

[277] *The following words, to the end of the verse, are omitted by some ancient authorities.*

[278] *Or, of such is*

[279] *Some ancient authorities read Good Teacher. See Mk. 10:17; Lk. 18:18.*

[280] *Some ancient authorities read Why callest thou me good? None is good save one, even God. See Mk. 10:18; Lk. 18:19.*

[281] **Textual Restoration:** The KJV reads "Why callest thou me good?" matching Mark. However, the older manuscripts read "Why askest thou me concerning that which is good?" The RV restores this unique Matthean phrasing, distinguishing Jesus from God (the Source of Good).

[282] *Ex. 20:12–16; Dt. 5:16–20.*

19 Honor thy father and thy mother; and, [283]Thou shalt love thy neighbor as thyself.

20 The young man saith unto him, All these things have I observed: what lack I yet?

21 Jesus said unto him, If thou wouldest be perfect, go, sell that which thou hast, and give to the poor, and thou shalt have treasure in heaven: and come, follow me.

22 But when the young man heard the saying, he went away sorrowful; for he was one that had great possessions.

23 And Jesus said unto his disciples, Verily I say unto you, It is hard for a rich man to enter into the kingdom of heaven.

24 And again I say unto you, It is easier for a camel to go through a needle's eye, than for a rich man to enter into the kingdom of God.

25 And when the disciples heard it, they were astonished exceedingly, saying, Who then can be saved?

26 And Jesus looking upon *them* said to them, With men this is impossible; but with God all things are possible.

27 Then answered Peter and said unto him, Lo, we have left all, and followed thee; what then shall we have?

28 And Jesus said unto them, Verily I say unto you, that ye who have followed me, in the regeneration when the Son of man shall sit on the throne of his glory, ye also shall sit upon twelve thrones, judging the twelve tribes of Israel.

29 And every one that hath left houses, or brethren, or sisters, or father, or mother, [284]or children, or lands, for my name's sake, shall receive [285]a hundredfold, and shall inherit eternal life.

30 But many shall be last *that are* first; and first *that are* last.

---

[283] *Lev. 19:18.*
[284] *Many ancient authorities add or wife: as in Lk. 18:29.*
[285] *Some ancient authorities read manifold.*

Chapter 20

1 For the kingdom of heaven is like unto a man that was a householder, who went out early in the morning to hire laborers into his vineyard.

2 And when he had agreed with the laborers for a ²⁸⁶shilling a day, he sent them into his vineyard.

3 And he went out about the third hour, and saw others standing in the marketplace idle;

4 and to them he said, Go ye also into the vineyard, and whatsoever is right I will give you. And they went their way.

5 Again he went out about the sixth and the ninth hour, and did likewise.

6 And about the eleventh *hour* he went out, and found others standing; and he saith unto them, Why stand ye here all the day idle?

7 They say unto him, Because no man hath hired us. He saith unto them, Go ye also into the vineyard.

8 And when even was come, the lord of the vineyard saith unto his steward, Call the laborers, and pay them their hire, beginning from the last unto the first.

9 And when they came that *were hired* about the eleventh hour, they received every man a ²⁸⁷shilling.

10 And when the first came, they supposed that they would receive more; and they likewise received every man a ²⁸⁸shilling.

11 And when they received it, they murmured against the householder,

12 saying, These last have spent *but* one hour, and thou hast made them equal unto us, who have borne the burden of the day and the ²⁸⁹scorching heat.

13 But he answered and said to one of them, Friend, I do thee no wrong: didst not thou agree with me for a ²⁹⁰shilling?

---

²⁸⁶ *See marginal note on 18:28.*
²⁸⁷ *See marginal note on 18:28.*
²⁸⁸ *See marginal note on 18:28.*
²⁸⁹ *Or, hot wind*
²⁹⁰ *See marginal note on 18:28.*

14 Take up that which is thine, and go thy way; it is my will to give unto this last, even as unto thee.

15 Is it not lawful for me to do what I will with mine own? or is thine eye evil, because I am good?

16 So the last shall be first, and the first last.

17 And as Jesus was going up to Jerusalem, he took the twelve disciples apart, and on the way he said unto them,

18 Behold, we go up to Jerusalem; and the Son of man shall be [291]delivered unto the chief priests and scribes; and they shall condemn him to death,

19 and shall deliver him unto the Gentiles to mock, and to scourge, and to crucify: and the third day he shall be raised up.

20 Then came to him the mother of the sons of Zebedee with her sons, [292]worshipping *him*, and asking a certain thing of him.

21 And he said unto her, What wouldest thou? She saith unto him, Command that these my two sons may sit, one on thy right hand, and one on thy left hand, in thy kingdom.

22 But Jesus answered and said, Ye know not what ye ask. Are ye able to drink the cup that I am about to drink? They say unto him, We are able.

† ✓ **The Limit of Authority.** Jesus explicitly denies having the authority to assign positions in the Kingdom, deferring that power solely to the Father. If Jesus were the "Co-Equal" Almighty, there would be no realm of authority withheld from him.

23 He saith unto them, My cup indeed ye shall drink: but to sit on my right hand, and on *my* left hand, is not mine to give; but *it is for them* for whom it hath been prepared of my Father.

24 And when the ten heard it, they were moved with indignation concerning the two brethren.

25 But Jesus called them unto him, and said, Ye know that the rulers of the Gentiles lord it over them, and their great ones exercise authority over them.

26 Not so shall it be among you: but whosoever would become great among you shall be your [293]minister;

27 and whosoever would be first among you shall be your [294]servant:

---

[291] *See 10:4.*
[292] *See marginal note on 2:2.*
[293] *Or, servant*
[294] *Greek bondservant.*

28 even as the Son of man came not to be ministered unto, but to minister, and to give his life a ransom for many.

29 And as they went out from Jericho, a great multitude followed him.

30 And behold, two blind men sitting by the way side, when they heard that Jesus was passing by, cried out, saying, Lord, have mercy on us, thou son of David.

31 And the multitude rebuked them, that they should hold their peace: but they cried out the more, saying, Lord, have mercy on us, thou son of David.

32 And Jesus stood still, and called them, and said, What will ye that I should do unto you?

33 They say unto him, Lord, that our eyes may be opened.

34 And Jesus, being moved with compassion, touched their eyes; and straightway they received their sight, and followed him.

Chapter 21

1 And when they drew nigh unto Jerusalem, and came unto Bethphage, unto the mount of Olives, then Jesus sent two disciples,

2 saying unto them, Go into the village that is over against you, and straightway ye shall find an ass tied, and a colt with her: loose *them*, and bring *them* unto me.

3 And if any one say aught unto you, ye shall say, The Lord hath need of them; and straightway he will send them.

4 Now this is come to pass, that it might be fulfilled which was spoken through the prophet, saying,

5 [295]Tell ye the daughter of Zion,
 Behold, thy King cometh unto thee,
 Meek, and riding upon an ass,
 And upon a colt the foal of an ass.

6 And the disciples went, and did even as Jesus appointed them,

7 and brought the ass, and the colt, and put on them their garments; and he sat thereon.

---

[295] *Isa. 62:11; Zech. 9:9.*

8 And the most part of the multitude spread their garments in the way; and others cut branches from the trees, and spread them in the way.

9 And the multitudes that went before him, and that followed, cried, saying, Hosanna to the son of David: Blessed *is* he that cometh in the name of the Lord; Hosanna in the highest.

10 And when he was come into Jerusalem, all the city was stirred, saying, Who is this?

11 And the multitudes said, This is the prophet, Jesus, from Nazareth of Galilee.

12 And Jesus entered into the temple [296]of God, and cast out all them that sold and bought in the temple, and overthrew the tables of the money-changers, and the seats of them that sold the doves;

13 and he saith unto them, It is written, [297]My house shall be called a house of prayer: [298]but ye make it a den of robbers.

14 And the blind and the lame came to him in the temple; and he healed them.

15 But when the chief priests and the scribes saw the wonderful things that he did, and the children that were crying in the temple and saying, Hosanna to the son of David; they were moved with indignation,

16 and said unto him, Hearest thou what these are saying? And Jesus saith unto them, Yea: did ye never read, [299]Out of the mouth of babes and sucklings thou hast perfected praise?

17 And he left them, and went forth out of the city to Bethany, and lodged there.

18 Now in the morning as he returned to the city, he hungered.

19 And seeing [300]a fig tree by the way side, he came to it, and found nothing thereon, but leaves only; and he saith unto it, Let there be no fruit from thee henceforward for ever. And immediately the fig tree withered away.

20 And when the disciples saw it, they marvelled, saying, How did the fig tree immediately wither away?

---

[296] *Many ancient authorities omit of God.*
[297] *Isa. 56:7.*
[298] *Jer. 7:11.*
[299] *Ps. 8:2.*
[300] *Or, a single*

21 And Jesus answered and said unto them, Verily I say unto you, If ye have faith, and doubt not, ye shall not only do what is done to the fig tree, but even if ye shall say unto this mountain, Be thou taken up and cast into the sea, it shall be done.

22 And all things, whatsoever ye shall ask in prayer, believing, ye shall receive.

23 And when he was come into the temple, the chief priests and the elders of the people came unto him as he was teaching, and said, By what authority doest thou these things? and who gave thee this authority?

24 And Jesus answered and said unto them, I also will ask you one [301]question, which if ye tell me, I likewise will tell you by what authority I do these things.

25 The baptism of John, whence was it? from heaven or from men? And they reasoned with themselves, saying, If we shall say, From heaven; he will say unto us, Why then did ye not believe him?

26 But if we shall say, From men; we fear the multitude; for all hold John as a prophet.

27 And they answered Jesus, and said, We know not. He also said unto them, Neither tell I you by what authority I do these things.

28 But what think ye? A man had two [302]sons; and he came to the first, and said, [303]Son, go work to-day in the vineyard.

29 And he answered and said, I will not: but afterward he repented himself, and went.

30 And he came to the second, and said likewise. And he answered and said, I *go*, sir: and went not.

31 Which of the two did the will of his father? They say, The first. Jesus saith unto them, Verily I say unto you, that the [304]publicans and the harlots go into the kingdom of God before you.

32 For John came unto you in the way of righteousness, and ye believed him not; but the [305]publicans and the harlots believed him: and ye,

---

[301] *Greek word.*
[302] *Greek children.*
[303] *Greek Child.*
[304] *See marginal note on 5:46.*
[305] *See marginal note on 5:46.*

when ye saw it, did not even repent yourselves afterward, that ye might believe him.

33 Hear another parable: There was a man that was a householder, who planted a vineyard, and set a hedge about it, and digged a winepress in it, and built a tower, and let it out to husbandmen, and went into another country.

34 And when the season of the fruits drew near, he sent his [306]servants to the husbandmen, to receive [307]his fruits.

35 And the husbandmen took his [308]servants, and beat one, and killed another, and stoned another.

36 Again, he sent other [309]servants more than the first: and they did unto them in like manner.

37 But afterward he sent unto them his son, saying, They will reverence my son.

38 But the husbandmen, when they saw the son, said among themselves, This is the heir; come, let us kill him, and take his inheritance.

39 And they took him, and cast him forth out of the vineyard, and killed him.

40 When therefore the lord of the vineyard shall come, what will he do unto those husbandmen?

41 They say unto him, He will miserably destroy those miserable men, and will let out the vineyard unto other husbandmen, who shall render him the fruits in their seasons.

42 Jesus saith unto them, Did ye never read in the scriptures,
> [310]The stone which the builders rejected,
> The same was made the head of the corner;
> This was from the Lord,
> And it is marvellous in our eyes?

43 Therefore say I unto you, The kingdom of God shall be taken away from you, and shall be given to a nation bringing forth the fruits thereof.

---

[306] *Greek bondservants.*
[307] *Or, the fruits of it*
[308] *Greek bondservants.*
[309] *Greek bondservants.*
[310] *Ps. 118:22f.*

44 [311]And he that falleth on this stone shall be broken to pieces: but on whomsoever it shall fall, it will scatter him as dust.

45 And when the chief priests and the Pharisees heard his parables, they perceived that he spake of them.

46 And when they sought to lay hold on him, they feared the multitudes, because they took him for a prophet.

Chapter 22

1 And Jesus answered and spake again in parables unto them, saying,

2 The kingdom of heaven is likened unto a certain king, who made a marriage feast for his son,

3 and sent forth his [312]servants to call them that were bidden to the marriage feast: and they would not come.

4 Again he sent forth other [313]servants, saying, Tell them that are bidden, Behold, I have made ready my dinner; my oxen and my fatlings are killed, and all things are ready: come to the marriage feast.

5 But they made light of it, and went their ways, one to his own farm, another to his merchandise;

6 and the rest laid hold on his [314]servants, and treated them shamefully, and killed them.

7 But the king was wroth; and he sent his armies, and destroyed those murderers, and burned their city.

8 Then saith he to his [315]servants, The wedding is ready, but they that were bidden were not worthy.

9 Go ye therefore unto the partings of the highways, and as many as ye shall find, bid to the marriage feast.

10 And those [316]servants went out into the highways, and gathered together all as many as they found, both bad and good: and the wedding was filled with guests.

---

[311] *Some ancient authorities omit verse 44.*
[312] *Greek bondservants.*
[313] *Greek bondservants.*
[314] *Greek bondservants.*
[315] *Greek bondservants.*
[316] *Greek bondservants.*

11 But when the king came in to behold the guests, he saw there a man who had not on a wedding-garment:

12 and he saith unto him, Friend, how camest thou in hither not having a wedding-garment? And he was speechless.

13 Then the king said to the [317]servants, Bind him hand and foot, and cast him out into the outer darkness; there shall be the weeping and the gnashing of teeth.

14 For many are called, but few chosen.

15 Then went the Pharisees, and took counsel how they might ensnare him in *his* talk.

16 And they send to him their disciples, with the Herodians, saying, Teacher, we know that thou art true, and teachest the way of God in truth, and carest not for any one: for thou regardest not the person of men.

17 Tell us therefore, What thinkest thou? Is it lawful to give tribute unto Caesar, or not?

18 But Jesus perceived their wickedness, and said, Why make ye trial of me, ye hypocrites?

19 Show me the tribute money. And they brought unto him a [318]denarius.

20 And he saith unto them, Whose is this image and superscription?

21 They say unto him, Caesar's. Then saith he unto them, Render therefore unto Caesar the things that are Caesar's; and unto God the things that are God's.

22 And when they heard it, they marvelled, and left him, and went away.

23 On that day there came to him Sadducees, [319]they that say that there is no resurrection: and they asked him,

24 saying, Teacher, Moses said, [320]If a man die, having no children, his brother [321]shall marry his wife, and raise up seed unto his brother.

25 Now there were with us seven brethren: and the first married and deceased, and having no seed left his wife unto his brother;

---

[317] *Or, ministers*
[318] *See marginal note on 18:28.*
[319] *Many ancient authorities read saying.*
[320] *Dt. 25:5.*
[321] *Greek shall perform the duty of a husband's brother to his wife.*

26 in like manner the second also, and the third, unto the [322]seventh.

27 And after them all, the woman died.

28 In the resurrection therefore whose wife shall she be of the seven? for they all had her.

29 But Jesus answered and said unto them, Ye do err, not knowing the scriptures, nor the power of God.

30 For in the resurrection they neither marry, nor are given in marriage, but are as angels [323]in heaven.

31 But as touching the resurrection of the dead, have ye not read that which was spoken unto you by God, saying,

32 [324]I am the God of Abraham, and the God of Isaac, and the God of Jacob? God is not *the God* of the dead, but of the living.

33 And when the multitudes heard it, they were astonished at his teaching.

34 But the Pharisees, when they heard that he had put the Sadducees to silence, gathered themselves together.

35 And one of them, a lawyer, asked him a question, trying him:

36 Teacher, which is the great commandment in the law?

37 And he said unto him, [325]Thou shalt love the Lord thy God with all thy heart, and with all thy soul, and with all thy mind.

38 This is the great and first commandment.

39 [326]And a second like *unto it* is this, [327]Thou shalt love thy neighbor as thyself.

40 On these two commandments the whole law hangeth, and the prophets.

41 Now while the Pharisees were gathered together, Jesus asked them a question,

42 saying, What think ye of the Christ? whose son is he? They say unto him, *The son* of David.

---

[322] *Greek seven.*
[323] *Many ancient authorities add of God.*
[324] *Ex. 3:6.*
[325] *Dt. 6:5.*
[326] *Or, And a second is like unto it, Thou shalt love etc.*
[327] *Lev. 19:18.*

43 He saith unto them, How then doth David in the Spirit call him Lord, saying,

44 [328]The Lord said unto my Lord,
   Sit thou on my right hand,
   Till I put thine enemies underneath thy feet?

45 If David then calleth him Lord, how is he his son?

46 And no one was able to answer him a word, neither durst any man from that day forth ask him any more questions.

Chapter 23

1 Then spake Jesus to the multitudes and to his disciples,

2 saying, The scribes and the Pharisees sit on Moses' seat:

3 all things therefore whatsoever they bid you, *these* do and observe: but do not ye after their works; for they say, and do not.

4 Yea, they bind heavy burdens [329]and grievous to be borne, and lay them on men's shoulders; but they themselves will not move them with their finger.

5 But all their works they do to be seen of men: for they make broad their phylacteries, and enlarge the borders *of their garments*,

6 and love the chief place at feasts, and the chief seats in the synagogues,

7 and the salutations in the marketplaces, and to be called of men, Rabbi.

†✓ **Jesus defines the "One Father."** Jesus forbids using "Father" as a religious title because that role belongs uniquely to the One God in heaven. He distinguishes the One Father from the one Master (Christ) in verse 10.

8 But be not ye called Rabbi: for one is your teacher, and all ye are brethren.

9 And call no man your father on the earth: for one is your Father, [330]*even* he who is in heaven.

10 Neither be ye called masters: for one is your master, *even* the Christ.

11 But he that is [331]greatest among you shall be your [332]servant.

---

[328] *Ps. 110:1.*
[329] *Many ancient authorities omit and grievous to be borne.*
[330] *Greek the heavenly.*
[331] *Greek greater.*
[332] *Or, minister*

12 And whosoever shall exalt himself shall be humbled; and whosoever shall humble himself shall be exalted.

13 But woe unto you, scribes and Pharisees, hypocrites! because ye shut the kingdom of heaven [333]against men: for ye enter not in yourselves, neither suffer ye them that are entering in to enter.[334]

15 Woe unto you, scribes and Pharisees, hypocrites! for ye compass sea and land to make one proselyte; and when he is become so, ye make him twofold more a son of [335]hell than yourselves.

16 Woe unto you, ye blind guides, that say, Whosoever shall swear by the [336]temple, it is nothing; but whosoever shall swear by the gold of the [337]temple, he is [338]a debtor.

17 Ye fools and blind: for which is greater, the gold, or the [339]temple that hath sanctified the gold?

18 And, Whosoever shall swear by the altar, it is nothing; but whosoever shall swear by the gift that is upon it, he is [340]a debtor.

19 Ye blind: for which is greater, the gift, or the altar that sanctifieth the gift?

20 He therefore that sweareth by the altar, sweareth by it, and by all things thereon.

21 And he that sweareth by the [341]temple, sweareth by it, and by him that dwelleth therein.

22 And he that sweareth by the heaven, sweareth by the throne of God, and by him that sitteth thereon.

23 Woe unto you, scribes and Pharisees, hypocrites! for ye tithe mint and [342]anise and cummin, and have left undone the weightier matters of

---

[333] *Greek before.*

[334] *Some authorities insert here, or after verse 12, verse 14 Woe unto you, scribes and Pharisees, hypocrites! for ye devour widows' houses, even while for a pretence ye make long prayers: therefore ye shall receive great condemnation. See Mk. 12:40; Lk. 20:47.*

[335] *Greek Gehenna.*

[336] *Or, sanctuary: as in verse 35.*

[337] *Or, sanctuary: as in verse 35.*

[338] *Or, bound by his oath*

[339] *Or, sanctuary: as in verse 35.*

[340] *Or, bound by his oath*

[341] *Or, sanctuary: as in verse 35.*

[342] *Or, dill*

the law, justice, and mercy, and faith: but these ye ought to have done, and not to have left the other undone.

24 Ye blind guides, that strain out the gnat, and swallow the camel!

25 Woe unto you, scribes and Pharisees, hypocrites! for ye cleanse the outside of the cup and of the platter, but within they are full from extortion and excess.

26 Thou blind Pharisee, cleanse first the inside of the cup and of the platter, that the outside thereof may become clean also.

27 Woe unto you, scribes and Pharisees, hypocrites! for ye are like unto whited sepulchres, which outwardly appear beautiful, but inwardly are full of dead men's bones, and of all uncleanness.

28 Even so ye also outwardly appear righteous unto men, but inwardly ye are full of hypocrisy and iniquity.

29 Woe unto you, scribes and Pharisees, hypocrites! for ye build the sepulchres of the prophets, and garnish the tombs of the righteous,

30 and say, If we had been in the days of our fathers, we should not have been partakers with them in the blood of the prophets.

31 Wherefore ye witness to yourselves, that ye are sons of them that slew the prophets.

32 Fill ye up then the measure of your fathers.

33 Ye serpents, ye offspring of vipers, how shall ye escape the judgment of [343]hell?

34 Therefore, behold, I send unto you prophets, and wise men, and scribes: some of them shall ye kill and crucify; and some of them shall ye scourge in your synagogues, and persecute from city to city:

35 that upon you may come all the righteous blood shed on the earth, from the blood of Abel the righteous unto the blood of Zachariah son of Barachiah, whom ye slew between the sanctuary and the altar.

36 Verily I say unto you, All these things shall come upon this generation.

37 O Jerusalem, Jerusalem, that killeth the prophets, and stoneth them that are sent unto her! how often would I have gathered thy children together, even as a hen gathereth her chickens under her wings, and ye would not!

---

[343] *Greek Gehenna.*

38 Behold, your house is left unto you [344]desolate.

39 For I say unto you, Ye shall not see me henceforth, till ye shall say, Blessed *is* he that cometh in the name of the Lord.

Chapter 24

1 And Jesus went out from the temple, and was going on his way; and his disciples came to him to show him the buildings of the temple.

2 But he answered and said unto them, See ye not all these things? verily I say unto you, There shall not be left here one stone upon another, that shall not be thrown down.

3 And as he sat on the mount of Olives, the disciples came unto him privately, saying, Tell us, when shall these things be? and what *shall be* the sign of thy [345]coming, and of [346]the end of the world?

4 And Jesus answered and said unto them, Take heed that no man lead you astray.

5 For many shall come in my name, saying, I am the Christ; and shall lead many astray.

6 And ye shall hear of wars and rumors of wars; see that ye be not troubled: for *these things* must needs come to pass; but the end is not yet.

7 For nation shall rise against nation, and kingdom against kingdom; and there shall be famines and earthquakes in divers places.

8 But all these things are the beginning of travail.

9 Then shall they deliver you up unto tribulation, and shall kill you: and ye shall be hated of all the nations for my name's sake.

10 And then shall many stumble, and shall [347]deliver up one another, and shall hate one another.

11 And many false prophets shall arise, and shall lead many astray.

12 And because iniquity shall be multiplied, the love of the many shall wax cold.

13 But he that endureth to the end, the same shall be saved.

---

[344] *Some ancient authorities omit desolate.*
[345] *Greek presence.*
[346] *Or, the consummation of the age*
[347] *See 10:4.*

14 And ³⁴⁸this gospel of the kingdom shall be preached in the whole ³⁴⁹world for a testimony unto all the nations; and then shall the end come.

15 When therefore ye see the abomination of desolation, which was ³⁵⁰spoken of through Daniel the prophet, standing in ³⁵¹the holy place (let him that readeth understand),

16 then let them that are in Judaea flee unto the mountains:

17 let him that is on the housetop not go down to take out the things that are in his house:

18 and let him that is in the field not return back to take his cloak.

19 But woe unto them that are with child and to them that give suck in those days!

20 And pray ye that your flight be not in the winter, neither on a sabbath:

21 for then shall be great tribulation, such as hath not been from the beginning of the world until now, no, nor ever shall be.

22 And except those days had been shortened, no flesh would have been saved: but for the elect's sake those days shall be shortened.

23 Then if any man shall say unto you, Lo, here is the Christ, or, Here; believe [352]*it* not.

24 For there shall arise false Christs, and false prophets, and shall show great signs and wonders; so as to lead astray, if possible, even the elect.

25 Behold, I have told you beforehand.

26 If therefore they shall say unto you, Behold, he is in the wilderness; go not forth: Behold, he is in the inner chambers; believe [353]*it* not.

27 For as the lightning cometh forth from the east, and is seen even unto the west; so shall be the [354]coming of the Son of man.

28 Wheresoever the carcase is, there will the [355]eagles be gathered together.

---

[348] *Or, these good tidings*
[349] *Greek inhabited earth.*
[350] *Dan. 9:27; 11:31; 12:11.*
[351] *Or, a holy place*
[352] *Or, him*
[353] *Or, them*
[354] *Greek presence.*
[355] *Or, vultures*

MATTHEW 24

29 But immediately after the tribulation of those days the sun shall be darkened, and the moon shall not give her light, and the stars shall fall from heaven, and the powers of the heavens shall be shaken:

30 and then shall appear the sign of the Son of man in heaven: and then shall all the tribes of the earth mourn, and they shall see the Son of man coming on the clouds of heaven with power and great glory.

31 And he shall send forth his angels [356]with [357]a great sound of a trumpet, and they shall gather together his elect from the four winds, from one end of heaven to the other.

32 Now from the fig tree learn her parable: when her branch is now become tender, and putteth forth its leaves, ye know that the summer is nigh;

33 even so ye also, when ye see all these things, know ye that [358]he is nigh, *even* at the doors.

34 Verily I say unto you, This generation shall not pass away, till all these things be accomplished.

35 Heaven and earth shall pass away, but my words shall not pass away.

36 But of that day and hour knoweth no one, not even the angels of heaven, [359]neither the Son, but the Father only.[360]

37 And as *were* the days of Noah, so shall be the [361]coming of the Son of man.

38 For as in those days which were before the flood they were eating and drinking, marrying and giving in marriage, until the day that Noah entered into the ark,

39 and they knew not until the flood came, and took them all away; so shall be the [362]coming of the Son of man.

40 Then shall two men be in the field; one is taken, and one is left:

†✓ **Jesus is not Omniscient.** KJV omits "neither the Son." RV restores it, proving the Son does not know what the Father knows.

---

[356] *Many ancient authorities read with a great trumpet, and they shall gather etc.*
[357] *Or, a trumpet of great sound*
[358] *Or, it*
[359] *Many authorities, some ancient, omit neither the Son.*
[360] **Omission Restoration:** The KJV omits "neither the Son," even though it appears in Mark 13:32. The best manuscripts include it here. The RV restores it, confirming that Jesus lacks omniscience regarding the Final Day.
[361] *Greek presence.*
[362] *Greek presence.*

41 two women *shall be* grinding at the mill; one is taken, and one is left.

42 Watch therefore: for ye know not on what day your Lord cometh.

43 [363]But know this, that if the master of the house had known in what watch the thief was coming, he would have watched, and would not have suffered his house to be [364]broken through.

44 Therefore be ye also ready; for in an hour that ye think not the Son of man cometh.

45 Who then is the faithful and wise [365]servant, whom his lord hath set over his household, to give them their food in due season?

46 Blessed is that [366]servant, whom his lord when he cometh shall find so doing.

47 Verily I say unto you, that he will set him over all that he hath.

48 But if that evil [367]servant shall say in his heart, My lord tarrieth;

49 and shall begin to beat his fellow-servants, and shall eat and drink with the drunken;

50 the lord of that [368]servant shall come in a day when he expecteth not, and in an hour when he knoweth not,

51 and shall [369]cut him asunder, and appoint his portion with the hypocrites: there shall be the weeping and the gnashing of teeth.

Chapter 25

1 Then shall the kingdom of heaven be likened unto ten virgins, who took their [370]lamps, and went forth to meet the bridegroom.

2 And five of them were foolish, and five were wise.

3 For the foolish, when they took their [371]lamps, took no oil with them:

4 but the wise took oil in their vessels with their [372]lamps.

---

[363] *Or, But this ye know*
[364] *Greek digged through.*
[365] *Greek bondservant.*
[366] *Greek bondservant.*
[367] *Greek bondservant.*
[368] *Greek bondservant.*
[369] *Or, severely scourge him*
[370] *Or, torches*
[371] *Or, torches*
[372] *Or, torches*

5 Now while the bridegroom tarried, they all slumbered and slept.

6 But at midnight there is a cry, Behold, the bridegroom! Come ye forth to meet him.

7 Then all those virgins arose, and trimmed their [373]lamps.

8 And the foolish said unto the wise, Give us of your oil; for our [374]lamps are going out.

9 But the wise answered, saying, Peradventure there will not be enough for us and you: go ye rather to them that sell, and buy for yourselves.

10 And while they went away to buy, the bridegroom came; and they that were ready went in with him to the marriage feast: and the door was shut.

11 Afterward came also the other virgins, saying, Lord, Lord, open to us.

12 But he answered and said, Verily I say unto you, I know you not.

13 Watch therefore, for ye know not the day nor the hour.

14 For *it is* as *when* a man, going into another country, called his own [375]servants, and delivered unto them his goods.

15 And unto one he gave five talents, to another two, to another one; to each according to his several ability; and he went on his journey.

16 Straightway he that received the five talents went and traded with them, and made other five talents.

17 In like manner he also that *received* the two gained other two.

18 But he that received the one went away and digged in the earth, and hid his lord's money.

19 Now after a long time the lord of those [376]servants cometh, and maketh a reckoning with them.

20 And he that received the five talents came and brought other five talents, saying, Lord, thou deliveredst unto me five talents: lo, I have gained other five talents.

---

[373] *Or, torches*
[374] *Or, torches*
[375] *Greek bondservants.*
[376] *Greek bondservants.*

21 His lord said unto him, Well done, good and faithful [377]servant: thou hast been faithful over a few things, I will set thee over many things; enter thou into the joy of thy lord.

22 And he also that *received* the two talents came and said, Lord, thou deliveredst unto me two talents: lo, I have gained other two talents.

23 His lord said unto him, Well done, good and faithful [378]servant: thou hast been faithful over a few things, I will set thee over many things; enter thou into the joy of thy lord.

24 And he also that had received the one talent came and said, Lord, I knew thee that thou art a hard man, reaping where thou didst not sow, and gathering where thou didst not scatter;

25 and I was afraid, and went away and hid thy talent in the earth: lo, thou hast thine own.

26 But his lord answered and said unto him, Thou wicked and slothful [379]servant, thou knewest that I reap where I sowed not, and gather where I did not scatter;

27 thou oughtest therefore to have put my money to the bankers, and at my coming I should have received back mine own with interest.

28 Take ye away therefore the talent from him, and give it unto him that hath the ten talents.

29 For unto every one that hath shall be given, and he shall have abundance: but from him that hath not, even that which he hath shall be taken away.

30 And cast ye out the unprofitable [380]servant into the outer darkness: there shall be the weeping and the gnashing of teeth.

31 But when the Son of man shall come in his glory, and all the angels with him, then shall he sit on the throne of his glory:

32 and before him shall be gathered all the nations: and he shall separate them one from another, as the shepherd separateth the sheep from the goats;

33 and he shall set the sheep on his right hand, but the goats on the left.

---

[377] *Greek bondservant.*
[378] *Greek bondservant.*
[379] *Greek bondservant.*
[380] *Greek bondservant.*

34 Then shall the King say unto them on his right hand, Come, ye blessed of my Father, inherit the kingdom prepared for you from the foundation of the world:

35 for I was hungry, and ye gave me to eat; I was thirsty, and ye gave me drink; I was a stranger, and ye took me in;

36 naked, and ye clothed me; I was sick, and ye visited me; I was in prison, and ye came unto me.

37 Then shall the righteous answer him, saying, Lord, when saw we thee hungry, and fed thee? or athirst, and gave thee drink?

38 And when saw we thee a stranger, and took thee in? or naked, and clothed thee?

39 And when saw we thee sick, or in prison, and came unto thee?

40 And the King shall answer and say unto them, Verily I say unto you, Inasmuch as ye did it unto one of these my brethren, *even* these least, ye did it unto me.

41 Then shall he say also unto them on the left hand, [381]Depart from me, ye cursed, into the eternal fire which is prepared for the devil and his angels:

42 for I was hungry, and ye did not give me to eat; I was thirsty, and ye gave me no drink;

43 I was a stranger, and ye took me not in; naked, and ye clothed me not; sick, and in prison, and ye visited me not.

44 Then shall they also answer, saying, Lord, when saw we thee hungry, or athirst, or a stranger, or naked, or sick, or in prison, and did not minister unto thee?

45 Then shall he answer them, saying, Verily I say unto you, Inasmuch as ye did it not unto one of these least, ye did it not unto me.

46 And these shall go away into eternal punishment: but the righteous into eternal life.

---

[381] *Or, Depart from me under a curse*

Chapter 26

1 And it came to pass, when Jesus had finished all these words, he said unto his disciples,

2 Ye know that after two days the passover cometh, and the Son of man is [382]delivered up to be crucified.

3 Then were gathered together the chief priests, and the elders of the people, unto the court of the high priest, who was called Caiaphas;

4 and they took counsel together that they might take Jesus by subtlety, and kill him.

5 But they said, Not during the feast, lest a tumult arise among the people.

6 Now when Jesus was in Bethany, in the house of Simon the leper,

7 there came unto him a woman having [383]an alabaster cruse of exceeding precious ointment, and she poured it upon his head, as [384]he sat at meat.

8 But when the disciples saw it, they had indignation, saying, To what purpose is this waste?

9 For this *ointment* might have been sold for much, and given to the poor.

10 But Jesus perceiving it said unto them, Why trouble ye the woman? for she hath wrought a good work upon me.

11 For ye have the poor always with you; but me ye have not always.

12 For in that she [385]poured this ointment upon my body, she did it to prepare me for burial.

13 Verily I say unto you, Wheresoever [386]this gospel shall be preached in the whole world, that also which this woman hath done shall be spoken of for a memorial of her.

14 Then one of the twelve, who was called Judas Iscariot, went unto the chief priests,

---

[382] *See 10:4.*
[383] *Or, a flask*
[384] *Or, reclined at table*
[385] *Greek cast.*
[386] *Or, these good tidings*

15 and said, What are ye willing to give me, and I will [387]deliver him unto you? And they weighed unto him thirty pieces of silver.

16 And from that time he sought opportunity to [388]deliver him *unto them*.

17 Now on the first *day* of unleavened bread the disciples came to Jesus, saying, Where wilt thou that we make ready for thee to eat the passover?

18 And he said, Go into the city to such a man, and say unto him, The Teacher saith, My time is at hand; I keep the passover at thy house with my disciples.

19 And the disciples did as Jesus appointed them; and they made ready the passover.

20 Now when even was come, he was [389]sitting at meat with the twelve [390]disciples;

21 and as they were eating, he said, Verily I say unto you, that one of you shall [391]betray me.

22 And they were exceeding sorrowful, and began to say unto him every one, Is it I, Lord?

23 And he answered and said, He that dipped his hand with me in the dish, the same shall [392]betray me.

24 The Son of man goeth, even as it is written of him: but woe unto that man through whom the Son of man is [393]betrayed! good were it [394]for that man if he had not been born.

25 And Judas, who [395]betrayed him, answered and said, Is it I, Rabbi? He saith unto him, Thou hast said.

26 And as they were eating, Jesus took [396]bread, and blessed, and brake it; and he gave to the disciples, and said, Take, eat; this is my body.

---

[387] *See 10:4.*
[388] *See 10:4.*
[389] *Or, reclining at table*
[390] *Many authorities, some ancient, omit disciples.*
[391] *See marginal note on 10:4.*
[392] *See marginal note on 10:4.*
[393] *See marginal note on 10:4.*
[394] *Greek for him if that man.*
[395] *See marginal note on 10:4.*
[396] *Or, a loaf*

27 And he took [397]a cup, and gave thanks, and gave to them, saying, Drink ye all of it;

28 for this is my blood of the [398]covenant, which is poured out for many unto remission of sins.

29 But I say unto you, I shall not drink henceforth of this fruit of the vine, until that day when I drink it new with you in my Father's kingdom.

30 And when they had sung a hymn, they went out into the mount of Olives.

31 Then saith Jesus unto them, All ye shall be offended in me this night: for it is written, [399]I will smite the shepherd, and the sheep of the flock shall be scattered abroad.

32 But after I am raised up, I will go before you into Galilee.

33 But Peter answered and said unto him, If all shall be [400]offended in thee, I will never be [401]offended.

34 Jesus said unto him, Verily I say unto thee, that this night, before the cock crow, thou shalt deny me thrice.

35 Peter saith unto him, Even if I must die with thee, *yet* will I not deny thee. Likewise also said all the disciples.

36 Then cometh Jesus with them unto [402]a place called Gethsemane, and saith unto his disciples, Sit ye here, while I go yonder and pray.

37 And he took with him Peter and the two sons of Zebedee, and began to be sorrowful and sore troubled.

38 Then saith he unto them, My soul is exceeding sorrowful, even unto death: abide ye here, and watch with me.

39 And he went forward a little, and fell on his face, and prayed, saying, My Father, if it be possible, let this cup pass away from me: nevertheless, not as I will, but as thou wilt.

40 And he cometh unto the disciples, and findeth them sleeping, and saith unto Peter, What, could ye not watch with me one hour?

---

[397] *Some ancient authorities read the cup.*
[398] *Many ancient authorities insert new.*
[399] *Zech. 13:7.*
[400] *Greek caused to stumble.*
[401] *Greek caused to stumble.*
[402] *Greek an enclosed piece of ground.*

41 [403]Watch and pray, that ye enter not into temptation: the spirit indeed is willing, but the flesh is weak.

42 Again a second time he went away, and prayed, saying, My Father, if this cannot pass away, except I drink it, thy will be done.

43 And he came again and found them sleeping, for their eyes were heavy.

44 And he left them again, and went away, and prayed a third time, saying again the same words.

45 Then cometh he to the disciples, and saith unto them, [404]Sleep on now, and take your rest: behold, the hour is at hand, and the Son of man is [405]betrayed into the hands of sinners.

46 Arise, let us be going: behold, he is at hand that [406]betrayeth me.

47 And while he yet spake, lo, Judas, one of the twelve, came, and with him a great multitude with swords and staves, from the chief priests and elders of the people.

48 Now he that [407]betrayed him gave them a sign, saying, Whomsoever I shall kiss, that is he: take him.

49 And straightway he came to Jesus, and said, Hail, Rabbi; and [408]kissed him.

50 And Jesus said unto him, Friend, *do* that for which thou art come. Then they came and laid hands on Jesus, and took him.

51 And behold, one of them that were with Jesus stretched out his hand, and drew his sword, and smote the [409]servant of the high priest, and struck off his ear.

52 Then saith Jesus unto him, Put up again thy sword into its place: for all they that take the sword shall perish with the sword.

53 Or thinkest thou that I cannot beseech my Father, and he shall even now send me more than twelve legions of angels?

54 How then should the scriptures be fulfilled, that thus it must be?

---

[403] *Or, Watch ye, and pray that ye enter not*
[404] *Or, Do ye sleep on, then, and take your rest?*
[405] *See marginal note on 10:4.*
[406] *See marginal note on 10:4.*
[407] *See marginal note on 10:4.*
[408] *Greek kissed him much.*
[409] *Greek bondservant.*

55 In that hour said Jesus to the multitudes, Are ye come out as against a robber with swords and staves to seize me? I sat daily in the temple teaching, and ye took me not.

56 But all this is come to pass, that the scriptures of the prophets might be fulfilled. Then all the disciples left him, and fled.

57 And they that had taken Jesus led him away to *the house of* Caiaphas the high priest, where the scribes and the elders were gathered together.

58 But Peter followed him afar off, unto the court of the high priest, and entered in, and sat with the officers, to see the end.

59 Now the chief priests and the whole council sought false witness against Jesus, that they might put him to death;

60 and they found it not, though many false witnesses came. But afterward came two,

61 and said, This man said, I am able to destroy the [410]temple of God, and to build it in three days.

62 And the high priest stood up, and said unto him, Answerest thou nothing? what is it which these witness against thee?

63 But Jesus held his peace. And the high priest said unto him, I adjure thee by the living God, that thou tell us whether thou art the Christ, the Son of God.

64 Jesus saith unto him, Thou hast said: nevertheless I say unto you, Henceforth ye shall see the Son of man sitting at the right hand of Power, and coming on the clouds of heaven.

65 Then the high priest rent his garments, saying, He hath spoken blasphemy: what further need have we of witnesses? behold, now ye have heard the blasphemy:

66 what think ye? They answered and said, He is [411]worthy of death.

67 Then did they spit in his face and buffet him: and some smote him [412]with the palms of their hands,

68 saying, Prophesy unto us, thou Christ: who is he that struck thee?

---

[410] *Or, sanctuary: as in 23:35; 27:5.*
[411] *Greek liable to.*
[412] *Or, with rods*

69 Now Peter was sitting without in the court: and a maid came unto him, saying, Thou also wast with Jesus the Galilaean.

70 But he denied before them all, saying, I know not what thou sayest.

71 And when he was gone out into the porch, another *maid* saw him, and saith unto them that were there, This man also was with Jesus of Nazareth.

72 And again he denied with an oath, I know not the man.

73 And after a little while they that stood by came and said to Peter, Of a truth thou also art *one* of them; for thy speech maketh thee known.

74 Then began he to curse and to swear, I know not the man. And straightway the cock crew.

75 And Peter remembered the word which Jesus had said, Before the cock crow, thou shalt deny me thrice. And he went out, and wept bitterly.

Chapter 27

1 Now when morning was come, all the chief priests and the elders of the people took counsel against Jesus to put him to death:

2 and they bound him, and led him away, and delivered him up to Pilate the governor.

3 Then Judas, who [413]betrayed him, when he saw that he was condemned, repented himself, and brought back the thirty pieces of silver to the chief priests and elders,

4 saying, I have sinned in that I [414]betrayed [415]innocent blood. But they said, What is that to us? see thou *to it*.

5 And he cast down the pieces of silver into the sanctuary, and departed; and he went away and hanged himself.

6 And the chief priests took the pieces of silver, and said, It is not lawful to put them into the [416]treasury, since it is the price of blood.

7 And they took counsel, and bought with them the potter's field, to bury strangers in.

---

[413] *See marginal note on 10:4.*
[414] *See marginal note on 10:4.*
[415] *Many ancient authorities read righteous.*
[416] *Greek corbanas, that is, sacred treasury. Compare Mk. 7:11.*

8 Wherefore that field was called, The field of blood, unto this day.

9 Then was fulfilled that which was spoken through Jeremiah the prophet, saying, [417]And [418]they took the thirty pieces of silver, the price of him that was priced, [419]whom *certain* of the children of Israel did price;

10 and [420]they gave them for the potter's field, as the Lord appointed me.

11 Now Jesus stood before the governor: and the governor asked him, saying, Art thou the King of the Jews? And Jesus said unto him, Thou sayest.

12 And when he was accused by the chief priests and elders, he answered nothing.

13 Then saith Pilate unto him, Hearest thou not how many things they witness against thee?

14 And he gave him no answer, not even to one word: insomuch that the governor marvelled greatly.

15 Now at [421]the feast the governor was wont to release unto the multitude one prisoner, whom they would.

16 And they had then a notable prisoner, called Barabbas.

17 When therefore they were gathered together, Pilate said unto them, Whom will ye that I release unto you? Barabbas, or Jesus who is called Christ?

18 For he knew that for envy they had delivered him up.

19 And while he was sitting on the judgment-seat, his wife sent unto him, saying, Have thou nothing to do with that righteous man; for I have suffered many things this day in a dream because of him.

20 Now the chief priests and the elders persuaded the multitudes that they should ask for Barabbas, and destroy Jesus.

21 But the governor answered and said unto them, Which of the two will ye that I release unto you? And they said, Barabbas.

---

[417] *Zech. 11:12, 13.*
[418] *Or, I took*
[419] *Or, whom they priced on the part of the sons of Israel*
[420] *Some ancient authorities read I gave.*
[421] *Or, a feast*

MATTHEW 27

22 Pilate saith unto them, What then shall I do unto Jesus who is called Christ? They all say, Let him be crucified.

23 And he said, Why, what evil hath he done? But they cried out exceedingly, saying, Let him be crucified.

24 So when Pilate saw that he prevailed nothing, but rather that a tumult was arising, he took water, and washed his hands before the multitude, saying, I am innocent [422]of the blood of this righteous man; see ye *to it*.

25 And all the people answered and said, His blood *be* on us, and on our children.

26 Then released he unto them Barabbas; but Jesus he scourged and delivered to be crucified.

27 Then the soldiers of the governor took Jesus into the [423]Praetorium, and gathered unto him the whole [424]band.

28 And they [425]stripped him, and put on him a scarlet robe.

29 And they platted a crown of thorns and put it upon his head, and a reed in his right hand; and they kneeled down before him, and mocked him, saying, Hail, King of the Jews!

30 And they spat upon him, and took the reed and smote him on the head.

31 And when they had mocked him, they took off from him the robe, and put on him his garments, and led him away to crucify him.

32 And as they came out, they found a man of Cyrene, Simon by name: him they [426]compelled to go *with them*, that he might bear his cross.

33 And when they were come unto a place called Golgotha, that is to say, The place of a skull,

34 they gave him wine to drink mingled with gall: and when he had tasted it, he would not drink.

35 And when they had crucified him, they parted his garments among them, casting lots;

36 and they sat and watched him there.

---

[422] *Some ancient authorities read of this blood: see ye etc.*
[423] *Or, palace See Mk. 15:16.*
[424] *Or, cohort*
[425] *Some ancient authorities read clothed.*
[426] *Greek impressed.*

37 And they set up over his head his accusation written, This is Jesus the King of the Jews.

38 Then are there crucified with him two robbers, one on the right hand and one on the left.

39 And they that passed by railed on him, wagging their heads,

40 and saying, Thou that destroyest the [427]temple, and buildest it in three days, save thyself: if thou art the Son of God, come down from the cross.

41 In like manner also the chief priests mocking *him*, with the scribes and elders, said,

42 He saved others; [428]himself he cannot save. He is the King of Israel; let him now come down from the cross, and we will believe on him.

43 He trusteth on God; let him deliver him now, if he desireth him: for he said, I am the Son of God.

44 And the robbers also that were crucified with him cast upon him the same reproach.

45 Now from the sixth hour there was darkness over all the [429]land until the ninth hour.

†✓ **The Forsaken Cry.** This is the ultimate proof of separate persons. God cannot "forsake" Himself, nor can God "die." The sufferer (Jesus) is crying out to his Superior (God) in a moment of genuine abandonment.

46 And about the ninth hour Jesus cried with a loud voice, saying, [430]Eli, Eli, lama sabachthani? that is, My God, my God, [431]why hast thou forsaken me?

47 And some of them that stood there, when they heard it, said, This man calleth Elijah.

48 And straightway one of them ran, and took a sponge, and filled it with vinegar, and put it on a reed, and gave him to drink.

49 And the rest said, Let be; let us see whether Elijah cometh to save him.[432]

50 And Jesus cried again with a loud voice, and yielded up his spirit.

---

[427] Or, sanctuary
[428] Or, can he not save himself?
[429] Or, earth
[430] Ps. 22:1.
[431] Or, why didst thou forsake me?
[432] Many ancient authorities add And another took a spear and pierced his side, and there came out water and blood. See Jn. 19:34.

51 And behold, the veil of the ⁴³³temple was rent in two from the top to the bottom; and the earth did quake; and the rocks were rent;

52 and the tombs were opened; and many bodies of the saints that had fallen asleep were raised;

53 and coming forth out of the tombs after his resurrection they entered into the holy city and appeared unto many.

54 Now the centurion, and they that were with him watching Jesus, when they saw the earthquake, and the things that were done, feared exceedingly, saying, Truly this was ⁴³⁴the Son of God.

55 And many women were there beholding from afar, who had followed Jesus from Galilee, ministering unto him:

56 among whom was Mary Magdalene, and Mary the mother of ⁴³⁵James and Joses, and the mother of the sons of Zebedee.

57 And when even was come, there came a rich man from Arimathaea, named Joseph, who also himself was Jesus' disciple:

58 this man went to Pilate, and asked for the body of Jesus. Then Pilate commanded it to be given up.

59 And Joseph took the body, and wrapped it in a clean linen cloth,

60 and laid it in his own new tomb, which he had hewn out in the rock: and he rolled a great stone to the door of the tomb, and departed.

61 And Mary Magdalene was there, and the other Mary, sitting over against the sepulchre.

62 Now on the morrow, which is *the day* after the Preparation, the chief priests and the Pharisees were gathered together unto Pilate,

63 saying, Sir, we remember that that deceiver said while he was yet alive, After three days I rise again.

64 Command therefore that the sepulchre be made sure until the third day, lest haply his disciples come and steal him away, and say unto the people, He is risen from the dead: and the last error will be worse than the first.

---

⁴³³ *Or, sanctuary*
⁴³⁴ *Or, a son of God*
⁴³⁵ *Or, Jacob*

65 Pilate said unto them, [436]Ye have a guard: go, [437]make it *as* sure as ye can.

66 So they went, and made the sepulchre sure, sealing the stone, the guard being with them.

Chapter 28

1 Now late on the sabbath day, as it began to dawn toward the first *day* of the week, came Mary Magdalene and the other Mary to see the sepulchre.

2 And behold, there was a great earthquake; for an angel of the Lord descended from heaven, and came and rolled away the stone, and sat upon it.

3 His appearance was as lightning, and his raiment white as snow:

4 and for fear of him the watchers did quake, and became as dead men.

5 And the angel answered and said unto the women, Fear not ye; for I know that ye seek Jesus, who hath been crucified.

6 He is not here; for he is risen, even as he said. Come, see the place [438]where the Lord lay.

7 And go quickly, and tell his disciples, He is risen from the dead; and lo, he goeth before you into Galilee; there shall ye see him: lo, I have told you.

8 And they departed quickly from the tomb with fear and great joy, and ran to bring his disciples word.

9 And behold, Jesus met them, saying, All hail. And they came and took hold of his feet, and [439]worshipped him.

10 Then saith Jesus unto them, Fear not: go tell my brethren that they depart into Galilee, and there shall they see me.

11 Now while they were going, behold, some of the guard came into the city, and told unto the chief priests all the things that were come to pass.

---

[436] *Or, Take a guard*
[437] *Greek make it sure, as ye know.*
[438] *Many ancient authorities read where he lay.*
[439] *See marginal note on 2:2.*

12 And when they were assembled with the elders, and had taken counsel, they gave much money unto the soldiers,

13 saying, Say ye, His disciples came by night, and stole him away while we slept.

14 And if this ⁴⁴⁰come to the governor's ears, we will persuade him, and rid you of care.

15 So they took the money, and did as they were taught: and this saying was spread abroad among the Jews, *and continueth* until this day.

16 But the eleven disciples went into Galilee, unto the mountain where Jesus had appointed them.

17 And when they saw him, they ⁴⁴¹worshipped *him*; but some doubted.

18 And Jesus came to them and spake unto them, saying, All authority hath been given unto me in heaven and on earth.

19 Go ye therefore, and make disciples of all the nations, baptizing them into the name of the Father and of the Son and of the Holy Spirit:⁴⁴²⁴⁴³

20 teaching them to observe all things whatsoever I commanded you: and lo, I am with you ⁴⁴⁴always, even unto ⁴⁴⁵the end of the world.

† **The triadic baptism formula is missing from early quotations.** Traditional reading: Trinitarian baptismal formula. Eusebius quotes 17× pre-Nicaea as "in my name" only. Acts baptisms always "in Jesus' name." Likely liturgical expansion (Buzzard).

---

⁴⁴⁰ *Or, come to a hearing before the governor*
⁴⁴¹ *See marginal note on 2:2.*
⁴⁴²**Textual Variant:** Eusebius (c. 260–339 AD) quotes this verse 17 times in his pre-Nicene writings as "Go ye and make disciples of all the nations in my name," omitting the triadic formula. The longer phrase may be a later liturgical expansion.
⁴⁴³**False Friend:** The KJV reads "Holy Ghost." In 1611, "ghost" simply meant a spirit. Today, it implies a spooky phantom of the dead. The RV uses the accurate title "Spirit" (*pneuma*), emphasizing God's active power rather than a haunting presence.
⁴⁴⁴*Greek all the days.*
⁴⁴⁵*Or, the consummation of the age*

Timeline for Mark

Mark presents an urgent, action-oriented narrative of Jesus as the powerful Son of God, emphasizing service and suffering.

MARK'S NARRATIVE STRUCTURE

SECTION / THEMATIC BLOCK	CHAPTER REFERENCE / NARRATIVE FOCUS
Preparation & Early Ministry	**Ch 1:** John the Baptist, Baptism, Temptation, and the call of the first disciples. Immediate emphasis on Jesus's authority over demons.
The Galilean Campaign	**Ch 2 – 4:** Conflicts with religious authorities; calls for repentance; parables used to teach the secrets of the Kingdom (Sower, Mustard Seed).
Power and Opposition	**Ch 5 – 8:26:** Miracles demonstrating divine power (raising the dead, walking on water). *Note:* Jesus frequently commands silence regarding his identity (**The Messianic Secret**) to prevent political misunderstanding.
The Turning Point	**Ch 8:27 – 10:52:** Peter's Confession ("You are the Christ"). Jesus shifts focus to the Cross. **Key Verse (10:45):** "For even the Son of Man came not to be ministered unto, but to minister, and to give his life a ransom for many."

MARK'S NARRATIVE STRUCTURE

SECTION / THEMATIC BLOCK	CHAPTER REFERENCE / NARRATIVE FOCUS
Jerusalem Authority	**Ch 11 – 13:** The Triumphal Entry; Cleansing the Temple; intense conflict with leaders; and the teaching on the End Times (Olivet Discourse).
The Passion and Abrupt Conclusion	**Ch 14 – 16:8:** The Last Supper, Gethsemane, Trials, Crucifixion, and the Resurrection. The narrative ends abruptly at **16:8** with the women fleeing in fear. (*Note: Verses 16:9-20 are absent from the oldest manuscripts and considered a later addition.*)

Chapter 1

1 The beginning of the [446]gospel of Jesus Christ, [447]the Son of God.

2 Even as it is written [448]in Isaiah the prophet,
[449]Behold, I send my messenger before thy face,
Who shall prepare thy way;

3 [450]The voice of one crying in the wilderness,
Make ye ready the way of the Lord,
Make his paths straight;

4 John came, who baptized in the wilderness and preached the baptism of repentance unto remission of sins.

5 And there went out unto him all the country of Judaea, and all they of Jerusalem; and they were baptized of him in the river Jordan, confessing their sins.

6 And John was clothed with camel's hair, and *had* a leathern girdle about his loins, and did eat locusts and wild honey.

7 And he preached, saying, There cometh after me he that is mightier than I, the latchet of whose shoes I am not [451]worthy to stoop down and unloose.

8 I baptized you [452]in water; but he shall baptize you [453]in the Holy Spirit.

9 And it came to pass in those days, that Jesus came from Nazareth of Galilee, and was baptized of John [454]in the Jordan.

10 And straightway coming up out of the water, he saw the heavens rent asunder, and the Spirit as a dove descending upon him:

11 and a voice came out of the heavens, Thou art my beloved Son, in thee I am well pleased.

12 And straightway the Spirit driveth him forth into the wilderness.

---

[446] *Or, good tidings: and so elsewhere.*
[447] *Some ancient authorities omit the Son of God.*
[448] *Some ancient authorities read in the prophets.*
[449] *Mal. 3:1.*
[450] *Isa. 40:3.*
[451] *Greek sufficient.*
[452] *Or, with*
[453] *Or, with*
[454] *Greek into.*

13 And he was in the wilderness forty days tempted of Satan; and he was with the wild beasts; and the angels ministered unto him.

14 Now after John was delivered up, Jesus came into Galilee, preaching the [455]gospel of God,

15 and saying, The time is fulfilled, and the kingdom of God is at hand: repent ye, and believe in the [456]gospel.

16 And passing along by the sea of Galilee, he saw Simon and Andrew the brother of Simon casting a net in the sea; for they were fishers.

17 And Jesus said unto them, Come ye after me, and I will make you to become fishers of men.

18 And straightway they left the nets, and followed him.

19 And going on a little further, he saw [457]James the *son* of Zebedee, and John his brother, who also were in the boat mending the nets.

20 And straightway he called them: and they left their father Zebedee in the boat with the hired servants, and went after him.

21 And they go into Capernaum; and straightway on the sabbath day he entered into the synagogue and taught.

22 And they were astonished at his teaching: for he taught them as having authority, and not as the scribes.

23 And straightway there was in their synagogue a man with an unclean spirit; and he cried out,

24 saying, What have we to do with thee, Jesus thou Nazarene? art thou come to destroy us? I know thee who thou art, the Holy One of God.

25 And Jesus rebuked [458]him, saying, Hold thy peace, and come out of him.

26 And the unclean spirit, [459]tearing him and crying with a loud voice, came out of him.

27 And they were all amazed, insomuch that they questioned among themselves, saying, What is this? a new teaching! with authority he commandeth even the unclean spirits, and they obey him.

---

[455] *Or, good tidings: and so elsewhere*
[456] *Or, good tidings: and so elsewhere*
[457] *Or, Jacob*
[458] *Or, it*
[459] *Or, convulsing*

28 And the report of him went out straightway everywhere into all the region of Galilee round about.

29 And straightway, [460]when they were come out of the synagogue, they came into the house of Simon and Andrew, with [461]James and John.

30 Now Simon's wife's mother lay sick of a fever; and straightway they tell him of her:

31 and he came and took her by the hand, and raised her up; and the fever left her, and she ministered unto them.

32 And at even, when the sun did set, they brought unto him all that were sick, and them that were [462]possessed with demons.

33 And all the city was gathered together at the door.

34 And he healed many that were sick with divers diseases, and cast out many demons; and he suffered not the demons to speak, because they knew him[463].

35 And in the morning, a great while before day, he rose up and went out, and departed into a desert place, and there prayed.

36 And Simon and they that were with him followed after him;

37 and they found him, and say unto him, All are seeking thee.

38 And he saith unto them, Let us go elsewhere into the next towns, that I may preach there also; for to this end came I forth.

39 And he went into their synagogues throughout all Galilee, preaching and casting out demons.

40 And there cometh to him a leper, beseeching him, [464]and kneeling down to him, and saying unto him, If thou wilt, thou canst make me clean.

41 And being moved with compassion, he stretched forth his hand, and touched him, and saith unto him, I will; be thou made clean.

42 And straightway the leprosy departed from him, and he was made clean.

---

[460] *Some ancient authorities read when he was come out of the synagogue, he came etc.*
[461] *Or, Jacob*
[462] *Or, demoniacs*
[463] *Many ancient authorities add to be Christ. See Lk. 4:41.*
[464] *Some ancient authorities omit and kneeling down to him.*

43 And he [465]strictly charged him, and straightway sent him out,

44 and saith unto him, See thou say nothing to any man: but go show thyself to the priest, and offer for thy cleansing the things which Moses [466]commanded, for a testimony unto them.

45 But he went out, and began to publish it much, and to spread abroad the [467]matter, insomuch that [468]Jesus could no more openly enter into [469]a city, but was without in desert places: and they came to him from every quarter.

Chapter 2

1 And when he entered again into Capernaum after some days, it was noised that he was [470]in the house.

2 And many were gathered together, so that there was no longer room *for them*, no, not even about the door: and he spake the word unto them.

3 And they come, bringing unto him a man sick of the palsy, borne of four.

4 And when they could not [471]come nigh unto him for the crowd, they uncovered the roof where he was: and when they had broken it up, they let down the [472]bed whereon the sick of the palsy lay.

5 And Jesus seeing their faith saith unto the sick of the palsy, [473]Son, thy sins are forgiven.

6 But there were certain of the scribes sitting there, and reasoning in their hearts,

7 Why doth this man thus speak? he blasphemeth: who can forgive sins but one, *even* God?

---

[465] *Or, sternly*
[466] *Lev. 13:49; 14:2ff.*
[467] *Greek word.*
[468] *Greek he.*
[469] *Or, the city*
[470] *Or, at home*
[471] *Many ancient authorities read bring him unto him.*
[472] *Or, pallet*
[473] *Greek Child.*

8 And straightway Jesus, perceiving in his spirit that they so reasoned within themselves, saith unto them, Why reason ye these things in your hearts?

9 Which is easier, to say to the sick of the palsy, Thy sins are forgiven; or to say, Arise, and take up thy [474]bed, and walk?

10 But that ye may know that the Son of man hath authority on earth to forgive sins (he saith to the sick of the palsy),

11 I say unto thee, Arise, take up thy [475]bed, and go unto thy house.

12 And he arose, and straightway took up the [476]bed, and went forth before them all; insomuch that they were all amazed, and glorified God, saying, We never saw it on this fashion.

13 And he went forth again by the sea side; and all the multitude resorted unto him, and he taught them.

14 And as he passed by, he saw Levi the *son* of Alphaeus sitting at the place of toll, and he saith unto him, Follow me. And he arose and followed him.

15 And it came to pass, that he was sitting at meat in his house, and many [477]publicans and sinners sat down with Jesus and his disciples: for there were many, and they followed him.

16 And the scribes [478]of the Pharisees, when they saw that he was eating with the sinners and [479]publicans, said unto his disciples, [480]*How is it that he eateth* [481]*and drinketh with* [482]*publicans and sinners?*

17 And when Jesus heard it, he saith unto them, They that are [483]whole have no need of a physician, but they that are sick: I came not to call the righteous, but sinners.

---

[474]*Or, pallet*
[475]*Or, pallet*
[476]*Or, pallet*
[477]*That is, collectors or renters of Roman taxes.*
[478]*Some ancient authorities read and the Pharisees.*
[479]*That is, collectors or renters of Roman taxes.*
[480]*Or, He eateth . . . sinners*
[481]*Some ancient authorities omit and drinketh.*
[482]*That is, collectors or renters of Roman taxes.*
[483]*Greek strong.*

18 And John's disciples and the Pharisees were fasting: and they come and say unto him, Why do John's disciples and the disciples of the Pharisees fast, but thy disciples fast not?

19 And Jesus said unto them, Can the [484]sons of the bridechamber fast, while the bridegroom is with them? as long as they have the bridegroom with them, they cannot fast.

20 But the days will come, when the bridegroom shall be taken away from them, and then will they fast in that day.

21 No man seweth a piece of undressed cloth on an old garment: else that which should fill it up taketh from it, the new from the old, and a worse rent is made.

22 And no man putteth new wine into old [485]wine-skins; else the wine will burst the skins, and the wine perisheth, and the skins: but *they put* new wine into fresh wine-skins.

23 And it came to pass, that he was going on the sabbath day through the grainfields; and his disciples [486]began, as they went, to pluck the ears.[487]

24 And the Pharisees said unto him, Behold, why do they on the sabbath day that which is not lawful?

25 And he said unto them, [488]Did ye never read what David did, when he had need, and was hungry, he, and they that were with him?

26 How he entered into the house of God [489]when Abiathar was high priest, and ate the showbread, which it is not lawful to eat save for the priests, and gave also to them that were with him?

27 And he said unto them, The sabbath was made for man, and not man for the sabbath:

28 so that the Son of man is lord even of the sabbath.

---

[484]*That is, companions of the bridegroom.*
[485]*That is, skins used as bottles.*
[486]*Greek began to make their way plucking.*
[487]**False Friend:** The KJV reads "corn." Modern readers imagine Maize (Yellow Corn), an American crop that did not exist in ancient Israel. The RV "ears" refers to the *heads of wheat or barley*. The disciples were snapping off the grain heads and rubbing them to eat the kernels (Lk 6:1), not shucking corn cobs.
[488]*1 Sam. 21:6.*
[489]*Some ancient authorities read in the days of Abiathar the high priest.*

Chapter 3

1 And he entered again into the synagogue; and there was a man there who had his hand withered.

2 And they watched him, whether he would heal him on the sabbath day; that they might accuse him.

3 And he saith unto the man that had his hand withered, [490]Stand forth.

4 And he saith unto them, Is it lawful on the sabbath day to do good, or to do harm? to save a life, or to kill? But they held their peace.

5 And when he had looked round about on them with anger, being grieved at the hardening of their heart, he saith unto the man, Stretch forth thy hand. And he stretched it forth; and his hand was restored.

6 And the Pharisees went out, and straightway with the Herodians took counsel against him, how they might destroy him.

7 And Jesus with his disciples withdrew to the sea: and a great multitude from Galilee followed; and from Judaea,

8 and from Jerusalem, and from Idumaea, and beyond the Jordan, and about Tyre and Sidon, a great multitude, hearing [491]what great things he did, came unto him.

9 And he spake to his disciples, that a little boat should wait on him because of the crowd, lest they should throng him:

10 for he had healed many; insomuch that as many as had [492]plagues [493]pressed upon him that they might touch him.

11 And the unclean spirits, whensoever they beheld him, fell down before him, and cried, saying, Thou art the Son of God.

12 And he charged them much that they should not make him known.

13 And he goeth up into the mountain, and calleth unto him whom he himself would; and they went unto him.

14 And he appointed twelve, [494]that they might be with him, and that he might send them forth to preach,

---

[490] *Greek Arise into the midst.*
[491] *Or, all the things that he did*
[492] *Greek scourges.*
[493] *Greek fell.*
[494] *Some ancient authorities add whom also he named apostles. See Lk. 6:13; compare 6:30.*

15 and to have authority to cast out demons:

16 [495]and Simon he surnamed Peter;

17 and [496]James the *son* of Zebedee, and John the brother of [497]James; and them he surnamed Boanerges, which is, Sons of thunder:

18 and Andrew, and Philip, and Bartholomew, and Matthew, and Thomas, and [498]James the *son* of Alphaeus, and Thaddaeus, and Simon the [499]Cananaean,

19 and Judas Iscariot, who also [500]betrayed him.

And he cometh [501]into a house.

20 And the multitude cometh together again, so that they could not so much as eat bread.

21 And when his friends heard it, they went out to lay hold on him: for they said, He is beside himself.

22 And the scribes that came down from Jerusalem said, He hath [502]Beelzebub, and, [503]By the prince of the demons casteth he out the demons.

23 And he called them unto him, and said unto them in parables, How can Satan cast out Satan?

24 And if a kingdom be divided against itself, that kingdom cannot stand.

25 And if a house be divided against itself, that house will not be able to stand.

26 And if Satan hath risen up against himself, and is divided, he cannot stand, but hath an end.

27 But no one can enter into the house of the strong *man*, and spoil his goods, except he first bind the strong *man*; and then he will spoil his house.

---

[495]*Some ancient authorities insert and he appointed twelve.*
[496]*Or, Jacob*
[497]*Or, Jacob*
[498]*Or, Jacob*
[499]*Or, Zealot. See Lk. 6:15; Acts 1:13.*
[500]*Or, delivered him up*
[501]*Or, home*
[502]*Greek Beelzebul.*
[503]*Or, In*

28 Verily I say unto you, All their sins shall be forgiven unto the sons of men, and their blasphemies wherewith soever they shall blaspheme:

29 but whosoever shall blaspheme against the Holy Spirit hath never forgiveness, but is guilty of an eternal sin:

30 because they said, He hath an unclean spirit.

31 And there come his mother and his brethren; and, standing without, they sent unto him, calling him.

32 And a multitude was sitting about him; and they say unto him, Behold, thy mother and thy brethren without seek for thee.

33 And he answereth them, and saith, Who is my mother and my brethren?

34 And looking round on them that sat round about him, he saith, Behold, my mother and my brethren!

35 For whosoever shall do the will of God, the same is my brother, and sister, and mother.

Chapter 4

1 And again he began to teach by the sea side. And there is gathered unto him a very great multitude, so that he entered into a boat, and sat in the sea; and all the multitude were by the sea on the land.

2 And he taught them many things in parables, and said unto them in his teaching,

3 Hearken: Behold, the sower went forth to sow:

4 and it came to pass, as he sowed, some *seed* fell by the way side, and the birds came and devoured it.

5 And other fell on the rocky *ground*, where it had not much earth; and straightway it sprang up, because it had no deepness of earth:

6 and when the sun was risen, it was scorched; and because it had no root, it withered away.

7 And other fell among the thorns, and the thorns grew up, and choked it, and it yielded no fruit.

8 And others fell into the good ground, and yielded fruit, growing up and increasing; and brought forth, thirtyfold, and sixtyfold, and a hundredfold.

9 And he said, Who hath ears to hear, let him hear.

10 And when he was alone, they that were about him with the twelve asked of him the parables.

11 And he said unto them, Unto you is given the mystery of the kingdom of God: but unto them that are without, all things are done in parables:

12 that seeing they may see, and not perceive; and hearing they may hear, and not understand; lest haply they should turn again, and it should be forgiven them.

13 And he saith unto them, Know ye not this parable? and how shall ye know all the parables?

14 The sower soweth the word.

15 And these are they by the way side, where the word is sown; and when they have heard, straightway cometh Satan, and taketh away the word which hath been sown in them.

16 And these in like manner are they that are sown upon the rocky *places*, who, when they have heard the word, straightway receive it with joy;

17 and they have no root in themselves, but endure for a while; then, when tribulation or persecution ariseth because of the word, straightway they stumble.

18 And others are they that are sown among the thorns; these are they that have heard the word,

19 and the cares of the [504]world, and the deceitfulness of riches, and the lusts of other things entering in, choke the word, and it becometh unfruitful.

20 And those are they that were sown upon the good ground; such as hear the word, and accept it, and bear fruit, thirtyfold, and sixtyfold, and a hundredfold.

21 And he said unto them, Is the lamp brought to be put under the bushel, or under the bed, *and* not to be put on the stand?

22 For there is nothing hid, save that it should be manifested; neither was *anything* made secret, but that it should come to light.

23 If any man hath ears to hear, let him hear.

---

[504] *Or, age*

24 And he said unto them, Take heed what ye hear: with what measure ye mete it shall be measured unto you; and more shall be given unto you.

25 For he that hath, to him shall be given: and he that hath not, from him shall be taken away even that which he hath.

26 And he said, So is the kingdom of God, as if a man should cast seed upon the earth;

27 and should sleep and rise night and day, and the seed should spring up and grow, he knoweth not how.

28 The earth [505]beareth fruit of herself; first the blade, then the ear, then the full grain in the ear.

29 But when the fruit [506]is ripe, straightway he [507]putteth forth the sickle, because the harvest is come.

30 And he said, How shall we liken the kingdom of God? or in what parable shall we set it forth?

31 [508]It is like a grain of mustard seed, which, when it is sown upon the earth, though it be less than all the seeds that are upon the earth,

32 yet when it is sown, groweth up, and becometh greater than all the herbs, and putteth out great branches; so that the birds of the heaven can lodge under the shadow thereof.

33 And with many such parables spake he the word unto them, as they were able to hear it;

34 and without a parable spake he not unto them: but privately to his own disciples he expounded all things.

35 And on that day, when even was come, he saith unto them, Let us go over unto the other side.

36 And leaving the multitude, they take him with them, even as he was, in the boat. And other boats were with him.

37 And there ariseth a great storm of wind, and the waves beat into the boat, insomuch that the boat was now filling.

---

[505] *Or, yieldeth*
[506] *Or, alloweth*
[507] *Or, sendeth forth*
[508] *Greek As unto.*

38 And he himself was in the stern, asleep on the cushion: and they awake him, and say unto him, Teacher, carest thou not that we perish?

39 And he awoke, and rebuked the wind, and said unto the sea, Peace, be still. And the wind ceased, and there was a great calm.

40 And he said unto them, Why are ye fearful? have ye not yet faith?

41 And they feared exceedingly, and said one to another, Who then is this, that even the wind and the sea obey him?

Chapter 5

1 And they came to the other side of the sea, into the country of the Gerasenes.

2 And when he was come out of the boat, straightway there met him out of the tombs a man with an unclean spirit,

3 who had his dwelling in the tombs: and no man could any more bind him, no, not with a chain;

4 because that he had been often bound with fetters and chains, and the chains had been rent asunder by him, and the fetters broken in pieces: and no man had strength to tame him.

5 And always, night and day, in the tombs and in the mountains, he was crying out, and cutting himself with stones.

6 And when he saw Jesus from afar, he ran and [509]worshipped him;

7 and crying out with a loud voice, he saith, What have I to do with thee, Jesus, thou Son of the Most High God? I adjure thee by God, torment me not.

8 For he said unto him, Come forth, thou unclean spirit, out of the man.

9 And he asked him, What is thy name? And he saith unto him, My name is Legion; for we are many.

10 And he besought him much that he would not send them away out of the country.

11 Now there was there on the mountain side a great herd of swine feeding.

---

[509]*The Greek word denotes an act of reverence, whether paid to a creature (see Mt. 4:9; 18:26) or to the Creator (see Mt. 4:10)*

12 And they besought him, saying, Send us into the swine, that we may enter into them.

13 And he gave them leave. And the unclean spirits came out, and entered into the swine: and the herd rushed down the steep into the sea, *in number* about two thousand; and they were drowned in the sea.

14 And they that fed them fled, and told it in the city, and in the country. And they came to see what it was that had come to pass.

15 And they come to Jesus, and behold [510]him that was possessed with demons sitting, clothed and in his right mind, *even* him that had the legion: and they were afraid.

16 And they that saw it declared unto them how it befell [511]him that was possessed with demons, and concerning the swine.

17 And they began to beseech him to depart from their borders.

18 And as he was entering into the boat, [512]he that had been possessed with demons besought him that he might be with him.

19 And he suffered him not, but saith unto him, Go to thy house unto thy friends, and tell them how great things the Lord hath done for thee, and *how* he had mercy on thee.

20 And he went his way, and began to publish in Decapolis how great things Jesus had done for him: and all men marvelled.

21 And when Jesus had crossed over again in the boat unto the other side, a great multitude was gathered unto him; and he was by the sea.

22 And there cometh one of the rulers of the synagogue, Jairus by name; and seeing him, he falleth at his feet,

23 and beseecheth him much, saying, My little daughter is at the point of death: *I pray thee,* that thou come and lay thy hands on her, that she may be [513]made whole, and live.

24 And he went with him; and a great multitude followed him, and they thronged him.

25 And a woman, who had an issue of blood twelve years,

---

[510] *Or, the demoniac*
[511] *Or, the demoniac*
[512] *Or, the demoniac*
[513] *Or, saved*

26 and had suffered many things of many physicians, and had spent all that she had, and was nothing bettered, but rather grew worse,

27 having heard the things concerning Jesus, came in the crowd behind, and touched his garment.

28 For she said, If I touch but his garments, I shall be [514]made whole.

29 And straightway the fountain of her blood was dried up; and she felt in her body that she was healed of her [515]plague.

30 And straightway Jesus, perceiving in himself that the power *proceeding* from him had gone forth, turned him about in the crowd, and said, Who touched my garments?

31 And his disciples said unto him, Thou seest the multitude thronging thee, and sayest thou, Who touched me?

32 And he looked round about to see her that had done this thing.

33 But the woman fearing and trembling, knowing what had been done to her, came and fell down before him, and told him all the truth.

34 And he said unto her, Daughter, thy faith hath [516]made thee whole; go in peace, and be whole of thy [517]plague.

35 While he yet spake, they come from the ruler of the synagogue's *house*, saying, Thy daughter is dead: why troublest thou the Teacher any further?

36 But Jesus, [518]not heeding the word spoken, saith unto the ruler of the synagogue, Fear not, only believe.

37 And he suffered no man to follow with him, save Peter, and [519]James, and John the brother of [520]James.

38 And they come to the house of the ruler of the synagogue; and he beholdeth a tumult, and *many* weeping and wailing greatly.

39 And when he was entered in, he saith unto them, Why make ye a tumult, and weep? the child is not dead, but sleepeth.

---

[514] *Or, saved*
[515] *Greek scourge.*
[516] *Or, saved thee*
[517] *Greek scourge.*
[518] *Or, overhearing*
[519] *Or, Jacob*
[520] *Or, Jacob*

40 And they laughed him to scorn. But he, having put them all forth, taketh the father of the child and her mother and them that were with him, and goeth in where the child was.

41 And taking the child by the hand, he saith unto her, Talitha cumi; which is, being interpreted, Damsel, I say unto thee, Arise.

42 And straightway the damsel rose up, and walked; for she was twelve years old. And they were amazed straightway with a great amazement.

43 And he charged them much that no man should know this: and he commanded that *something* should be given her to eat.

Chapter 6

1 And he went out from thence; and he cometh into his own country; and his disciples follow him.

2 And when the sabbath was come, he began to teach in the synagogue: and [521]many hearing him were astonished, saying, Whence hath this man these things? and, What is the wisdom that is given unto this man, and *what mean* such [522]mighty works wrought by his hands?

3 Is not this the carpenter, the son of Mary, and brother of [523]James, and Joses, and Judas, and Simon? and are not his sisters here with us? And they were [524]offended in him.

4 And Jesus said unto them, A prophet is not without honor, save in his own country, and among his own kin, and in his own house.

5 And he could there do no [525]mighty work, save that he laid his hands upon a few sick folk, and healed them.

6 And he marvelled because of their unbelief.

And he went round about the villages teaching.

7 And he calleth unto him the twelve, and began to send them forth by two and two; and he gave them authority over the unclean spirits;

---

[521] *Some ancient authorities insert the.*
[522] *Greek powers.*
[523] *Or, Jacob*
[524] *Greek caused to stumble.*
[525] *Greek power.*

8 and he charged them that they should take nothing for *their* journey, save a staff only; no bread, no wallet, no [526]money in their [527]purse;

9 but *to go* shod with sandals: and, *said he*, put not on two coats.

10 And he said unto them, Wheresoever ye enter into a house, there abide till ye depart thence.

11 And whatsoever place shall not receive you, and they hear you not, as ye go forth thence, shake off the dust that is under your feet for a testimony unto them.

12 And they went out, and preached that *men* should repent.

13 And they cast out many demons, and anointed with oil many that were sick, and healed them.

14 And king Herod heard *thereof*; for his name had become known: and [528]he said, John the Baptizer is risen from the dead, and therefore do these powers work in him.

15 But others said, It is Elijah. And others said, *It is* a prophet, *even* as one of the prophets.

16 But Herod, when he heard *thereof*, said, John, whom I beheaded, he is risen.

17 For Herod himself had sent forth and laid hold upon John, and bound him in prison for the sake of Herodias, his brother Philip's wife; for he had married her.

18 For John said unto Herod, It is not lawful for thee to have thy brother's wife.

19 And Herodias set herself against him, and desired to kill him; and she could not;

20 for Herod feared John, knowing that he was a righteous and holy man, and kept him safe. And when he heard him, he [529]was much perplexed; and he heard him gladly.

---

[526] *Greek brass.*
[527] *Greek girdle.*
[528] *Some ancient authorities read they.*
[529] *Many ancient authorities read did many things.*

21 And when a convenient day was come, that Herod on his birthday made a supper to his lords, and the [530]high captains, and the chief men of Galilee;

22 and when [531]the daughter of Herodias herself came in and danced, [532]she pleased Herod and them that sat at meat with him; and the king said unto the damsel, Ask of me whatsoever thou wilt, and I will give it thee.

23 And he sware unto her, Whatsoever thou shalt ask of me, I will give it thee, unto the half of my kingdom.

24 And she went out, and said unto her mother, What shall I ask? And she said, The head of John the Baptizer.

25 And she came in straightway with haste unto the king, and asked, saying, I will that thou forthwith give me on a platter the head of John the Baptist.

26 And the king was exceeding sorry; but for the sake of his oaths, and of them that sat at meat, he would not reject her.

27 And straightway the king sent forth a soldier of his guard, and commanded to bring his head: and he went and beheaded him in the prison,

28 and brought his head on a platter, and gave it to the damsel; and the damsel gave it to her mother.

29 And when his disciples heard *thereof*, they came and took up his corpse, and laid it in a tomb.

30 And the apostles gather themselves together unto Jesus; and they told him all things, whatsoever they had done, and whatsoever they had taught.

31 And he saith unto them, Come ye yourselves apart into a desert place, and rest a while. For there were many coming and going, and they had no leisure so much as to eat.

32 And they went away in the boat to a desert place apart.

---

[530] *Or, military tribunes. Greek chiliarchs.*
[531] *Some ancient authorities read his daughter Herodias.*
[532] *Or, it*

33 And *the people* saw them going, and many knew *them*, and they ran together there [533]on foot from all the cities, and outwent them.

34 And he came forth and saw a great multitude, and he had compassion on them, because they were as sheep not having a shepherd: and he began to teach them many things.

35 And when the day was now far spent, his disciples came unto him, and said, The place is desert, and the day is now far spent;

36 send them away, that they may go into the country and villages round about, and buy themselves somewhat to eat.

37 But he answered and said unto them, Give ye them to eat. And they say unto him, Shall we go and buy two hundred [534]shillings' worth of bread, and give them to eat?

38 And he saith unto them, How many loaves have ye? go *and* see. And when they knew, they say, Five, and two fishes.

39 And he commanded them that all should [535]sit down by companies upon the green grass.

40 And they sat down in ranks, by hundreds, and by fifties.

41 And he took the five loaves and the two fishes, and looking up to heaven, he blessed, and brake the loaves; and he gave to the disciples to set before them; and the two fishes divided he among them all.

42 And they all ate, and were filled.

43 And they took up broken pieces, twelve basketfuls, and also of the fishes.

44 And they that ate the loaves were five thousand men.

45 And straightway he constrained his disciples to enter into the boat, and to go before *him* unto the other side to Bethsaida, while he himself sendeth the multitude away.

46 And after he had taken leave of them, he departed into the mountain to pray.

47 And when even was come, the boat was in the midst of the sea, and he alone on the land.

---

[533] *Or, by land*

[534] *The word in the Greek denotes a coin worth about eight pence half-penny, or nearly seventeen cents.*

[535] *Greek recline.*

48 And seeing them distressed in rowing, for the wind was contrary unto them, about the fourth watch of the night he cometh unto them, walking on the sea; and he would have passed by them:

49 but they, when they saw him walking on the sea, supposed that it was a ghost, and cried out;

50 for they all saw him, and were troubled. But he straightway spake with them, and saith unto them, Be of good cheer: it is I; be not afraid.

51 And he went up unto them into the boat; and the wind ceased: and they were sore amazed in themselves;

52 for they understood not concerning the loaves, but their heart was hardened.

53 And when they had [536]crossed over, they came to the land unto Gennesaret, and moored to the shore.

54 And when they were come out of the boat, straightway *the people* knew him,

55 and ran round about that whole region, and began to carry about on their [537]beds those that were sick, where they heard he was.

56 And wheresoever he entered, into villages, or into cities, or into the country, they laid the sick in the marketplaces, and besought him that they might touch if it were but the border of his garment: and as many as touched [538]him were made whole.

---

[536] *Or, crossed over to the land, they came unto Gennesaret*
[537] *Or, pallets*
[538] *Or, it*

Chapter 7

1 And there are gathered together unto him the Pharisees, and certain of the scribes, who had come from Jerusalem,

2 and had seen that some of his disciples ate their bread with [539]defiled, that is, unwashen, hands.

3 (For the Pharisees, and all the Jews, except they wash their hands [540]diligently, eat not, holding the tradition of the elders;

4 and *when they come* from the marketplace, except they [541]bathe themselves, they eat not; and many other things there are, which they have received to hold, [542]washings of cups, and pots, and brasen vessels[543].)

5 And the Pharisees and the scribes ask him, Why walk not thy disciples according to the tradition of the elders, but eat their bread with [544]defiled hands?

6 And he said unto them, Well did Isaiah prophesy of you hypocrites, as it is written,

> [545]This people honoreth me with their lips,
> But their heart is far from me.

7 But in vain do they worship me,
Teaching *as their* doctrines the precepts of men.

8 Ye leave the commandment of God, and hold fast the tradition of men.

9 And he said unto them, Full well do ye reject the commandment of God, that ye may keep your tradition.

10 For Moses said, [546]Honor thy father and thy mother; and, He that speaketh evil of father or mother, let him [547]die the death:

11 but ye say, If a man shall say to his father or his mother, That wherewith thou mightest have been profited by me is Corban, that is to say, Given *to God*;

---

[539] *Or, common*
[540] *Or, up to the elbow. Greek with the fist.*
[541] *Greek baptize. Some ancient authorities read sprinkle themselves.*
[542] *Greek baptizings.*
[543] *Many ancient authorities add and couches.*
[544] *Or, common*
[545] *Isa. 29:13.*
[546] *Ex. 20:12; Dt. 5:16; Ex. 21:17; Lev. 20:9.*
[547] *Or, surely die*

12 ye no longer suffer him to do aught for his father or his mother;

13 making void the word of God by your tradition, which ye have delivered: and many such like things ye do.

14 And he called to him the multitude again, and said unto them, Hear me all of you, and understand:

15 there is nothing from without the man, that going into him can defile him; but the things which proceed out of the man are those that defile the man.[548]

17 And when he was entered into the house from the multitude, his disciples asked of him the parable.

18 And he saith unto them, Are ye so without understanding also? Perceive ye not, that whatsoever from without goeth into the man, *it* cannot defile him;

19 because it goeth not into his heart, but into his belly, and goeth out into the draught? *This he said*, making all meats clean.

20 And he said, That which proceedeth out of the man, that defileth the man.

21 For from within, out of the heart of men, [549]evil thoughts proceed, fornications, thefts, murders, adulteries,

22 covetings, wickednesses, deceit, lasciviousness, an evil eye, railing, pride, foolishness:

23 all these evil things proceed from within, and defile the man.

24 And from thence he arose, and went away into the borders of Tyre [550]and Sidon. And he entered into a house, and would have no man know it; and he could not be hid.

25 But straightway a woman, whose little daughter had an unclean spirit, having heard of him, came and fell down at his feet.

26 Now the woman was a [551]Greek, a Syrophoenician by race. And she besought him that he would cast forth the demon out of her daughter.

---

[548] Many ancient authorities insert verse 16 *If any man hath ears to hear, let him hear.* See 4:9.
[549] Greek *thoughts that are evil.*
[550] Some ancient authorities omit *and Sidon.*
[551] Or, *Gentile*

27 And he said unto her, Let the children first be filled: for it is not meet to take the children's [552]bread and cast it to the dogs.

28 But she answered and saith unto him, Yea, Lord; even the dogs under the table eat of the children's crumbs.

29 And he said unto her, For this saying go thy way; the demon is gone out of thy daughter.

30 And she went away unto her house, and found the child laid upon the bed, and the demon gone out.

31 And again he went out from the borders of Tyre, and came through Sidon unto the sea of Galilee, through the midst of the borders of Decapolis.

32 And they bring unto him one that was deaf, and had an impediment in his speech; and they beseech him to lay his hand upon him.

33 And he took him aside from the multitude privately, and put his fingers into his ears, and he spat, and touched his tongue;

34 and looking up to heaven, he sighed, and saith unto him, Ephphatha, that is, Be opened.

35 And his ears were opened, and the bond of his tongue was loosed, and he spake plain.

36 And he charged them that they should tell no man: but the more he charged them, so much the more a great deal they published it.

37 And they were beyond measure astonished, saying, He hath done all things well; he maketh even the deaf to hear, and the dumb to speak.

---

[552] *Or, loaf*

Chapter 8

1 In those days, when there was again a great multitude, and they had nothing to eat, he called unto him his disciples, and saith unto them,

2 I have compassion on the multitude, because they continue with me now three days, and have nothing to eat:

3 and if I send them away fasting to their home, they will faint on the way; and some of them are come from far.

4 And his disciples answered him, Whence shall one be able to fill these men with [553]bread here in a desert place?

5 And he asked them, How many loaves have ye? And they said, Seven.

6 And he commandeth the multitude to sit down on the ground: and he took the seven loaves, and having given thanks, he brake, and gave to his disciples, to set before them; and they set them before the multitude.

7 And they had a few small fishes: and having blessed them, he commanded to set these also before them.

8 And they ate, and were filled: and they took up, of broken pieces that remained over, seven baskets.

9 And they were about four thousand: and he sent them away.

10 And straightway he entered into the boat with his disciples, and came into the parts of Dalmanutha.

11 And the Pharisees came forth, and began to question with him, seeking of him a sign from heaven, trying him.

12 And he sighed deeply in his spirit, and saith, Why doth this generation seek a sign? verily I say unto you, There shall no sign be given unto this generation.

13 And he left them, and again entering into *the boat* departed to the other side.

14 And they forgot to take bread; and they had not in the boat with them more than one loaf.

15 And he charged them, saying, Take heed, beware of the leaven of the Pharisees and the leaven of Herod.

---

[553] *Greek loaves.*

16 And they reasoned one with another, [554]saying, [555]We have no bread.

17 And Jesus perceiving it saith unto them, Why reason ye, because ye have no bread? do ye not yet perceive, neither understand? have ye your heart hardened?

18 Having eyes, see ye not? and having ears, hear ye not? and do ye not remember?

19 When I brake the five loaves among the five thousand, how many [556]baskets full of broken pieces took ye up? They say unto him, Twelve.

20 And when the seven among the four thousand, how many [557]basketfuls of broken pieces took ye up? And they say unto him, Seven.

21 And he said unto them, Do ye not yet understand?

22 And they come unto Bethsaida. And they bring to him a blind man, and beseech him to touch him.

23 And he took hold of the blind man by the hand, and brought him out of the village; and when he had spit on his eyes, and laid his hands upon him, he asked him, Seest thou aught?

24 And he looked up, and said, I see men; for I behold *them* as trees, walking.

25 Then again he laid his hands upon his eyes; and he looked stedfastly, and was restored, and saw all things clearly.

26 And he sent him away to his home, saying, Do not even enter into the village.

27 And Jesus went forth, and his disciples, into the villages of Caesarea Philippi: and on the way he asked his disciples, saying unto them, Who do men say that I am?

28 And they told him, saying, John the Baptist; and others, Elijah; but others, One of the prophets.

29 And he asked them, But who say ye that I am? Peter answereth and saith unto him, Thou art the Christ.

30 And he charged them that they should tell no man of him.

---

[554] *Some ancient authorities read because they had no bread.*
[555] *Or, It is because we have no bread.*
[556] *Basket in verses 19 and 20 represent different Greek words.*
[557] *Basket in verses 19 and 20 represent different Greek words.*

31 And he began to teach them, that the Son of man must suffer many things, and be rejected by the elders, and the chief priests, and the scribes, and be killed, and after three days rise again.

32 And he spake the saying openly. And Peter took him, and began to rebuke him.

33 But he turning about, and seeing his disciples, rebuked Peter, and saith, Get thee behind me, Satan; for thou mindest not the things of God, but the things of men.

34 And he called unto him the multitude with his disciples, and said unto them, If any man would come after me, let him deny himself, and take up his cross, and follow me.

35 For whosoever would save his life shall lose it; and whosoever shall lose his life for my sake and the [558]gospel's shall save it.

36 For what doth it profit a man, to gain the whole world, and forfeit his life?

37 For what should a man give in exchange for his life?

38 For whosoever shall be ashamed of me and of my words in this adulterous and sinful generation, the Son of man also shall be ashamed of him, when he cometh in the glory of his Father with the holy angels.

---

[558]*See marginal note on 1:1.*

Chapter 9

1 And he said unto them, Verily I say unto you, There are some here of them that stand *by*, who shall in no wise taste of death, till they see the kingdom of God come with power.

2 And after six days Jesus taketh with him Peter, and [559]James, and John, and bringeth them up into a high mountain apart by themselves: and he was transfigured before them;

3 and his garments became glistering, exceeding white, so as no fuller on earth can whiten them.

4 And there appeared unto them Elijah with Moses: and they were talking with Jesus.

5 And Peter answereth and saith to Jesus, Rabbi, it is good for us to be here: and let us make three [560]tabernacles; one for thee, and one for Moses, and one for Elijah.

6 For he knew not what to answer; for they became sore afraid.

7 And there came a cloud overshadowing them: and there came a voice out of the cloud, This is my beloved Son: hear ye him.

8 And suddenly looking round about, they saw no one any more, save Jesus only with themselves.

9 And as they were coming down from the mountain, he charged them that they should tell no man what things they had seen, save when the Son of man should have risen again from the dead.

10 And they kept the saying, questioning among themselves what the rising again from the dead should mean.

11 And they asked him, saying, [561]*How is it* that the scribes say that Elijah must first come?

12 And he said unto them, Elijah indeed cometh first, and restoreth all things: and how is it written of the Son of man, that he should suffer many things and be set at nought?

13 But I say unto you, that Elijah is come, and they have also done unto him whatsoever they would, even as it is written of him.

---

[559] *Or, Jacob*
[560] *Or, booths*
[561] *Or, The scribes say . . . come*

14 And when they came to the disciples, they saw a great multitude about them, and scribes questioning with them.

15 And straightway all the multitude, when they saw him, were greatly amazed, and running to him saluted him.

16 And he asked them, What question ye with them?

17 And one of the multitude answered him, Teacher, I brought unto thee my son, who hath a dumb spirit;

18 and wheresoever it taketh him, it [562]dasheth him down: and he foameth, and grindeth his teeth, and pineth away: and I spake to thy disciples that they should cast it out; and they were not able.

19 And he answereth them and saith, O faithless generation, how long shall I be with you? how long shall I bear with you? bring him unto me.

20 And they brought him unto him: and when he saw him, straightway the spirit [563]tare him grievously; and he fell on the ground, and wallowed foaming.

21 And he asked his father, How long time is it since this hath come unto him? And he said, From a child.

22 And oft-times it hath cast him both into the fire and into the waters, to destroy him: but if thou canst do anything, have compassion on us, and help us.

23 And Jesus said unto him, If thou canst! All things are possible to him that believeth.

24 Straightway the father of the child cried out, and said, [564]I believe; help thou mine unbelief.

25 And when Jesus saw that a multitude came running together, he rebuked the unclean spirit, saying unto him, Thou dumb and deaf spirit, I command thee, come out of him, and enter no more into him.

26 And having cried out, and [565]torn him much, he came out: and *the boy* became as one dead; insomuch that the more part said, He is dead.

27 But Jesus took him by the hand, and raised him up; and he arose.

---

[562] *Or, rendeth him. See Mt. 7:6.*
[563] *Or, convulsed. See 1:26.*
[564] *Many ancient authorities add with tears.*
[565] *Or, convulsed. See 1:26.*

MARK 9

28 And when he was come into the house, his disciples asked him privately, [566]*How is it* that we could not cast it out?

29 And he said unto them, This kind can come out by nothing, save by prayer[567].

30 And they went forth from thence, and passed through Galilee; and he would not that any man should know it.

31 For he taught his disciples, and said unto them, The Son of man is [568]delivered up into the hands of men, and they shall kill him; and when he is killed, after three days he shall rise again.

32 But they understood not the saying, and were afraid to ask him.

33 And they came to Capernaum: and when he was in the house he asked them, What were ye reasoning on the way?

34 But they held their peace: for they had disputed one with another on the way, who *was* the [569]greatest.

35 And he sat down, and called the twelve; and he saith unto them, If any man would be first, he shall be last of all, and [570]servant of all.

36 And he took a little child, and set him in the midst of them: and taking him in his arms, he said unto them,

37 Whosoever shall receive one of such little children in my name, receiveth me: and whosoever receiveth me, receiveth not me, but him that sent me.

38 John said unto him, Teacher, we saw one casting out demons in thy name; and we forbade him, because he followed not us.

39 But Jesus said, Forbid him not: for there is no man who shall do a [571]mighty work in my name, and be able quickly to speak evil of me.

40 For he that is not against us is for us.

41 For whosoever shall give you a cup of water to drink, [572]because ye are Christ's, verily I say unto you, he shall in no wise lose his reward.

---

[566] *Or, saying, We could not cast it out*
[567] *Many ancient authorities add with fasting.*
[568] *See 3:19.*
[569] *Greek greater.*
[570] *Or, minister*
[571] *Greek power.*
[572] *Greek in name that ye are.*

42 And whosoever shall cause one of these little ones that believe [573]on me to stumble, it were better for him if [574]a great millstone were hanged about his neck, and he were cast into the sea.

43 And if thy hand cause thee to stumble, cut it off: it is good for thee to enter into life maimed, rather than having thy two hands to go into [575]hell, into the unquenchable fire.[576]

45 And if thy foot cause thee to stumble, cut it off: it is good for thee to enter into life halt, rather than having thy two feet to be cast into [577]hell.

47 And if thine eye cause thee to stumble, cast it out: it is good for thee to enter into the kingdom of God with one eye, rather than having two eyes to be cast into [578]hell;

48 where their worm dieth not, and the fire is not quenched.

49 For every one shall be salted with fire[579].

50 Salt is good: but if the salt have lost its saltness, wherewith will ye season it? Have salt in yourselves, and be at peace one with another.

---

[573] *Many ancient authorities omit on me.*
[574] *Greek a millstone turned by an ass.*
[575] *Greek Gehenna.*
[576] *Verses 44 and 46 (which are identical with verse 48) are omitted by the best ancient authorities.*
[577] *Greek Gehenna.*
[578] *Greek Gehenna.*
[579] *Many ancient authorities add and every sacrifice shall be salted with salt. See Lev. 2:13.*

Chapter 10

1 And he arose from thence, and cometh into the borders of Judaea and beyond the Jordan: and multitudes come together unto him again; and, as he was wont, he taught them again.

2 And there came unto him Pharisees, and asked him, Is it lawful for a man to put away *his* wife? trying him.

3 And he answered and said unto them, [580]What did Moses command you?

4 And they said, Moses suffered to write a bill of divorcement, and to put her away.

5 But Jesus said unto them, For your hardness of heart he wrote you this commandment.

6 But from the beginning of the creation, Male and female made he them.

7 For this cause shall a man leave his father and mother, [581]and shall cleave to his wife;

8 and the two shall become one flesh: so that they are no more two, but one flesh.

9 What therefore God hath joined together, let not man put asunder.

10 And in the house the disciples asked him again of this matter.

11 And he saith unto them, Whosoever shall put away his wife, and marry another, committeth adultery against her:

12 and if she herself shall put away her husband, and marry another, she committeth adultery.

13 And they were bringing unto him little children, that he should touch them: and the disciples rebuked them.

14 But when Jesus saw it, he was moved with indignation, and said unto them, Suffer the little children to come unto me; forbid them not: for [582]to such belongeth the kingdom of God.

15 Verily I say unto you, Whosoever shall not receive the kingdom of God as a little child, he shall in no wise enter therein.

---

[580] Dt. 24:1, 3.
[581] *Some ancient authorities omit and shall cleave to his wife.*
[582] *Or, of such is*

16 And he took them in his arms, and blessed them, laying his hands upon them.

17 And as he was going forth ⁵⁸³into the way, there ran one to him, and kneeled to him, and asked him, Good Teacher, what shall I do that I may inherit eternal life?

18 And Jesus said unto him, Why callest thou me good? none is good save one, *even* God.

19 Thou knowest the commandments, ⁵⁸⁴Do not kill, Do not commit adultery, Do not steal, Do not bear false witness, Do not defraud, Honor thy father and mother.

20 And he said unto him, Teacher, all these things have I observed from my youth.

21 And Jesus looking upon him loved him, and said unto him, One thing thou lackest: go, sell whatsoever thou hast, and give to the poor, and thou shalt have treasure in heaven: and come, follow me.

22 But his countenance fell at the saying, and he went away sorrowful: for he was one that had great possessions.

23 And Jesus looked round about, and saith unto his disciples, How hardly shall they that have riches enter into the kingdom of God!

24 And the disciples were amazed at his words. But Jesus answereth again, and saith unto them, Children, how hard is it ⁵⁸⁵for them that trust in riches to enter into the kingdom of God!

25 It is easier for a camel to go through a needle's eye, than for a rich man to enter into the kingdom of God.

26 And they were astonished exceedingly, saying ⁵⁸⁶unto him, Then who can be saved?

27 Jesus looking upon them saith, With men it is impossible, but not with God: for all things are possible with God.

28 Peter began to say unto him, Lo, we have left all, and have followed thee.

---

†✓ **Jesus Distinguishes Himself from God.** Jesus deflects the title of 'absolute goodness' to the Father alone. If Jesus possessed inherent, uncreated deity co-equal with the Father, he would have accepted this attribution without qualification. His response is a deliberate theological distinction, proving a separation of person and nature. This is a clear statement of subordination, asserting that 'Good' is an attribute belonging solely to the One God (the Father).

---

⁵⁸³*Or, on his way*
⁵⁸⁴*Ex. 20:12–16; Dt. 5:16–20.*
⁵⁸⁵*Some ancient authorities omit* for them that trust in riches.
⁵⁸⁶*Many ancient authorities read* among themselves.

29 Jesus said, Verily I say unto you, There is no man that hath left house, or brethren, or sisters, or mother, or father, or children, or lands, for my sake, and for the [587]gospel's sake,

30 but he shall receive a hundredfold now in this time, houses, and brethren, and sisters, and mothers, and children, and lands, with persecutions; and in the [588]world to come eternal life.

31 But many *that are* first shall be last; and the last first.

32 And they were on the way, going up to Jerusalem; and Jesus was going before them: and they were amazed; and they that followed were afraid. And he took again the twelve, and began to tell them the things that were to happen unto him,

33 *saying*, Behold, we go up to Jerusalem; and the Son of man shall be delivered unto the chief priests and the scribes; and they shall condemn him to death, and shall deliver him unto the Gentiles:

34 and they shall mock him, and shall spit upon him, and shall scourge him, and shall kill him; and after three days he shall rise again.

35 And there come near unto him [589]James and John, the sons of Zebedee, saying unto him, Teacher, we would that thou shouldest do for us whatsoever we shall ask of thee.

36 And he said unto them, What would ye that I should do for you?

37 And they said unto him, Grant unto us that we may sit, one on thy right hand, and one on *thy* left hand, in thy glory.

38 But Jesus said unto them, Ye know not what ye ask. Are ye able to drink the cup that I drink? or to be baptized with the baptism that I am baptized with?

39 And they said unto him, We are able. And Jesus said unto them, The cup that I drink ye shall drink; and with the baptism that I am baptized withal shall ye be baptized:

40 but to sit on my right hand or on *my* left hand is not mine to give; but *it is for them* for whom it hath been prepared.

---

[587] *See marginal note on 1:1.*
[588] *Or, age*
[589] *Or, Jacob*

41 And when the ten heard it, they began to be moved with indignation concerning [590]James and John.

42 And Jesus called them to him, and saith unto them, Ye know that they who are accounted to rule over the Gentiles lord it over them; and their great ones exercise authority over them.

43 But it is not so among you: but whosoever would become great among you, shall be your [591]minister;

44 and whosoever would be first among you, shall be [592]servant of all.

45 For the Son of man also came not to be ministered unto, but to minister, and to give his life a ransom for many.

46 And they come to Jericho: and as he went out from Jericho, with his disciples and a great multitude, the son of Timaeus, Bartimaeus, a blind beggar, was sitting by the way side.

47 And when he heard that it was Jesus the Nazarene, he began to cry out, and say, Jesus, thou son of David, have mercy on me.

48 And many rebuked him, that he should hold his peace: but he cried out the more a great deal, Thou son of David, have mercy on me.

49 And Jesus stood still, and said, Call ye him. And they call the blind man, saying unto him, Be of good cheer: rise, he calleth thee.

50 And he, casting away his garment, sprang up, and came to Jesus.

51 And Jesus answered him, and said, What wilt thou that I should do unto thee? And the blind man said unto him, [593]Rabboni, that I may receive my sight.

52 And Jesus said unto him, Go thy way; thy faith hath [594]made thee whole. And straightway he received his sight, and followed him in the way.

---

[590] *Or, Jacob*
[591] *Or, servant*
[592] *Greek bondservant.*
[593] *See Jn. 20:16.*
[594] *Or, saved thee*

Chapter 11

1 And when they draw nigh unto Jerusalem, unto Bethphage and Bethany, at the mount of Olives, he sendeth two of his disciples,

2 and saith unto them, Go your way into the village that is over against you: and straightway as ye enter into it, ye shall find a colt tied, whereon no man ever yet sat; loose him, and bring him.

3 And if any one say unto you, Why do ye this? say ye, The Lord hath need of him; and straightway he [595]will send him [596]back hither.

4 And they went away, and found a colt tied at the door without in the open street; and they loose him.

5 And certain of them that stood there said unto them, What do ye, loosing the colt?

6 And they said unto them even as Jesus had said: and they let them go.

7 And they bring the colt unto Jesus, and cast on him their garments; and he sat upon him.

8 And many spread their garments upon the way; and others [597]branches, which they had cut from the fields.

9 And they that went before, and they that followed, cried, Hosanna; Blessed *is* he that cometh in the name of the Lord:

10 Blessed *is* the kingdom that cometh, *the kingdom* of our father David: Hosanna in the highest.

11 And he entered into Jerusalem, into the temple; and when he had looked round about upon all things, it being now eventide, he went out unto Bethany with the twelve.

12 And on the morrow, when they were come out from Bethany, he hungered.

13 And seeing a fig tree afar off having leaves, he came, if haply he might find anything thereon: and when he came to it, he found nothing but leaves; for it was not the season of figs.

14 And he answered and said unto it, No man eat fruit from thee henceforward for ever. And his disciples heard it.

---

[595] *Greek sendeth.*
[596] *Or, again*
[597] *Greek layers of leaves.*

15 And they come to Jerusalem: and he entered into the temple, and began to cast out them that sold and them that bought in the temple, and overthrew the tables of the money-changers, and the seats of them that sold the doves;

16 and he would not suffer that any man should carry a vessel through the temple.

17 And he taught, and said unto them, Is it not written, [598]My house shall be called a house of prayer for all the nations? [599]but ye have made it a den of robbers.

18 And the chief priests and the scribes heard it, and sought how they might destroy him: for they feared him, for all the multitude was astonished at his teaching.

19 And [600]every evening [601]he went forth out of the city.

20 And as they passed by in the morning, they saw the fig tree withered away from the roots.

21 And Peter calling to remembrance saith unto him, Rabbi, behold, the fig tree which thou cursedst is withered away.

22 And Jesus answering saith unto them, Have faith in God.

23 Verily I say unto you, Whosoever shall say unto this mountain, Be thou taken up and cast into the sea; and shall not doubt in his heart, but shall believe that what he saith cometh to pass; he shall have it.

24 Therefore I say unto you, All things whatsoever ye pray and ask for, believe that ye [602]receive them, and ye shall have them.

25 And whensoever ye stand praying, forgive, if ye have aught against any one; that your Father also who is in heaven may forgive you your trespasses.[603]

27 And they come again to Jerusalem: and as he was walking in the temple, there come to him the chief priests, and the scribes, and the elders;

---

[598] *Isa. 56:7.*
[599] *Jer. 7:11.*
[600] *Greek whenever evening came.*
[601] *Some ancient authorities read they.*
[602] *Greek received.*
[603] *Many ancient authorities add verse 26 But if ye do not forgive, neither will your Father who is in heaven forgive your trespasses. Compare Mt. 6:15; 18:35.*

28 and they said unto him, By what authority doest thou these things? or who gave thee this authority to do these things?

29 And Jesus said unto them, I will ask of you one [604]question, and answer me, and I will tell you by what authority I do these things.

30 The baptism of John, was it from heaven, or from men? answer me.

31 And they reasoned with themselves, saying, If we shall say, From heaven; he will say, Why then did ye not believe him?

32 [605]But should we say, From men—they feared the people: [606]for all verily held John to be a prophet.

33 And they answered Jesus and say, We know not. And Jesus saith unto them, Neither tell I you by what authority I do these things.

Chapter 12

1 And he began to speak unto them in parables. A man planted a vineyard, and set a hedge about it, and digged a pit for the winepress, and built a tower, and let it out to husbandmen, and went into another country.

2 And at the season he sent to the husbandmen a [607]servant, that he might receive from the husbandmen of the fruits of the vineyard.

3 And they took him, and beat him, and sent him away empty.

4 And again he sent unto them another [608]servant; and him they wounded in the head, and handled shamefully.

5 And he sent another; and him they killed: and many others; beating some, and killing some.

6 He had yet one, a beloved son: he sent him last unto them, saying, They will reverence my son.

7 But those husbandmen said among themselves, This is the heir; come, let us kill him, and the inheritance shall be ours.

8 And they took him, and killed him, and cast him forth out of the vineyard.

---

[604] *Greek word.*
[605] *Or, But shall we say, From men?*
[606] *Or, for all held John to be a prophet indeed*
[607] *Greek bondservant.*
[608] *Greek bondservant.*

9 What therefore will the lord of the vineyard do? he will come and destroy the husbandmen, and will give the vineyard unto others.

10 Have ye not read even this scripture:
> [609]The stone which the builders rejected,
> The same was made the head of the corner;

11 This was from the Lord,
> And it is marvellous in our eyes?

12 And they sought to lay hold on him; and they feared the multitude; for they perceived that he spake the parable against them: and they left him, and went away.

13 And they send unto him certain of the Pharisees and of the Herodians, that they might catch him in talk.

14 And when they were come, they say unto him, Teacher, we know that thou art true, and carest not for any one; for thou regardest not the person of men, but of a truth teachest the way of God: Is it lawful to give tribute unto Caesar, or not?

15 Shall we give, or shall we not give? But he, knowing their hypocrisy, said unto them, Why make ye trial of me? bring me a [610]denarius, that I may see it.

16 And they brought it. And he saith unto them, Whose is this image and superscription? And they said unto him, Caesar's.

17 And Jesus said unto them, Render unto Caesar the things that are Caesar's, and unto God the things that are God's. And they marvelled greatly at him.

18 And there come unto him Sadducees, who say that there is no resurrection; and they asked him, saying,

19 Teacher, Moses wrote unto us, [611]If a man's brother die, and leave a wife behind him, and leave no child, that his brother should take his wife, and raise up seed unto his brother.

20 There were seven brethren: and the first took a wife, and dying left no seed;

---

[609] *Ps. 118:22f.*
[610] *See marginal note on 6:37.*
[611] *Dt. 25:5.*

21 and the second took her, and died, leaving no seed behind him; and the third likewise:

22 and the seven left no seed. Last of all the woman also died.

23 In the resurrection whose wife shall she be of them? for the seven had her to wife.

24 Jesus said unto them, Is it not for this cause that ye err, that ye know not the scriptures, nor the power of God?

25 For when they shall rise from the dead, they neither marry, nor are given in marriage; but are as angels in heaven.

26 But as touching the dead, that they are raised; have ye not read in the book of Moses, in *the place concerning* the Bush, how God spake unto him, saying, [612]I *am* the God of Abraham, and the God of Isaac, and the God of Jacob?

27 He is not the God of the dead, but of the living: ye do greatly err.

28 And one of the scribes came, and heard them questioning together, and knowing that he had answered them well, asked him, What commandment is the first of all?

29 Jesus answered, The first is, [613]Hear, O Israel; [614]The Lord our God, the Lord is one:

30 and thou shalt love the Lord thy God [615]with all thy heart, and [616]with all thy soul, and [617]with all thy mind, and [618]with all thy strength.

31 The second is this, [619]Thou shalt love thy neighbor as thyself. There is none other commandment greater than these.

32 And the scribe said unto him, Of a truth, Teacher, thou hast well said that he is one; and there is none other but he:

33 and to love him with all the heart, and with all the understanding, and with all the strength, and to love his neighbor as himself, is much more than all whole burnt-offerings and sacrifices.

---

[612] *Ex. 3:6.*
[613] *Dt. 6:4ff.*
[614] *Or, The Lord is our God; the Lord is one*
[615] *Greek from.*
[616] *Greek from.*
[617] *Greek from.*
[618] *Greek from.*
[619] *Lev. 19:18.*

†✓ **Jesus Affirms the Shema.** Jesus explicitly affirms the standard Jewish creed (Deut 6:4) that God is numerically One. He quotes this to the scribe, who agrees. The declaration that "The Lord is one" is the bedrock of Monotheism and serves as a direct counter-witness against Trinitarian assertions regarding the Father's sole identity as the One God.

34 And when Jesus saw that he answered discreetly, he said unto him, Thou art not far from the kingdom of God. And no man after that durst ask him any question.

35 And Jesus answered and said, as he taught in the temple, How say the scribes that the Christ is the son of David?

36 David himself said in the Holy Spirit,
   [620]The Lord said unto my Lord,
   Sit thou on my right hand,
   Till I make thine enemies [621]the footstool of thy feet.

37 David himself calleth him Lord; and whence is he his son? And [622]the common people heard him gladly.

38 And in his teaching he said, Beware of the scribes, who desire to walk in long robes, and *to have* salutations in the marketplaces,

39 and chief seats in the synagogues, and chief places at feasts:

40 they that devour widows' houses, [623]and for a pretence make long prayers; these shall receive greater condemnation.

41 And he sat down over against the treasury, and beheld how the multitude cast [624]money into the treasury: and many that were rich cast in much.

42 And there came [625]a poor widow, and she cast in two mites, which make a farthing.

43 And he called unto him his disciples, and said unto them, Verily I say unto you, This poor widow cast in more than all they that are casting into the treasury:

44 for they all did cast in of their superfluity; but she of her want did cast in all that she had, *even* all her living.

---

[620]*Ps. 110:1.*
[621]*Some ancient authorities read underneath thy feet.*
[622]*Or, the great multitude*
[623]*Or, even while for a pretence they make*
[624]*Greek brass.*
[625]*Greek one.*

Chapter 13

1 And as he went forth out of the temple, one of his disciples saith unto him, Teacher, behold, what manner of stones and what manner of buildings!

2 And Jesus said unto him, Seest thou these great buildings? there shall not be left here one stone upon another, which shall not be thrown down.

3 And as he sat on the mount of Olives over against the temple, Peter and [626]James and John and Andrew asked him privately,

4 Tell us, when shall these things be? and what *shall be* the sign when these things are all about to be accomplished?

5 And Jesus began to say unto them, Take heed that no man lead you astray.

6 Many shall come in my name, saying, I am *he*; and shall lead many astray.

7 And when ye shall hear of wars and rumors of wars, be not troubled: *these things* must needs come to pass; but the end is not yet.

8 For nation shall rise against nation, and kingdom against kingdom; there shall be earthquakes in divers places; there shall be famines: these things are the beginning of travail.

9 But take ye heed to yourselves: for they shall deliver you up to councils; and in synagogues shall ye be beaten; and before governors and kings shall ye stand for my sake, for a testimony unto them.

10 And the [627]gospel must first be preached unto all the nations.

11 And when they lead you *to judgment*, and deliver you up, be not anxious beforehand what ye shall speak: but whatsoever shall be given you in that hour, that speak ye; for it is not ye that speak, but the Holy Spirit.

12 And brother shall [628]deliver up brother to death, and the father his child; and children shall rise up against parents, and [629]cause them to be put to death.

---

[626] *Or, Jacob*
[627] *See marginal note on 1:1.*
[628] *See 3:19.*
[629] *Or, put them to death*

13 And ye shall be hated of all men for my name's sake: but he that endureth to the end, the same shall be saved.

14 But when ye see the abomination of desolation standing where he ought not (let him that readeth understand), then let them that are in Judaea flee unto the mountains:

15 and let him that is on the housetop not go down, nor enter in, to take anything out of his house:

16 and let him that is in the field not return back to take his cloak.

17 But woe unto them that are with child and to them that give suck in those days!

18 And pray ye that it be not in the winter.

19 For those days shall be tribulation, such as there hath not been the like from the beginning of the creation which God created until now, and never shall be.

20 And except the Lord had shortened the days, no flesh would have been saved; but for the elect's sake, whom he chose, he shortened the days.

21 And then if any man shall say unto you, Lo, here is the Christ; or, Lo, there; believe [630]*it* not:

22 for there shall arise false Christs and false prophets, and shall show signs and wonders, that they may lead astray, if possible, the elect.

23 But take ye heed: behold, I have told you all things beforehand.

24 But in those days, after that tribulation, the sun shall be darkened, and the moon shall not give her light,

25 and the stars shall be falling from heaven, and the powers that are in the heavens shall be shaken.

26 And then shall they see the Son of man coming in clouds with great power and glory.

27 And then shall he send forth the angels, and shall gather together his elect from the four winds, from the uttermost part of the earth to the uttermost part of heaven.

---

[630] *Or, him*

28 Now from the fig tree learn her parable: when her branch is now become tender, and putteth forth its leaves, ye know that the summer is nigh;

29 even so ye also, when ye see these things coming to pass, know ye that [631]he is nigh, *even* at the doors.

30 Verily I say unto you, This generation shall not pass away, until all these things be accomplished.

31 Heaven and earth shall pass away: but my words shall not pass away.

32 But of that day or that hour knoweth no one, not even the angels in heaven, neither the Son, but the Father.

33 Take ye heed, watch [632]and pray: for ye know not when the time is.

34 *It is* as *when* a man, sojourning in another country, having left his house, and given authority to his [633]servants, to each one his work, commanded also the porter to watch.

35 Watch therefore: for ye know not when the lord of the house cometh, whether at even, or at midnight, or at cockcrowing, or in the morning;

36 lest coming suddenly he find you sleeping.

37 And what I say unto you I say unto all, Watch.

†√ **The Son's Limited Knowledge.** If Jesus were the Omniscient God, He could not be ignorant of the "day or hour." This verse proves a distinction in nature and mind between the Father and the Son.

---

[631] *Or, it*
[632] *Some ancient authorities omit and pray.*
[633] *Greek bondservants.*

Chapter 14

1 Now after two days was *the feast of* the passover and the unleavened bread: and the chief priests and the scribes sought how they might take him with subtlety, and kill him:

2 for they said, Not during the feast, lest haply there shall be a tumult of the people.

3 And while he was in Bethany in the house of Simon the leper, as he sat at meat, there came a woman having [634]an alabaster cruse of ointment of [635]pure nard very costly; *and* she brake the cruse, and poured it over his head.

4 But there were some that had indignation among themselves, *saying*, To what purpose hath this waste of the ointment been made?

5 For this ointment might have been sold for above three hundred [636]shillings, and given to the poor. And they murmured against her.

6 But Jesus said, Let her alone; why trouble ye her? she hath wrought a good work on me.

7 For ye have the poor always with you, and whensoever ye will ye can do them good: but me ye have not always.

8 She hath done what she could; she hath anointed my body beforehand for the burying.

9 And verily I say unto you, Wheresoever the [637]gospel shall be preached throughout the whole world, that also which this woman hath done shall be spoken of for a memorial of her.

10 And Judas Iscariot, [638]he that was one of the twelve, went away unto the chief priests, that he might [639]deliver him unto them.

11 And they, when they heard it, were glad, and promised to give him money. And he sought how he might conveniently [640]deliver him *unto them*.

---

[634] *Or, a flask*
[635] *Or, liquid nard*
[636] *See marginal note on 6:37.*
[637] *See marginal note on 1:1.*
[638] *Greek the one of the twelve.*
[639] *See 3:19.*
[640] *See 3:19.*

12 And on the first day of unleavened bread, when they sacrificed the passover, his disciples say unto him, Where wilt thou that we go and make ready that thou mayest eat the passover?

13 And he sendeth two of his disciples, and saith unto them, Go into the city, and there shall meet you a man bearing a pitcher of water: follow him;

14 and wheresoever he shall enter in, say to the master of the house, The Teacher saith, Where is my guest-chamber, where I shall eat the passover with my disciples?

15 And he will himself show you a large upper room furnished *and* ready: and there make ready for us.

16 And the disciples went forth, and came into the city, and found as he had said unto them: and they made ready the passover.

17 And when it was evening he cometh with the twelve.

18 And as they [641]sat and were eating, Jesus said, Verily I say unto you, One of you shall [642]betray me, *even* he that eateth with me.

19 They began to be sorrowful, and to say unto him one by one, Is it I?

20 And he said unto them, *It is* one of the twelve, he that dippeth with me in the dish.

21 For the Son of man goeth, even as it is written of him: but woe unto that man through whom the Son of man is [643]betrayed! good were it [644]for that man if he had not been born.

22 And as they were eating, he took [645]bread, and when he had blessed, he brake it, and gave to them, and said, Take ye: this is my body.

23 And he took a cup, and when he had given thanks, he gave to them: and they all drank of it.

24 And he said unto them, This is my blood of the [646]covenant, which is poured out for many.

25 Verily I say unto you, I shall no more drink of the fruit of the vine, until that day when I drink it new in the kingdom of God.

---

[641] *Greek reclined.*
[642] *See marginal note on 3:19.*
[643] *See marginal note on 3:19.*
[644] *Greek for him if that man.*
[645] *Or, a loaf*
[646] *Some ancient authorities insert new.*

26 And when they had sung a hymn, they went out unto the mount of Olives.

27 And Jesus saith unto them, All ye shall be [647]offended: for it is written, [648]I will smite the shepherd, and the sheep shall be scattered abroad.

28 Howbeit, after I am raised up, I will go before you into Galilee.

29 But Peter said unto him, Although all shall be [649]offended, yet will not I.

30 And Jesus saith unto him, Verily I say unto thee, that thou to-day, *even* this night, before the cock crow twice, shalt deny me thrice.

31 But he spake exceeding vehemently, If I must die with thee, I will not deny thee. And in like manner also said they all.

32 And they come unto [650]a place which was named Gethsemane: and he saith unto his disciples, Sit ye here, while I pray.

33 And he taketh with him Peter and [651]James and John, and began to be greatly amazed, and sore troubled.

34 And he saith unto them, My soul is exceeding sorrowful even unto death: abide ye here, and watch.

35 And he went forward a little, and fell on the ground, and prayed that, if it were possible, the hour might pass away from him.

36 And he said, Abba, Father, all things are possible unto thee; remove this cup from me: howbeit not what I will, but what thou wilt.

37 And he cometh, and findeth them sleeping, and saith unto Peter, Simon, sleepest thou? couldest thou not watch one hour?

38 [652]Watch and pray, that ye enter not into temptation: the spirit indeed is willing, but the flesh is weak.

39 And again he went away, and prayed, saying the same words.

40 And again he came, and found them sleeping, for their eyes were very heavy; and they knew not what to answer him.

---

[647] *Greek caused to stumble.*
[648] *Zech. 13:7.*
[649] *Greek caused to stumble.*
[650] *Greek an enclosed piece of ground.*
[651] *Or, Jacob*
[652] *Or, Watch ye, and pray that ye enter not*

41 And he cometh the third time, and saith unto them, [653]Sleep on now, and take your rest: it is enough; the hour is come; behold, the Son of man is [654]betrayed into the hands of sinners.

42 Arise, let us be going: behold, he that [655]betrayeth me is at hand.

43 And straightway, while he yet spake, cometh Judas, one of the twelve, and with him a multitude with swords and staves, from the chief priests and the scribes and the elders.

44 Now he that [656]betrayed him had given them a token, saying, Whomsoever I shall kiss, that is he; take him, and lead him away safely.

45 And when he was come, straightway he came to him, and saith, Rabbi; and [657]kissed him.

46 And they laid hands on him, and took him.

47 But a certain one of them that stood by drew his sword, and smote the [658]servant of the high priest, and struck off his ear.

48 And Jesus answered and said unto them, Are ye come out, as against a robber, with swords and staves to seize me?

49 I was daily with you in the temple teaching, and ye took me not: but *this is done* that the scriptures might be fulfilled.

50 And they all left him, and fled.

51 And a certain young man followed with him, having a linen cloth cast about him, over *his* naked *body*: and they lay hold on him;

52 but he left the linen cloth, and fled naked.

53 And they led Jesus away to the high priest: and there come together with him all the chief priests and the elders and the scribes.

54 And Peter had followed him afar off, even within, into the court of the high priest; and he was sitting with the officers, and warming himself in the light *of the fire*.

55 Now the chief priests and the whole council sought witness against Jesus to put him to death; and found it not.

---

[653] *Or, Do ye sleep on, then, and take your rest?*
[654] *See marginal note on 3:19.*
[655] *See marginal note on 3:19.*
[656] *See marginal note on 3:19.*
[657] *Greek kissed him much.*
[658] *Greek bondservant.*

56 For many bare false witness against him, and their witness agreed not together.

57 And there stood up certain, and bare false witness against him, saying,

58 We heard him say, I will destroy this [659]temple that is made with hands, and in three days I will build another made without hands.

59 And not even so did their witness agree together.

60 And the high priest stood up in the midst, and asked Jesus, saying, Answerest thou nothing? what is it which these witness against thee?

61 But he held his peace, and answered nothing. Again the high priest asked him, and saith unto him, Art thou the Christ, the Son of the Blessed?

62 And Jesus said, I am: and ye shall see the Son of man sitting at the right hand of Power, and coming with the clouds of heaven.

63 And the high priest rent his clothes, and saith, What further need have we of witnesses?

64 Ye have heard the blasphemy: what think ye? And they all condemned him to be [660]worthy of death.

65 And some began to spit on him, and to cover his face, and to buffet him, and to say unto him, Prophesy: and the officers received him with [661]blows of their hands.

66 And as Peter was beneath in the court, there cometh one of the maids of the high priest;

67 and seeing Peter warming himself, she looked upon him, and saith, Thou also wast with the Nazarene, *even* Jesus.

68 But he denied, saying, [662]I neither know, nor understand what thou sayest: and he went out into the [663]porch; [664]and the cock crew.

69 And the maid saw him, and began again to say to them that stood by, This is *one* of them.

---

[659] *Or, sanctuary*
[660] *Greek liable to.*
[661] *Or, strokes of rods*
[662] *Or, I neither know, nor understand: thou, what sayest thou?*
[663] *Greek forecourt.*
[664] *Many ancient authorities omit and the cock crew.*

70 But he again denied it. And after a little while again they that stood by said to Peter, Of a truth thou art *one* of them; for thou art a Galilaean.

71 But he began to curse, and to swear, I know not this man of whom ye speak.

72 And straightway the second time the cock crew. And Peter called to mind the word, how that Jesus said unto him, Before the cock crow twice, thou shalt deny me thrice. [665]And when he thought thereon, he wept.

Chapter 15

1 And straightway in the morning the chief priests with the elders and scribes, and the whole council, held a consultation, and bound Jesus, and carried him away, and delivered him up to Pilate.

2 And Pilate asked him, Art thou the King of the Jews? And he answering saith unto him, Thou sayest.

3 And the chief priests accused him of many things.

4 And Pilate again asked him, saying, Answerest thou nothing? behold how many things they accuse thee of.

5 But Jesus no more answered anything; insomuch that Pilate marvelled.

6 Now at [666]the feast he used to release unto them one prisoner, whom they asked of him.

7 And there was one called Barabbas, *lying* bound with them that had made insurrection, men who in the insurrection had committed murder.

8 And the multitude went up and began to ask him *to do* as he was wont to do unto them.

9 And Pilate answered them, saying, Will ye that I release unto you the King of the Jews?

10 For he perceived that for envy the chief priests had delivered him up.

11 But the chief priests stirred up the multitude, that he should rather release Barabbas unto them.

---

[665] *Or, And he began to weep*
[666] *Or, a feast*

12 And Pilate again answered and said unto them, What then shall I do unto him whom ye call the King of the Jews?

13 And they cried out again, Crucify him.

14 And Pilate said unto them, Why, what evil hath he done? But they cried out exceedingly, Crucify him.

15 And Pilate, wishing to content the multitude, released unto them Barabbas, and delivered Jesus, when he had scourged him, to be crucified.

16 And the soldiers led him away within the court, which is the [667]Praetorium; and they call together the whole [668]band.

17 And they clothe him with purple, and platting a crown of thorns, they put it on him;

18 and they began to salute him, Hail, King of the Jews!

19 And they smote his head with a reed, and spat upon him, and bowing their knees [669]worshipped him.

20 And when they had mocked him, they took off from him the purple, and put on him his garments. And they lead him out to crucify him.

21 And they [670]compel one passing by, Simon of Cyrene, coming from the country, the father of Alexander and Rufus, to go *with them*, that he might bear his cross.

22 And they bring him unto the place Golgotha, which is, being interpreted, The place of a skull.

23 And they offered him wine mingled with myrrh: but he received it not.

24 And they crucify him, and part his garments among them, casting lots upon them, what each should take.

25 And it was the third hour, and they crucified him.

26 And the superscription of his accusation was written over, the King of the Jews.

---

[667] *Or, palace*
[668] *Or, cohort*
[669] *See marginal note on 5:6.*
[670] *Greek impress.*

27 And with him they crucify two robbers; one on his right hand, and one on his left.⁶⁷¹

29 And they that passed by railed on him, wagging their heads, and saying, Ha! thou that destroyest the ⁶⁷²temple, and buildest it in three days,

30 save thyself, and come down from the cross.

31 In like manner also the chief priests mocking *him* among themselves with the scribes said, He saved others; ⁶⁷³himself he cannot save.

32 Let the Christ, the King of Israel, now come down from the cross, that we may see and believe. And they that were crucified with him reproached him.

33 And when the sixth hour was come, there was darkness over the whole ⁶⁷⁴land until the ninth hour.

34 And at the ninth hour Jesus cried with a loud voice, Eloi, Eloi, lama sabachthani? which is, being interpreted, ⁶⁷⁵My God, my God, ⁶⁷⁶why hast thou forsaken me?

35 And some of them that stood by, when they heard it, said, Behold, he calleth Elijah.

36 And one ran, and filling a sponge full of vinegar, put it on a reed, and gave him to drink, saying, Let be; let us see whether Elijah cometh to take him down.

37 And Jesus uttered a loud voice, and gave up the ghost.

38 And the veil of the ⁶⁷⁷temple was rent in two from the top to the bottom.

39 And when the centurion, who stood by over against him, saw that he ⁶⁷⁸so gave up the ghost, he said, Truly this man was ⁶⁷⁹the Son of God.

---

⁶⁷¹*Many ancient authorities insert verse 28 And the scripture was fulfilled, which saith, And he was reckoned with transgressors. See Lk. 22:37.*
⁶⁷²*Or, sanctuary*
⁶⁷³*Or, can he not save himself?*
⁶⁷⁴*Or, earth*
⁶⁷⁵*Ps. 22:1.*
⁶⁷⁶*Or, why didst thou forsake me?*
⁶⁷⁷*Or, sanctuary*
⁶⁷⁸*Many ancient authorities read so cried out, and gave up the ghost.*
⁶⁷⁹*Or, a son of God*

40 And there were also women beholding from afar: among whom *were* both Mary Magdalene, and Mary the mother of [680]James the [681]less and of Joses, and Salome;

41 who, when he was in Galilee, followed him, and ministered unto him; and many other women that came up with him unto Jerusalem.

42 And when even was now come, because it was the Preparation, that is, the day before the sabbath,

43 there came Joseph of Arimathaea, a councillor of honorable estate, who also himself was looking for the kingdom of God; and he boldly went in unto Pilate, and asked for the body of Jesus.

44 And Pilate marvelled if he were already dead: and calling unto him the centurion, he asked him whether [682]he had been any while dead.

45 And when he learned it of the centurion, he granted the corpse to Joseph.

46 And he bought a linen cloth, and taking him down, wound him in the linen cloth, and laid him in a tomb which had been hewn out of a rock; and he rolled a stone against the door of the tomb.

47 And Mary Magdalene and Mary the *mother* of Joses beheld where he was laid.

---

[680] *Or, Jacob*
[681] *Greek little.*
[682] *Many ancient authorities read were already dead.*

Chapter 16

1 And when the sabbath was past, Mary Magdalene, and Mary the *mother* of [683]James, and Salome, bought spices, that they might come and anoint him.

2 And very early on the first day of the week, they come to the tomb when the sun was risen.

3 And they were saying among themselves, Who shall roll us away the stone from the door of the tomb?

4 and looking up, they see that the stone is rolled back: for it was exceeding great.

5 And entering into the tomb, they saw a young man sitting on the right side, arrayed in a white robe; and they were amazed.

6 And he saith unto them, Be not amazed: ye seek Jesus, the Nazarene, who hath been crucified: he is risen; he is not here: behold, the place where they laid him!

7 But go, tell his disciples and Peter, He goeth before you into Galilee: there shall ye see him, as he said unto you.

8 And they went out, and fled from the tomb; for trembling and astonishment had come upon them: and they said nothing to any one; for they were afraid.

9 [684]Now when he was risen early on the first day of the week, he appeared first to Mary Magdalene, from whom he had cast out seven demons.

10 She went and told them that had been with him, as they mourned and wept.

11 And they, when they heard that he was alive, and had been seen of her, disbelieved.

12 And after these things he was manifested in another form unto two of them, as they walked, on their way into the country.

13 And they went away and told it unto the rest: neither believed they them.

---

[683] *Or, Jacob*
[684] *The two oldest Greek manuscripts, and some other authorities, omit from verse 9 to the end. Some other authorities have a different ending to the Gospel.*

14 And afterward he was manifested unto the eleven themselves as they sat at meat; and he upbraided them with their unbelief and hardness of heart, because they believed not them that had seen him after he was risen.

15 And he said unto them, Go ye into all the world, and preach the [685]gospel to the whole creation.

16 He that believeth and is baptized shall be saved; but he that disbelieveth shall be condemned.

17 And these signs shall accompany them that believe: in my name shall they cast out demons; they shall speak with [686]new tongues;

18 they shall take up serpents, and if they drink any deadly thing, it shall in no wise hurt them; they shall lay hands on the sick, and they shall recover.

19 So then the Lord Jesus, after he had spoken unto them, was received up into heaven, and sat down at the right hand of God.

20 And they went forth, and preached everywhere, the Lord working with them, and confirming the word by the signs that followed. Amen.

---

[685]*See marginal note on 1:1.*
[686]*Some ancient authorities omit new.*

Timeline for Luke

Luke provides a meticulous historical account, emphasizing Jesus as the Savior of all nations, with special attention to the marginalized, prayer, and the Holy Spirit.

LUKE'S NARRATIVE STRUCTURE

SECTION / THEMATIC BLOCK	CHAPTER REFERENCE / NARRATIVE FOCUS
Prologue & Infancy Narratives	**Ch 1 – 2:** The births of John the Baptist and Jesus; the songs of Mary (Magnificat) and Zechariah (Benedictus); Jesus in the Temple at age twelve.
Preparation for Ministry	**Ch 3 – 4:13:** Ministry of John; the genealogy of Jesus (traced back to **Adam**, not just Abraham, portraying Jesus as the Savior of all humanity); Baptism; Temptation.
Galilean Ministry	**Ch 4:14 – 9:50:** Rejection at Nazareth (Mission Statement of Jubilee); calling of disciples; Sermon on the Plain; miracles demonstrating compassion for outcasts and Gentiles.
The Journey to Jerusalem	**Ch 9:51 – 19:27:** The "Travel Narrative"—a distinct section unique to Luke containing famous parables (Good Samaritan, Prodigal Son) and teachings on the cost of discipleship.

LUKE'S NARRATIVE STRUCTURE

SECTION / THEMATIC BLOCK	CHAPTER REFERENCE / NARRATIVE FOCUS
Ministry in Jerusalem	**Ch 19:28 – 21:** The Triumphal Entry; weeping over Jerusalem; cleansing the Temple; warnings about the destruction of the Temple and the End Times.
Passion & Resurrection	**Ch 22 – 24:** The Last Supper; trials before Pilate and Herod; Crucifixion; the Walk to Emmaus (unique to Luke); and the **Ascension** (the hinge connecting this Gospel to Luke's second volume, Acts).

Chapter 1

1 Forasmuch as many have taken in hand to draw up a narrative concerning those matters which have been [687]fulfilled among us,

2 even as they delivered them unto us, who from the beginning were eyewitnesses and ministers of the word,

3 it seemed good to me also, having traced the course of all things accurately from the first, to write unto thee in order, most excellent Theophilus;

4 that thou mightest know the certainty concerning the [688]things [689]wherein thou wast instructed.

5 There was in the days of Herod, king of Judaea, a certain priest named Zacharias, of the course of Abijah: and he had a wife of the daughters of Aaron, and her name was Elisabeth.

6 And they were both righteous before God, walking in all the commandments and ordinances of the Lord blameless.

7 And they had no child, because that Elisabeth was barren, and they both were *now* [690]well stricken in years.

8 Now it came to pass, while he executed the priest's office before God in the order of his course,

9 according to the custom of the priest's office, his lot was to enter into the [691]temple of the Lord and burn incense.

10 And the whole multitude of the people were praying without at the hour of incense.

11 And there appeared unto him an angel of the Lord standing on the right side of the altar of incense.

12 And Zacharias was troubled when he saw *him*, and fear fell upon him.

13 But the angel said unto him, Fear not, Zacharias: because thy supplication is heard, and thy wife Elisabeth shall bear thee a son, and thou shalt call his name John.

---

[687] *Or, fully established*
[688] *Greek words.*
[689] *Or, which thou wast taught by word of mouth*
[690] *Greek advanced in their days.*
[691] *Or, sanctuary*

14 And thou shalt have joy and gladness; and many shall rejoice at his birth.

15 For he shall be great in the sight of the Lord, and he shall drink no wine nor [692]strong drink; and he shall be filled with the Holy Spirit, even from his mother's womb.

16 And many of the children of Israel shall he turn unto the Lord their God.

17 And he shall [693]go before his face in the spirit and power of Elijah, to turn the hearts of the fathers to the children, and the disobedient *to walk* in the wisdom of the just; to make ready for the Lord a people prepared *for him.*

18 And Zacharias said unto the angel, Whereby shall I know this? for I am an old man, and my wife [694]well stricken in years.

19 And the angel answering said unto him, I am Gabriel, that stand in the presence of God; and I was sent to speak unto thee, and to bring thee these good tidings.

20 And behold, thou shalt be silent and not able to speak, until the day that these things shall come to pass, because thou believedst not my words, which shall be fulfilled in their season.

21 And the people were waiting for Zacharias, and they marvelled [695]while he tarried in the [696]temple.

22 And when he came out, he could not speak unto them: and they perceived that he had seen a vision in the [697]temple: and he continued making signs unto them, and remained dumb.

23 And it came to pass, when the days of his ministration were fulfilled, he departed unto his house.

24 And after these days Elisabeth his wife conceived; and she hid herself five months, saying,

25 Thus hath the Lord done unto me in the days wherein he looked upon *me*, to take away my reproach among men.

---

[692] *Greek sikera.*
[693] *Some ancient authorities read come nigh before his face.*
[694] *Greek advanced in her days.*
[695] *Or, at his tarrying*
[696] *Or, sanctuary*
[697] *Or, sanctuary*

26 Now in the sixth month the angel Gabriel was sent from God unto a city of Galilee, named Nazareth,

27 to a virgin betrothed to a man whose name was Joseph, of the house of David; and the virgin's name was Mary.

28 And he came in unto her, and said, Hail, thou that art [698]highly favored, the Lord *is* with thee[699].

29 But she was greatly troubled at the saying, and cast in her mind what manner of salutation this might be.

30 And the angel said unto her, Fear not, Mary: for thou hast found [700]favor with God.

31 And behold, thou shalt conceive in thy womb, and bring forth a son, and shalt call his name Jesus.

32 He shall be great, and shall be called the Son of the Most High: and the Lord God shall give unto him the throne of his father David:

33 and he shall reign over the house of Jacob [701]for ever; and of his kingdom there shall be no end.

34 And Mary said unto the angel, How shall this be, seeing I know not a man?

35 And the angel answered and said unto her, The Holy Spirit shall come upon thee, and the power of the Most High shall overshadow thee: wherefore also [702]the holy thing which is begotten [703]shall be called the Son of God.

36 And behold, Elisabeth thy kinswoman, she also hath conceived a son in her old age; and this is the sixth month with her that [704]was called barren.

37 For no word from God shall be void of power.

38 And Mary said, Behold, the [705]handmaid of the Lord; be it unto me according to thy word. And the angel departed from her.

---

[698] *Or, endued with grace*
[699] *Many ancient authorities add* blessed art thou among women. *See verse 42.*
[700] *Or, grace*
[701] *Greek* unto the ages.
[702] *Or, that which is to be born shall be called holy, the Son of God*
[703] *Some ancient authorities insert* of thee.
[704] *Or, is*
[705] *Greek* bondmaid.

39 And Mary arose in these days and went into the hill country with haste, into a city of Judah;

40 and entered into the house of Zacharias and saluted Elisabeth.

41 And it came to pass, when Elisabeth heard the salutation of Mary, the babe leaped in her womb; and Elisabeth was filled with the Holy Spirit;

42 and she lifted up her voice with a loud cry, and said, Blessed *art* thou among women, and blessed *is* the fruit of thy womb.

43 And whence is this to me, that the mother of my Lord should come unto me?

44 For behold, when the voice of thy salutation came into mine ears, the babe leaped in my womb for joy.

45 And blessed *is* she that [706]believed; for there shall be a fulfilment of the things which have been spoken to her from the Lord.

46 And Mary said,
    My soul doth magnify the Lord,

47 And my spirit hath rejoiced in God my Saviour.

48 For he hath looked upon the low estate of his [707]handmaid:
    For behold, from henceforth all generations shall call me blessed.

49 For he that is mighty hath done to me great things;
    And holy is his name.

50 And his mercy is unto generations and generations
    On them that fear him.

51 He hath showed strength with his arm;
    He hath scattered the proud [708]in the imagination of their heart.

52 He hath put down princes from *their* thrones,
    And hath exalted them of low degree.

53 The hungry he hath filled with good things;
    And the rich he hath sent empty away.

54 He hath given help to Israel his servant,
    That he might remember mercy

---

[706] *Or, believed that there shall be*
[707] *Greek bondmaid.*
[708] *Or, by*

55 (As he spake unto our fathers)
    Toward Abraham and his seed for ever.

56 And Mary abode with her about three months, and returned unto her house.

57 Now Elisabeth's time was fulfilled that she should be delivered; and she brought forth a son.

58 And her neighbors and her kinsfolk heard that the Lord had magnified his mercy towards her; and they rejoiced with her.

59 And it came to pass on the eighth day, that they came to circumcise the child; and they would have called him Zacharias, after the name of his father.

60 And his mother answered and said, Not so; but he shall be called John.

61 And they said unto her, There is none of thy kindred that is called by this name.

62 And they made signs to his father, what he would have him called.

63 And he asked for a writing tablet, and wrote, saying, His name is John. And they marvelled all.

64 And his mouth was opened immediately, and his tongue *loosed*, and he spake, blessing God.

65 And fear came on all that dwelt round about them: and all these sayings were noised abroad throughout all the hill country of Judaea.

66 And all that heard them laid them up in their heart, saying, What then shall this child be? For the hand of the Lord was with him.

67 And his father Zacharias was filled with the Holy Spirit, and prophesied, saying,

68 Blessed *be* the Lord, the God of Israel;
    For he hath visited and wrought redemption for his people,

69 And hath raised up a horn of salvation for us
    In the house of his servant David

70 (As he spake by the mouth of his holy prophets that have been from of old),

71 Salvation from our enemies, and from the hand of all that hate us;

72 To show mercy towards our fathers,
    And to remember his holy covenant;

73 The oath which he sware unto Abraham our father,
74 To grant unto us that we being delivered out of the hand of our enemies
   Should serve him without fear,
75 In holiness and righteousness before him all our days.
76 Yea and thou, child, shalt be called the prophet of the Most High:
   For thou shalt go before the face of the Lord to make ready his ways;
77 To give knowledge of salvation unto his people
   In the remission of their sins,
78 Because of the [709]tender mercy of our God,
   [710]Whereby the dayspring from on high [711]shall visit us,
79 To shine upon them that sit in darkness and the shadow of death;
   To guide our feet into the way of peace.
80 And the child grew, and waxed strong in spirit, and was in the deserts till the day of his showing unto Israel.

---

[709] *Or, heart of mercy*
[710] *Or, Wherein*
[711] *Many ancient authorities read hath visited us.*

Chapter 2

1 Now it came to pass in those days, there went out a decree from Caesar Augustus, that all [712]the world should be enrolled.

2 This was the first enrolment made when Quirinius was governor of Syria.

3 And all went to enrol themselves, every one to his own city.

4 And Joseph also went up from Galilee, out of the city of Nazareth, into Judaea, to the city of David, which is called Bethlehem, because he was of the house and family of David;

5 to enrol himself with Mary, who was betrothed to him, being great with child.

6 And it came to pass, while they were there, the days were fulfilled that she should be delivered.

7 And she brought forth her firstborn son; and she wrapped him in swaddling clothes, and laid him in a manger, because there was no room for them in the inn.

8 And there were shepherds in the same country abiding in the field, and keeping [713]watch by night over their flock.

9 And an angel of the Lord stood by them, and the glory of the Lord shone round about them: and they were sore afraid.

10 And the angel said unto them, Be not afraid; for behold, I bring you good tidings of great joy which shall be to all the people:

11 for there is born to you this day in the city of David a Saviour, who is [714]Christ the Lord.

12 And this *is* the sign unto you: Ye shall find a babe wrapped in swaddling clothes, and lying in a manger.

13 And suddenly there was with the angel a multitude of the heavenly host praising God, and saying,

14 Glory to God in the highest,

---

[712]*Greek the inhabited earth.*
[713]*Or, night-watches*
[714]*Or, Anointed Lord*

And on earth [715]peace among [716]men in whom he is well pleased.

15 And it came to pass, when the angels went away from them into heaven, the shepherds said one to another, Let us now go even unto Bethlehem, and see this [717]thing that is come to pass, which the Lord hath made known unto us.

16 And they came with haste, and found both Mary and Joseph, and the babe lying in the manger.

17 And when they saw it, they made known concerning the saying which was spoken to them about this child.

18 And all that heard it wondered at the things which were spoken unto them by the shepherds.

19 But Mary kept all these [718]sayings, pondering them in her heart.

20 And the shepherds returned, glorifying and praising God for all the things that they had heard and seen, even as it was spoken unto them.

21 And when eight days were fulfilled for circumcising him, his name was called Jesus, which was so called by the angel before he was conceived in the womb.

22 And when the days of their purification [719]according to the law of Moses were fulfilled, they brought him up to Jerusalem, to present him to the Lord

23 (as it is written in the law of the Lord, [720]Every male that openeth the womb shall be called holy to the Lord),

24 and to offer a sacrifice according to that which is said in the law of the Lord, [721]A pair of turtledoves, or two young pigeons.

25 And behold, there was a man in Jerusalem, whose name was Simeon; and this man was righteous and devout, looking for the consolation of Israel: and the Holy Spirit was upon him.

26 And it had been revealed unto him by the Holy Spirit, that he should not see death, before he had seen the Lord's Christ.

---

[715] *Many ancient authorities read peace, good pleasure among men.*
[716] *Greek men of good pleasure.*
[717] *Or, saying*
[718] *Or, things*
[719] *Lev. 12:2–6.*
[720] *Ex. 13:2, 12.*
[721] *Lev. 12:8; 5:11.*

27 And he came in the Spirit into the temple: and when the parents brought in the child Jesus, that they might do concerning him after the custom of the law,

28 then he received him into his arms, and blessed God, and said,

29 Now lettest thou thy [722]servant depart, [723]Lord,
   According to thy word, in peace;

30 For mine eyes have seen thy salvation,

31 Which thou hast prepared before the face of all peoples;

32 A light for [724]revelation to the Gentiles,
   And the glory of thy people Israel.

33 And his father and his mother were marvelling at the things which were spoken concerning him;

34 and Simeon blessed them, and said unto Mary his mother, Behold, this *child* is set for the falling and the rising of many in Israel; and for a sign which is spoken against;

35 yea and a sword shall pierce through thine own soul; that thoughts out of many hearts may be revealed.

36 And there was one Anna, a prophetess, the daughter of Phanuel, of the tribe of Asher (she was [725]of a great age, having lived with a husband seven years from her virginity,

37 and she had been a widow even unto fourscore and four years), who departed not from the temple, worshipping with fastings and supplications night and day.

38 And coming up at that very hour she gave thanks unto God, and spake of him to all them that were looking for the redemption of Jerusalem.

39 And when they had accomplished all things that were according to the law of the Lord, they returned into Galilee, to their own city Nazareth.

40 And the child grew, and waxed strong, [726]filled with wisdom: and the grace of God was upon him.

---

[722] *Greek bondservant.*
[723] *Greek Master.*
[724] *Or, the unveiling of the Gentiles*
[725] *Greek advanced in many days.*
[726] *Greek becoming full of wisdom.*

41 And his parents went every year to Jerusalem at the feast of the passover.

42 And when he was twelve years old, they went up after the custom of the feast;

43 and when they had fulfilled the days, as they were returning, the boy Jesus tarried behind in Jerusalem; and his parents knew it not;

44 but supposing him to be in the company, they went a day's journey; and they sought for him among their kinsfolk and acquaintance:

45 and when they found him not, they returned to Jerusalem, seeking for him.

46 And it came to pass, after three days they found him in the temple, sitting in the midst of the [727]teachers, both hearing them, and asking them questions:

47 and all that heard him were amazed at his understanding and his answers.

48 And when they saw him, they were astonished; and his mother said unto him, [728]Son, why hast thou thus dealt with us? behold, thy father and I sought thee sorrowing.

49 And he said unto them, How is it that ye sought me? knew ye not that I must be [729]in my Father's house?

50 And they understood not the saying which he spake unto them. vnum51 And he went down with them, and came to Nazareth; and he was subject unto them: and his mother kept all *these* [730]sayings in her heart.

†✓ **Jesus Grew.** God is immutable and perfect in wisdom. Jesus "advanced" or "increased" in wisdom. This development is the hallmark of a perfect human, not an already-omniscient Deity.

52 And Jesus advanced in wisdom and [731]stature, and in [732]favor with God and men.

---

[727] *Or, doctors. See 5:17; Acts 5:34.*
[728] *Greek Child.*
[729] *Or, about my Father's business. Greek in the things of my Father.*
[730] *Or, things*
[731] *Or, age*
[732] *Or, grace*

Chapter 3

1 Now in the fifteenth year of the reign of Tiberius Caesar, Pontius Pilate being governor of Judaea, and Herod being tetrarch of Galilee, and his brother Philip tetrarch of the region of Ituraea and Trachonitis, and Lysanias tetrarch of Abilene,

2 in the high-priesthood of Annas and Caiaphas, the word of God came unto John the son of Zacharias in the wilderness.

3 And he came into all the region round about the Jordan, preaching the baptism of repentance unto remission of sins;

4 as it is written in the book of the words of Isaiah the prophet,
[733]The voice of one crying in the wilderness,
Make ye ready the way of the Lord,
Make his paths straight.

5 Every valley shall be filled,
And every mountain and hill shall be brought low;
And the crooked shall become straight,
And the rough ways smooth;

6 And all flesh shall see the salvation of God.

7 He said therefore to the multitudes that went out to be baptized of him, Ye offspring of vipers, who warned you to flee from the wrath to come?

8 Bring forth therefore fruits worthy of [734]repentance, and begin not to say within yourselves, We have Abraham to our father: for I say unto you, that God is able of these stones to raise up children unto Abraham.

9 And even now the axe also lieth at the root of the trees: every tree therefore that bringeth not forth good fruit is hewn down, and cast into the fire.

10 And the multitudes asked him, saying, What then must we do?

11 And he answered and said unto them, He that hath two coats, let him impart to him that hath none; and he that hath food, let him do likewise.

---

[733] *Isa. 40:3ff.*
[734] *Or, your repentance*

12 And there came also [735]publicans to be baptized, and they said unto him, Teacher, what must we do?

13 And he said unto them, Extort no more than that which is appointed you.

14 And [736]soldiers also asked him, saying, And we, what must we do? And he said unto them, Extort from no man by violence, neither accuse *any one* wrongfully; and be content with your wages.

15 And as the people were in expectation, and all men reasoned in their hearts concerning John, whether haply he were the Christ;

16 John answered, saying unto them all, I indeed baptize you with water; but there cometh he that is mightier than I, the latchet of whose shoes I am not [737]worthy to unloose: he shall baptize you [738]in the Holy Spirit and *in* fire:

17 whose fan is in his hand, thoroughly to cleanse his threshing-floor, and to gather the wheat into his garner; but the chaff he will burn up with unquenchable fire.

18 With many other exhortations therefore preached he [739]good tidings unto the people;

19 but Herod the tetrarch, being reproved by him for Herodias his brother's wife, and for all the evil things which Herod had done,

20 added this also to them all, that he shut up John in prison.

21 Now it came to pass, when all the people were baptized, that, Jesus also having been baptized, and praying, the heaven was opened,

22 and the Holy Spirit descended in a bodily form, as a dove, upon him, and a voice came out of heaven, Thou art my beloved Son; in thee I am well pleased.

23 And Jesus himself, when he began *to teach*, was about thirty years of age, being the son (as was supposed) of Joseph, the *son* of Heli,

24 the *son* of Matthat, the *son* of Levi, the *son* of Melchi, the *son* of Jannai, the *son* of Joseph,

---

[735] *That is, collectors or renters of Roman taxes.*
[736] *Greek soldiers on service.*
[737] *Greek sufficient.*
[738] *Or, with*
[739] *Or, the gospel*

25 the *son* of Mattathias, the *son* of Amos, the *son* of Nahum, the *son* of Esli, the *son* of Naggai,

26 the *son* of Maath, the *son* of Mattathias, the *son* of Semein, the *son* of Josech, the *son* of Joda,

27 the *son* of Joanan, the *son* of Rhesa, the *son* of Zerubbabel, the *son* of [740]Shealtiel, the *son* of Neri,

28 the *son* of Melchi, the *son* of Addi, the *son* of Cosam, the *son* of Elmadam, the *son* of Er,

29 the *son* of Jesus, the *son* of Eliezer, the *son* of Jorim, the *son* of Matthat, the *son* of Levi,

30 the *son* of Symeon, the *son* of Judas, the *son* of Joseph, the *son* of Jonam, the *son* of Eliakim,

31 the *son* of Melea, the *son* of Menna, the *son* of Mattatha, the *son* of Nathan, the *son* of David,

32 the *son* of Jesse, the *son* of Obed, the *son* of Boaz, the *son* of [741]Salmon, the *son* of Nahshon,

33 the *son* of Amminadab, [742]the *son* of [743]Arni, the *son* of Hezron, the *son* of Perez, the *son* of Judah,

34 the *son* of Jacob, the *son* of Isaac, the *son* of Abraham, the *son* of Terah, the *son* of Nahor,

35 the *son* of Serug, the *son* of Reu, the *son* of Peleg, the *son* of Eber, the *son* of Shelah,

36 the *son* of Cainan, the *son* of Arphaxad, the *son* of Shem, the *son* of Noah, the *son* of Lamech,

37 the *son* of Methuselah, the *son* of Enoch, the *son* of Jared, the *son* of Mahalaleel, the *son* of Cainan,

38 the *son* of Enos, the *son* of Seth, the *son* of Adam, the *son* of God.

---

[740] *Greek Salathiel.*
[741] *Some ancient authorities write Sala.*
[742] *Many ancient authorities insert the son of Admin: and one writes Admin for Amminadab.*
[743] *Some ancient authorities write Aram.*

Chapter 4

1 And Jesus, full of the Holy Spirit, returned from the Jordan, and was led in the Spirit in the wilderness

2 during forty days, being tempted of the devil. And he did eat nothing in those days: and when they were completed, he hungered.

3 And the devil said unto him, If thou art the Son of God, command this stone that it become [744]bread.

4 And Jesus answered unto him, It is written, [745]Man shall not live by bread alone.

5 And he led him up, and showed him all the kingdoms of [746]the world in a moment of time.

6 And the devil said unto him, To thee will I give all this authority, and the glory of them: for it hath been delivered unto me; and to whomsoever I will I give it.

7 If thou therefore wilt [747]worship before me, it shall all be thine.

8 And Jesus answered and said unto him, It is written, Thou shalt worship the Lord thy God, and him only shalt thou serve.

9 And he led him to Jerusalem, and set him on the [748]pinnacle of the temple, and said unto him, If thou art the Son of God, cast thyself down from hence:

10 for it is written,

[749]He shall give his angels charge concerning thee, to guard thee:

11 and,

On their hands they shall bear thee up,

Lest haply thou dash thy foot against a stone.

12 And Jesus answering said unto him, It is said, [750]Thou shalt not make trial of the Lord thy God.

---

[744] *Or, a loaf*
[745] Dt. 8:3.
[746] *Greek the inhabited earth.*
[747] *The Greek word denotes an act of reverence, whether paid to a creature, or to the Creator (compare marginal note on Mt. 2:2)*
[748] *Greek wing.*
[749] Ps. 91:11, 12.
[750] Dt. 6:16.

13 And when the devil had completed every temptation, he departed from him [751]for a season.

14 And Jesus returned in the power of the Spirit into Galilee: and a fame went out concerning him through all the region round about.

15 And he taught in their synagogues, being glorified of all.

16 And he came to Nazareth, where he had been brought up: and he entered, as his custom was, into the synagogue on the sabbath day, and stood up to read.

17 And there was delivered unto him [752]the book of the prophet Isaiah. And he opened the [753]book, and found the place where it was written,

18 [754]The Spirit of the Lord is upon me,
[755]Because he anointed me to preach [756]good tidings to the poor:
He hath sent me to proclaim release to the captives,
And recovering of sight to the blind,
To set at liberty them that are bruised,

19 To proclaim the acceptable year of the Lord.

20 And he closed the [757]book, and gave it back to the attendant, and sat down: and the eyes of all in the synagogue were fastened on him.

21 And he began to say unto them, To-day hath this scripture been fulfilled in your ears.

22 And all bare him witness, and wondered at the words of grace which proceeded out of his mouth: and they said, Is not this Joseph's son?

23 And he said unto them, Doubtless ye will say unto me this parable, Physician, heal thyself: whatsoever we have heard done at Capernaum, do also here in thine own country.

24 And he said, Verily I say unto you, No prophet is acceptable in his own country.

---

[751] *Or, until*
[752] *Or, a roll*
[753] *Or, roll*
[754] *Isa. 61:1f.*
[755] *Or, Wherefore*
[756] *Or, the gospel*
[757] *Or, roll*

25 But of a truth I say unto you, There were many widows in Israel in the days of Elijah, when the heaven was shut up three years and six months, when there came a great famine over all the land;

26 and unto none of them was Elijah sent, but only to [758]Zarephath, in the land of Sidon, unto a woman that was a widow.

27 And there were many lepers in Israel in the time of Elisha the prophet; and none of them was cleansed, but only Naaman the Syrian.

28 And they were all filled with wrath in the synagogue, as they heard these things;

29 and they rose up, and cast him forth out of the city, and led him unto the brow of the hill whereon their city was built, that they might throw him down headlong.

30 But he passing through the midst of them went his way.

31 And he came down to Capernaum, a city of Galilee. And he was teaching them on the sabbath day:

32 and they were astonished at his teaching; for his word was with authority.

33 And in the synagogue there was a man, that had a spirit of an unclean demon; and he cried out with a loud voice,

34 [759]Ah! what have we to do with thee, Jesus thou Nazarene? art thou come to destroy us? I know thee who thou art, the Holy One of God.

35 And Jesus rebuked him, saying, Hold thy peace, and come out of him. And when the demon had thrown him down in the midst, he came out of him, having done him no hurt.

36 And amazement came upon all, and they spake together, one with another, saying, What is [760]this word? for with authority and power he commandeth the unclean spirits, and they come out.

37 And there went forth a rumor concerning him into every place of the region round about.

38 And he rose up from the synagogue, and entered into the house of Simon. And Simon's wife's mother was holden with a great fever; and they besought him for her.

---

[758] *Greek Sarepta.*
[759] *Or, Let alone*
[760] *Or, this word, that with authority . . . come out?*

39 And he stood over her, and rebuked the fever; and it left her: and immediately she rose up and ministered unto them.

40 And when the sun was setting, all they that had any sick with divers diseases brought them unto him; and he laid his hands on every one of them, and healed them.

41 And demons also came out from many, crying out, and saying, Thou art the Son of God. And rebuking them, he suffered them not to speak, because they knew that he was the Christ.

42 And when it was day, he came out and went into a desert place: and the multitudes sought after him, and came unto him, and would have stayed him, that he should not go from them.

43 But he said unto them, I must preach [761]the good tidings of the kingdom of God to the other cities also: for therefore was I sent.

44 And he was preaching in the synagogues of [762]Galilee.

Chapter 5

1 Now it came to pass, while the multitude pressed upon him and heard the word of God, that he was standing by the lake of Gennesaret;

2 and he saw two boats standing by the lake: but the fishermen had gone out of them, and were washing their nets.

3 And he entered into one of the boats, which was Simon's, and asked him to put out a little from the land. And he sat down and taught the multitudes out of the boat.

4 And when he had left speaking, he said unto Simon, Put out into the deep, and let down your nets for a draught.

5 And Simon answered and said, Master, we toiled all night, and took nothing: but at thy word I will let down the nets.

6 And when they had done this, they inclosed a great multitude of fishes; and their nets were breaking;

7 and they beckoned unto their partners in the other boat, that they should come and help them. And they came, and filled both the boats, so that they began to sink.

---

[761] *Or, the gospel*
[762] *Very many ancient authorities read Judaea.*

8 But Simon Peter, when he saw it, fell down at Jesus' knees, saying, Depart from me; for I am a sinful man, O Lord.

9 For he was amazed, and all that were with him, at the draught of the fishes which they had taken;

10 and so were also [763]James and John, sons of Zebedee, who were partners with Simon. And Jesus said unto Simon, Fear not; from henceforth thou shalt [764]catch men.

11 And when they had brought their boats to land, they left all, and followed him.

12 And it came to pass, while he was in one of the cities, behold, a man full of leprosy: and when he saw Jesus, he fell on his face, and besought him, saying, Lord, if thou wilt, thou canst make me clean.

13 And he stretched forth his hand, and touched him, saying, I will; be thou made clean. And straightway the leprosy departed from him.

14 And he charged him to tell no man: but go thy way, and show thyself to the priest, and offer for thy cleansing, [765]according as Moses commanded, for a testimony unto them.

15 But so much the more went abroad the report concerning him: and great multitudes came together to hear, and to be healed of their infirmities.

16 But he withdrew himself in the deserts, and prayed.

17 And it came to pass on one of those days, that he was teaching; and there were Pharisees and doctors of the law sitting by, who were come out of every village of Galilee and Judaea and Jerusalem: and the power of the Lord was with him [766]to heal.

18 And behold, men bring on a bed a man that was palsied: and they sought to bring him in, and to lay him before him.

19 And not finding by what *way* they might bring him in because of the multitude, they went up to the housetop, and let him down through the tiles with his couch into the midst before Jesus.

20 And seeing their faith, he said, Man, thy sins are forgiven thee.

---

[763] *Or, Jacob*
[764] *Greek take alive.*
[765] *Lev. 13:49; 14:2ff.*
[766] *Greek that he should heal. Many ancient authorities read that he should heal them.*

21 And the scribes and the Pharisees began to reason, saying, Who is this that speaketh blasphemies? Who can forgive sins, but God alone?

22 But Jesus perceiving their [767]reasonings, answered and said unto them, [768]Why reason ye in your hearts?

23 Which is easier, to say, Thy sins are forgiven thee; or to say, Arise and walk?

24 But that ye may know that the Son of man hath authority on earth to forgive sins (he said unto him that was palsied), I say unto thee, Arise, and take up thy couch, and go unto thy house.

25 And immediately he rose up before them, and took up that whereon he lay, and departed to his house, glorifying God.

26 And amazement took hold on all, and they glorified God; and they were filled with fear, saying, We have seen strange things to-day.

27 And after these things he went forth, and beheld a [769]publican, named Levi, sitting at the place of toll, and said unto him, Follow me.

28 And he forsook all, and rose up and followed him.

29 And Levi made him a great feast in his house: and there was a great multitude of [770]publicans and of others that were sitting at meat with them.

30 And [771]the Pharisees and their scribes murmured against his disciples, saying, Why do ye eat and drink with the [772]publicans and sinners?

31 And Jesus answering said unto them, They that are [773]in health have no need of a physician; but they that are sick.

32 I am not come to call the righteous but sinners to repentance.

33 And they said unto him, The disciples of John fast often, and make supplications; likewise also the *disciples* of the Pharisees; but thine eat and drink.

---

[767] *Or, questionings*
[768] *Or, What*
[769] *See marginal note on 3:12.*
[770] *See marginal note on 3:12.*
[771] *Or, the Pharisees and the scribes among them*
[772] *See marginal note on 3:12.*
[773] *Greek sound.*

34 And Jesus said unto them, Can ye make the [774]sons of the bride-chamber fast, while the bridegroom is with them?

35 But the days will come; and when the bridegroom shall be taken away from them, then will they fast in those days.

36 And he spake also a parable unto them: No man rendeth a piece from a new garment and putteth it upon an old garment; else he will rend the new, and also the piece from the new will not agree with the old.

37 And no man putteth new wine into old [775]wine-skins; else the new wine will burst the skins, and itself will be spilled, and the skins will perish.

38 But new wine must be put into fresh wine-skins.

39 And no man having drunk old *wine* desireth new; for he saith, The old is [776]good.

Chapter 6

1 Now it came to pass on a [777]sabbath, that he was going through the grainfields; and his disciples plucked the ears, and did eat, rubbing them in their hands.

2 But certain of the Pharisees said, Why do ye that which it is not lawful to do on the sabbath day?

3 And Jesus answering them said, [778]Have ye not read even this, what David did, when he was hungry, he, and they that were with him;

4 how he entered into the house of God, and took and ate the showbread, and gave also to them that were with him; which it is not lawful to eat save for the priests alone?

5 And he said unto them, The Son of man is lord of the sabbath.

6 And it came to pass on another sabbath, that he entered into the synagogue and taught: and there was a man there, and his right hand was withered.

---

[774]*That is, companions of the bridegroom.*
[775]*That is, skins used as bottles.*
[776]*Many ancient authorities read* better.
[777]*Many ancient authorities insert* second-first.
[778]*1 Sam. 21:6.*

7 And the scribes and the Pharisees watched him, whether he would heal on the sabbath; that they might find how to accuse him.

8 But he knew their thoughts; and he said to the man that had his hand withered, Rise up, and stand forth in the midst. And he arose and stood forth.

9 And Jesus said unto them, I ask you, Is it lawful on the sabbath to do good, or to do harm? to save a life, or to destroy it?

10 And he looked round about on them all, and said unto him, Stretch forth thy hand. And he did *so*: and his hand was restored.

11 But they were filled with [779]madness; and communed one with another what they might do to Jesus.

12 And it came to pass in these days, that he went out into the mountain to pray; and he continued all night in prayer to God.

13 And when it was day, he called his disciples; and he chose from them twelve, whom also he named apostles:

14 Simon, whom he also named Peter, and Andrew his brother, and [780]James and John, and Philip and Bartholomew,

15 and Matthew and Thomas, and [781]James *the son* of Alphaeus, and Simon who was called the Zealot,

16 and Judas *the* [782]*son* of [783]James, and Judas Iscariot, who became a traitor;

17 and he came down with them, and stood on a level place, and a great multitude of his disciples, and a great number of the people from all Judaea and Jerusalem, and the sea coast of Tyre and Sidon, who came to hear him, and to be healed of their diseases;

18 and they that were troubled with unclean spirits were healed.

19 And all the multitude sought to touch him; for power came forth from him, and healed *them* all.

20 And he lifted up his eyes on his disciples, and said, Blessed *are* ye poor: for yours is the kingdom of God.

---

[779] *Or, foolishness*
[780] *Or, Jacob*
[781] *Or, Jacob*
[782] *Or, brother. See Jude 1.*
[783] *Or, Jacob*

21 Blessed *are* ye that hunger now: for ye shall be filled. Blessed *are* ye that weep now: for ye shall laugh.

22 Blessed are ye, when men shall hate you, and when they shall separate you *from their company*, and reproach you, and cast out your name as evil, for the Son of man's sake.

23 Rejoice in that day, and leap *for joy*: for behold, your reward is great in heaven; for in the same manner did their fathers unto the prophets.

24 But woe unto you that are rich! for ye have received your consolation.

25 Woe unto you, ye that are full now! for ye shall hunger. Woe *unto you*, ye that laugh now! for ye shall mourn and weep.

26 Woe *unto you*, when all men shall speak well of you! for in the same manner did their fathers to the false prophets.

27 But I say unto you that hear, Love your enemies, do good to them that hate you,

28 bless them that curse you, pray for them that despitefully use you.

29 To him that smiteth thee on the *one* cheek offer also the other; and from him that taketh away thy cloak withhold not thy coat also.

30 Give to every one that asketh thee; and of him that taketh away thy goods ask them not again.

31 And as ye would that men should do to you, do ye also to them likewise.

32 And if ye love them that love you, what thank have ye? for even sinners love those that love them.

33 And if ye do good to them that do good to you, what thank have ye? for even sinners do the same.

34 And if ye lend to them of whom ye hope to receive, what thank have ye? even sinners lend to sinners, to receive again as much.

35 But love your enemies, and do *them* good, and lend, [784]never despairing; and your reward shall be great, and ye shall be sons of the Most High: for he is kind toward the unthankful and evil.

36 Be ye merciful, even as your Father is merciful.

37 And judge not, and ye shall not be judged: and condemn not, and ye shall not be condemned: release, and ye shall be released:

---

[784]*Some ancient authorities read despairing of no man.*

38 give, and it shall be given unto you; good measure, pressed down, shaken together, running over, shall they give into your bosom. For with what measure ye mete it shall be measured to you again.

39 And he spake also a parable unto them, Can the blind guide the blind? shall they not both fall into a pit?

40 The disciple is not above his teacher: but every one when he is perfected shall be as his teacher.

41 And why beholdest thou the mote that is in thy brother's eye, but considerest not the beam that is in thine own eye?

42 Or how canst thou say to thy brother, Brother, let me cast out the mote that is in thine eye, when thou thyself beholdest not the beam that is in thine own eye? Thou hypocrite, cast out first the beam out of thine own eye, and then shalt thou see clearly to cast out the mote that is in thy brother's eye.

43 For there is no good tree that bringeth forth corrupt fruit; nor again a corrupt tree that bringeth forth good fruit.

44 For each tree is known by its own fruit. For of thorns men do not gather figs, nor of a bramble bush gather they grapes.

45 The good man out of the good treasure of his heart bringeth forth that which is good; and the evil *man* out of the evil *treasure* bringeth forth that which is evil: for out of the abundance of the heart his mouth speaketh.

46 And why call ye me, Lord, Lord, and do not the things which I say?

47 Every one that cometh unto me, and heareth my words, and doeth them, I will show you to whom he is like:

48 he is like a man building a house, who digged and went deep, and laid a foundation upon the rock: and when a flood arose, the stream brake against that house, and could not shake it: [785]because it had been well builded.

49 But he that [786]heareth, and [787]doeth not, is like a man that built a house upon the earth without a foundation; against which the stream brake, and straightway it fell in; and the ruin of that house was great.

---

[785] *Many ancient authorities read for it had been founded upon the rock: as in Mt. 7:25.*
[786] *Greek heard.*
[787] *Greek did not.*

Chapter 7

1 After he had ended all his sayings in the ears of the people, he entered into Capernaum.

2 And a certain centurion's [788]servant, who was [789]dear unto him, was sick and at the point of death.

3 And when he heard concerning Jesus, he sent unto him elders of the Jews, asking him that he would come and save his [790]servant.

4 And they, when they came to Jesus, besought him earnestly, saying, He is worthy that thou shouldest do this for him;

5 for he loveth our nation, and himself built us our synagogue.

6 And Jesus went with them. And when he was now not far from the house, the centurion sent friends to him, saying unto him, Lord, trouble not thyself; for I am not [791]worthy that thou shouldest come under my roof:

7 wherefore neither thought I myself worthy to come unto thee: but say [792]the word, and my [793]servant shall be healed.

8 For I also am a man set under authority, having under myself soldiers: and I say to this one, Go, and he goeth; and to another, Come, and he cometh; and to my [794]servant, Do this, and he doeth it.

9 And when Jesus heard these things, he marvelled at him, and turned and said unto the multitude that followed him, I say unto you, I have not found so great faith, no, not in Israel.

10 And they that were sent, returning to the house, found the [795]servant whole.

11 And it came to pass [796]soon afterwards, that he went to a city called Nain; and his disciples went with him, and a great multitude.

---

[788] *Greek bondservant.*
[789] *Or, precious to him. Or, honorable with him*
[790] *Greek bondservant.*
[791] *Greek sufficient.*
[792] *Greek with a word.*
[793] *Or, boy*
[794] *Greek bondservant.*
[795] *Greek bondservant.*
[796] *Many ancient authorities read on the next day.*

12 Now when he drew near to the gate of the city, behold, there was carried out one that was dead, the only son of his mother, and she was a widow: and much people of the city was with her.

13 And when the Lord saw her, he had compassion on her, and said unto her, Weep not.

14 And he came nigh and touched the bier: and the bearers stood still. And he said, Young man, I say unto thee, Arise.

15 And he that was dead sat up, and began to speak. And he gave him to his mother.

16 And fear took hold on all: and they glorified God, saying, A great prophet is arisen among us: and, God hath visited his people.

17 And this report went forth concerning him in the whole of Judaea, and all the region round about.

18 And the disciples of John told him of all these things.

19 And John calling unto him [797] two of his disciples sent them to the Lord, saying, Art thou he that cometh, or look we for another?

20 And when the men were come unto him, they said, John the Baptist hath sent us unto thee, saying, Art thou he that cometh, or look we for another?

21 In that hour he cured many of diseases and [798] plagues and evil spirits; and on many that were blind he bestowed sight.

22 And he answered and said unto them, Go and tell John the things which ye have seen and heard; the blind receive their sight, the lame walk, the lepers are cleansed, and the deaf hear, the dead are raised up, the poor have [799] good tidings preached to them.

23 And blessed is he, whosoever shall find no occasion of stumbling in me.

24 And when the messengers of John were departed, he began to say unto the multitudes concerning John, What went ye out into the wilderness to behold? a reed shaken with the wind?

---

[797] *Greek certain two.*
[798] *Greek scourges.*
[799] *Or, the gospel*

25 But what went ye out to see? a man clothed in soft raiment? Behold, they that are gorgeously apparelled, and live delicately, are in kings' courts.

26 But what went ye out to see? a prophet? Yea, I say unto you, and much more than a prophet.

27 This is he of whom it is written,
[800]Behold, I send my messenger before thy face,
Who shall prepare thy way before thee.

28 I say unto you, Among them that are born of women there is none greater than John: yet he that is [801]but little in the kingdom of God is greater than he.

29 And all the people when they heard, and the [802]publicans, justified God, [803]being baptized with the baptism of John.

30 But the Pharisees and the lawyers rejected for themselves the counsel of God, [804]being not baptized of him.

31 Whereunto then shall I liken the men of this generation, and to what are they like?

32 They are like unto children that sit in the marketplace, and call one to another; who say, We piped unto you, and ye did not dance; we wailed, and ye did not weep.

33 For John the Baptist is come eating no bread nor drinking wine; and ye say, He hath a demon.

34 The Son of man is come eating and drinking; and ye say, Behold, a gluttonous man, and a winebibber, a friend of [805]publicans and sinners!

35 And wisdom [806]is justified of all her children.

36 And one of the Pharisees desired him that he would eat with him. And he entered into the Pharisee's house, and [807]sat down to meat.

---

[800] *Mal. 3:1.*
[801] *Greek lesser.*
[802] *See marginal note on 3:12.*
[803] *Or, having been*
[804] *Or, not having been*
[805] *See marginal note on 3:12.*
[806] *Or, was*
[807] *Or, reclined at table*

37 And behold, a woman who was in the city, a sinner; and when she knew that he was [808]sitting at meat in the Pharisee's house, she brought [809]an alabaster cruse of ointment,

38 and standing behind at his feet, weeping, she began to wet his feet with her tears, and wiped them with the hair of her head, and [810]kissed his feet, and anointed them with the ointment.

39 Now when the Pharisee that had bidden him saw it, he spake within himself, saying, This man, if he were [811]a prophet, would have perceived who and what manner of woman this is that toucheth him, that she is a sinner.

40 And Jesus answering said unto him, Simon, I have somewhat to say unto thee. And he saith, Teacher, say on.

41 A certain lender had two debtors: the one owed five hundred [812]shillings, and the other fifty.

42 When they had not *wherewith* to pay, he forgave them both. Which of them therefore will love him most?

43 Simon answered and said, He, I suppose, to whom he forgave the most. And he said unto him, Thou hast rightly judged.

44 And turning to the woman, he said unto Simon, Seest thou this woman? I entered into thy house, thou gavest me no water for my feet: but she hath wetted my feet with her tears, and wiped them with her hair.

45 Thou gavest me no kiss: but she, since the time I came in, hath not ceased to [813]kiss my feet.

46 My head with oil thou didst not anoint: but she hath anointed my feet with ointment.

47 Wherefore I say unto thee, Her sins, which are many, are forgiven; for she loved much: but to whom little is forgiven, *the same* loveth little.

48 And he said unto her, Thy sins are forgiven.

---

[808] *Or, reclining at table*
[809] *Or, a flask*
[810] *Greek kissed much.*
[811] *Some ancient authorities read the prophet. See Jn. 1:21, 25.*
[812] *The word in the Greek denotes a coin worth about eight pence half-penny, or nearly seventeen cents.*
[813] *Greek kiss much.*

49 And they that [814]sat at meat with him began to say [815]within themselves, Who is this that even forgiveth sins?

50 And he said unto the woman, Thy faith hath saved thee; go in peace.

Chapter 8

1 And it came to pass soon afterwards, that he went about through cities and villages, preaching and bringing the [816]good tidings of the kingdom of God, and with him the twelve,

2 and certain women who had been healed of evil spirits and infirmities: Mary that was called Magdalene, from whom seven demons had gone out,

3 and Joanna the wife of Chuzas Herod's steward, and Susanna, and many others, who ministered unto [817]them of their substance.

4 And when a great multitude came together, and they of every city resorted unto him, he spake by a parable:

5 The sower went forth to sow his seed: and as he sowed, some fell by the way side; and it was trodden under foot, and the birds of the heaven devoured it.

6 And other fell on the rock; and as soon as it grew, it withered away, because it had no moisture.

7 And other fell amidst the thorns; and the thorns grew with it, and choked it.

8 And other fell into the good ground, and grew, and brought forth fruit a hundredfold. As he said these things, he cried, He that hath ears to hear, let him hear.

9 And his disciples asked him what this parable might be.

10 And he said, Unto you it is given to know the mysteries of the kingdom of God: but to the rest in parables; that seeing they may not see, and hearing they may not understand.

11 Now the parable is this: The seed is the word of God.

---

[814] *Greek reclined.*
[815] *Or, among*
[816] *Or, gospel*
[817] *Many ancient authorities read him.*

12 And those by the way side are they that have heard; then cometh the devil, and taketh away the word from their heart, that they may not believe and be saved.

13 And those on the rock *are* they who, when they have heard, receive the word with joy; and these have no root, who for a while believe, and in time of temptation fall away.

14 And that which fell among the thorns, these are they that have heard, and as they go on their way they are choked with cares and riches and pleasures of *this* life, and bring no fruit to perfection.

15 And that in the good ground, these are such as in an honest and good heart, having heard the word, hold it fast, and bring forth fruit with [818]patience.

16 And no man, when he hath lighted a lamp, covereth it with a vessel, or putteth it under a bed; but putteth it on a stand, that they that enter in may see the light.

17 For nothing is hid, that shall not be made manifest; nor *anything* secret, that shall not be known and come to light.

18 Take heed therefore how ye hear: for whosoever hath, to him shall be given; and whosoever hath not, from him shall be taken away even that which he [819]thinketh he hath.

19 And there came to him his mother and brethren, and they could not come at him for the crowd.

20 And it was told him, Thy mother and thy brethren stand without, desiring to see thee.

21 But he answered and said unto them, My mother and my brethren are these that hear the word of God, and do it.

22 Now it came to pass on one of those days, that he entered into a boat, himself and his disciples; and he said unto them, Let us go over unto the other side of the lake: and they launched forth.

23 But as they sailed he fell asleep: and there came down a storm of wind on the lake; and they were filling *with water*, and were in jeopardy.

---

[818] *Or, stedfastness*
[819] *Or, seemeth to have*

24 And they came to him, and awoke him, saying, Master, master, we perish. And he awoke, and rebuked the wind and the raging of the water: and they ceased, and there was a calm.

25 And he said unto them, Where is your faith? And being afraid they marvelled, saying one to another, Who then is this, that he commandeth even the winds and the water, and they obey him?

26 And they arrived at the country of the [820]Gerasenes, which is over against Galilee.

27 And when he was come forth upon the land, there met him a certain man out of the city, who had demons; and for a long time he had worn no clothes, and abode not in *any* house, but in the tombs.

28 And when he saw Jesus, he cried out, and fell down before him, and with a loud voice said, What have I to do with thee, Jesus, thou Son of the Most High God? I beseech thee, torment me not.

29 For he was commanding the unclean spirit to come out from the man. For [821]oftentimes it had seized him: and he was kept under guard, and bound with chains and fetters; and breaking the bands asunder, he was driven of the demon into the deserts.

30 And Jesus asked him, What is thy name? And he said, Legion; for many demons were entered into him.

31 And they entreated him that he would not command them to depart into the abyss.

32 Now there was there a herd of many swine feeding on the mountain: and they entreated him that he would give them leave to enter into them. And he gave them leave.

33 And the demons came out from the man, and entered into the swine: and the herd rushed down the steep into the lake, and were drowned.

34 And when they that fed them saw what had come to pass, they fled, and told it in the city and in the country.

35 And they went out to see what had come to pass; and they came to Jesus, and found the man, from whom the demons were gone out, sitting, clothed and in his right mind, at the feet of Jesus: and they were afraid.

---

[820] *Many ancient authorities read Gergesenes others Gadarenes: and so in verse 37*
[821] *Or, of a long time*

36 And they that saw it told them how he that was possessed with demons was [822]made whole.

37 And all the people of the country of the Gerasenes round about asked him to depart from them; for they were holden with great fear: and he entered into a boat, and returned.

38 But the man from whom the demons were gone out prayed him that he might be with him: but he sent him away, saying,

39 Return to thy house, and declare how great things God hath done for thee. And he went his way, publishing throughout the whole city how great things Jesus had done for him.

40 And as Jesus returned, the multitude welcomed him; for they were all waiting for him.

41 And behold, there came a man named Jairus, and he was a ruler of the synagogue: and he fell down at Jesus' feet, and besought him to come into his house;

42 for he had an only daughter, about twelve years of age, and she was dying. But as he went the multitudes thronged him.

43 And a woman having an issue of blood twelve years, who [823]had spent all her living upon physicians, and could not be healed of any,

44 came behind him, and touched the border of his garment: and immediately the issue of her blood stanched.

45 And Jesus said, Who is it that touched me? And when all denied, Peter said, [824]and they that were with him, Master, the multitudes press thee and crush *thee*.

46 But Jesus said, Some one did touch me; for I perceived that power had gone forth from me.

47 And when the woman saw that she was not hid, she came trembling, and falling down before him declared in the presence of all the people for what cause she touched him, and how she was healed immediately.

---

[822] *Or, saved*
[823] *Some ancient authorities omit* had spent all her living upon physicians, and.
[824] *Some ancient authorities omit* and they that were with him.

48 And he said unto her, Daughter, thy faith hath [825]made thee whole; go in peace.

49 While he yet spake, there cometh one from the ruler of the synagogue's *house*, saying, Thy daughter is dead; trouble not the Teacher.

50 But Jesus hearing it, answered him, Fear not: only believe, and she shall be [826]made whole.

51 And when he came to the house, he suffered not any man to enter in with him, save Peter, and John, and James, and the father of the maiden and her mother.

52 And all were weeping, and bewailing her: but he said, Weep not; for she is not dead, but sleepeth.

53 And they laughed him to scorn, knowing that she was dead.

54 But he, taking her by the hand, called, saying, Maiden, arise.

55 And her spirit returned, and she rose up immediately: and he commanded that *something* be given her to eat.

56 And her parents were amazed: but he charged them to tell no man what had been done.

Chapter 9

1 And he called the twelve together, and gave them power and authority over all demons, and to cure diseases.

2 And he sent them forth to preach the kingdom of God, and to heal [827]the sick.

3 And he said unto them, Take nothing for your journey, neither staff, nor wallet, nor bread, nor money; neither have two coats.

4 And into whatsoever house ye enter, there abide, and thence depart.

5 And as many as receive you not, when ye depart from that city, shake off the dust from your feet for a testimony against them.

6 And they departed, and went throughout the villages, preaching the [828]gospel, and healing everywhere.

---

[825] *Or, saved thee*
[826] *Or, saved*
[827] *Some ancient authorities omit the sick.*
[828] *Or, good tidings*

7 Now Herod the tetrarch heard of all that was done: and he was much perplexed, because that it was said by some, that John was risen from the dead;

8 and by some, that Elijah had appeared; and by others, that one of the old prophets was risen again.

9 And Herod said, John I beheaded: but who is this, about whom I hear such things? And he sought to see him.

10 And the apostles, when they were returned, declared unto him what things they had done. And he took them, and withdrew apart to a city called Bethsaida.

11 But the multitudes perceiving it followed him: and he welcomed them, and spake to them of the kingdom of God, and them that had need of healing he cured.

12 And the day began to wear away; and the twelve came, and said unto him, Send the multitude away, that they may go into the villages and country round about, and lodge, and get provisions: for we are here in a desert place.

13 But he said unto them, Give ye them to eat. And they said, We have no more than five loaves and two fishes; except we should go and buy food for all this people.

14 For they were about five thousand men. And he said unto his disciples, Make them [829] sit down in companies, about fifty each.

15 And they did so, and made them all sit down.

16 And he took the five loaves and the two fishes, and looking up to heaven, he blessed them, and brake; and gave to the disciples to set before the multitude.

17 And they ate, and were all filled: and there was taken up that which remained over to them of broken pieces, twelve baskets.

18 And it came to pass, as he was praying apart, the disciples were with him: and he asked them, saying, Who do the multitudes say that I am?

19 And they answering said, John the Baptist; but others *say*, Elijah; and others, that one of the old prophets is risen again.

---

[829] *Greek recline.*

20 And he said unto them, But who say ye that I am? And Peter answering said, The Christ of God.

21 But he charged them, and commanded *them* to tell this to no man;

22 saying, The Son of man must suffer many things, and be rejected of the elders and chief priests and scribes, and be killed, and the third day be raised up.

23 And he said unto all, If any man would come after me, let him deny himself, and take up his cross daily, and follow me.

24 For whosoever would save his life shall lose it; but whosoever shall lose his life for my sake, the same shall save it.

25 For what is a man profited, if he gain the whole world, and lose or forfeit his own self?

26 For whosoever shall be ashamed of me and of my words, of him shall the Son of man be ashamed, when he cometh in his own glory, and *the glory* of the Father, and of the holy angels.

27 But I tell you of a truth, There are some of them that stand here, who shall in no wise taste of death, till they see the kingdom of God.

28 And it came to pass about eight days after these sayings, that he took with him Peter and John and James, and went up into the mountain to pray.

29 And as he was praying, the fashion of his countenance was altered, and his raiment *became* white *and* dazzling.

30 And behold, there talked with him two men, who were Moses and Elijah;

31 who appeared in glory, and spake of his [830]decease which he was about to accomplish at Jerusalem.

32 Now Peter and they that were with him were heavy with sleep: but [831]when they were fully awake, they saw his glory, and the two men that stood with him.

33 And it came to pass, as they were parting from him, Peter said unto Jesus, Master, it is good for us to be here: and let us make three

---

[830]*Or, departure*
[831]*Or, having remained awake*

[832]tabernacles; one for thee, and one for Moses, and one for Elijah: not knowing what he said.

34 And while he said these things, there came a cloud, and overshadowed them: and they feared as they entered into the cloud.

35 And a voice came out of the cloud, saying, This is [833]my Son, my chosen: hear ye him.

36 And when the voice [834]came, Jesus was found alone. And they held their peace, and told no man in those days any of the things which they had seen.

37 And it came to pass, on the next day, when they were come down from the mountain, a great multitude met him.

38 And behold, a man from the multitude cried, saying, Teacher, I beseech thee to look upon my son; for he is mine only child:

39 and behold, a spirit taketh him, and he suddenly crieth out; and it [835]teareth him that he foameth, and it hardly departeth from him, bruising him sorely.

40 And I besought thy disciples to cast it out; and they could not.

41 And Jesus answered and said, O faithless and perverse generation, how long shall I be with you, and bear with you? bring hither thy son.

42 And as he was yet a coming, the demon [836]dashed him down, and [837]tare *him* grievously. But Jesus rebuked the unclean spirit, and healed the boy, and gave him back to his father.

43 And they were all astonished at the majesty of God.

But while all were marvelling at all the things which he did, he said unto his disciples,

44 Let these words sink into your ears: for the Son of man shall be [838]delivered up into the hands of men.

---

[832] *Or, booths*
[833] *Many ancient authorities read my beloved Son. See Mt. 17:5; Mk. 9:7.*
[834] *Or, was past*
[835] *Or, convulseth*
[836] *Or, rent him*
[837] *Or, convulsed*
[838] *Or, betrayed*

45 But they understood not this saying, and it was concealed from them, that they should not perceive it; and they were afraid to ask him about this saying.

46 And there arose a [839]reasoning among them, which of them was the [840]greatest.

47 But when Jesus saw the [841]reasoning of their heart, he took a little child, and set him by his side,

48 and said unto them, Whosoever shall receive this little child in my name receiveth me: and whosoever shall receive me receiveth him that sent me: for he that is [842]least among you all, the same is great.

49 And John answered and said, Master, we saw one casting out demons in thy name; and we forbade him, because he followeth not with us.

50 But Jesus said unto him, Forbid *him* not: for he that is not against you is for you.

51 And it came to pass, when the days [843]were well-nigh come that he should be received up, he stedfastly set his face to go to Jerusalem,

52 and sent messengers before his face: and they went, and entered into a village of the Samaritans, to make ready for him.

53 And they did not receive him, because his face was *as though he were* going to Jerusalem.

54 And when his disciples James and John saw *this*, they said, Lord, wilt thou that we bid fire to come down from heaven, and consume them[844]?

55 But he turned, and rebuked them[845].

56 And they went to another village.

57 And as they went on the way, a certain man said unto him, I will follow thee whithersoever thou goest.

---

[839] *Or, questioning*
[840] *Greek greater.*
[841] *Or, questioning*
[842] *Greek lesser.*
[843] *Greek were being fulfilled.*
[844] *Many ancient authorities add even as Elijah did. Compare 2 Kin. 1:10–12.*
[845] *Some ancient authorities add and said, Ye know not what manner of spirit ye are of. Some, but fewer, add also For the Son of man came not to destroy men's lives but to save them. Compare 19:10; Jn. 3:17; 12:47.*

58 And Jesus said unto him, The foxes have holes, and the birds of the heaven *have* [846]nests; but the Son of man hath not where to lay his head.

59 And he said unto another, Follow me. But he said, Lord, suffer me first to go and bury my father.

60 But he said unto him, Leave the dead to bury their own dead; but go thou and publish abroad the kingdom of God.

61 And another also said, I will follow thee, Lord; but first suffer me to bid farewell to them that are at my house.

62 But Jesus said unto him, No man, having put his hand to the plow, and looking back, is fit for the kingdom of God.

Chapter 10

1 Now after these things the Lord appointed seventy [847]others, and sent them two and two before his face into every city and place, whither he himself was about to come.

2 And he said unto them, The harvest indeed is plenteous, but the laborers are few: pray ye therefore the Lord of the harvest, that he send forth laborers into his harvest.

3 Go your ways; behold, I send you forth as lambs in the midst of wolves.

4 Carry no purse, no wallet, no shoes; and salute no man on the way.

5 And into whatsoever house ye shall [848]enter, first say, Peace *be* to this house.

6 And if a son of peace be there, your peace shall rest upon [849]him: but if not, it shall turn to you again.

7 And in that same house remain, eating and drinking such things as they give: for the laborer is worthy of his hire. Go not from house to house.

8 And into whatsoever city ye enter, and they receive you, eat such things as are set before you:

---

[846] *Greek lodging-places.*
[847] *Many ancient authorities add and two: and so in verse 17*
[848] *Or, enter first, say*
[849] *Or, it*

9 and heal the sick that are therein, and say unto them, The kingdom of God is come nigh unto you.

10 But into whatsoever city ye shall enter, and they receive you not, go out into the streets thereof and say,

11 Even the dust from your city, that cleaveth to our feet, we wipe off against you: nevertheless know this, that the kingdom of God is come nigh.

12 I say unto you, It shall be more tolerable in that day for Sodom, than for that city.

13 Woe unto thee, Chorazin! woe unto thee, Bethsaida! for if the [850]mighty works had been done in Tyre and Sidon, which were done in you, they would have repented long ago, sitting in sackcloth and ashes.

14 But it shall be more tolerable for Tyre and Sidon in the judgment, than for you.

15 And thou, Capernaum, shalt thou be exalted unto heaven? thou shalt be brought down unto Hades.

16 He that heareth you heareth me; and he that rejecteth you rejecteth me; and he that rejecteth me rejecteth him that sent me.

17 And the seventy returned with joy, saying, Lord, even the demons are subject unto us in thy name.

18 And he said unto them, I beheld Satan fallen as lightning from heaven.

19 Behold, I have given you authority to tread upon serpents and scorpions, and over all the power of the enemy: and nothing shall in any wise hurt you.

20 Nevertheless in this rejoice not, that the spirits are subject unto you; but rejoice that your names are written in heaven.

21 In that same hour he rejoiced [851]in the Holy Spirit, and said, I [852]thank thee, O Father, Lord of heaven and earth, that thou didst hide these things from the wise and understanding, and didst reveal them unto babes: yea, Father; [853]for so it was well-pleasing in thy sight.

---

[850] *Greek powers.*
[851] *Or, by*
[852] *Or, praise*
[853] *Or, that*

22 All things have been delivered unto me of my Father: and no one knoweth who the Son is, save the Father; and who the Father is, save the Son, and he to whomsoever the Son willeth to reveal *him*.

23 And turning to the disciples, he said privately, Blessed *are* the eyes which see the things that ye see:

24 for I say unto you, that many prophets and kings desired to see the things which ye see, and saw them not; and to hear the things which ye hear, and heard them not.

25 And behold, a certain lawyer stood up and made trial of him, saying, Teacher, what shall I do to inherit eternal life?

26 And he said unto him, What is written in the law? how readest thou?

27 And he answering said, [854]'Thou shalt love the Lord thy God [855]with all thy heart, and with all thy soul, and with all thy strength, and with all thy mind; [856]and thy neighbor as thyself.

28 And he said unto him, Thou hast answered right: this do, and thou shalt live.

29 But he, desiring to justify himself, said unto Jesus, And who is my neighbor?

30 Jesus made answer and said, A certain man was going down from Jerusalem to Jericho; and he fell among robbers, who both stripped him and beat him, and departed, leaving him half dead.

31 And by chance a certain priest was going down that way: and when he saw him, he passed by on the other side.

32 And in like manner a Levite also, when he came to the place, and saw him, passed by on the other side.

33 But a certain Samaritan, as he journeyed, came where he was: and when he saw him, he was moved with compassion,

34 and came to him, and bound up his wounds, pouring on *them* oil and wine; and he set him on his own beast, and brought him to an inn, and took care of him.

---

[854] *Dt. 6:5.*
[855] *Greek from.*
[856] *Lev. 19:18.*

35 And on the morrow he took out two [857]shillings, and gave them to the host, and said, Take care of him; and whatsoever thou spendest more, I, when I come back again, will repay thee.

36 Which of these three, thinkest thou, proved neighbor unto him that fell among the robbers?

37 And he said, He that showed mercy on him. And Jesus said unto him, Go, and do thou likewise.

38 Now as they went on their way, he entered into a certain village: and a certain woman named Martha received him into her house.

39 And she had a sister called Mary, who also sat at the Lord's feet, and heard his word.

40 But Martha was [858]cumbered about much serving; and she came up to him, and said, Lord, dost thou not care that my sister did leave me to serve alone? bid her therefore that she help me.

41 But the Lord answered and said unto her, [859]Martha, Martha, thou art anxious and troubled about many things:

42 [860]but one thing is needful: for Mary hath chosen the good part, which shall not be taken away from her.

Chapter 11

1 And it came to pass, as he was praying in a certain place, that when he ceased, one of his disciples said unto him, Lord, teach us to pray, even as John also taught his disciples.

2 And he said unto them, When ye pray, say, [861]Father, Hallowed be thy name. Thy kingdom come. [862]

3 Give us day by day [863]our daily bread.

4 And forgive us our sins; for we ourselves also forgive every one that is indebted to us. And bring us not into temptation[864].

---

[857] *See marginal note on 7:41.*
[858] *Greek distracted.*
[859] *A few ancient authorities read Martha, Martha, thou art troubled; Mary hath chosen etc.*
[860] *Many ancient authorities read but few things are needful, or one.*
[861] *Many ancient authorities read Our Father, who art in heaven. See Mt. 6:9.*
[862] *Many ancient authorities add Thy will be done, as in heaven, so on earth. See Mt. 6:10.*
[863] *Greek our bread for the coming day. Or, our needful bread: as in Mt. 6:11.*
[864] *Many ancient authorities add but deliver us from the evil one (or, from evil). See Mt. 6:13.*

5 And he said unto them, Which of you shall have a friend, and shall go unto him at midnight, and say to him, Friend, lend me three loaves;

6 for a friend of mine is come to me from a journey, and I have nothing to set before him;

7 and he from within shall answer and say, Trouble me not: the door is now shut, and my children are with me in bed; I cannot rise and give thee?

8 I say unto you, Though he will not rise and give him because he is his friend, yet because of his importunity he will arise and give him [865]as many as he needeth.

9 And I say unto you, Ask, and it shall be given you; seek, and ye shall find; knock, and it shall be opened unto you.

10 For every one that asketh receiveth; and he that seeketh findeth; and to him that knocketh it shall be opened.

11 And of which of you that is a father shall his son ask [866]a loaf, and he give him a stone? or a fish, and he for a fish give him a serpent?

12 Or *if* he shall ask an egg, will he give him a scorpion?

13 If ye then, being evil, know how to give good gifts unto your children, how much more shall *your* heavenly Father give the Holy Spirit to them that ask him?

14 And he was casting out a demon *that was* dumb. And it came to pass, when the demon was gone out, the dumb man spake; and the multitudes marvelled.

15 But some of them said, [867]By [868]Beelzebub the prince of the demons casteth he out demons.

16 And others, trying *him*, sought of him a sign from heaven.

17 But he, knowing their thoughts, said unto them, Every kingdom divided against itself is brought to desolation; [869]and a house *divided* against a house falleth.

---

[865] *Or, whatsoever things*
[866] *Some ancient authorities omit a loaf, and he give him a stone? or.*
[867] *Or, In*
[868] *Greek Beelzebul.*
[869] *Or, and house falleth upon house*

18 And if Satan also is divided against himself, how shall his kingdom stand? because ye say that I cast out demons [870]by [871]Beelzebub.

19 And if I [872]by [873]Beelzebub cast out demons, by whom do your sons cast them out? therefore shall they be your judges.

20 But if I by the finger of God cast out demons, then is the kingdom of God come upon you.

21 When the strong *man* fully armed guardeth his own court, his goods are in peace:

22 but when a stronger than he shall come upon him, and overcome him, he taketh from him his whole armor wherein he trusted, and divideth his spoils.

23 He that is not with me is against me; and he that gathereth not with me scattereth.

24 The unclean spirit when [874]he is gone out of the man, passeth through waterless places, seeking rest, and finding none, he saith, I will turn back unto my house whence I came out.

25 And when [875]he is come, [876]he findeth it swept and garnished.

26 Then goeth [877]he, and taketh *to him* seven other spirits more evil than [878]himself; and they enter in and dwell there: and the last state of that man becometh worse than the first.

27 And it came to pass, as he said these things, a certain woman out of the multitude lifted up her voice, and said unto him, Blessed is the womb that bare thee, and the breasts which thou didst suck.

28 But he said, Yea rather, blessed are they that hear the word of God, and keep it.

29 And when the multitudes were gathering together unto him, he began to say, This generation is an evil generation: it seeketh after a sign; and there shall no sign be given to it but the sign of Jonah.

---

[870] *Or, In*
[871] *Greek Beelzebul.*
[872] *Or, In*
[873] *Greek Beelzebul.*
[874] *Or, it*
[875] *Or, it*
[876] *Or, it*
[877] *Or, it*
[878] *Or, itself*

30 For even as Jonah became a sign unto the Ninevites, so shall also the Son of man be to this generation.

31 The queen of the south shall rise up in the judgment with the men of this generation, and shall condemn them: for she came from the ends of the earth to hear the wisdom of Solomon; and behold, [879]a greater than Solomon is here.

32 The men of Nineveh shall stand up in the judgment with this generation, and shall condemn it: for they repented at the preaching of Jonah; and behold, [880]a greater than Jonah is here.

33 No man, when he hath lighted a lamp, putteth it in a cellar, neither under the bushel, but on the stand, that they which enter in may see the light.

34 The lamp of thy body is thine eye: when thine eye is single, thy whole body also is full of light; but when it is evil, thy body also is full of darkness.

35 Look therefore whether the light that is in thee be not darkness.

36 If therefore thy whole body be full of light, having no part dark, it shall be wholly full of light, as when the lamp with its bright shining doth give thee light.

37 Now as he spake, a Pharisee asketh him to [881]dine with him: and he went in, and sat down to meat.

38 And when the Pharisee saw it, he marvelled that he had not first bathed himself before [882]dinner.

39 And the Lord said unto him, Now ye the Pharisees cleanse the outside of the cup and of the platter; but your inward part is full of extortion and wickedness.

40 Ye foolish ones, did not he that made the outside make the inside also?

41 But give for alms those things which [883]are within; and behold, all things are clean unto you.

---

[879] *Greek more than.*
[880] *Greek more than.*
[881] *Greek breakfast.*
[882] *Greek breakfast.*
[883] *Or, ye can*

42 But woe unto you Pharisees! for ye tithe mint and rue and every herb, and pass over justice and the love of God: but these ought ye to have done, and not to leave the other undone.

43 Woe unto you Pharisees! for ye love the chief seats in the synagogues, and the salutations in the marketplaces.

44 Woe unto you! for ye are as the tombs which appear not, and the men that walk over *them* know it not.

45 And one of the lawyers answering saith unto him, Teacher, in saying this thou reproachest us also.

46 And he said, Woe unto you lawyers also! for ye load men with burdens grievous to be borne, and ye yourselves touch not the burdens with one of your fingers.

47 Woe unto you! for ye build the tombs of the prophets, and your fathers killed them.

48 So ye are witnesses and consent unto the works of your fathers: for they killed them, and ye build *their tombs*.

49 Therefore also said the wisdom of God, I will send unto them prophets and apostles; and *some* of them they shall kill and persecute;

50 that the blood of all the prophets, which was shed from the foundation of the world, may be required of this generation;

51 from the blood of Abel unto the blood of Zachariah, who perished between the altar and the [884]sanctuary: yea, I say unto you, it shall be required of this generation.

52 Woe unto you lawyers! for ye took away the key of knowledge: ye entered not in yourselves, and them that were entering in ye hindered.

53 And when he was come out from thence, the scribes and the Pharisees began to [885]press upon *him* vehemently, and to provoke him to speak of [886]many things;

54 laying wait for him, to catch something out of his mouth.

---

[884] *Greek house.*
[885] *Or, set themselves vehemently against him*
[886] *Or, more*

Chapter 12

1 In the mean time, when [887]the many thousands of the multitude were gathered together, insomuch that they trod one upon another, he began to [888]say unto his disciples first of all, Beware ye of the leaven of the Pharisees, which is hypocrisy.

2 But there is nothing covered up, that shall not be revealed; and hid, that shall not be known.

3 Wherefore whatsoever ye have said in the darkness shall be heard in the light; and what ye have spoken in the ear in the inner chambers shall be proclaimed upon the housetops.

4 And I say unto you my friends, Be not afraid of them that kill the body, and after that have no more that they can do.

5 But I will warn you whom ye shall fear: Fear him, who after he hath killed hath [889]power to cast into [890]hell; yea, I say unto you, Fear him.

6 Are not five sparrows sold for two pence? and not one of them is forgotten in the sight of God.

7 But the very hairs of your head are all numbered. Fear not: ye are of more value than many sparrows.

8 And I say unto you, Every one who shall confess [891]me before men, [892]him shall the Son of man also confess before the angels of God:

9 but he that denieth me in the presence of men shall be denied in the presence of the angels of God.

10 And every one who shall speak a word against the Son of man, it shall be forgiven him: but unto him that blasphemeth against the Holy Spirit it shall not be forgiven.

11 And when they bring you before the synagogues, and the rulers, and the authorities, be not anxious how or what ye shall answer, or what ye shall say:

---

[887] *Greek the myriads of.*
[888] *Or, say unto his disciples, First of all beware ye*
[889] *Or, authority*
[890] *Greek Gehenna.*
[891] *Greek in me.*
[892] *Greek in him.*

12 for the Holy Spirit shall teach you in that very hour what ye ought to say.

13 And one out of the multitude said unto him, Teacher, bid my brother divide the inheritance with me.

14 But he said unto him, Man, who made me a judge or a divider over you?

15 And he said unto them, Take heed, and keep yourselves from all covetousness: [893] for a man's life consisteth not in the abundance of the things which he possesseth.

16 And he spake a parable unto them, saying, The ground of a certain rich man brought forth plentifully:

17 and he reasoned within himself, saying, What shall I do, because I have not where to bestow my fruits?

18 And he said, This will I do: I will pull down my barns, and build greater; and there will I bestow all my grain and my goods.

19 And I will say to my [894]soul, [895]Soul, thou hast much goods laid up for many years; take thine ease, eat, drink, be merry.

20 But God said unto him, Thou foolish one, this night [896]is thy [897]soul required of thee; and the things which thou hast prepared, whose shall they be?

21 So is he that layeth up treasure for himself, and is not rich toward God.

22 And he said unto his disciples, Therefore I say unto you, Be not anxious for *your* [898]life, what ye shall eat; nor yet for your body, what ye shall put on.

23 For the [899]life is more than the food, and the body than the raiment.

24 Consider the ravens, that they sow not, neither reap; which have no store-chamber nor barn; and God feedeth them: of how much more value are ye than the birds!

---

[893] *Or, for even in a man's abundance his life is not from the things which he possesseth*
[894] *Or, life*
[895] *Or, life*
[896] *Greek they require thy soul.*
[897] *Or, life*
[898] *Or, soul*
[899] *Or, soul*

25 And which of you by being anxious can add a cubit unto [900]the measure of his life?

26 If then ye are not able to do even that which is least, why are ye anxious concerning the rest?

27 Consider the lilies, how they grow: they toil not, neither do they spin; yet I say unto you, Even Solomon in all his glory was not arrayed like one of these.

28 But if God doth so clothe the grass in the field, which to-day is, and to-morrow is cast into the oven; how much more *shall he clothe* you, O ye of little faith?

29 And seek not ye what ye shall eat, and what ye shall drink, neither be ye of doubtful mind.

30 For all these things do the nations of the world seek after: but your Father knoweth that ye have need of these things.

31 Yet seek ye [901]his kingdom, and these things shall be added unto you.

32 Fear not, little flock; for it is your Father's good pleasure to give you the kingdom.

33 Sell that which ye have, and give alms; make for yourselves purses which wax not old, a treasure in the heavens that faileth not, where no thief draweth near, neither moth destroyeth.

34 For where your treasure is, there will your heart be also.

35 Let your loins be girded about, and your lamps burning;

36 and be ye yourselves like unto men looking for their lord, when he shall return from the marriage feast; that, when he cometh and knocketh, they may straightway open unto him.

37 Blessed are those [902]servants, whom the lord when he cometh shall find watching: verily I say unto you, that he shall gird himself, and make them sit down to meat, and shall come and serve them.

38 And if he shall come in the second watch, and if in the third, and find *them* so, blessed are those *servants*.

---

[900] *Or, his stature*
[901] *Many ancient authorities read the kingdom of God.*
[902] *Greek bondservants.*

39 [903]But know this, that if the master of the house had known in what hour the thief was coming, he would have watched, and not have left his house to be [904]broken through.

40 Be ye also ready: for in an hour that ye think not the Son of man cometh.

41 And Peter said, Lord, speakest thou this parable unto us, or even unto all?

42 And the Lord said, Who then is [905]the faithful and wise steward, whom his lord shall set over his household, to give them their portion of food in due season?

43 Blessed is that [906]servant, whom his lord when he cometh shall find so doing.

44 Of a truth I say unto you, that he will set him over all that he hath.

45 But if that [907]servant shall say in his heart, My lord delayeth his coming; and shall begin to beat the menservants and the maidservants, and to eat and drink, and to be drunken;

46 the lord of that [908]servant shall come in a day when he expecteth not, and in an hour when he knoweth not, and shall [909]cut him asunder, and appoint his portion with the unfaithful.

47 And that [910]servant, who knew his lord's will, and made not ready, nor did according to his will, shall be beaten with many *stripes*;

48 but he that knew not, and did things worthy of stripes, shall be beaten with few *stripes*. And to whomsoever much is given, of him shall much be required: and to whom they commit much, of him will they ask the more.

49 I came to cast fire upon the earth; and [911]what do I desire, if it is already kindled?

---

[903] *Or, But this ye know*
[904] *Greek digged through.*
[905] *Or, the faithful steward, the wise man whom etc.*
[906] *Greek bondservant.*
[907] *Greek bondservant.*
[908] *Greek bondservant.*
[909] *Or, severely scourge him*
[910] *Greek bondservant.*
[911] *Or, how would I that it were already kindled!*

50 But I have a baptism to be baptized with; and how am I straitened till it be accomplished!

51 Think ye that I am come to give peace in the earth? I tell you, Nay; but rather division:

52 for there shall be from henceforth five in one house divided, three against two, and two against three.

53 They shall be divided, father against son, and son against father; mother against daughter, and daughter against her mother; mother in law against her daughter in law, and daughter in law against her mother in law.

54 And he said to the multitudes also, When ye see a cloud rising in the west, straightway ye say, There cometh a shower; and so it cometh to pass.

55 And when *ye see* a south wind blowing, ye say, There will be a [912]scorching heat; and it cometh to pass.

56 Ye hypocrites, ye know how to [913]interpret the face of the earth and the heaven; but how is it that ye know not how to [914]interpret this time?

57 And why even of yourselves judge ye not what is right?

58 For as thou art going with thine adversary before the magistrate, on the way give diligence to be quit of him; lest haply he drag thee unto the judge, and the judge shall deliver thee to the [915]officer, and the [916]officer shall cast thee into prison.

59 I say unto thee, Thou shalt by no means come out thence, till thou have paid the very last mite.

---

[912] *Or, hot wind*
[913] *Greek prove.*
[914] *Greek prove.*
[915] *Greek exactor.*
[916] *Greek exactor.*

Chapter 13

1 Now there were some present at that very season who told him of the Galilaeans, whose blood Pilate had mingled with their sacrifices.

2 And he answered and said unto them, Think ye that these Galilaeans were sinners above all the Galilaeans, because they have suffered these things?

3 I tell you, Nay: but, except ye repent, ye shall all in like manner perish.

4 Or those eighteen, upon whom the tower in Siloam fell, and killed them, think ye that they were [917]offenders above all the men that dwell in Jerusalem?

5 I tell you, Nay: but, except ye repent, ye shall all likewise perish.

6 And he spake this parable; A certain man had a fig tree planted in his vineyard; and he came seeking fruit thereon, and found none.

7 And he said unto the vinedresser, Behold, these three years I come seeking fruit on this fig tree, and find none: cut it down; why doth it also cumber the ground?

8 And he answering saith unto him, Lord, let it alone this year also, till I shall dig about it, and dung it:

9 and if it bear fruit thenceforth, *well*; but if not, thou shalt cut it down.

10 And he was teaching in one of the synagogues on the sabbath day.

11 And behold, a woman that had a spirit of infirmity eighteen years; and she was bowed together, and could in no wise lift herself up.

12 And when Jesus saw her, he called her, and said to her, Woman, thou art loosed from thine infirmity.

13 And he laid his hands upon her: and immediately she was made straight, and glorified God.

14 And the ruler of the synagogue, being moved with indignation because Jesus had healed on the sabbath, answered and said to the multitude, There are six days in which men ought to work: in them therefore come and be healed, and not on the day of the sabbath.

---

[917] *Greek debtors.*

15 But the Lord answered him, and said, Ye hypocrites, doth not each one of you on the sabbath loose his ox or his ass from the [918]stall, and lead him away to watering?

16 And ought not this woman, being a daughter of Abraham, whom Satan had bound, lo, *these* eighteen years, to have been loosed from this bond on the day of the sabbath?

17 And as he said these things, all his adversaries were put to shame: and all the multitude rejoiced for all the glorious things that were done by him.

18 He said therefore, Unto what is the kingdom of God like? and whereunto shall I liken it?

19 It is like unto a grain of mustard seed, which a man took, and cast into his own garden; and it grew, and became a tree; and the birds of the heaven lodged in the branches thereof.

20 And again he said, Whereunto shall I liken the kingdom of God?

21 It is like unto leaven, which a woman took and hid in three [919]measures of meal, till it was all leavened.

22 And he went on his way through cities and villages, teaching, and journeying on unto Jerusalem.

23 And one said unto him, Lord, are they few that are saved? And he said unto them,

24 Strive to enter in by the narrow door: for many, I say unto you, shall seek to enter in, and shall not be [920]able.

25 When once the master of the house is risen up, and hath shut to the door, and ye begin to stand without, and to knock at the door, saying, Lord, open to us; and he shall answer and say to you, I know you not whence ye are;

26 then shall ye begin to say, We did eat and drink in thy presence, and thou didst teach in our streets;

27 and he shall say, I tell you, I know not whence ye are; depart from me, all ye workers of iniquity.

---

[918] *Greek manger.*
[919] *See marginal note on Mt. 13:33.*
[920] *Or, able, when once*

28 There shall be the weeping and the gnashing of teeth, when ye shall see Abraham, and Isaac, and Jacob, and all the prophets, in the kingdom of God, and yourselves cast forth without.

29 And they shall come from the east and west, and from the north and south, and shall [921]sit down in the kingdom of God.

30 And behold, there are last who shall be first, and there are first who shall be last.

31 In that very hour there came certain Pharisees, saying to him, Get thee out, and go hence: for Herod would fain kill thee.

32 And he said unto them, Go and say to that fox, Behold, I cast out demons and perform cures to-day and to-morrow, and the third *day* I [922]am perfected.

33 Nevertheless I must go on my way to-day and to-morrow and the *day* following: for it cannot be that a prophet perish out of Jerusalem.

34 O Jerusalem, Jerusalem, that killeth the prophets, and stoneth them that are sent unto her! how often would I have gathered thy children together, even as a hen *gathereth* her own brood under her wings, and ye would not!

35 Behold, your house is left unto you *desolate*: and I say unto you, Ye shall not see me, until ye shall say, Blessed *is* he that cometh in the name of the Lord.

Chapter 14

1 And it came to pass, when he went into the house of one of the rulers of the Pharisees on a sabbath to eat bread, that they were watching him.

2 And behold, there was before him a certain man that had the dropsy.

3 And Jesus answering spake unto the lawyers and Pharisees, saying, Is it lawful to heal on the sabbath, or not?

4 But they held their peace. And he took him, and healed him, and let him go.

5 And he said unto them, Which of you shall have [923]an ass or an ox fallen into a well, and will not straightway draw him up on a sabbath day?

---

[921] *Greek recline.*
[922] *Or, end my course*
[923] *Many ancient authorities read a son. See 13:15.*

LUKE 14

6 And they could not answer again unto these things.

7 And he spake a parable unto those that were bidden, when he marked how they chose out the chief seats; saying unto them,

8 When thou art bidden of any man to a marriage feast, [924]sit not down in the chief seat; lest haply a more honorable man than thou be bidden of him,

9 and he that bade thee and him shall come and say to thee, Give this man place; and then thou shalt begin with shame to take the lowest place.

10 But when thou art bidden, go and sit down in the lowest place; that when he that hath bidden thee cometh, he may say to thee, Friend, go up higher: then shalt thou have glory in the presence of all that [925]sit at meat with thee.[926]

11 For every one that exalteth himself shall be humbled; and he that humbleth himself shall be exalted.

12 And he said to him also that had bidden him, When thou makest a dinner or a supper, call not thy friends, nor thy brethren, nor thy kinsmen, nor rich neighbors; lest haply they also bid thee again, and a recompense be made thee.

13 But when thou makest a feast, bid the poor, the maimed, the lame, the blind:

14 and thou shalt be blessed; because they have not *wherewith* to recompense thee: for thou shalt be recompensed in the resurrection of the just.

15 And when one of them that [927]sat at meat with him heard these things, he said unto him, Blessed is he that shall eat bread in the kingdom of God.

16 But he said unto him, A certain man made a great supper; and he bade many:

---

[924]*Greek recline not.*

[925]*Greek recline. Compare 7:36, 37 margin.*

[926]**False Friend:** The KJV reads "then shalt thou have worship." In 1611, "worship" could mean respect for a human (like "Your Worship" in court). Today, it implies deity. The RV "glory" protects the reader from the error of worshipping men.

[927]*Greek reclined. Compare 7:36, 37 margin.*

17 and he sent forth his ⁹²⁸servant at supper time to say to them that were bidden, Come; for *all* things are now ready.

18 And they all with one *consent* began to make excuse. The first said unto him, I have bought a field, and I must needs go out and see it; I pray thee have me excused.

19 And another said, I have bought five yoke of oxen, and I go to prove them; I pray thee have me excused.

20 And another said, I have married a wife, and therefore I cannot come.

21 And the ⁹²⁹servant came, and told his lord these things. Then the master of the house being angry said to his ⁹³⁰servant, Go out quickly into the streets and lanes of the city, and bring in hither the poor and maimed and blind and lame.

22 And the ⁹³¹servant said, Lord, what thou didst command is done, and yet there is room.

23 And the lord said unto the ⁹³²servant, Go out into the highways and hedges, and constrain *them* to come in, that my house may be filled.

24 For I say unto you, that none of those men that were bidden shall taste of my supper.

25 Now there went with him great multitudes: and he turned, and said unto them,

26 If any man cometh unto me, and hateth not his own father, and mother, and wife, and children, and brethren, and sisters, yea, and his own life also, he cannot be my disciple.

27 Whosoever doth not bear his own cross, and come after me, cannot be my disciple.

28 For which of you, desiring to build a tower, doth not first sit down and count the cost, whether he have *wherewith* to complete it?

29 Lest haply, when he hath laid a foundation, and is not able to finish, all that behold begin to mock him,

30 saying, This man began to build, and was not able to finish.

---

⁹²⁸ *Greek bondservant.*
⁹²⁹ *Greek bondservant.*
⁹³⁰ *Greek bondservant.*
⁹³¹ *Greek bondservant.*
⁹³² *Greek bondservant.*

31 Or what king, as he goeth to encounter another king in war, will not sit down first and take counsel whether he is able with ten thousand to meet him that cometh against him with twenty thousand?

32 Or else, while the other is yet a great way off, he sendeth an ambassage, and asketh conditions of peace.

33 So therefore whosoever he be of you that renounceth not all that he hath, he cannot be my disciple.

34 Salt therefore is good: but if even the salt have lost its savor, wherewith shall it be seasoned?

35 It is fit neither for the land nor for the dunghill: *men* cast it out. He that hath ears to hear, let him hear.

Chapter 15

1 Now all the [933]publicans and sinners were drawing near unto him to hear him.

2 And both the Pharisees and the scribes murmured, saying, This man receiveth sinners, and eateth with them.

3 And he spake unto them this parable, saying,

4 What man of you, having a hundred sheep, and having lost one of them, doth not leave the ninety and nine in the wilderness, and go after that which is lost, until he find it?

5 And when he hath found it, he layeth it on his shoulders, rejoicing.

6 And when he cometh home, he calleth together his friends and his neighbors, saying unto them, Rejoice with me, for I have found my sheep which was lost.

7 I say unto you, that even so there shall be joy in heaven over one sinner that repenteth, *more* than over ninety and nine righteous persons, who need no repentance.

8 Or what woman having ten [934]pieces of silver, if she lose one piece, doth not light a lamp, and sweep the house, and seek diligently until she find it?

---

[933]*See marginal note on 3:12.*
[934]*Greek drachma, a coin worth about eight pence, or sixteen cents.*

9 And when she hath found it, she calleth together her friends and neighbors, saying, Rejoice with me, for I have found the piece which I had lost.

10 Even so, I say unto you, there is joy in the presence of the angels of God over one sinner that repenteth.

11 And he said, A certain man had two sons:

12 and the younger of them said to his father, Father, give me the portion of [935]*thy* substance that falleth to me. And he divided unto them his living.

13 And not many days after, the younger son gathered all together and took his journey into a far country; and there he wasted his substance with riotous living.

14 And when he had spent all, there arose a mighty famine in that country; and he began to be in want.

15 And he went and joined himself to one of the citizens of that country; and he sent him into his fields to feed swine.

16 And he would fain [936]have filled his belly with [937]the husks that the swine did eat: and no man gave unto him.

17 But when he came to himself he said, How many hired servants of my father's have bread enough and to spare, and I perish here with hunger!

18 I will arise and go to my father, and will say unto him, Father, I have sinned against heaven, and in thy sight:

19 I am no more worthy to be called thy son: make me as one of thy hired servants.

20 And he arose, and came to his father. But while he was yet afar off, his father saw him, and was moved with compassion, and ran, and fell on his neck, and [938]kissed him.

21 And the son said unto him, Father, I have sinned against heaven, and in thy sight: I am no more worthy to be called thy son[939].

---

[935] *Greek the.*
[936] *Many ancient authorities read have been filled.*
[937] *Greek the pods of the carob tree.*
[938] *Greek kissed him much. See 7:38, 45.*
[939] *Some ancient authorities add make me as one of thy hired servants. See verse 19.*

22 But the father said to his ⁹⁴⁰servants, Bring forth quickly the best robe, and put it on him; and put a ring on his hand, and shoes on his feet:

23 and bring the fatted calf, *and* kill it, and let us eat, and make merry:

24 for this my son was dead, and is alive again; he was lost, and is found. And they began to be merry.

25 Now his elder son was in the field: and as he came and drew nigh to the house, he heard music and dancing.

26 And he called to him one of the servants, and inquired what these things might be.

27 And he said unto him, Thy brother is come; and thy father hath killed the fatted calf, because he hath received him safe and sound.

28 But he was angry, and would not go in: and his father came out, and entreated him.

29 But he answered and said to his father, Lo, these many years do I serve thee, and I never transgressed a commandment of thine; and *yet* thou never gavest me a kid, that I might make merry with my friends:

30 but when this thy son came, who hath devoured thy living with harlots, thou killedst for him the fatted calf.

31 And he said unto him, ⁹⁴¹Son, thou art ever with me, and all that is mine is thine.

32 But it was meet to make merry and be glad: for this thy brother was dead, and is alive *again*; and *was* lost, and is found.

---

⁹⁴⁰ *Greek bondservants.*
⁹⁴¹ *Greek Child.*

Chapter 16

1 And he said also unto the disciples, There was a certain rich man, who had a steward; and the same was accused unto him that he was wasting his goods.

2 And he called him, and said unto him, What is this that I hear of thee? render the account of thy stewardship; for thou canst be no longer steward.

3 And the steward said within himself, What shall I do, seeing that my lord taketh away the stewardship from me? I have not strength to dig; to beg I am ashamed.

4 I am resolved what to do, that, when I am put out of the stewardship, they may receive me into their houses.

5 And calling to him each one of his lord's debtors, he said to the first, How much owest thou unto my lord?

6 And he said, A hundred [942]measures of oil. And he said unto him, Take thy [943]bond, and sit down quickly and write fifty.

7 Then said he to another, And how much owest thou? And he said, A hundred [944]measures of wheat. He saith unto him, Take thy [945]bond, and write fourscore.

8 And his lord commended [946]the unrighteous steward because he had done wisely: for the sons of this [947]world are for their own generation wiser than the sons of the light.

9 And I say unto you, Make to yourselves friends [948]by means of the mammon of unrighteousness; that, when it shall fail, they may receive you into the eternal tabernacles.

10 He that is faithful in a very little is faithful also in much: and he that is unrighteous in a very little is unrighteous also in much.

11 If therefore ye have not been faithful in the unrighteous mammon, who will commit to your trust the true *riches*?

---

[942] *Greek baths, the bath being a Hebrew measure. See Ezek. 45:10, 11, 14.*
[943] *Greek writings.*
[944] *Greek cors, the cor being a Hebrew measure. See Ezek. 45:14.*
[945] *Greek writings.*
[946] *Greek the steward of unrighteousness.*
[947] *Or, age*
[948] *Greek out of.*

12 And if ye have not been faithful in that which is another's, who will give you that which is ⁹⁴⁹your own?

13 No ⁹⁵⁰servant can serve two masters: for either he will hate the one, and love the other; or else he will hold to one, and despise the other. Ye cannot serve God and mammon.

14 And the Pharisees, who were lovers of money, heard all these things; and they scoffed at him.

15 And he said unto them, Ye are they that justify yourselves in the sight of men; but God knoweth your hearts: for that which is exalted among men is an abomination in the sight of God.

16 The law and the prophets *were* until John: from that time the ⁹⁵¹gospel of the kingdom of God is preached, and every man entereth violently into it.

17 But it is easier for heaven and earth to pass away, than for one tittle of the law to fall.

18 Every one that putteth away his wife, and marrieth another, committeth adultery: and he that marrieth one that is put away from a husband committeth adultery.

19 Now there was a certain rich man, and he was clothed in purple and fine linen, ⁹⁵²faring sumptuously every day:

20 and a certain beggar named Lazarus was laid at his gate, full of sores,

21 and desiring to be fed with the *crumbs* that fell from the rich man's table; yea, even the dogs came and licked his sores.

22 And it came to pass, that the beggar died, and that he was carried away by the angels into Abraham's bosom: and the rich man also died, and was buried.

23 And in Hades he lifted up his eyes, being in torments, and seeth Abraham afar off, and Lazarus in his bosom.

24 And he cried and said, Father Abraham, have mercy on me, and send Lazarus, that he may dip the tip of his finger in water, and cool my tongue; for I am in anguish in this flame.

---

⁹⁴⁹ *Some ancient authorities read our own.*
⁹⁵⁰ *Greek household-servant.*
⁹⁵¹ *Or, good tidings: compare 3:18.*
⁹⁵² *Or, living in mirth and splendor every day*

25 But Abraham said, [953]Son, remember that thou in thy lifetime receivedst thy good things, and Lazarus in like manner evil things: but now here he is comforted, and thou art in anguish.

26 And [954]besides all this, between us and you there is a great gulf fixed, that they that would pass from hence to you may not be able, and that none may cross over from thence to us.

27 And he said, I pray thee therefore, father, that thou wouldest send him to my father's house;

28 for I have five brethren; that he may testify unto them, lest they also come into this place of torment.

29 But Abraham saith, They have Moses and the prophets; let them hear them.

30 And he said, Nay, father Abraham: but if one go to them from the dead, they will repent.

31 And he said unto him, If they hear not Moses and the prophets, neither will they be persuaded, if one rise from the dead.

---

[953] *Greek Child.*
[954] *Or, in all these things*

Chapter 17

1 And he said unto his disciples, It is impossible but that occasions of stumbling should come; but woe unto him, through whom they come!

2 It were well for him if a millstone were hanged about his neck, and he were thrown into the sea, rather than that he should cause one of these little ones to stumble.

3 Take heed to yourselves: if thy brother sin, rebuke him; and if he repent, forgive him.

4 And if he sin against thee seven times in the day, and seven times turn again to thee, saying, I repent; thou shalt forgive him.

5 And the apostles said unto the Lord, Increase our faith.

6 And the Lord said, If ye had faith as a grain of mustard seed, ye would say unto this sycamine tree, Be thou rooted up, and be thou planted in the sea; and it would obey you.

7 But who is there of you, having a [955]servant plowing or keeping sheep, that will say unto him, when he is come in from the field, Come straightway and sit down to meat;

8 and will not rather say unto him, Make ready wherewith I may sup, and gird thyself, and serve me, till I have eaten and drunken; and afterward thou shalt eat and drink?

9 Doth he thank the [956]servant because he did the things that were commanded?

10 Even so ye also, when ye shall have done all the things that are commanded you, say, We are unprofitable [957]servants; we have done that which it was our duty to do.

11 And it came to pass, [958]as they were on the way to Jerusalem, that he was passing [959]along the borders of Samaria and Galilee.

12 And as he entered into a certain village, there met him ten men that were lepers, who stood afar off:

---
[955] *Greek bondservant.*
[956] *Greek bondservant.*
[957] *Greek bondservants.*
[958] *Or, as he was*
[959] *Or, through the midst of etc.*

13 and they lifted up their voices, saying, Jesus, Master, have mercy on us.

14 And when he saw them, he said unto them, Go and show yourselves unto the priests. And it came to pass, as they went, they were cleansed.

15 And one of them, when he saw that he was healed, turned back, with a loud voice glorifying God;

16 and he fell upon his face at his feet, giving him thanks: and he was a Samaritan.

17 And Jesus answering said, Were not the ten cleansed? but where are the nine?

18 [960]Were there none found that returned to give glory to God, save this [961]stranger?

19 And he said unto him, Arise, and go thy way: thy faith hath [962]made thee whole.

20 And being asked by the Pharisees, when the kingdom of God cometh, he answered them and said, The kingdom of God cometh not with observation:

21 neither shall they say, Lo, here! or, There! for lo, the kingdom of God is [963]within you.

22 And he said unto the disciples, The days will come, when ye shall desire to see one of the days of the Son of man, and ye shall not see it.

23 And they shall say to you, Lo, there! Lo, here! go not away, nor follow after *them*:

24 for as the lightning, when it lighteneth out of the one part under the heaven, shineth unto the other part under heaven; so shall the Son of man be [964]in his day.

25 But first must he suffer many things and be rejected of this generation.

26 And as it came to pass in the days of Noah, even so shall it be also in the days of the Son of man.

---

[960] *Or, There were none found . . . save this stranger.*
[961] *Or, alien*
[962] *Or, saved thee*
[963] *Or, in the midst of you*
[964] *Some ancient authorities omit in his day.*

27 They ate, they drank, they married, they were given in marriage, until the day that Noah entered into the ark, and the flood came, and destroyed them all.

28 Likewise even as it came to pass in the days of Lot; they ate, they drank, they bought, they sold, they planted, they builded;

29 but in the day that Lot went out from Sodom it rained fire and brimstone from heaven, and destroyed them all:

30 after the same manner shall it be in the day that the Son of man is revealed.

31 In that day, he that shall be on the housetop, and his goods in the house, let him not go down to take them away: and let him that is in the field likewise not return back.

32 Remember Lot's wife.

33 Whosoever shall seek to gain his life shall lose it: but whosoever shall lose *his life* shall [965]preserve it.

34 I say unto you, In that night there shall be two men on one bed; the one shall be taken, and the other shall be left.

35 There shall be two women grinding together; the one shall be taken, and the other shall be left.[966]

37 And they answering say unto him, Where, Lord? And he said unto them, Where the body *is*, thither will the [967]eagles also be gathered together.

Chapter 18

1 And he spake a parable unto them to the end that they ought always to pray, and not to faint;

2 saying, There was in a city a judge, who feared not God, and regarded not man:

3 and there was a widow in that city; and she came oft unto him, saying, [968]Avenge me of mine adversary.

---

[965] *Greek save it alive.*
[966] *Some ancient authorities add verse 36 There shall be two men in the field; the one shall be taken, and the other shall be left. Mt. 24:40.*
[967] *Or, vultures*
[968] *Or, Do me justice of: and so in verses 5, 7, 8.*

4 And he would not for a while: but afterward he said within himself, Though I fear not God, nor regard man;

5 yet because this widow troubleth me, I will avenge her, ⁹⁶⁹lest she ⁹⁷⁰wear me out by her continual coming.

6 And the Lord said, Hear what ⁹⁷¹the unrighteous judge saith.

7 And shall not God avenge his elect, that cry to him day and night, ⁹⁷²and *yet* he is longsuffering over them?

8 I say unto you, that he will avenge them speedily. Nevertheless, when the Son of man cometh, shall he find ⁹⁷³faith on the earth?

9 And he spake also this parable unto certain who trusted in themselves that they were righteous, and set ⁹⁷⁴all others at nought:

10 Two men went up into the temple to pray; the one a Pharisee, and the other a ⁹⁷⁵publican.

11 The Pharisee stood and prayed thus with himself, God, I thank thee, that I am not as the rest of men, extortioners, unjust, adulterers, or even as this ⁹⁷⁶publican.

12 I fast twice in the week; I give tithes of all that I get.

13 But the ⁹⁷⁷publican, standing afar off, would not lift up so much as his eyes unto heaven, but smote his breast, saying, God, ⁹⁷⁸be thou merciful to me ⁹⁷⁹a sinner.

14 I say unto you, This man went down to his house justified rather than the other: for every one that exalteth himself shall be humbled; but he that humbleth himself shall be exalted.

15 And they were bringing unto him also their babes, that he should touch them: but when the disciples saw it, they rebuked them.

---

⁹⁶⁹ *Or, lest at last by her coming she wear me out*
⁹⁷⁰ *Greek bruise.*
⁹⁷¹ *Greek the judge of unrighteousness.*
⁹⁷² *Or, and is he slow to punish on their behalf?*
⁹⁷³ *Or, the faith*
⁹⁷⁴ *Greek the rest.*
⁹⁷⁵ *See marginal note on 3:12.*
⁹⁷⁶ *See marginal note on 3:12.*
⁹⁷⁷ *See marginal note on 3:12.*
⁹⁷⁸ *Or, be thou propitiated*
⁹⁷⁹ *Or, the sinner*

16 But Jesus called them unto him, saying, Suffer the little children to come unto me, and forbid them not: for [980]to such belongeth the kingdom of God.

17 Verily I say unto you, Whosoever shall not receive the kingdom of God as a little child, he shall in no wise enter therein.

18 And a certain ruler asked him, saying, Good Teacher, what shall I do to inherit eternal life?

19 And Jesus said unto him, Why callest thou me good? none is good, save one, *even* God.

20 Thou knowest the commandments, [981]Do not commit adultery, Do not kill, Do not steal, Do not bear false witness, Honor thy father and mother.

21 And he said, All these things have I observed from my youth up.

22 And when Jesus heard it, he said unto him, One thing thou lackest yet: sell all that thou hast, and distribute unto the poor, and thou shalt have treasure in heaven: and come, follow me.

23 But when he heard these things, he became exceeding sorrowful; for he was very rich.

24 And Jesus seeing him said, How hardly shall they that have riches enter into the kingdom of God!

25 For it is easier for a camel to enter in through a needle's eye, than for a rich man to enter into the kingdom of God.

26 And they that heard it said, Then who can be saved?

27 But he said, The things which are impossible with men are possible with God.

28 And Peter said, Lo, we have left [982]our own, and followed thee.

29 And he said unto them, Verily I say unto you, There is no man that hath left house, or wife, or brethren, or parents, or children, for the kingdom of God's sake,

30 who shall not receive manifold more in this time, and in the [983]world to come eternal life.

---

[980] *Or, of such is*
[981] *Ex. 20:12–16; Dt. 5:16–20.*
[982] *Or, our own homes. See Jn. 19:27.*
[983] *Or, age*

31 And he took unto him the twelve, and said unto them, Behold, we go up to Jerusalem, and all the things that are written through the prophets shall be accomplished unto the Son of man.

32 For he shall be [984]delivered up unto the Gentiles, and shall be mocked, and shamefully treated, and spit upon:

33 and they shall scourge and kill him: and the third day he shall rise again.

34 And they understood none of these things; and this saying was hid from them, and they perceived not the things that were said.

35 And it came to pass, as he drew nigh unto Jericho, a certain blind man sat by the way side begging:

36 and hearing a multitude going by, he inquired what this meant.

37 And they told him, that Jesus of Nazareth passeth by.

38 And he cried, saying, Jesus, thou son of David, have mercy on me.

39 And they that went before rebuked him, that he should hold his peace: but he cried out the more a great deal, Thou son of David, have mercy on me.

40 And Jesus stood, and commanded him to be brought unto him: and when he was come near, he asked him,

41 What wilt thou that I should do unto thee? And he said, Lord, that I may receive my sight.

42 And Jesus said unto him, Receive thy sight: thy faith hath [985]made thee whole.

43 And immediately he received his sight, and followed him, glorifying God: and all the people, when they saw it, gave praise unto God.

Chapter 19

1 And he entered and was passing through Jericho.

2 And behold, a man called by name Zacchaeus; and he was a chief publican, and he was rich.

3 And he sought to see Jesus who he was; and could not for the crowd, because he was little of stature.

---

[984] *Or, betrayed*
[985] *Or, saved thee*

4 And he ran on before, and climbed up into a sycomore tree to see him: for he was to pass that way.

5 And when Jesus came to the place, he looked up, and said unto him, Zacchaeus, make haste, and come down; for to-day I must abide at thy house.

6 And he made haste, and came down, and received him joyfully.

7 And when they saw it, they all murmured, saying, He is gone in to lodge with a man that is a sinner.

8 And Zacchaeus stood, and said unto the Lord, Behold, Lord, the half of my goods I give to the poor; and if I have wrongfully exacted aught of any man, I restore fourfold.

9 And Jesus said unto him, To-day is salvation come to this house, forasmuch as he also is a son of Abraham.

10 For the Son of man came to seek and to save that which was lost.

11 And as they heard these things, he added and spake a parable, because he was nigh to Jerusalem, and *because* they supposed that the kingdom of God was immediately to appear.

12 He said therefore, A certain nobleman went into a far country, to receive for himself a kingdom, and to return.

13 And he called ten [986]servants of his, and gave them ten [987]pounds, and said unto them, Trade ye *herewith* till I come.

14 But his citizens hated him, and sent an ambassage after him, saying, We will not that this man reign over us.

15 And it came to pass, when he was come back again, having received the kingdom, that he commanded these [988]servants, unto whom he had given the money, to be called to him, that he might know what they had gained by trading.

16 And the first came before him, saying, Lord, thy pound hath made ten pounds more.

17 And he said unto him, Well done, thou good [989]servant: because thou wast found faithful in a very little, have thou authority over ten cities.

---

[986] *Greek bondservants.*
[987] *Mina, here translated a pound, is equal to one hundred drachmas. See 15:8.*
[988] *Greek bondservants.*
[989] *Greek bondservant.*

18 And the second came, saying, Thy pound, Lord, hath made five pounds.

19 And he said unto him also, Be thou also over five cities.

20 And [990]another came, saying, Lord, behold, *here is* thy pound, which I kept laid up in a napkin:

21 for I feared thee, because thou art an austere man: thou takest up that which thou layedst not down, and reapest that which thou didst not sow.

22 He saith unto him, Out of thine own mouth will I judge thee, thou wicked [991]servant. Thou knewest that I am an austere man, taking up that which I laid not down, and reaping that which I did not sow;

23 then wherefore gavest thou not my money into the bank, and [992]I at my coming should have required it with interest?

24 And he said unto them that stood by, Take away from him the pound, and give it unto him that hath the ten pounds.

25 And they said unto him, Lord, he hath ten pounds.

26 I say unto you, that unto every one that hath shall be given; but from him that hath not, even that which he hath shall be taken away from him.

27 But these mine enemies, that would not that I should reign over them, bring hither, and slay them before me.

28 And when he had thus spoken, he went on before, going up to Jerusalem.

29 And it came to pass, when he drew nigh unto Bethphage and Bethany, at the mount that is called Olivet, he sent two of the disciples,

30 saying, Go your way into the village over against *you*; in which as ye enter ye shall find a colt tied, whereon no man ever yet sat: loose him, and bring him.

31 And if any one ask you, Why do ye loose him? thus shall ye say, The Lord hath need of him.

32 And they that were sent went away, and found even as he had said unto them.

---

[990] *Greek the other.*
[991] *Greek bondservant.*
[992] *Or, I should have gone and required*

33 And as they were loosing the colt, the owners thereof said unto them, Why loose ye the colt?

34 And they said, The Lord hath need of him.

35 And they brought him to Jesus: and they threw their garments upon the colt, and set Jesus thereon.

36 And as he went, they spread their garments in the way.

37 And as he was now drawing nigh, *even* at the descent of the mount of Olives, the whole multitude of the disciples began to rejoice and praise God with a loud voice for all the [993]mighty works which they had seen;

38 saying, Blessed *is* the King that cometh in the name of the Lord: peace in heaven, and glory in the highest.

39 And some of the Pharisees from the multitude said unto him, Teacher, rebuke thy disciples.

40 And he answered and said, I tell you that, if these shall hold their peace, the stones will cry out.

41 And when he drew nigh, he saw the city and wept over it,

42 saying, [994]If thou hadst known in [995]this day, even thou, the things which belong unto [996]peace! but now they are hid from thine eyes.

43 For the days shall come upon thee, when thine enemies shall cast up a [997]bank about thee, and compass thee round, and keep thee in on every side,

44 and shall dash thee to the ground, and thy children within thee; and they shall not leave in thee one stone upon another; because thou knewest not the time of thy visitation.

45 And he entered into the temple, and began to cast out them that sold,

46 saying unto them, It is written, [998]And my house shall be a house of prayer: but [999]ye have made it a den of robbers.

47 And he was teaching daily in the temple. But the chief priests and the scribes and the principal men of the people sought to destroy him:

---

[993] *Greek powers.*
[994] *Or, O that thou hadst known*
[995] *Some ancient authorities read this thy day.*
[996] *Some ancient authorities read thy peace.*
[997] *Greek palisade.*
[998] *Isa. 56:7.*
[999] *Jer. 7:11.*

48 and they could not find what they might do; for the people all hung upon him, listening.

Chapter 20

1 And it came to pass, on one of the days, as he was teaching the people in the temple, and preaching the [1000]gospel, there came upon him the chief priests and the scribes with the elders;

2 and they spake, saying unto him, Tell us: By what authority doest thou these things? or who is he that gave thee this authority?

3 And he answered and said unto them, I also will ask you a [1001]question; and tell me:

4 The baptism of John, was it from heaven, or from men?

5 And they reasoned with themselves, saying, If we shall say, From heaven; he will say, Why did ye not believe him?

6 But if we shall say, From men; all the people will stone us: for they are persuaded that John was a prophet.

7 And they answered, that they knew not whence *it was*.

8 And Jesus said unto them, Neither tell I you by what authority I do these things.

9 And he began to speak unto the people this parable: A man planted a vineyard, and let it out to husbandmen, and went into another country for a long time.

10 And at the season he sent unto the husbandmen a [1002]servant, that they should give him of the fruit of the vineyard: but the husbandmen beat him, and sent him away empty.

11 And he sent yet another [1003]servant: and him also they beat, and handled him shamefully, and sent him away empty.

12 And he sent yet a third: and him also they wounded, and cast him forth.

13 And the lord of the vineyard said, What shall I do? I will send my beloved son; it may be they will reverence him.

[1000] *Or, good tidings: compare 3:18.*
[1001] *Greek word.*
[1002] *Greek bondservant.*
[1003] *Greek bondservant.*

14 But when the husbandmen saw him, they reasoned one with another, saying, This is the heir; let us kill him, that the inheritance may be ours.

15 And they cast him forth out of the vineyard, and killed him. What therefore will the lord of the vineyard do unto them?

16 He will come and destroy these husbandmen, and will give the vineyard unto others. And when they heard it, they said, [1004]God forbid.

17 But he looked upon them, and said, What then is this that is written,
[1005]The stone which the builders rejected,
The same was made the head of the corner?

18 Every one that falleth on that stone shall be broken to pieces; but on whomsoever it shall fall, it will scatter him as dust.

19 And the scribes and the chief priests sought to lay hands on him in that very hour; and they feared the people: for they perceived that he spake this parable against them.

20 And they watched him, and sent forth spies, who feigned themselves to be righteous, that they might take hold of his speech, so as to deliver him up to the [1006]rule and to the authority of the governor.

21 And they asked him, saying, Teacher, we know that thou sayest and teachest rightly, and acceptest not the person *of any*, but of a truth teachest the way of God:

22 Is it lawful for us to give tribute unto Caesar, or not?

23 But he perceived their craftiness, and said unto them,

24 Show me a [1007]denarius. Whose image and superscription hath it? And they said, Caesar's.

25 And he said unto them, Then render unto Caesar the things that are Caesar's, and unto God the things that are God's.

26 And they were not able to take hold of the saying before the people: and they marvelled at his answer, and held their peace.

27 And there came to him certain of the Sadducees, they that say that there is no resurrection;

[1004] *Greek Be it not so.*
[1005] *Ps. 118:22.*
[1006] *Or, ruling power*
[1007] *See marginal note on 7:41.*

28 and they asked him, saying, Teacher, [1008]Moses wrote unto us, that if a man's brother die, having a wife, and he be childless, his brother should take the wife, and raise up seed unto his brother.

29 There were therefore seven brethren: and the first took a wife, and died childless;

30 and the second:

31 and the third took her; and likewise the seven also left no children, and died.

32 Afterward the woman also died.

33 In the resurrection therefore whose wife of them shall she be? for the seven had her to wife.

34 And Jesus said unto them, The sons of this [1009]world marry, and are given in marriage:

35 but they that are accounted worthy to attain to that [1010]world, and the resurrection from the dead, neither marry, nor are given in marriage:

36 for neither can they die any more: for they are equal unto the angels; and are sons of God, being sons of the resurrection.

37 But that the dead are raised, even Moses showed, in [1011]*the place concerning* the Bush, when he calleth the Lord the God of Abraham, and the God of Isaac, and the God of Jacob.

38 Now he is not the God of the dead, but of the living: for all live unto him.

39 And certain of the scribes answering said, Teacher, thou hast well said.

40 For they durst not any more ask him any question.

41 And he said unto them, How say they that the Christ is David's son?

42 For David himself saith in the book of Psalms,
    [1012]The Lord said unto my Lord,
    Sit thou on my right hand,

43 Till I make thine enemies the footstool of thy feet.

44 David therefore calleth him Lord, and how is he his son?

[1008] Dt. 25:5.
[1009] Or, *age*
[1010] Or, *age*
[1011] Ex. 3:6.
[1012] Ps. 110:1.

45 And in the hearing of all the people he said unto his disciples,

46 Beware of the scribes, who desire to walk in long robes, and love salutations in the marketplaces, and chief seats in the synagogues, and chief places at feasts;

47 who devour widows' houses, and for a pretence make long prayers: these shall receive greater condemnation.

Chapter 21

1 And he looked up, [1013]and saw the rich men that were casting their gifts into the treasury.

2 And he saw a certain poor widow casting in thither two mites.

3 And he said, Of a truth I say unto you, This poor widow cast in more than they all:

4 for all these did of their superfluity cast in unto the gifts; but she of her want did cast in all the living that she had.

5 And as some spake of the temple, how it was adorned with goodly stones and offerings, he said,

6 As for these things which ye behold, the days will come, in which there shall not be left here one stone upon another, that shall not be thrown down.

7 And they asked him, saying, Teacher, when therefore shall these things be? and what *shall be* the sign when these things are about to come to pass?

8 And he said, Take heed that ye be not led astray: for many shall come in my name, saying, I am *he*; and, The time is at hand: go ye not after them.

9 And when ye shall hear of wars and tumults, be not terrified: for these things must needs come to pass first; but the end is not immediately.

10 Then said he unto them, Nation shall rise against nation, and kingdom against kingdom;

11 and there shall be great earthquakes, and in divers places famines and pestilences; and there shall be terrors and great signs from heaven.

[1013]*Or, and saw them that . . . treasury, and they were rich.*

12 But before all these things, they shall lay their hands on you, and shall persecute you, delivering you up to the synagogues and prisons, [1014]bringing you before kings and governors for my name's sake.

13 It shall turn out unto you for a testimony.

14 Settle it therefore in your hearts, not to meditate beforehand how to answer:

15 for I will give you a mouth and wisdom, which all your adversaries shall not be able to withstand or to gainsay.

16 But ye shall be [1015]delivered up even by parents, and brethren, and kinsfolk, and friends; and *some* of you [1016]shall they cause to be put to death.

17 And ye shall be hated of all men for my name's sake.

18 And not a hair of your head shall perish.

19 In your [1017]patience ye shall win your [1018]souls.

20 But when ye see Jerusalem compassed with armies, then know that her desolation is at hand.

21 Then let them that are in Judaea flee unto the mountains; and let them that are in the midst of her depart out; and let not them that are in the country enter therein.

22 For these are days of vengeance, that all things which are written may be fulfilled.

23 Woe unto them that are with child and to them that give suck in those days! for there shall be great distress upon the [1019]land, and wrath unto this people.

24 And they shall fall by the edge of the sword, and shall be led captive into all the nations: and Jerusalem shall be trodden down of the Gentiles, until the times of the Gentiles be fulfilled.

25 And there shall be signs in sun and moon and stars; and upon the earth distress of nations, in perplexity for the roaring of the sea and the billows;

[1014] *Greek you being brought.*
[1015] *Or, betrayed*
[1016] *Or, shall they put to death*
[1017] *Or, stedfastness*
[1018] *Or, lives*
[1019] *Or, earth*

26 men [1020]fainting for fear, and for expectation of the things which are coming on [1021]the world: for the powers of the heavens shall be shaken.

27 And then shall they see the Son of man coming in a cloud with power and great glory.

28 But when these things begin to come to pass, look up, and lift up your heads; because your redemption draweth nigh.

29 And he spake to them a parable: Behold the fig tree, and all the trees:

30 when they now shoot forth, ye see it and know of your own selves that the summer is now nigh.

31 Even so ye also, when ye see these things coming to pass, know ye that the kingdom of God is nigh.

32 Verily I say unto you, This generation shall not pass away, till all things be accomplished.

33 Heaven and earth shall pass away: but my words shall not pass away.

34 But take heed to yourselves, lest haply your hearts be overcharged with surfeiting, and drunkenness, and cares of this life, and that day come on you suddenly as a snare:

35 for *so* shall it come upon all them that dwell on the face of all the earth.

36 But watch ye at every season, making supplication, that ye may prevail to escape all these things that shall come to pass, and to stand before the Son of man.

37 And every day he was teaching in the temple; and every night he went out, and lodged in the mount that is called Olivet.

38 And all the people came early in the morning to him in the temple, to hear him.

[1020] *Or, expiring*
[1021] *Greek the inhabited earth.*

Chapter 22

1 Now the feast of unleavened bread drew nigh, which is called the Passover.

2 And the chief priests and the scribes sought how they might put him to death; for they feared the people.

3 And Satan entered into Judas who was called Iscariot, being of the number of the twelve.

4 And he went away, and communed with the chief priests and captains, how he might [1022]deliver him unto them.

5 And they were glad, and covenanted to give him money.

6 And he consented, and sought opportunity to [1023]deliver him unto them [1024]in the absence of the multitude.

7 And the day of unleavened bread came, on which the passover must be sacrificed.

8 And he sent Peter and John, saying, Go and make ready for us the passover, that we may eat.

9 And they said unto him, Where wilt thou that we make ready?

10 And he said unto them, Behold, when ye are entered into the city, there shall meet you a man bearing a pitcher of water; follow him into the house whereinto he goeth.

11 And ye shall say unto the master of the house, The Teacher saith unto thee, Where is the guest-chamber, where I shall eat the passover with my disciples?

12 And he will show you a large upper room furnished: there make ready.

13 And they went, and found as he had said unto them: and they made ready the passover.

14 And when the hour was come, he sat down, and the apostles with him.

15 And he said unto them, With desire I have desired to eat this passover with you before I suffer:

[1022] *Or, betray*
[1023] *Or, betray*
[1024] *Or, without tumult*

16 for I say unto you, I shall not eat it, until it be fulfilled in the kingdom of God.

17 And he received a cup, and when he had given thanks, he said, Take this, and divide it among yourselves:

18 for I say unto you, I shall not drink from henceforth of the fruit of the vine, until the kingdom of God shall come.

19 And he took [1025]bread, and when he had given thanks, he brake it, and gave to them, saying, This is my body [1026]which is given for you: this do in remembrance of me.

20 And the cup in like manner after supper, saying, This cup is the new covenant in my blood, *even* that which is poured out for you.

21 But behold, the hand of him that [1027]betrayeth me is with me on the table.

22 For the Son of man indeed goeth, as it hath been determined: but woe unto that man through whom he is [1028]betrayed!

23 And they began to question among themselves, which of them it was that should do this thing.

24 And there arose also a contention among them, which of them was accounted to be [1029]greatest.

25 And he said unto them, The kings of the Gentiles have lordship over them; and they that have authority over them are called Benefactors.

26 But ye *shall* not *be* so: but he that is the greater among you, let him become as the younger; and he that is chief, as he that doth serve.

27 For which is greater, he that [1030]sitteth at meat, or he that serveth? is not he that [1031]sitteth at meat? but I am in the midst of you as he that serveth.

28 But ye are they that have continued with me in my temptations;

[1025] *Or, a loaf*
[1026] *Some ancient authorities omit which is given for you . . . which is poured out for you.*
[1027] *See verse 4.*
[1028] *See verse 4.*
[1029] *Greek greater.*
[1030] *Greek reclineth.*
[1031] *Greek reclineth.*

29 and ¹⁰³²I appoint unto you a kingdom, even as my Father appointed unto me,

30 that ye may eat and drink at my table in my kingdom; and ye shall sit on thrones judging the twelve tribes of Israel.

31 Simon, Simon, behold, Satan ¹⁰³³asked to have you, that he might sift you as wheat:

32 but I made supplication for thee, that thy faith fail not; and do thou, when once thou hast turned again, establish thy brethren.

33 And he said unto him, Lord, with thee I am ready to go both to prison and to death.

34 And he said, I tell thee, Peter, the cock shall not crow this day, until thou shalt thrice deny that thou knowest me.

35 And he said unto them, When I sent you forth without purse, and wallet, and shoes, lacked ye anything? And they said, Nothing.

36 And he said unto them, But now, he that hath a purse, let him take it, and likewise a wallet; ¹⁰³⁴and he that hath none, let him sell his cloak, and buy a sword.

37 For I say unto you, that this which is written must be fulfilled in me, ¹⁰³⁵And he was reckoned with transgressors: for that which concerneth me hath ¹⁰³⁶fulfilment.

38 And they said, Lord, behold, here are two swords. And he said unto them, It is enough.

39 And he came out, and went, as his custom was, unto the mount of Olives; and the disciples also followed him.

40 And when he was at the place, he said unto them, Pray that ye enter not into temptation.

41 And he was parted from them about a stone's cast; and he kneeled down and prayed,

†✓ **Two Distinct Wills.** Jesus submits His human will to the Father's divine will. One God cannot have two opposing wills or "negotiate" with Himself. This is the prayer of a subordinate Son to His God.

42 saying, Father, if thou be willing, remove this cup from me: nevertheless not my will, but thine, be done.

---

¹⁰³²*Or, I appoint unto you, even as my Father appointed unto me a kingdom, that ye may eat and drink etc.*

¹⁰³³*Or, obtained you by asking*

¹⁰³⁴*Or, and he that hath no sword, let him sell his cloak, and buy one*

¹⁰³⁵*Isa. 53:12.*

¹⁰³⁶*Greek end.*

43 [1037] And there appeared unto him an angel from heaven, strengthening him.

44 And being in an agony he prayed more earnestly; and his sweat became as it were great drops of blood falling down upon the ground.

45 And when he rose up from his prayer, he came unto the disciples, and found them sleeping for sorrow,

46 and said unto them, Why sleep ye? rise and pray, that ye enter not into temptation.

47 While he yet spake, behold, a multitude, and he that was called Judas, one of the twelve, went before them; and he drew near unto Jesus to kiss him.

48 But Jesus said unto him, Judas, [1038] betrayest thou the Son of man with a kiss?

49 And when they that were about him saw what would follow, they said, Lord, shall we smite with the sword?

50 And a certain one of them smote the [1039] servant of the high priest, and struck off his right ear.

51 But Jesus answered and said, Suffer ye *them* thus far. And he touched his ear, and healed him.

52 And Jesus said unto the chief priests, and captains of the temple, and elders, that were come against him, Are ye come out, as against a robber, with swords and staves?

53 When I was daily with you in the temple, ye stretched not forth your hands against me: but this is your hour, and the power of darkness.

54 And they seized him, and led him *away*, and brought him into the high priest's house. But Peter followed afar off.

55 And when they had kindled a fire in the midst of the court, and had sat down together, Peter sat in the midst of them.

56 And a certain maid seeing him as he sat in the light *of the fire*, and looking stedfastly upon him, said, This man also was with him.

57 But he denied, saying, Woman, I know him not.

[1037] *Many ancient authorities omit verses 43, 44*
[1038] *See verse 4.*
[1039] *Greek bondservant.*

58 And after a little while another saw him, and said, Thou also art *one* of them. But Peter said, Man, I am not.

59 And after the space of about one hour another confidently affirmed, saying, Of a truth this man also was with him; for he is a Galilaean.

60 But Peter said, Man, I know not what thou sayest. And immediately, while he yet spake, the cock crew.

61 And the Lord turned, and looked upon Peter. And Peter remembered the word of the Lord, how that he said unto him, Before the cock crow this day thou shalt deny me thrice.

62 And he went out, and wept bitterly.

63 And the men that held [1040]*Jesus* mocked him, and beat him.

64 And they blindfolded him, and asked him, saying, Prophesy: who is he that struck thee?

65 And many other things spake they against him, reviling him.

66 And as soon as it was day, the assembly of the elders of the people was gathered together, both chief priests and scribes; and they led him away into their council, saying,

67 If thou art the Christ, tell us. But he said unto them, If I tell you, ye will not believe:

68 and if I ask *you*, ye will not answer.

69 But from henceforth shall the Son of man be seated at the right hand of the power of God.

70 And they all said, Art thou then the Son of God? And he said unto them, [1041]Ye say that I am.

71 And they said, What further need have we of witness? for we ourselves have heard from his own mouth.

[1040] *Greek him.*
[1041] *Or, Ye say it, because I am*

Chapter 23

1 And the whole company of them rose up, and brought him before Pilate.

2 And they began to accuse him, saying, We found this man perverting our nation, and forbidding to give tribute to Caesar, and saying that he himself is Christ a king.

3 And Pilate asked him, saying, Art thou the King of the Jews? And he answered him and said, Thou sayest.

4 And Pilate said unto the chief priests and the multitudes, I find no fault in this man.

5 But they were the more urgent, saying, He stirreth up the people, teaching throughout all Judaea, and beginning from Galilee even unto this place.

6 But when Pilate heard it, he asked whether the man were a Galilaean.

7 And when he knew that he was of Herod's jurisdiction, he sent him unto Herod, who himself also was at Jerusalem in these days.

8 Now when Herod saw Jesus, he was exceeding glad: for he was of a long time desirous to see him, because he had heard concerning him; and he hoped to see some [1042]miracle done by him.

9 And he questioned him in many words; but he answered him nothing.

10 And the chief priests and the scribes stood, vehemently accusing him.

11 And Herod with his soldiers set him at nought, and mocked him, and arraying him in gorgeous apparel sent him back to Pilate.

12 And Herod and Pilate became friends with each other that very day: for before they were at enmity between themselves.

13 And Pilate called together the chief priests and the rulers and the people,

14 and said unto them, Ye brought unto me this man, as one that perverteth the people: and behold, I, having examined him before you, found no fault in this man touching those things whereof ye accuse him:

[1042] *Greek sign.*

15 no, nor yet Herod: for [1043]he sent him back unto us; and behold, nothing worthy of death hath been done by him.

16 I will therefore chastise him, and release him.[1044]

18 But they cried out all together, saying, Away with this man, and release unto us Barabbas:—

19 one who for a certain insurrection made in the city, and for murder, was cast into prison.

20 And Pilate spake unto them again, desiring to release Jesus;

21 but they shouted, saying, Crucify, crucify him.

22 And he said unto them the third time, Why, what evil hath this man done? I have found no cause of death in him: I will therefore chastise him and release him.

23 But they were urgent with loud voices, asking that he might be crucified. And their voices prevailed.

24 And Pilate gave sentence that what they asked for should be done.

25 And he released him that for insurrection and murder had been cast into prison, whom they asked for; but Jesus he delivered up to their will.

26 And when they led him away, they laid hold upon one Simon of Cyrene, coming from the country, and laid on him the cross, to bear it after Jesus.

27 And there followed him a great multitude of the people, and of women who bewailed and lamented him.

28 But Jesus turning unto them said, Daughters of Jerusalem, weep not for me, but weep for yourselves, and for your children.

29 For behold, the days are coming, in which they shall say, Blessed are the barren, and the wombs that never bare, and the breasts that never gave suck.

30 Then shall they begin to say to the mountains, Fall on us; and to the hills, Cover us.

[1043] *Many ancient authorities read I sent you to him.*

[1044] *Many ancient authorities insert verse 17 Now he must needs release unto them at the feast one prisoner. Compare Mt. 27:15; Mk. 15:6; Jn. 18:39. Others add the same words after verse 19.*

31 For if they do these things in the green tree, what shall be done in the dry?

32 And there were also two others, malefactors, led with him to be put to death.

33 And when they came unto the place which is called [1045]The skull, there they crucified him, and the malefactors, one on the right hand and the other on the left.

34 [1046]And Jesus said, Father, forgive them; for they know not what they do. And parting his garments among them, they cast lots.

35 And the people stood beholding. And the rulers also scoffed at him, saying, He saved others; let him save himself, if this is the Christ of God, his chosen.

36 And the soldiers also mocked him, coming to him, offering him vinegar,

37 and saying, If thou art the King of the Jews, save thyself.

38 And there was also a superscription over him, This is the King of the Jews.

39 And one of the malefactors that were hanged railed on him, saying, Art not thou the Christ? save thyself and us.

40 But the other answered, and rebuking him said, Dost thou not even fear God, seeing thou art in the same condemnation?

41 And we indeed justly; for we receive the due reward of our deeds: but this man hath done nothing amiss.

42 And he said, Jesus, remember me when thou comest [1047]in thy kingdom.

43 And he said unto him, Verily I say unto thee, To-day shalt thou be with me in Paradise.

44 And it was now about the sixth hour, and a darkness came over the whole [1048]land until the ninth hour,

---

[1045] *According to the Latin, Calvary, which has the same meaning.*

[1046] *Some ancient authorities omit And Jesus said, Father, forgive them; for they know not what they do.*

[1047] *Some ancient authorities read into thy kingdom.*

[1048] *Or, earth*

45 [1049]the sun's light failing: and the veil of the [1050]temple was rent in the midst.

46 [1051]And Jesus, crying with a loud voice, said, Father, into thy hands I commend my spirit: and having said this, he gave up the ghost.

47 And when the centurion saw what was done, he glorified God, saying, Certainly this was a righteous man.

48 And all the multitudes that came together to this sight, when they beheld the things that were done, returned smiting their breasts.

49 And all his acquaintance, and the women that followed with him from Galilee, stood afar off, seeing these things.

50 And behold, a man named Joseph, who was a councillor, a good and righteous man

51 (he had not consented to their counsel and deed), *a man* of Arimathaea, a city of the Jews, who was looking for the kingdom of God:

52 this man went to Pilate, and asked for the body of Jesus.

53 And he took it down, and wrapped it in a linen cloth, and laid him in a tomb that was hewn in stone, where never man had yet lain.

54 And it was the day of the Preparation, and the sabbath [1052]drew on.

55 And the women, who had come with him out of Galilee, followed after, and beheld the tomb, and how his body was laid.

56 And they returned, and prepared spices and ointments.
 And on the sabbath they rested according to the commandment.

[1049] *Greek the sun failing.*
[1050] *Or, sanctuary*
[1051] *Or, And when Jesus had cried with a loud voice, he said*
[1052] *Greek began to dawn.*

Chapter 24

1 But on the first day of the week, at early dawn, they came unto the tomb, bringing the spices which they had prepared.

2 And they found the stone rolled away from the tomb.

3 And they entered in, and found not the body [1053]of the Lord Jesus.

4 And it came to pass, while they were perplexed thereabout, behold, two men stood by them in dazzling apparel:

5 and as they were affrighted and bowed down their faces to the earth, they said unto them, Why seek ye [1054]the living among the dead?

6 [1055]He is not here, but is risen: remember how he spake unto you when he was yet in Galilee,

7 saying that the Son of man must be delivered up into the hands of sinful men, and be crucified, and the third day rise again.

8 And they remembered his words,

9 and returned [1056]from the tomb, and told all these things to the eleven, and to all the rest.

10 Now they were Mary Magdalene, and Joanna, and Mary the *mother* of James: and the other women with them told these things unto the apostles.

11 And these words appeared in their sight as idle talk; and they disbelieved them.

12 [1057]But Peter arose, and ran unto the tomb; and stooping and looking in, he seeth the linen cloths by themselves; and he [1058]departed to his home, wondering at that which was come to pass.

13 And behold, two of them were going that very day to a village named Emmaus, which was threescore furlongs from Jerusalem.

14 And they communed with each other of all these things which had happened.

[1053] *Some ancient authorities omit of the Lord Jesus.*
[1054] *Greek him that liveth.*
[1055] *Some ancient authorities omit He is not here, but is risen.*
[1056] *Some ancient authorities omit from the tomb.*
[1057] *Some ancient authorities omit verse 12.*
[1058] *Or, departed, wondering with himself*

15 And it came to pass, while they communed and questioned together, that Jesus himself drew near, and went with them.

16 But their eyes were holden that they should not know him.

17 And he said unto them, [1059]What communications are these that ye have one with another, as ye walk? And they stood still, looking sad.

18 And one of them, named Cleopas, answering said unto him, [1060]Dost thou alone sojourn in Jerusalem and not know the things which are come to pass there in these days?

19 And he said unto them, What things? And they said unto him, The things concerning Jesus the Nazarene, who was a prophet mighty in deed and word before God and all the people:

20 and how the chief priests and our rulers delivered him up to be condemned to death, and crucified him.

21 But we hoped that it was he who should redeem Israel. Yea and besides all this, it is now the third day since these things came to pass.

22 Moreover certain women of our company amazed us, having been early at the tomb;

23 and when they found not his body, they came, saying, that they had also seen a vision of angels, who said that he was alive.

24 And certain of them that were with us went to the tomb, and found it even so as the women had said: but him they saw not.

25 And he said unto them, O foolish men, and slow of heart to believe [1061]in all that the prophets have spoken!

26 Behooved it not the Christ to suffer these things, and to enter into his glory?

27 And beginning from Moses and from all the prophets, he interpreted to them in all the scriptures the things concerning himself.

28 And they drew nigh unto the village, whither they were going: and he made as though he would go further.

29 And they constrained him, saying, Abide with us; for it is toward evening, and the day is now far spent. And he went in to abide with them.

[1059] *Greek What words are these that ye exchange one with another.*
[1060] *Or, Dost thou sojourn alone in Jerusalem, and knowest thou not the things*
[1061] *Or, after*

30 And it came to pass, when he had sat down with them to meat, he took the [1062]bread and blessed; and breaking *it* he gave to them.

31 And their eyes were opened, and they knew him; and he vanished out of their sight.

32 And they said one to another, Was not our heart burning within us, while he spake to us in the way, while he opened to us the scriptures?

33 And they rose up that very hour, and returned to Jerusalem, and found the eleven gathered together, and them that were with them,

34 saying, The Lord is risen indeed, and hath appeared to Simon.

35 And they rehearsed the things *that happened* in the way, and how he was known of them in the breaking of the bread.

36 And as they spake these things, he himself stood in the midst of them, [1063]and saith unto them, Peace *be* unto you.

37 But they were terrified and affrighted, and supposed that they beheld a spirit.

38 And he said unto them, Why are ye troubled? and wherefore do questionings arise in your heart?

39 See my hands and my feet, that it is I myself: handle me, and see; for a spirit hath not flesh and bones, as ye behold me having.

40 [1064]And when he had said this, he showed them his hands and his feet.

41 And while they still disbelieved for joy, and wondered, he said unto them, Have ye here anything to eat?

42 And they gave him a piece of a broiled fish[1065].

43 And he took it, and ate before them.

44 And he said unto them, These are my words which I spake unto you, while I was yet with you, that all things must needs be fulfilled, which are written in the law of Moses, and the prophets, and the psalms, concerning me.

45 Then opened he their mind, that they might understand the scriptures;

[1062] *Or, loaf*
[1063] *Some ancient authorities omit and saith unto them, Peace be unto you*
[1064] *Some ancient authorities omit verse 40.*
[1065] *Many ancient authorities add and a honeycomb.*

46 and he said unto them, Thus it is written, that the Christ should suffer, and rise again from the dead the third day;

47 and that repentance [1066] and remission of sins should be preached in his name unto all the [1067] nations, beginning from Jerusalem.

48 Ye are witnesses of these things.

49 And behold, I send forth the promise of my Father upon you: but tarry ye in the city, until ye be clothed with power from on high.

50 And he led them out until *they were* over against Bethany: and he lifted up his hands, and blessed them.

51 And it came to pass, while he blessed them, he parted from them, [1068] and was carried up into heaven.

52 And they [1069] worshipped him, and returned to Jerusalem with great joy:

53 and were continually in the temple, blessing God.

[1066] *Some ancient authorities read unto.*
[1067] *Or, nations. Beginning from Jerusalem, ye are witnesses*
[1068] *Some ancient authorities omit and was carried up into heaven.*
[1069] *Some ancient authorities omit worshipped him, and. See marginal note on 4:7.*

Timeline for John

John presents a theological portrait of Jesus as the eternal Logos and the "I AM," organized around seven miraculous signs and extended discourses.

JOHN'S NARRATIVE STRUCTURE

SECTION / THEMATIC BLOCK	CHAPTER REFERENCE / NARRATIVE FOCUS
The Prologue	**Ch 1:1–18:** The Word (*Logos*) made flesh. John identifies Jesus not as a second God, but as the **Tabernacle** of God ("dwelt among us"), replacing the physical Temple with a human life.
The Book of Signs (Part I)	**Ch 1:19 – 4:** The witness of John the Baptist, the first sign (Water to Wine), the cleansing of the Temple, and encounters with Nicodemus and the Samaritan Woman.
The Book of Signs (Part II)	**Ch 5 – 10:** Increasing controversy; the Predicated "I AM" statements (Bread of Life, Light of the World); healing the lame man and the man born blind.
The Climax of Signs	**Ch 11 – 12:** The raising of Lazarus (the pivotal sign leading to the plot to kill Jesus) and the Triumphal Entry into Jerusalem.
The Book of Glory	**Ch 13 – 17:** The Upper Room, foot washing, the Farewell Discourse (promising the Paraclete/Spirit), and the High Priestly Prayer for unity.

JOHN'S NARRATIVE STRUCTURE

SECTION / THEMATIC BLOCK	CHAPTER REFERENCE / NARRATIVE FOCUS
Passion & Resurrection	**Ch 18 – 21:** Arrest, trials (Jesus's Kingdom "not of this world"), Crucifixion, Resurrection appearances, and the Epilogue (restoration of Peter).

Chapter 1

John the Apostle (The "Disciple Whom Jesus Loved") This Gospel is the primary battleground of Christology. Unlike the Synoptic Gospels (Matthew, Mark, Luke), which focus on Jesus' actions, John focuses on his *identity*. Because of its high poetic language ("The Word," "I Am"), it is frequently cited as the ultimate proof of the Trinity. The challenge is to read these Jewish idioms without imposing later Greek philosophical definitions upon them. The reader must distinguish between *representation* (Jesus revealing the Father) and *identity* (Jesus being the Father). The key to unlocking John is found in the author's own purpose statement in **John 20:31**: *"...these are written, that ye may believe that Jesus is the Christ, the Son of God."* John did not write to prove Jesus *is* God, but to prove he is God's *Son*. The Lens is **Transparency**. In John, Jesus is the perfect Agent who speaks only what he hears (5:19, 8:28). When Jesus says, "I and the Father are one" (10:30), he is describing a unity of *purpose* and *agency*, not a unity of *essence*. We must interpret the poetic prologue (1:1-14) through the clear, explicit creed of Jesus himself in **John 17:3**: *"that they should know thee, the only true God."*

1 In the beginning was the Word, and the Word was with God, and the Word was God.[1070]

2 The same was in the beginning with God.

3 All things were made through him; and without him [1071]was not anything made that hath been made.

4 In him was life; and the life was the light of men.

5 And the light shineth in the darkness; and the darkness [1072]apprehended it not.

6 There came a man, sent from God, whose name was John.

7 The same came for witness, that he might bear witness of the light, that all might believe through him.

8 He was not the light, but *came* that he might bear witness of the light.

†✓ **The Word was divine in nature, but not the same person as God.** Traditional reading: Identity ("Jesus is the Father"). Actual Greek: *theos en ho logos*. Theos lacks the article, making it qualitative (describing nature), not definite.

[1070]**Grammar:** The Greek text reads *kai theos en ho logos*. The word *theos* (God) lacks the definite article (*ho*). In Greek grammar, an anarthrous noun often indicates *quality*, not identity. A precise translation is "and the Word was divine" or "god-like," distinguishing the Word from The God (The Father) mentioned previously.

[1071]*Or, was not anything made. That which hath been made was life in him; and the life etc.*

[1072]*Or, overcame. See 12:35 (Greek).*

9 [1073]There was the true light, *even the light* which lighteth [1074]every man, coming into the world.

10 He was in the world, and the world was made through him, and the world knew him not.

11 He came unto [1075]his own, and they that were his own received him not.

12 But as many as received him, to them gave he the right to become children of God, *even* to them that believe on his name:

13 who were [1076]born, not of [1077]blood, nor of the will of the flesh, nor of the will of man, but of God.

14 And the Word became flesh, and [1078]dwelt among us (and we beheld his glory, glory as of [1079]the only begotten from the Father), full of grace and truth.

15 John beareth witness of him, and crieth, saying, [1080]This was he of whom I said, He that cometh after me is become before me: for he was [1081]before me.

16 For of his fulness we all received, and [1082]grace for grace.

17 For the law was given through Moses; grace and truth came through Jesus Christ.

18 No man hath seen God at any time; [1083]the only begotten Son, who is in the bosom of the Father, he hath declared *him*.[1084]

19 And this is the witness of John, when the Jews sent unto him from Jerusalem priests and Levites to ask him, Who art thou?

20 And he confessed, and denied not; and he confessed, I am not the Christ.

[1073] *Or, the true light, which lighteth every man, was coming*
[1074] *Or, every man as he cometh*
[1075] *Greek his own things.*
[1076] *Or, begotten*
[1077] *Greek bloods.*
[1078] *Greek tabernacled.*
[1079] *Or, an only begotten from a father. Compare Heb. 11:17.*
[1080] *Some ancient authorities read (this was he that said).*
[1081] *Greek first in regard of me.*
[1082] *Or, grace upon grace*
[1083] *Many very ancient authorities read God only begotten.*
[1084] **Critical Variant:** The earliest manuscripts (P66, P75, Sinaiticus) read *monogenes theos* ("unique god" or "only begotten god") instead of "only begotten Son." If original, this describes Jesus as a "begotten" (created/generated) divine being, distinct from the Unbegotten Father.

JOHN 1

21 And they asked him, What then? Art thou Elijah? And he saith, I am not. Art thou the prophet? And he answered, No.

22 They said therefore unto him, Who art thou? that we may give an answer to them that sent us. What sayest thou of thyself?

23 He said, I am the voice of one crying in the wilderness, Make straight the way of the Lord, as [1085]said Isaiah the prophet.

24 [1086]And they had been sent from the Pharisees.

25 And they asked him, and said unto him, Why then baptizest thou, if thou art not the Christ, neither Elijah, neither the prophet?

26 John answered them, saying, I baptize [1087]in water: in the midst of you standeth one whom ye know not,

27 *even* he that cometh after me, the latchet of whose shoe I am not worthy to unloose.

28 These things were done in [1088]Bethany beyond the Jordan, where John was baptizing.

29 On the morrow he seeth Jesus coming unto him, and saith, Behold, the Lamb of God, that [1089]taketh away the sin of the world!

30 This is he of whom I said, After me cometh a man who is become before me: for he was [1090]before me.

31 And I knew him not; but that he should be made manifest to Israel, for this cause came I baptizing [1091]in water.

32 And John bare witness, saying, I have beheld the Spirit descending as a dove out of heaven; and it abode upon him.

33 And I knew him not: but he that sent me to baptize [1092]in water, he said unto me, Upon whomsoever thou shalt see the Spirit descending, and abiding upon him, the same is he that baptizeth [1093]in the Holy Spirit.

[1085] *Isa. 40:3.*
[1086] *Or, And certain had been sent from among the Pharisees.*
[1087] *Or, with*
[1088] *Many ancient authorities read Bethabarah, some Betharabah. Compare Josh. 15:6, 61; 18:22.*
[1089] *Or, beareth the sin*
[1090] *Greek first in regard of me.*
[1091] *Or, with*
[1092] *Or, with*
[1093] *Or, with*

34 And I have seen, and have borne witness that this is the Son of God.

35 Again on the morrow John was standing, and two of his disciples;

36 and he looked upon Jesus as he walked, and saith, Behold, the Lamb of God!

37 And the two disciples heard him speak, and they followed Jesus.

38 And Jesus turned, and beheld them following, and saith unto them, What seek ye? And they said unto him, Rabbi (which is to say, being interpreted, Teacher), where abidest thou?

39 He saith unto them, Come, and ye shall see. They came therefore and saw where he abode; and they abode with him that day: it was about the tenth hour.

40 One of the two that heard John *speak*, and followed him, was Andrew, Simon Peter's brother.

41 He findeth first his own brother Simon, and saith unto him, We have found the Messiah (which is, being interpreted, [1094]Christ).

42 He brought him unto Jesus. Jesus looked upon him, and said, Thou art Simon the son of [1095]John: thou shalt be called Cephas (which is by interpretation, [1096]Peter).

43 On the morrow he was minded to go forth into Galilee, and he findeth Philip: and Jesus saith unto him, Follow me.

44 Now Philip was from Bethsaida, of the city of Andrew and Peter.

45 Philip findeth Nathanael, and saith unto him, We have found him, of whom Moses in the law, and the prophets, wrote, Jesus of Nazareth, the son of Joseph.

46 And Nathanael said unto him, Can any good thing come out of Nazareth? Philip saith unto him, Come and see.

47 Jesus saw Nathanael coming to him, and saith of him, Behold, an Israelite indeed, in whom is no guile!

48 Nathanael saith unto him, Whence knowest thou me? Jesus answered and said unto him, Before Philip called thee, when thou wast under the fig tree, I saw thee.

[1094]*That is, Anointed. Compare Ps. 2:2.*
[1095]*Greek Joanes: called in Mt. 16:17 Jonah.*
[1096]*That is, Rock or Stone.*

49 Nathanael answered him, Rabbi, thou art the Son of God; thou art King of Israel.

50 Jesus answered and said unto him, Because I said unto thee, I saw thee underneath the fig tree, believest thou? thou shalt see greater things than these.

51 And he saith unto him, Verily, verily, I say unto you, Ye shall see the heaven opened, and the angels of God ascending and descending upon the Son of man.

Chapter 2

1 And the third day there was a marriage in Cana of Galilee; and the mother of Jesus was there:

2 and Jesus also was bidden, and his disciples, to the marriage.

3 And when the wine failed, the mother of Jesus saith unto him, They have no wine.

4 And Jesus saith unto her, Woman, what have I to do with thee? mine hour is not yet come.

5 His mother saith unto the servants, Whatsoever he saith unto you, do it.

6 Now there were six waterpots of stone set there after the Jews' manner of purifying, containing two or three firkins apiece.

7 Jesus saith unto them, Fill the waterpots with water. And they filled them up to the brim.

8 And he saith unto them, Draw out now, and bear unto the [1097]ruler of the feast. And they bare it.

9 And when the ruler of the feast tasted the water [1098]now become wine, and knew not whence it was (but the servants that had drawn the water knew), the ruler of the feast calleth the bridegroom,

10 and saith unto him, Every man setteth on first the good wine; and when *men* have drunk freely, *then* that which is worse: thou hast kept the good wine until now.

[1097] *Or, steward*
[1098] *Or, that it had become*

11 This beginning of his signs did Jesus in Cana of Galilee, and manifested his glory; and his disciples believed on him.

12 After this he went down to Capernaum, he, and his mother, and *his* brethren, and his disciples; and there they abode not many days.

13 And the passover of the Jews was at hand, and Jesus went up to Jerusalem.

14 And he found in the temple those that sold oxen and sheep and doves, and the changers of money sitting:

15 and he made a scourge of cords, and cast all out of the temple, both the sheep and the oxen; and he poured out the changers' money, and overthrew their tables;

16 and to them that sold the doves he said, Take these things hence; make not my Father's house a house of merchandise.

17 His disciples remembered that it was written, [1099]Zeal for thy house shall eat me up.

18 The Jews therefore answered and said unto him, What sign showest thou unto us, seeing that thou doest these things?

19 Jesus answered and said unto them, Destroy this [1100]temple, and in three days I will raise it up.

20 The Jews therefore said, Forty and six years was this [1101]temple in building, and wilt thou raise it up in three days?

21 But he spake of the [1102]temple of his body.

22 When therefore he was raised from the dead, his disciples remembered that he spake this; and they believed the scripture, and the word which Jesus had said.

23 Now when he was in Jerusalem at the passover, during the feast, many believed on his name, beholding his signs which he did.

24 But Jesus did not trust himself unto them, for that he knew all men,

25 and because he needed not that any one should bear witness concerning [1103]man; for he himself knew what was in man.

[1099] *Ps. 69:9.*
[1100] *Or, sanctuary*
[1101] *Or, sanctuary*
[1102] *Or, sanctuary*
[1103] *Or, a man; for ... the man.*

Chapter 3

1 Now there was a man of the Pharisees, named Nicodemus, a ruler of the Jews:

2 the same came unto him by night, and said to him, Rabbi, we know that thou art a teacher come from God; for no one can do these signs that thou doest, except God be with him.

3 Jesus answered and said unto him, Verily, verily, I say unto thee, Except one be born [1104]anew, he cannot see the kingdom of God.

4 Nicodemus saith unto him, How can a man be born when he is old? can he enter a second time into his mother's womb, and be born?

5 Jesus answered, Verily, verily, I say unto thee, Except one be born of water and the Spirit, he cannot enter into the kingdom of God.

6 That which is born of the flesh is flesh; and that which is born of the Spirit is spirit.

7 Marvel not that I said unto thee, Ye must be born [1105]anew.

8 [1106]The wind bloweth where it will, and thou hearest the voice thereof, but knowest not whence it cometh, and whither it goeth: so is every one that is born of the Spirit.

9 Nicodemus answered and said unto him, How can these things be?

10 Jesus answered and said unto him, Art thou the teacher of Israel, and understandest not these things?

11 Verily, verily, I say unto thee, We speak that which we know, and bear witness of that which we have seen; and ye receive not our witness.

12 If I told you earthly things and ye believe not, how shall ye believe if I tell you heavenly things?

13 And no one hath ascended into heaven, but he that descended out of heaven, *even* the Son of man, [1107]who is in heaven.

14 And as Moses lifted up the serpent in the wilderness, even so must the Son of man be lifted up;

[1104] *Or, from above. See verse 31; 19:11; Jas. 1:17; 3:15, 17.*
[1105] *Or, from above. See verse 31; 19:11; Jas. 1:17; 3:15, 17.*
[1106] *Or, The Spirit breatheth*
[1107] *Man ancient authorities omit who is in heaven.*

15 that whosoever [1108]believeth may in him have eternal life.

16 For God so loved the world, that he gave his only begotten Son, that whosoever believeth on him should not perish, but have eternal life.

17 For God sent not the Son into the world to judge the world; but that the world should be saved through him.

18 He that believeth on him is not judged: he that believeth not hath been judged already, because he hath not believed on the name of the only begotten Son of God.

19 And this is the judgment, that the light is come into the world, and men loved the darkness rather than the light; for their works were evil.

20 For every one that [1109]doeth evil hateth the light, and cometh not to the light, lest his works should be [1110]reproved.

21 But he that doeth the truth cometh to the light, that his works may be made manifest, [1111]that they have been wrought in God.

22 After these things came Jesus and his disciples into the land of Judaea; and there he tarried with them, and baptized.

23 And John also was baptizing in Aenon near to Salim, because there [1112]was much water there: and they came, and were baptized.

24 For John was not yet cast into prison.

25 There arose therefore a questioning on the part of John's disciples with a Jew about purifying.

26 And they came unto John, and said to him, Rabbi, he that was with thee beyond the Jordan, to whom thou hast borne witness, behold, the same baptizeth, and all men come to him.

27 John answered and said, A man can receive nothing, except it have been given him from heaven.

28 Ye yourselves bear me witness, that I said, I am not the Christ, but, that I am sent before him.

[1108] *Or, believeth in him may have*
[1109] *Or, practiseth*
[1110] *Or, convicted*
[1111] *Or, because*
[1112] *Greek were many waters.*

29 He that hath the bride is the bridegroom: but the friend of the bridegroom, that standeth and heareth him, rejoiceth greatly because of the bridegroom's voice: this my joy therefore is made full.

30 He must increase, but I must decrease.

31 He that cometh from above is above all: he that is of the earth is of the earth, and of the earth he speaketh: [1113]he that cometh from heaven is above all.

32 What he hath seen and heard, of that he beareth witness; and no man receiveth his witness.

33 He that hath received his witness hath set his seal to *this*, that God is true.

34 For he whom God hath sent speaketh the words of God: for he giveth not the Spirit by measure.

35 The Father loveth the Son, and hath given all things into his hand.

36 He that believeth on the Son hath eternal life; but he that [1114]obeyeth not the Son shall not see life, but the wrath of God abideth on him.

Chapter 4

1 When therefore the Lord knew that the Pharisees had heard that Jesus was making and baptizing more disciples than John

2 (although Jesus himself baptized not, but his disciples),

3 he left Judaea, and departed again into Galilee.

4 And he must needs pass through Samaria.

5 So he cometh to a city of Samaria, called Sychar, near to the parcel of ground that Jacob gave to his son Joseph:

6 and Jacob's [1115]well was there. Jesus therefore, being wearied with his journey, sat [1116]thus by the [1117]well. It was about the sixth hour.

7 There cometh a woman of Samaria to draw water: Jesus saith unto her, Give me to drink.

[1113] *Some ancient authorities read he that cometh from heaven beareth witness of what he hath seen and heard.*
[1114] *Or, believeth not*
[1115] *Greek spring: and so in verse 14; but not in verses 11, 12.*
[1116] *Or, as he was. Compare 13:25.*
[1117] *Greek spring: and so in verse 14; but not in verses 11, 12.*

8 For his disciples were gone away into the city to buy food.

9 The Samaritan woman therefore saith unto him, How is it that thou, being a Jew, askest drink of me, who am a Samaritan woman? [1118](For Jews have no dealings with Samaritans.)

10 Jesus answered and said unto her, If thou knewest the gift of God, and who it is that saith to thee, Give me to drink; thou wouldest have asked of him, and he would have given thee living water.

11 The woman saith unto him, [1119]Sir, thou hast nothing to draw with, and the well is deep: whence then hast thou that living water?

12 Art thou greater than our father Jacob, who gave us the well, and drank thereof himself, and his sons, and his cattle?

13 Jesus answered and said unto her, Every one that drinketh of this water shall thirst again:

14 but whosoever drinketh of the water that I shall give him shall never thirst; but the water that I shall give him shall become in him a well of water springing up unto eternal life.

15 The woman saith unto him, [1120]Sir, give me this water, that I thirst not, neither come all the way hither to draw.

16 Jesus saith unto her, Go, call thy husband, and come hither.

17 The woman answered and said unto him, I have no husband. Jesus saith unto her, Thou saidst well, I have no husband:

18 for thou hast had five husbands; and he whom thou now hast is not thy husband: this hast thou said truly.

19 The woman saith unto him, Sir, I perceive that thou art a prophet.

20 Our fathers worshipped in this mountain; and ye say, that in Jerusalem is the place where men ought to worship.

21 Jesus saith unto her, Woman, believe me, the hour cometh, when neither in this mountain, nor in Jerusalem, shall ye worship the Father.

22 Ye worship that which ye know not: we worship that which we know; for salvation is from the Jews.

†√ **Jesus identifies himself as a worshiper of God.** Traditional reading: Jesus is object of worship. Context: Jesus includes himself with the Jewish worshipers of the Father.

[1118]*Some ancient authorities omit For the Jews have no dealings with Samaritans.*
[1119]*Or, Lord*
[1120]*Or, Lord*

JOHN 4

23 But the hour cometh, and now is, when the true worshippers shall worship the Father in spirit and truth: [1121]for such doth the Father seek to be his worshippers.

24 [1122]God is a Spirit: and they that worship him must worship in spirit and truth.

25 The woman saith unto him, I know that Messiah cometh (he that is called Christ): when he is come, he will declare unto us all things.

26 Jesus saith unto her, I that speak unto thee am *he*.

27 And upon this came his disciples; and they marvelled that he was speaking with a woman; yet no man said, What seekest thou? or, Why speakest thou with her?

28 So the woman left her waterpot, and went away into the city, and saith to the people,

29 Come, see a man, who told me all things that *ever* I did: can this be the Christ?

30 They went out of the city, and were coming to him.

31 In the mean while the disciples prayed him, saying, Rabbi, eat.

32 But he said unto them, I have meat to eat that ye know not.

33 The disciples therefore said one to another, Hath any man brought him *aught* to eat?

34 Jesus saith unto them, My meat is to do the will of him that sent me, and to accomplish his work.

35 Say not ye, There are yet four months, and *then* cometh the harvest? behold, I say unto you, Lift up your eyes, and look on the fields, that they are [1123]white already unto harvest.

36 He that reapeth receiveth wages, and gathereth fruit unto life eternal; that he that soweth and he that reapeth may rejoice together.

37 For herein is the saying true, One soweth, and another reapeth.

38 I sent you to reap that whereon ye have not labored: others have labored, and ye are entered into their labor.

[1121] *Or, for such the Father also seeketh*
[1122] *Or, God is spirit*
[1123] *Or, white unto harvest. Already he that reapeth etc.*

39 And from that city many of the Samaritans believed on him because of the word of the woman, who testified, He told me all things that *ever* I did.

40 So when the Samaritans came unto him, they besought him to abide with them: and he abode there two days.

41 And many more believed because of his word;

42 and they said to the woman, Now we believe, not because of thy speaking: for we have heard for ourselves, and know that this is indeed the Saviour of the world.

43 And after the two days he went forth from thence into Galilee.

44 For Jesus himself testified, that a prophet hath no honor in his own country.

45 So when he came into Galilee, the Galilaeans received him, having seen all the things that he did in Jerusalem at the feast: for they also went unto the feast.

46 He came therefore again unto Cana of Galilee, where he made the water wine. And there was a certain [1124]nobleman, whose son was sick at Capernaum.

47 When he heard that Jesus was come out of Judaea into Galilee, he went unto him, and besought *him* that he would come down, and heal his son; for he was at the point of death.

48 Jesus therefore said unto him, Except ye see signs and wonders, ye will in no wise believe.

49 The [1125]nobleman saith unto him, [1126]Sir, come down ere my child die.

50 Jesus saith unto him, Go thy way; thy son liveth. The man believed the word that Jesus spake unto him, and he went his way.

51 And as he was now going down, his [1127]servants met him, saying, that his son lived.

52 So he inquired of them the hour when he began to amend. They said therefore unto him, Yesterday at the seventh hour the fever left him.

[1124] *Or, king's officer*
[1125] *Or, king's officer*
[1126] *Or, Lord*
[1127] *Greek bondservants.*

53 So the father knew that *it was* at that hour in which Jesus said unto him, Thy son liveth: and himself believed, and his whole house.

54 This is again the second sign that Jesus did, having come out of Judaea into Galilee.

Chapter 5

1 After these things there was [1128]a feast of the Jews; and Jesus went up to Jerusalem.

2 Now there is in Jerusalem by the sheep *gate* a pool, which is called in Hebrew [1129]Bethesda, having five porches.

3 In these lay a multitude of them that were sick, blind, halt, withered[1130].

5 And a certain man was there, who had been thirty and eight years in his infirmity.

6 When Jesus saw him lying, and knew that he had been now a long time *in that case*, he saith unto him, Wouldest thou be made whole?

7 The sick man answered him, [1131]Sir, I have no man, when the water is troubled, to put me into the pool: but while I am coming, another steppeth down before me.

8 Jesus saith unto him, Arise, take up thy [1132]bed, and walk.

9 And straightway the man was made whole, and took up his [1133]bed and walked.

Now it was the sabbath on that day.

10 So the Jews said unto him that was cured, It is the sabbath, and it is not lawful for thee to take up thy [1134]bed.

[1128] *Many ancient authorities read the feast (Compare 2:13?).*

[1129] *Some ancient authorities read Bethsaida, others Bethzatha*

[1130] *Many ancient authorities insert, wholly or in part, waiting for the moving of the water: 4for an angel of the Lord went down at certain seasons into the pool, and troubled the water: whosoever then first after the troubling of the water stepped in was made whole, with whatsoever disease he was holden.*

[1131] *Or, Lord*

[1132] *Or, pallet*

[1133] *Or, pallet*

[1134] *Or, pallet*

11 But he answered them, He that made me whole, the same said unto me, Take up thy [1135]bed, and walk.

12 They asked him, Who is the man that said unto thee, Take up *thy* [1136]*bed*, and walk?

13 But he that was healed knew not who it was; for Jesus had conveyed himself away, a multitude being in the place.

14 Afterward Jesus findeth him in the temple, and said unto him, Behold, thou art made whole: sin no more, lest a worse thing befall thee.

15 The man went away, and told the Jews that it was Jesus who had made him whole.

16 And for this cause the Jews persecuted Jesus, because he did these things on the sabbath.

17 But Jesus answered them, My Father worketh even until now, and I work.

18 For this cause therefore the Jews sought the more to kill him, because he not only brake the sabbath, but also called God his own Father, making himself equal with God.

19 Jesus therefore answered and said unto them, Verily, verily, I say unto you, The Son can do nothing of himself, but what he seeth the Father doing: for what things soever he doeth, these the Son also doeth in like manner.

†✓ **Jesus claims total dependency and delegated authority.** Traditional reading: Co-equal power. Context: Functional subordination. God does not need to "see" anyone else to act.

20 For the Father loveth the Son, and showeth him all things that himself doeth: and greater works than these will he show him, that ye may marvel.

21 For as the Father raiseth the dead and giveth them life, even so the Son also giveth life to whom he will.

22 For neither doth the Father judge any man, but he hath given all judgment unto the Son;

23 that all may honor the Son, even as they honor the Father. He that honoreth not the Son honoreth not the Father that sent him.

24 Verily, verily, I say unto you, He that heareth my word, and believeth him that sent me, hath eternal life, and cometh not into judgment, but hath passed out of death into life.

[1135] *Or, pallet*
[1136] *Or, pallet*

25 Verily, verily, I say unto you, The hour cometh, and now is, when the dead shall hear the voice of the Son of God; and they that [1137]hear shall live.

26 For as the Father hath life in himself, even so gave he to the Son also to have life in himself:

27 and he gave him authority to execute judgment, because he is a son of man.

28 Marvel not at this: for the hour cometh, in which all that are in the tombs shall hear his voice,

29 and shall come forth; they that have done good, unto the resurrection of life; and they that have [1138]done evil, unto the resurrection of judgment.

30 I can of myself do nothing: as I hear, I judge: and my judgment is righteous; because I seek not mine own will, but the will of him that sent me.

31 If I bear witness of myself, my witness is not true.

32 It is another that beareth witness of me; and I know that the witness which he witnesseth of me is true.

33 Ye have sent unto John, and he hath borne witness unto the truth.

34 But the witness which I receive is not from man: howbeit I say these things, that ye may be saved.

35 He was the lamp that burneth and shineth; and ye were willing to rejoice for a season in his light.

36 But the witness which I have is greater than *that of* John; for the works which the Father hath given me to accomplish, the very works that I do, bear witness of me, that the Father hath sent me.

37 And the Father that sent me, he hath borne witness of me. Ye have neither heard his voice at any time, nor seen his form.

38 And ye have not his word abiding in you: for whom he sent, him ye believe not.

39 [1139]Ye search the scriptures, because ye think that in them ye have eternal life; and these are they which bear witness of me;

[1137] *Or, hearken*
[1138] *Or, practised*
[1139] *Or, Search the scriptures*

40 and ye will not come to me, that ye may have life.

41 I receive not glory from men.

42 But I know you, that ye have not the love of God in yourselves.

43 I am come in my Father's name, and ye receive me not: if another shall come in his own name, him ye will receive.

44 How can ye believe, who receive glory one of another, and the glory that *cometh* from [1140]the only God ye seek not?

45 Think not that I will accuse you to the Father: there is one that accuseth you, *even* Moses, on whom ye have set your hope.

46 For if ye believed Moses, ye would believe me; for he wrote of me.

47 But if ye believe not his writings, how shall ye believe my words?

Chapter 6

1 After these things Jesus went away to the other side of the sea of Galilee, which is *the sea* of Tiberias.

2 And a great multitude followed him, because they beheld the signs which he did on them that were sick.

3 And Jesus went up into the mountain, and there he sat with his disciples.

4 Now the passover, the feast of the Jews, was at hand.

5 Jesus therefore lifting up his eyes, and seeing that a great multitude cometh unto him, saith unto Philip, Whence are we to buy [1141]bread, that these may eat?

6 And this he said to prove him: for he himself knew what he would do.

7 Philip answered him, Two hundred [1142]shillings' worth of [1143]bread is not sufficient for them, that every one may take a little.

8 One of his disciples, Andrew, Simon Peter's brother, saith unto him,

9 There is a lad here, who hath five barley loaves, and two fishes: but what are these among so many?

[1140] *Some ancient authorities read the only one.*
[1141] *Greek loaves.*
[1142] *The word in the Greek denotes a coin worth about eight pence halfpenny, or nearly seventeen cents.*
[1143] *Greek loaves.*

10 Jesus said, Make the people sit down. Now there was much grass in the place. So the men sat down, in number about five thousand.

11 Jesus therefore took the loaves; and having given thanks, he distributed to them that were set down; likewise also of the fishes as much as they would.

12 And when they were filled, he saith unto his disciples, Gather up the broken pieces which remain over, that nothing be lost.

13 So they gathered them up, and filled twelve baskets with broken pieces from the five barley loaves, which remained over unto them that had eaten.

14 When therefore the people saw the [1144]sign which he did, they said, This is of a truth the prophet that cometh into the world.

15 Jesus therefore perceiving that they were about to come and take him by force, to make him king, withdrew again into the mountain himself alone.

16 And when evening came, his disciples went down unto the sea;

17 and they entered into a boat, and were going over the sea unto Capernaum. And it was now dark, and Jesus had not yet come to them.

18 And the sea was rising by reason of a great wind that blew.

19 When therefore they had rowed about five and twenty or thirty furlongs, they behold Jesus walking on the sea, and drawing nigh unto the boat: and they were afraid.

20 But he saith unto them, It is I; be not afraid.

21 They were willing therefore to receive him into the boat: and straightway the boat was at the land whither they were going.

22 On the morrow the multitude that stood on the other side of the sea saw that there was no other [1145]boat there, save one, and that Jesus entered not with his disciples into the boat, but *that* his disciples went away alone

23 (howbeit there came [1146]boats from Tiberias nigh unto the place where they ate the bread after the Lord had given thanks):

[1144] *Some ancient authorities read signs.*
[1145] *Greek little boat.*
[1146] *Greek little boats.*

24 when the multitude therefore saw that Jesus was not there, neither his disciples, they themselves got into the [1147]boats, and came to Capernaum, seeking Jesus.

25 And when they found him on the other side of the sea, they said unto him, Rabbi, when camest thou hither?

26 Jesus answered them and said, Verily, verily, I say unto you, Ye seek me, not because ye saw signs, but because ye ate of the loaves, and were filled.

27 Work not for the food which perisheth, but for the food which abideth unto eternal life, which the Son of man shall give unto you: for him the Father, *even* God, hath sealed.

28 They said therefore unto him, What must we do, that we may work the works of God?

29 Jesus answered and said unto them, This is the work of God, that ye believe on him whom [1148]he hath sent.

30 They said therefore unto him, What then doest thou for a sign, that we may see, and believe thee? what workest thou?

31 Our fathers ate the manna in the wilderness; as it is written, He [1149]gave them bread out of heaven to eat.

32 Jesus therefore said unto them, Verily, verily, I say unto you, It was not Moses that gave you the bread out of heaven; but my Father giveth you the true bread out of heaven.

33 For the bread of God is that which cometh down out of heaven, and giveth life unto the world.

34 They said therefore unto him, Lord, evermore give us this bread.

35 Jesus said unto them, I am the bread of life: he that cometh to me shall not hunger, and he that believeth on me shall never thirst.

36 But I said unto you, that ye have seen me, and yet believe not.

37 All that which the Father giveth me shall come unto me; and him that cometh to me I will in no wise cast out.

38 For I am come down from heaven, not to do mine own will, but the will of him that sent me.

[1147] *Greek little boats.*
[1148] *Or, he sent*
[1149] Neh. 9:15; Ex. 16:4, 15; Ps. 78:24; 105:40.

39 And this is the will of him that sent me, that of all that which he hath given me I should lose nothing, but should raise it up at the last day.

40 For this is the will of my Father, that every one that beholdeth the Son, and believeth on him, should have eternal life; and [1150]I will raise him up at the last day.

41 The Jews therefore murmured concerning him, because he said, I am the bread which came down out of heaven.

42 And they said, Is not this Jesus, the son of Joseph, whose father and mother we know? how doth he now say, I am come down out of heaven?

43 Jesus answered and said unto them, Murmur not among yourselves.

44 No man can come to me, except the Father that sent me draw him: and I will raise him up in the last day.

45 It is written in the prophets, [1151]And they shall all be taught of God. Every one that hath heard from the Father, and hath learned, cometh unto me.

46 Not that any man hath seen the Father, save he that is from God, he hath seen the Father.

47 Verily, verily, I say unto you, He that believeth hath eternal life.

48 I am the bread of life.

49 Your fathers ate the manna in the wilderness, and they died.

50 This is the bread which cometh down out of heaven, that a man may eat thereof, and not die.

51 I am the living bread which came down out of heaven: if any man eat of this bread, he shall live for ever: yea and the bread which I will give is my flesh, for the life of the world.

52 The Jews therefore strove one with another, saying, How can this man give us his flesh to eat?

53 Jesus therefore said unto them, Verily, verily, I say unto you, Except ye eat the flesh of the Son of man and drink his blood, ye have not life in yourselves.

[1150] *Or, that I should raise him up*
[1151] *Isa. 54:13; (Jer. 31:34?).*

54 He that eateth my flesh and drinketh my blood hath eternal life; and I will raise him up at the last day.

55 For my flesh is [1152]meat indeed, and my blood is [1153]drink indeed.

56 He that eateth my flesh and drinketh my blood abideth in me, and I in him.

57 As the living Father sent me, and I live because of the Father; so he that eateth me, he also shall live because of me.

58 This is the bread which came down out of heaven: not as the fathers ate, and died; he that eateth this bread shall live for ever.

59 These things said he in [1154]the synagogue, as he taught in Capernaum.

60 Many therefore of his disciples, when they heard *this*, said, This is a hard saying; who can hear [1155]it?

61 But Jesus knowing in himself that his disciples murmured at this, said unto them, Doth this cause you to stumble?

62 *What* then if ye should behold the Son of man ascending where he was before?

63 It is the spirit that giveth life; the flesh profiteth nothing: the words that I have spoken unto you are spirit, and are life.

64 But there are some of you that believe not. For Jesus knew from the beginning who they were that believed not, and who it was that should [1156]betray him.

65 And he said, For this cause have I said unto you, that no man can come unto me, except it be given unto him of the Father.

66 Upon this many of his disciples went back, and walked no more with him.

67 Jesus said therefore unto the twelve, Would ye also go away?

68 Simon Peter answered him, Lord, to whom shall we go? thou [1157]hast the words of eternal life.

69 And we have believed and know that thou art the Holy One of God.

[1152] *Greek true meat.*
[1153] *Greek true drink.*
[1154] *Or, a synagogue*
[1155] *Or, him*
[1156] *Or, deliver him up*
[1157] *Or, hast words*

70 Jesus answered them, Did not I choose you the twelve, and one of you is a devil?

71 Now he spake of Judas *the son* of Simon Iscariot, for he it was that should [1158]betray him, *being* one of the twelve.

Chapter 7

1 And after these things Jesus walked in Galilee: for he would not walk in Judaea, because the Jews sought to kill him.

2 Now the feast of the Jews, the feast of tabernacles, was at hand.

3 His brethren therefore said unto him, Depart hence, and go into Judaea, that thy disciples also may behold thy works which thou doest.

4 For no man doeth anything in secret, [1159]and himself seeketh to be known openly. If thou doest these things, manifest thyself to the world.

5 For even his brethren did not believe on him.

6 Jesus therefore saith unto them, My time is not yet come; but your time is always ready.

7 The world cannot hate you; but me it hateth, because I testify of it, that its works are evil.

8 Go ye up unto the feast: I go not up [1160]unto this feast; because my time is not yet fulfilled.

9 And having said these things unto them, he abode *still* in Galilee.

10 But when his brethren were gone up unto the feast, then went he also up, not publicly, but as it were in secret.

11 The Jews therefore sought him at the feast, and said, Where is he?

12 And there was much murmuring among the multitudes concerning him: some said, He is a good man; others said, Not so, but he leadeth the multitude astray.

13 Yet no man spake openly of him for fear of the Jews.

14 But when it was now the midst of the feast Jesus went up into the temple, and taught.

[1158] *Or, deliver him up*
[1159] *Some ancient authorities read and seeketh it to be known openly.*
[1160] *Many ancient authorities add yet.*

15 The Jews therefore marvelled, saying, How knoweth this man letters, having never learned?

16 Jesus therefore answered them, and said, My teaching is not mine, but his that sent me.

17 If any man willeth to do his will, he shall know of the teaching, whether it is of God, or *whether* I speak from myself.

18 He that speaketh from himself seeketh his own glory: but he that seeketh the glory of him that sent him, the same is true, and no unrighteousness is in him.

19 Did not Moses give you the law, and *yet* none of you doeth the law? Why seek ye to kill me?

20 The multitude answered, Thou hast a demon: who seeketh to kill thee?

21 Jesus answered and said unto them, I did one work, and ye all marvel because thereof.

22 Moses hath given you circumcision (not that it is of Moses, but of the fathers); and on the sabbath ye circumcise a man.

23 If a man receiveth circumcision on the sabbath, that the law of Moses may not be broken; are ye wroth with me, because I made [1161]a man every whit whole on the sabbath?

24 Judge not according to appearance, but judge righteous judgment.

25 Some therefore of them of Jerusalem said, Is not this he whom they seek to kill?

26 And lo, he speaketh openly, and they say nothing unto him. Can it be that the rulers indeed know that this is the Christ?

27 Howbeit we know this man whence he is: but when the Christ cometh, no one knoweth whence he is.

28 Jesus therefore cried in the temple, teaching and saying, Ye both know me, and know whence I am; and I am not come of myself, but he that sent me is true, whom ye know not.

29 I know him; because I am from him, and he sent me.

30 They sought therefore to take him: and no man laid his hand on him, because his hour was not yet come.

[1161] *Greek a whole man sound.*

JOHN 7

31 But of the multitude many believed on him; and they said, When the Christ shall come, will he do more signs than those which this man hath done?

32 The Pharisees heard the multitude murmuring these things concerning him; and the chief priests and the Pharisees sent officers to take him.

33 Jesus therefore said, Yet a little while am I with you, and I go unto him that sent me.

34 Ye shall seek me, and shall not find me: and where I am, ye cannot come.

35 The Jews therefore said among themselves, Whither will this man go that we shall not find him? will he go unto the Dispersion [1162]among the Greeks, and teach the Greeks?

36 What is this word that he said, Ye shall seek me, and shall not find me; and where I am, ye cannot come?

37 Now on the last day, the great *day* of the feast, Jesus stood and cried, saying, If any man thirst, let him come unto me and drink.

38 He that believeth on me, as the scripture hath said, [1163]from within him shall flow rivers of living water.

39 But this spake he of the Spirit, which they that believed on him were to receive: [1164]for the Spirit was not yet *given*; because Jesus was not yet glorified.

40 *Some* of the multitude therefore, when they heard these words, said, This is of a truth the prophet.

41 Others said, This is the Christ. But some said, What, doth the Christ come out of Galilee?

42 [1165]Hath not the scripture said that the Christ cometh of the seed of David, and from Bethlehem, the village where David was?

43 So there arose a division in the multitude because of him.

44 And some of them would have taken him; but no man laid hands on him.

[1162] *Greek of.*
[1163] *Greek out of his belly.*
[1164] *Some ancient authorities read for the Holy Spirit was not yet given.*
[1165] *2 Sam. 7:12ff; Mic. 5:2.*

45 The officers therefore came to the chief priests and Pharisees; and they said unto them, Why did ye not bring him?

46 The officers answered, Never man so spake.

47 The Pharisees therefore answered them, Are ye also led astray?

48 Hath any of the rulers believed on him, or of the Pharisees?

49 But this multitude that knoweth not the law are accursed.

50 Nicodemus saith unto them (he that came to him before, being one of them),

51 Doth our law judge a man, except it first hear from himself and know what he doeth?

52 They answered and said unto him, Art thou also of Galilee? Search, and [1166] see that out of Galilee ariseth no prophet.

53 [1167] [And they went every man unto his own house:

Chapter 8

1 but Jesus went unto the mount of Olives.

2 And early in the morning he came again into the temple, and all the people came unto him; and he sat down, and taught them.

3 And the scribes and the Pharisees bring a woman taken in adultery; and having set her in the midst,

4 they say unto him, Teacher, this woman hath been taken in adultery, in the very act.

5 [1168] Now in the law Moses commanded us to stone such: what then sayest thou of her?

6 And this they said, trying him, that they might have *whereof* to accuse him. But Jesus stooped down, and with his finger wrote on the ground.

7 But when they continued asking him, he lifted up himself, and said unto them, He that is without sin among you, let him first cast a stone at her.

[1166] *Or, see: for out of Galilee etc.*

[1167] *Most of the ancient authorities omit 7:53–8:11. Those which contain it vary much from each other.*

[1168] *Lev. 20:10; Dt. 22:22f.*

8 And again he stooped down, and with his finger wrote on the ground.

9 And they, when they heard it, went out one by one, beginning from the eldest, *even* unto the last: and Jesus was left alone, and the woman, where she was, in the midst.

10 And Jesus lifted up himself, and said unto her, Woman, where are they? did no man condemn thee?

11 And she said, No man, Lord. And Jesus said, Neither do I condemn thee: go thy way; from henceforth sin no more.]

12 Again therefore Jesus spake unto them, saying, I am the light of the world: he that followeth me shall not walk in the darkness, but shall have the light of life.

13 The Pharisees therefore said unto him, Thou bearest witness of thyself; thy witness is not true.

14 Jesus answered and said unto them, Even if I bear witness of myself, my witness is true; for I know whence I came, and whither I go; but ye know not whence I come, or whither I go.

15 Ye judge after the flesh; I judge no man.

16 Yea and if I judge, my judgment is true; for I am not alone, but I and the Father that sent me.

17 Yea and in your law it is written, [1169] that the witness of two men is true.

18 I am he that beareth witness of myself, and the Father that sent me beareth witness of me.

19 They said therefore unto him, Where is thy Father? Jesus answered, Ye know neither me, nor my Father: if ye knew me, ye would know my Father also.

20 These words spake he in the treasury, as he taught in the temple: and no man took him; because his hour was not yet come.

21 He said therefore again unto them, I go away, and ye shall seek me, and shall die in your sin: whither I go, ye cannot come.

22 The Jews therefore said, Will he kill himself, that he saith, Whither I go, ye cannot come?

†✓ **The Law of Two Men.** Jesus utilizes the legal requirement for two distinct witnesses to prove his identity. He defines himself as the first "man" and the Father as the second "man." To merge them into one being would be to invalidate his own legal testimony.

[1169] *Compare Dt. 19:15; 17:6.*

23 And he said unto them, Ye are from beneath; I am from above: ye are of this world; I am not of this world.

24 I said therefore unto you, that ye shall die in your sins: for except ye believe that I am *he*, ye shall die in your sins.

25 They said therefore unto him, Who art thou? Jesus said unto them, [1170]Even that which I have also spoken unto you from the beginning.

26 I have many things to speak and to judge concerning you: howbeit he that sent me is true; and the things which I heard from him, these speak I unto the world.

27 They perceived not that he spake to them of the Father.

28 Jesus therefore said, When ye have lifted up the Son of man, then shall ye know that [1171]I am *he*, and *that* I do nothing of myself, but as the Father taught me, I speak these things.

29 And he that sent me is with me; he hath not left me alone; for I do always the things that are pleasing to him.

30 As he spake these things, many believed on him.

31 Jesus therefore said to those Jews that had believed him, If ye abide in my word, *then* are ye truly my disciples;

32 and ye shall know the truth, and the truth shall make you free.

33 They answered unto him, We are Abraham's seed, and have never yet been in bondage to any man: how sayest thou, Ye shall be made free?

34 Jesus answered them, Verily, verily, I say unto you, Every one that committeth sin is the bondservant of sin.

35 And the bondservant abideth not in the house for ever: the son abideth for ever.

36 If therefore the Son shall make you free, ye shall be free indeed.

37 I know that ye are Abraham's seed; yet ye seek to kill me, because my word [1172]hath not free course in you.

38 I speak the things which I have seen with [1173]*my* Father: and ye also do the things which ye heard from *your* father.

[1170] *Or, Altogether that which I also speak unto you*
[1171] *Or, I am he: and I do*
[1172] *Or, hath no place in you*
[1173] *Or, the Father: do ye also therefore the things which ye heard from the Father.*

39 They answered and said unto him, Our father is Abraham. Jesus saith unto them, If ye [1174]were Abraham's children, [1175]ye would do the works of Abraham.

40 But now ye seek to kill me, a man that hath told you the truth, which I heard from God: this did not Abraham.

41 Ye do the works of your father. They said unto him, We were not born of fornication; we have one Father, *even* God.

42 Jesus said unto them, If God were your Father, ye would love me: for I came forth and am come from God; for neither have I come of myself, but he sent me.

43 Why do ye not [1176]understand my speech? *Even* because ye cannot hear my word.

44 Ye are of *your* father the devil, and the lusts of your father it is your will to do. He was a murderer from the beginning, and standeth not in the truth, because there is no truth in him. [1177]When he speaketh a lie, he speaketh of his own: for he is a liar, and the father thereof.

45 But because I say the truth, ye believe me not.

46 Which of you convicteth me of sin? If I say truth, why do ye not believe me?

47 He that is of God heareth the words of God: for this cause ye hear *them* not, because ye are not of God.

48 The Jews answered and said unto him, Say we not well that thou art a Samaritan, and hast a demon?

49 Jesus answered, I have not a demon; but I honor my Father, and ye dishonor me.

50 But I seek not mine own glory: there is one that seeketh and judgeth.

51 Verily, verily, I say unto you, If a man keep my word, he shall never see death.

52 The Jews said unto him, Now we know that thou hast a demon. Abraham died, and the prophets; and thou sayest, If a man keep my word, he shall never taste of death.

[1174]*Greek are.*
[1175]*Some ancient authorities read ye do the works of Abraham.*
[1176]*Or, know*
[1177]*Or, When one speaketh a lie, he speaketh of his own: for his father also is a liar.*

53 Art thou greater than our father Abraham, who died? and the prophets died: whom makest thou thyself?

54 Jesus answered, If I glorify myself, my glory is nothing: it is my Father that glorifieth me; of whom ye say, that he is your God;

55 and ye have not known him: but I know him; and if I should say, I know him not, I shall be like unto you, a liar: but I know him, and keep his word.

56 Your father Abraham rejoiced [1178]to see my day; and he saw it, and was glad.

57 The Jews therefore said unto him, Thou art not yet fifty years old, and hast thou seen Abraham?

58 Jesus said unto them, Verily, verily, I say unto you, Before Abraham was born, I am.[1179]

†✓ **Jesus is claiming pre-existence, not the divine Name.** Traditional reading: Jesus claims the name "I AM" (YHWH). Actual Greek: *ego eimi* is standard grammar for "I am he". The Septuagint for Exod 3:14 is different (*ho on*).

59 They took up stones therefore to cast at him: but Jesus [1180]hid himself, and went out of the temple[1181].

Chapter 9

1 And as he passed by, he saw a man blind from his birth.

2 And his disciples asked him, saying, Rabbi, who sinned, this man, or his parents, that he should be born blind?

3 Jesus answered, Neither did this man sin, nor his parents: but that the works of God should be made manifest in him.

4 We must work the works of him that sent me, while it is day: the night cometh, when no man can work.

5 When I am in the world, I am the light of the world.

6 When he had thus spoken, he spat on the ground, and made clay of the spittle, [1182]and anointed his eyes with the clay,

---

[1178] *Or, that he should see*

[1179] **Translation:** Greek *ego eimi*. This is standard grammar for "I am he" or "I exist." The blind man uses the exact same phrase in John 9:9. It is distinct from the divine name in Exodus 3:14 (*ho on*). Jesus is claiming pre-eminence, not the Divine Name.

[1180] *Or, was hidden, and went etc.*

[1181] *Many ancient authorities add and going through the midst of them went his way and so passed by.*

[1182] *Or, and with the clay thereof anointed his eyes*

7 and said unto him, Go, wash in the pool of Siloam (which is by interpretation, Sent). He went away therefore, and washed, and came seeing.

8 The neighbors therefore, and they that saw him aforetime, that he was a beggar, said, Is not this he that sat and begged?

9 Others said, It is he: others said, No, but he is like him. He said, I am *he*.

10 They said therefore unto him, How then were thine eyes opened?

11 He answered, The man that is called Jesus made clay, and anointed mine eyes, and said unto me, Go to Siloam, and wash: so I went away and washed, and I received sight.

12 And they said unto him, Where is he? He saith, I know not.

13 They bring to the Pharisees him that aforetime was blind.

14 Now it was the sabbath on the day when Jesus made the clay, and opened his eyes.

15 Again therefore the Pharisees also asked him how he received his sight. And he said unto them, He put clay upon mine eyes, and I washed, and I see.

16 Some therefore of the Pharisees said, This man is not from God, because he keepeth not the sabbath. But others said, How can a man that is a sinner do such signs? And there was a division among them.

17 They say therefore unto the blind man again, What sayest thou of him, in that he opened thine eyes? And he said, He is a prophet.

18 The Jews therefore did not believe concerning him, that he had been blind, and had received his sight, until they called the parents of him that had received his sight,

19 and asked them, saying, Is this your son, who ye say was born blind? how then doth he now see?

20 His parents answered and said, We know that this is our son, and that he was born blind:

21 but how he now seeth, we know not; or who opened his eyes, we know not: ask him; he is of age; he shall speak for himself.

22 These things said his parents, because they feared the Jews: for the Jews had agreed already, that if any man should confess him *to be* Christ, he should be put out of the synagogue.

23 Therefore said his parents, He is of age; ask him.

24 So they called a second time the man that was blind, and said unto him, Give glory to God: we know that this man is a sinner.

25 He therefore answered, Whether he is a sinner, I know not: one thing I know, that, whereas I was blind, now I see.

26 They said therefore unto him, What did he to thee? how opened he thine eyes?

27 He answered them, I told you even now, and ye did not hear; wherefore would ye hear it again? would ye also become his disciples?

28 And they reviled him, and said, Thou art his disciple; but we are disciples of Moses.

29 We know that God hath spoken unto Moses: but as for this man, we know not whence he is.

30 The man answered and said unto them, Why, herein is the marvel, that ye know not whence he is, and *yet* he opened mine eyes.

31 We know that God heareth not sinners: but if any man be a worshipper of God, and do his will, him he heareth.

32 Since the world began it was never heard that any one opened the eyes of a man born blind.

33 If this man were not from God, he could do nothing.

34 They answered and said unto him, Thou wast altogether born in sins, and dost thou teach us? And they cast him out.

35 Jesus heard that they had cast him out; and finding him, he said, Dost thou believe on [1183]the Son of God?

36 He answered and said, And who is he, Lord, that I may believe on him?

37 Jesus said unto him, Thou hast both seen him, and he it is that speaketh with thee.

[1183] *Many ancient authorities read the Son of Man.*

38 And he said, Lord, I believe. And he [1184]worshipped him.

39 And Jesus said, For judgment came I into this world, that they that see not may see; and that they that see may become blind.

40 Those of the Pharisees who were with him heard these things, and said unto him, Are we also blind?

41 Jesus said unto them, If ye were blind, ye would have no sin: but now ye say, We see: your sin remaineth.

Chapter 10

1 Verily, verily, I say unto you, He that entereth not by the door into the fold of the sheep, but climbeth up some other way, the same is a thief and a robber.

2 But he that entereth in by the door is [1185]the shepherd of the sheep.

3 To him the porter openeth; and the sheep hear his voice: and he calleth his own sheep by name, and leadeth them out.

4 When he hath put forth all his own, he goeth before them, and the sheep follow him: for they know his voice.

5 And a stranger will they not follow, but will flee from him: for they know not the voice of strangers.

6 This [1186]parable spake Jesus unto them: but they understood not what things they were which he spake unto them.

7 Jesus therefore said unto them again, Verily, verily, I say unto you, I am the door of the sheep.

8 All that came [1187]before me are thieves and robbers: but the sheep did not hear them.

9 I am the door; by me if any man enter in, he shall be saved, and shall go in and go out, and shall find pasture.

10 The thief cometh not, but that he may steal, and kill, and destroy: I came that they may have life, and may [1188]have *it* abundantly.

[1184]*The Greek word denotes an act of reverence, whether paid to a creature (as here) or to the Creator (see 4:20).*
[1185]*Or, a shepherd*
[1186]*Or, proverb*
[1187]*Some ancient authorities omit before me.*
[1188]*Or, have abundance*

11 I am the good shepherd: the good shepherd layeth down his life for the sheep.

12 He that is a hireling, and not a shepherd, whose own the sheep are not, beholdeth the wolf coming, and leaveth the sheep, and fleeth, and the wolf snatcheth them, and scattereth *them*:

13 *he fleeth* because he is a hireling, and careth not for the sheep.

14 I am the good shepherd; and I know mine own, and mine own know me,

15 even as the Father knoweth me, and I know the Father; and I lay down my life for the sheep.

16 And other sheep I have, which are not of this fold: them also I must [1189]bring, and they shall hear my voice; and [1190]they shall become one flock, one shepherd.

17 Therefore doth the Father love me, because I lay down my life, that I may take it again.

18 No one [1191]taketh it away from me, but I lay it down of myself. I have [1192]power to lay it down, and I have [1193]power to take it again. This commandment received I from my Father.

19 There arose a division again among the Jews because of these words.

20 And many of them said, He hath a demon, and is mad; why hear ye him?

21 Others said, These are not the sayings of one possessed with a demon. Can a demon open the eyes of the blind?

22 [1194]And it was the feast of the dedication at Jerusalem:

23 it was winter; and Jesus was walking in the temple in Solomon's [1195]porch.

24 The Jews therefore came round about him, and said unto him, How long dost thou hold us in suspense? If thou art the Christ, tell us plainly.

[1189] *Or, lead*
[1190] *Or, there shall be one flock*
[1191] *Some ancient authorities read took it away.*
[1192] *Or, right*
[1193] *Or, right*
[1194] *Some ancient authorities read At that time was the feast.*
[1195] *Or, portico*

JOHN 10

25 Jesus answered them, I told you, and ye believe not: the works that I do in my Father's name, these bear witness of me.

26 But ye believe not, because ye are not of my sheep.

27 My sheep hear my voice, and I know them, and they follow me:

28 and I give unto them eternal life; and they shall never perish, and no one shall snatch them out of my hand.

29 [1196]My Father, who hath given *them* unto me, is greater than all; and no one is able to snatch [1197]*them* out of the Father's hand.

30 I and the Father are one.

31 The Jews took up stones again to stone him.

32 Jesus answered them, Many good works have I showed you from the Father; for which of those works do ye stone me?

33 The Jews answered him, For a good work we stone thee not, but for blasphemy; and because that thou, being a man, makest thyself God.

34 Jesus answered them, Is it not written in your law, [1198]I said, Ye are gods?

35 If he called them gods, unto whom the word of God came (and the scripture cannot be broken),

36 say ye of him, whom the Father [1199]sanctified and sent into the world, Thou blasphemest; because I said, I am *the* Son of God?

37 If I do not the works of my Father, believe me not.

38 But if I do them, though ye believe not me, believe the works: that ye may know and understand that the Father is in me, and I in the Father.

39 They sought again to take him: and he went forth out of their hand.

40 And he went away again beyond the Jordan into the place where John was at the first baptizing; and there he abode.

41 And many came unto him; and they said, John indeed did no sign: but all things whatsoever John spake of this man were true.

42 And many believed on him there.

> †✓ **One in purpose, not essence.** Traditional reading: One essence. Actual context: oneness in purpose/protection (John 17:21–22 prays disciples be one "as we are one").

[1196] *Some ancient authorities read That which my Father hath given unto me.*
[1197] *Or, aught*
[1198] *Ps. 82:6.*
[1199] *Or, consecrated*

Chapter 11

1 Now a certain man was sick, Lazarus of Bethany, of the village of Mary and her sister Martha.

2 And it was that Mary who anointed the Lord with ointment, and wiped his feet with her hair, whose brother Lazarus was sick.

3 The sisters therefore sent unto him, saying, Lord, behold, he whom thou lovest is sick.

4 But when Jesus heard it, he said, This sickness is not unto death, but for the glory of God, that the Son of God may be glorified thereby.

5 Now Jesus loved Martha, and her sister, and Lazarus.

6 When therefore he heard that he was sick, he abode at that time two days in the place where he was.

7 Then after this he saith to the disciples, Let us go into Judaea again.

8 The disciples say unto him, Rabbi, the Jews were but now seeking to stone thee; and goest thou thither again?

9 Jesus answered, Are there not twelve hours in the day? If a man walk in the day, he stumbleth not, because he seeth the light of this world.

10 But if a man walk in the night, he stumbleth, because the light is not in him.

11 These things spake he: and after this he saith unto them, Our friend Lazarus is fallen asleep; but I go, that I may awake him out of sleep.

12 The disciples therefore said unto him, Lord, if he is fallen asleep, he will [1200]recover.

13 Now Jesus had spoken of his death: but they thought that he spake of taking rest in sleep.

14 Then Jesus therefore said unto them plainly, Lazarus is dead.

15 And I am glad for your sakes that I was not there, to the intent ye may believe; nevertheless let us go unto him.

16 Thomas therefore, who is called [1201]Didymus, said unto his fellow-disciples, Let us also go, that we may die with him.

[1200]*Greek be saved.*
[1201]*That is, Twin.*

17 So when Jesus came, he found that he had been in the tomb four days already.

18 Now Bethany was nigh unto Jerusalem, about fifteen furlongs off;

19 and many of the Jews had come to Martha and Mary, to console them concerning their brother.

20 Martha therefore, when she heard that Jesus was coming, went and met him: but Mary still sat in the house.

21 Martha therefore said unto Jesus, Lord, if thou hadst been here, my brother had not died.

22 And even now I know that, whatsoever thou shalt ask of God, God will give thee.

23 Jesus saith unto her, Thy brother shall rise again.

24 Martha saith unto him, I know that he shall rise again in the resurrection at the last day.

25 Jesus said unto her, I am the resurrection, and the life: he that believeth on me, though he die, yet shall he live;

26 and whosoever liveth and believeth on me shall never die. Believest thou this?

27 She saith unto him, Yea, Lord: I have believed that thou art the Christ, the Son of God, *even* he that cometh into the world.

28 And when she had said this, she went away, and called Mary [1202]her sister secretly, saying, The Teacher is here, and calleth thee.

29 And she, when she heard it, arose quickly, and went unto him.

30 (Now Jesus was not yet come into the village, but was still in the place where Martha met him.)

31 The Jews then who were with her in the house, and were consoling her, when they saw Mary, that she rose up quickly and went out, followed her, supposing that she was going unto the tomb to [1203]weep there.

32 Mary therefore, when she came where Jesus was, and saw him, fell down at his feet, saying unto him, Lord, if thou hadst been here, my brother had not died.

[1202] *Or, her sister, saying secretly*
[1203] *Greek wail.*

33 When Jesus therefore saw her [1204]weeping, and the Jews *also* [1205]weeping who came with her, he [1206]groaned in the spirit, and [1207]was troubled,

34 and said, Where have ye laid him? They say unto him, Lord, come and see.

35 Jesus wept.

36 The Jews therefore said, Behold how he loved him!

37 But some of them said, Could not this man, who opened the eyes of him that was blind, have caused that this man also should not die?

38 Jesus therefore again [1208]groaning in himself cometh to the tomb. Now it was a cave, and a stone lay [1209]against it.

39 Jesus saith, Take ye away the stone. Martha, the sister of him that was dead, saith unto him, Lord, by this time [1210]the body decayeth; for he hath been *dead* four days.

40 Jesus saith unto her, Said I not unto thee, that, if thou believedst, thou shouldest see the glory of God?

41 So they took away the stone. And Jesus lifted up his eyes, and said, Father, I thank thee that thou heardest me.

42 And I knew that thou hearest me always: but because of the multitude that standeth around I said it, that they may believe that thou didst send me.

43 And when he had thus spoken, he cried with a loud voice, Lazarus, come forth.

44 He that was dead came forth, bound hand and foot with [1211]graveclothes; and his face was bound about with a napkin. Jesus saith unto them, Loose him, and let him go.

45 Many therefore of the Jews, who came to Mary and beheld [1212]that which he did, believed on him.

[1204] *Greek wailing.*
[1205] *Greek wailing.*
[1206] *Or, was moved with indignation in the spirit*
[1207] *Greek troubled himself.*
[1208] *Or, being moved with indignation in himself*
[1209] *Or, upon*
[1210] *Greek he stinketh.*
[1211] *Or, grave-bands*
[1212] *Many ancient authorities read the things which he did.*

46 But some of them went away to the Pharisees, and told them the things which Jesus had done.

47 The chief priests therefore and the Pharisees gathered a council, and said, What do we? for this man doeth many signs.

48 If we let him thus alone, all men will believe on him: and the Romans will come and take away both our place and our nation.

49 But a certain one of them, Caiaphas, being high priest that year, said unto them, Ye know nothing at all,

50 nor do ye take account that it is expedient for you that one man should die for the people, and that the whole nation perish not.

51 Now this he said not of himself: but being high priest that year, he prophesied that Jesus should die for the nation;

52 and not for the nation only, but that he might also gather together into one the children of God that are scattered abroad.

53 So from that day forth they took counsel that they might put him to death.

54 Jesus therefore walked no more openly among the Jews, but departed thence into the country near to the wilderness, into a city called Ephraim; and there he tarried with the disciples.

55 Now the passover of the Jews was at hand: and many went up to Jerusalem out of the country before the passover, to purify themselves.

56 They sought therefore for Jesus, and spake one with another, as they stood in the temple, What think ye? That he will not come to the feast?

57 Now the chief priests and the Pharisees had given commandment, that, if any man knew where he was, he should show it, that they might take him.

Chapter 12

1 Jesus therefore six days before the passover came to Bethany, where Lazarus was, whom Jesus raised from the dead.

2 So they made him a supper there: and Martha served; but Lazarus was one of them that [1213]sat at meat with him.

3 Mary therefore took a pound of ointment of [1214]pure nard, very precious, and anointed the feet of Jesus, and wiped his feet with her hair: and the house was filled with the odor of the ointment.

4 But Judas Iscariot, one of his disciples, that should [1215]betray him, saith,

5 Why was not this ointment sold for three hundred [1216]shillings, and given to the poor?

6 Now this he said, not because he cared for the poor; but because he was a thief, and having the [1217]bag [1218]took away what was put therein.

7 Jesus therefore said, [1219]Suffer her to keep it against the day of my burying.

8 For the poor ye have always with you; but me ye have not always.

9 The common people therefore of the Jews learned that he was there: and they came, not for Jesus' sake only, but that they might see Lazarus also, whom he had raised from the dead.

10 But the chief priests took counsel that they might put Lazarus also to death;

11 because that by reason of him many of the Jews went away, and believed on Jesus.

12 On the morrow [1220]a great multitude that had come to the feast, when they heard that Jesus was coming to Jerusalem,

---

[1213] *Greek reclined.*
[1214] *Or, liquid nard*
[1215] *Or, deliver him up*
[1216] *See marginal note on 6:7.*
[1217] *Or, box*
[1218] *Or, carried what was put therein*
[1219] *Or, Let her alone: it was that she might keep it*
[1220] *Some ancient authorities read the common people. See verse 9.*

JOHN 12

13 took the branches of the palm trees, and went forth to meet him, and cried out, Hosanna: Blessed *is* he that cometh in the name of the Lord, even the King of Israel.

14 And Jesus, having found a young ass, sat thereon; as it is written,

15 [1221]Fear not, daughter of Zion: behold, thy King cometh, sitting on an ass's colt.

16 These things understood not his disciples at the first: but when Jesus was glorified, then remembered they that these things were written of him, and that they had done these things unto him.

17 The multitude therefore that was with him when he called Lazarus out of the tomb, and raised him from the dead, bare witness.

18 For this cause also the multitude went and met him, for that they heard that he had done this sign.

19 The Pharisees therefore said among themselves, [1222]Behold how ye prevail nothing; lo, the world is gone after him.

20 Now there were certain Greeks among those that went up to worship at the feast:

21 these therefore came to Philip, who was of Bethsaida of Galilee, and asked him, saying, Sir, we would see Jesus.

22 Philip cometh and telleth Andrew: Andrew cometh, and Philip, and they tell Jesus.

23 And Jesus answereth them, saying, The hour is come, that the Son of man should be glorified.

24 Verily, verily, I say unto you, Except a grain of wheat fall into the earth and die, it abideth by itself alone; but if it die, it beareth much fruit.

25 He that loveth his [1223]life loseth it; and he that hateth his [1224]life in this world shall keep it unto [1225]life eternal.

26 If any man serve me, let him follow me; and where I am, there shall also my servant be: if any man serve me, him will the Father honor.

[1221] *Zech. 9:9.*
[1222] *Or, Ye behold*
[1223] *life in these places represents two different Greek words.*
[1224] *life in these places represents two different Greek words.*
[1225] *life in these places represents two different Greek words.*

27 Now is my soul troubled; and what shall I say? Father, save me from this [1226]hour. But for this cause came I unto this hour.

28 Father, glorify thy name. There came therefore a voice out of heaven, *saying*, I have both glorified it, and will glorify it again.

29 The multitude therefore, that stood by, and heard it, said that it had thundered: others said, An angel hath spoken to him.

30 Jesus answered and said, This voice hath not come for my sake, but for your sakes.

31 Now is [1227]the judgment of this world: now shall the prince of this world be cast out.

32 And I, if I be lifted up [1228]from the earth, will draw all men unto myself.

33 But this he said, signifying by what manner of death he should die.

34 The multitude therefore answered him, We have heard out of the law that the Christ abideth for ever: and how sayest thou, The Son of man must be lifted up? who is this Son of man?

35 Jesus therefore said unto them, Yet a little while is the light [1229]among you. Walk while ye have the light, that darkness overtake you not: and he that walketh in the darkness knoweth not whither he goeth.

36 While ye have the light, believe on the light, that ye may become sons of light.

These things spake Jesus, and he departed and [1230]hid himself from them.

37 But though he had done so many signs before them, yet they believed not on him:

38 that the word of Isaiah the prophet might be fulfilled, which he spake,
[1231]Lord, who hath believed our report?
And to whom hath the arm of the Lord been revealed?

39 For this cause they could not believe, for that Isaiah said again,

40 [1232]He hath blinded their eyes, and he hardened their heart;

[1226] *Or, hour?*
[1227] *Or, a judgment*
[1228] *Or, out of*
[1229] *Or, in*
[1230] *Or, was hidden from them*
[1231] *Isa. 53:1.*
[1232] *Isa. 6:10.*

> Lest they should see with their eyes, and perceive with their heart,
> And should turn,
> And I should heal them.

41 These things said Isaiah, because he saw his glory; and he spake of him.

42 Nevertheless even of the rulers many believed on him; but because of the Pharisees they did not confess [1233]*it*, lest they should be put out of the synagogue:

43 for they loved the glory *that is* of men more than the glory *that is* of God.

44 And Jesus cried and said, He that believeth on me, believeth not on me, but on him that sent me.

45 And he that beholdeth me beholdeth him that sent me.

46 I am come a light into the world, that whosoever believeth on me may not abide in the darkness.

47 And if any man hear my sayings, and keep them not, I judge him not: for I came not to judge the world, but to save the world.

48 He that rejecteth me, and receiveth not my sayings, hath one that judgeth him: the word that I spake, the same shall judge him in the last day.

49 For I spake not from myself; but the Father that sent me, he hath given me a commandment, what I should say, and what I should speak.

50 And I know that his commandment is life eternal; the things therefore which I speak, even as the Father hath said unto me, so I speak.

[1233] *Or,* him

Chapter 13

1 Now before the feast of the passover, Jesus knowing that his hour was come that he should depart out of this world unto the Father, having loved his own that were in the world, he loved them [1234]unto the end.

2 And during supper, the devil having already put into the heart of Judas Iscariot, Simon's *son*, to [1235]betray him,

3 *Jesus*, knowing that the Father had given all things into his hands, and that he came forth from God, and goeth unto God,

4 riseth from supper, and layeth aside his garments; and he took a towel, and girded himself.

5 Then he poureth water into the basin, and began to wash the disciples' feet, and to wipe them with the towel wherewith he was girded.

6 So he cometh to Simon Peter. He saith unto him, Lord, dost thou wash my feet?

7 Jesus answered and said unto him, What I do thou knowest not now; but thou shalt understand hereafter.

8 Peter saith unto him, Thou shalt never wash my feet. Jesus answered him, If I wash thee not, thou hast no part with me.

9 Simon Peter saith unto him, Lord, not my feet only, but also my hands and my head.

10 Jesus saith to him, He that is bathed needeth not [1236]save to wash his feet, but is clean every whit: and ye are clean, but not all.

11 For he knew him that should [1237]betray him; therefore said he, Ye are not all clean.

12 So when he had washed their feet, and taken his garments, and [1238]sat down again, he said unto them, Know ye what I have done to you?

13 Ye call me, Teacher, and, Lord: and ye say well; for so I am.

14 If I then, the Lord and the Teacher, have washed your feet, ye also ought to wash one another's feet.

[1234] *Or, to the uttermost*
[1235] *Or, deliver him up*
[1236] *Some ancient authorities omit save, and his feet.*
[1237] *Or, deliver him up*
[1238] *Greek reclined.*

15 For I have given you an example, that ye also should do as I have done to you.

16 Verily, verily, I say unto you, A [1239]servant is not greater than his lord; neither [1240]one that is sent greater than he that sent him.

17 If ye know these things, blessed are ye if ye do them.

18 I speak not of you all: I know whom I [1241]have chosen: but that the scripture may be fulfilled, [1242]He that eateth [1243]my bread lifted up his heel against me.

19 From henceforth I tell you before it come to pass, that, when it is come to pass, ye may believe that I am *he*.

20 Verily, verily, I say unto you, He that receiveth whomsoever I send receiveth me; and he that receiveth me receiveth him that sent me.

21 When Jesus had thus said, he was troubled in the spirit, and testified, and said, Verily, verily, I say unto you, that one of you shall [1244]betray me.

22 The disciples looked one on another, doubting of whom he spake.

23 There was at the table reclining in Jesus' bosom one of his disciples, whom Jesus loved.

24 Simon Peter therefore beckoneth to him, and saith unto him, Tell *us* who it is of whom he speaketh.

25 He leaning back, as he was, on Jesus' breast saith unto him, Lord, who is it?

26 Jesus therefore answereth, He it is, for whom I shall dip the sop, and give it him. So when he had dipped the sop, he taketh and giveth it to Judas, *the son* of Simon Iscariot.

27 And after the sop, then entered Satan into him. Jesus therefore saith unto him, What thou doest, do quickly.

28 Now no man at the table knew for what intent he spake this unto him.

[1239] *Greek bondservant.*
[1240] *Greek an apostle.*
[1241] *Or, chose*
[1242] *Ps. 41:9.*
[1243] *Many ancient authorities read his bread with me.*
[1244] *Or, deliver me up*

29 For some thought, because Judas had the [1245]bag, that Jesus said unto him, Buy what things we have need of for the feast; or, that he should give something to the poor.

30 He then having received the sop went out straightway: and it was night.

31 When therefore he was gone out, Jesus saith, Now [1246]is the Son of man glorified, and God [1247]is glorified in him;

32 and God shall glorify him in himself, and straightway shall he glorify him.

33 Little children, yet a little while I am with you. Ye shall seek me: and as I said unto the Jews, Whither I go, ye cannot come; so now I say unto you.

34 A new commandment I give unto you, that ye love one another; [1248]even as I have loved you, that ye also love one another.

35 By this shall all men know that ye are my disciples, if ye have love one to another.

36 Simon Peter saith unto him, Lord, whither goest thou? Jesus answered, Whither I go, thou canst not follow me now; but thou shalt follow afterwards.

37 Peter saith unto him, Lord, why cannot I follow thee even now? I will lay down my life for thee.

38 Jesus answereth, Wilt thou lay down thy life for me? Verily, verily, I say unto thee, The cock shall not crow, till thou hast denied me thrice.

[1245] *Or, box*
[1246] *Or, was*
[1247] *Or, was*
[1248] *Or, even as I loved you, that ye also may love one another.*

Chapter 14

1 Let not your heart be troubled: ¹²⁴⁹believe in God, believe also in me.

2 In my Father's house are many ¹²⁵⁰mansions; if it were not so, I would have told you; for I go to prepare a place for you.

3 And if I go and prepare a place for you, I come again, and will receive you unto myself; that where I am, *there* ye may be also.

4 ¹²⁵¹And whither I go, ye know the way.

5 Thomas saith unto him, Lord, we know not whither thou goest; how know we the way?

6 Jesus saith unto him, I am the way, and the truth, and the life: no one cometh unto the Father, but ¹²⁵²by me.

7 If ye had known me, ye would have known my Father also: from henceforth ye know him, and have seen him.

8 Philip saith unto him, Lord, show us the Father, and it sufficeth us.

9 Jesus saith unto him, Have I been so long time with you, and dost thou not know me, Philip? he that hath seen me hath seen the Father; how sayest thou, Show us the Father?

10 Believest thou not that I am in the Father, and the Father in me? the words that I say unto you I speak not from myself: but the Father abiding in me doeth his works.

11 Believe me that I am in the Father, and the Father in me: or else believe me for the very works' sake.

12 Verily, verily, I say unto you, He that believeth on me, the works that I do shall he do also; and greater *works* than these shall he do; because I go unto the Father.

13 And whatsoever ye shall ask in my name, that will I do, that the Father may be glorified in the Son.

14 If ye shall ask ¹²⁵³anything in my name, that will I do.

15 If ye love me, ye will keep my commandments.

---

¹²⁴⁹ *Or, ye believe in God*
¹²⁵⁰ *Or, abiding-places*
¹²⁵¹ *Many ancient authorities read And whither I go ye know, and the way ye know.*
¹²⁵² *Or, through*
¹²⁵³ *Many ancient authorities add me.*

16 And I will ¹²⁵⁴pray the Father, and he shall give you another ¹²⁵⁵Comforter, that he may be with you for ever,

17 *even* the Spirit of truth: whom the world cannot receive; for it beholdeth him not, neither knoweth him: ye know him; for he abideth with you, and shall be in you.

18 I will not leave you ¹²⁵⁶desolate: I come unto you.

19 Yet a little while, and the world beholdeth me no more; but ye behold me: because I live, ¹²⁵⁷ye shall live also.

20 In that day ye shall know that I am in my Father, and ye in me, and I in you.

21 He that hath my commandments, and keepeth them, he it is that loveth me: and he that loveth me shall be loved of my Father, and I will love him, and will manifest myself unto him.

22 Judas (not Iscariot) saith unto him, Lord, what is come to pass that thou wilt manifest thyself unto us, and not unto the world?

23 Jesus answered and said unto him, If a man love me, he will keep my word: and my Father will love him, and we will come unto him, and make our abode with him.

24 He that loveth me not keepeth not my words: and the word which ye hear is not mine, but the Father's who sent me.

25 These things have I spoken unto you, while *yet* abiding with you.

26 But the ¹²⁵⁸Comforter, *even* the Holy Spirit, whom the Father will send in my name, he shall teach you all things, and bring to your remembrance all that I said unto you.

27 Peace I leave with you; my peace I give unto you: not as the world giveth, give I unto you. Let not your heart be troubled, neither let it be fearful.

†✓ **The Father is Greater.** Jesus does not say the Father is "greater in office" but simply "greater than I." This categorical statement excludes co-equality. The Source is always greater than the Sent.

28 Ye heard how I said to you, I go away, and I come unto you. If ye loved me, ye would have rejoiced, because I go unto the Father: for the Father is greater than I.

---

¹²⁵⁴ *Greek make request of.*
¹²⁵⁵ *Or, Advocate. Or, Helper. Greek Paraclete.*
¹²⁵⁶ *Or, orphans*
¹²⁵⁷ *Or, and ye shall live.*
¹²⁵⁸ *Or, Advocate. Or, Helper. Greek Paraclete.*

29 And now I have told you before it come to pass, that, when it is come to pass, ye may believe.

30 I will no more speak much with you, for the prince of the world cometh: and he hath nothing [1259]in me;

31 but that the world may know that I love the Father, and as the Father gave me commandment, even so I do. Arise, let us go hence.

Chapter 15

1 I am the true vine, and my Father is the husbandman.

2 Every branch in me that beareth not fruit, he taketh it away: and every *branch* that beareth fruit, he cleanseth it, that it may bear more fruit.

3 Already ye are clean because of the word which I have spoken unto you.

4 Abide in me, and I in you. As the branch cannot bear fruit of itself, except it abide in the vine; so neither can ye, except ye abide in me.

5 I am the vine, ye are the branches: He that abideth in me, and I in him, the same beareth much fruit: for apart from me ye can do nothing.

6 If a man abide not in me, he is cast forth as a branch, and is withered; and they gather them, and cast them into the fire, and they are burned.

7 If ye abide in me, and my words abide in you, ask whatsoever ye will, and it shall be done unto you.

8 Herein [1260]is my Father glorified, [1261]that ye bear much fruit; and *so* shall ye be my disciples.

9 Even as the Father hath loved me, I also have loved you: abide ye in my love.

10 If ye keep my commandments, ye shall abide in my love; even as I have kept my Father's commandments, and abide in his love.

11 These things have I spoken unto you, that my joy may be in you, and *that* your joy may be made full.

12 This is my commandment, that ye love one another, even as I have loved you.

[1259] *Or, in me. But that etc. . . . I do, arise etc.*
[1260] *Or, was*
[1261] *Many ancient authorities read that ye bear much fruit, and be my disciples.*

13 Greater love hath no man than this, that a man lay down his life for his friends.

14 Ye are my friends, if ye do the things which I command you.

15 No longer do I call you [1262]servants; for the [1263]servant knoweth not what his lord doeth: but I have called you friends; for all things that I heard from my Father I have made known unto you.

16 Ye did not choose me, but I chose you, and appointed you, that ye should go and bear fruit, and *that* your fruit should abide: that whatsoever ye shall ask of the Father in my name, he may give it you.

17 These things I command you, that ye may love one another.

18 If the world hateth you, [1264]ye know that it hath hated me before *it hated* you.

19 If ye were of the world, the world would love its own: but because ye are not of the world, but I chose you out of the world, therefore the world hateth you.

20 Remember the word that I said unto you, A [1265]servant is not greater than his lord. If they persecuted me, they will also persecute you; if they kept my word, they will keep yours also.

21 But all these things will they do unto you for my name's sake, because they know not him that sent me.

22 If I had not come and spoken unto them, they had not had sin: but now they have no excuse for their sin.

23 He that hateth me hateth my Father also.

24 If I had not done among them the works which none other did, they had not had sin: but now have they both seen and hated both me and my Father.

25 But *this cometh to pass*, that the word may be fulfilled that is written in their law, [1266]They hated me without a cause.

[1262] *Greek bondservants.*
[1263] *Greek bondservant.*
[1264] *Or, know ye*
[1265] *Greek bondservant.*
[1266] Ps. 35:19; 69:4.

26 But when the [1267]Comforter is come, whom I will send unto you from the Father, *even* the Spirit of truth, which [1268]proceedeth from the Father, he shall bear witness of me:

27 [1269]and ye also bear witness, because ye have been with me from the beginning.

Chapter 16

1 These things have I spoken unto you, that ye should not be caused to stumble.

2 They shall put you out of the synagogues: yea, the hour cometh, that whosoever killeth you shall think that he offereth service unto God.

3 And these things will they do, because they have not known the Father, nor me.

4 But these things have I spoken unto you, that when their hour is come, ye may remember them, how that I told you. And these things I said not unto you from the beginning, because I was with you.

5 But now I go unto him that sent me; and none of you asketh me, Whither goest thou?

6 But because I have spoken these things unto you, sorrow hath filled your heart.

7 Nevertheless I tell you the truth: It is expedient for you that I go away; for if I go not away, the [1270]Comforter will not come unto you; but if I go, I will send him unto you.

8 And he, when he is come, will convict the world in respect of sin, and of righteousness, and of judgment:

9 of sin, because they believe not on me;

10 of righteousness, because I go to the Father, and ye behold me no more;

11 of judgment, because the prince of this world hath been judged.

12 I have yet many things to say unto you, but ye cannot bear them now.

[1267] *Or, Advocate. Or, Helper. Greek Paraclete.*
[1268] *Or, goeth forth from*
[1269] *Or, and bear ye also witness*
[1270] *Or, Advocate. Or, Helper. Greek Paraclete.*

13 Howbeit when he, the Spirit of truth, is come, he shall guide you into all the truth: for he shall not speak from himself; but what things soever he shall hear, *these* shall he speak: and he shall declare unto you the things that are to come.

14 He shall glorify me: for he shall take of mine, and shall declare *it* unto you.

15 All things whatsoever the Father hath are mine: therefore said I, that he taketh of mine, and shall declare *it* unto you.

16 A little while, and ye behold me no more; and again a little while, and ye shall see me.

17 *Some* of his disciples therefore said one to another, What is this that he saith unto us, A little while, and ye behold me not; and again a little while, and ye shall see me: and, Because I go to the Father?

18 They said therefore, What is this that he saith, A little while? We know not what he saith.

19 Jesus perceived that they were desirous to ask him, and he said unto them, Do ye inquire among yourselves concerning this, that I said, A little while, and ye behold me not, and again a little while, and ye shall see me?

20 Verily, verily, I say unto you, that ye shall weep and lament, but the world shall rejoice: ye shall be sorrowful, but your sorrow shall be turned into joy.

21 A woman when she is in travail hath sorrow, because her hour is come: but when she is delivered of the child, she remembereth no more the anguish, for the joy that a man is born into the world.

22 And ye therefore now have sorrow: but I will see you again, and your heart shall rejoice, and your joy no one taketh away from you.

23 And in that day ye shall [1271]ask me no question. Verily, verily, I say unto you, If ye shall ask anything of the Father, he will give it you in my name.

24 Hitherto have ye asked nothing in my name: ask, and ye shall receive, that your joy may be made full.

[1271] *Or, ask me nothing. Compare verse 26; 14:13, 20.*

25 These things have I spoken unto you in ¹²⁷²dark sayings: the hour cometh, when I shall no more speak unto you in dark sayings, but shall tell you plainly of the Father.

26 In that day ye shall ask in my name: and I say not unto you, that I will ¹²⁷³pray the Father for you;

27 for the Father himself loveth you, because ye have loved me, and have believed that I came forth from the Father.

28 I came out from the Father, and am come into the world: again, I leave the world, and go unto the Father.

29 His disciples say, Lo, now speakest thou plainly, and speakest no ¹²⁷⁴dark saying.

30 Now know we that thou knowest all things, and needest not that any man should ask thee: by this we believe that thou camest forth from God.

31 Jesus answered them, Do ye now believe?

32 Behold, the hour cometh, yea, is come, that ye shall be scattered, every man to his own, and shall leave me alone: and *yet* I am not alone, because the Father is with me.

33 These things have I spoken unto you, that in me ye may have peace. In the world ye have tribulation: but be of good cheer; I have overcome the world.

Chapter 17

1 These things spake Jesus; and lifting up his eyes to heaven, he said, Father, the hour is come; glorify thy Son, that the Son may glorify thee:

2 even as thou gavest him authority over all flesh, that ¹²⁷⁵to all whom thou hast given him, he should give eternal life.

3 And this is life eternal, that they should know thee the only true God, and him whom thou didst send, *even* Jesus Christ.¹²⁷⁶

---

¹²⁷²*Or, parables*
¹²⁷³*Greek make request of.*
¹²⁷⁴*Or, parable*
¹²⁷⁵*Greek whatsoever thou hast given him, to them he etc.*
¹²⁷⁶**Grammar:** Jesus uses the singular pronoun *se* ("Thee") to address the Father, identifying Him alone as the *monon alethinon theon*. This explicitly separates the Father from Jesus, who is defined in the next clause as the one "sent" by God.

†✓ **Jesus defines the Father as the "Only True God".** Traditional reading: Jesus is included in God. Text: "Thee" (Father) is exclusively the Only True God. Jesus is the agent sent by Him.

4 I glorified thee on the earth, having accomplished the work which thou hast given me to do.

5 And now, Father, glorify thou me with thine own self with the glory which I had with thee before the world was.

6 I manifested thy name unto the men whom thou gavest me out of the world: thine they were, and thou gavest them to me; and they have kept thy word.

7 Now they know that all things whatsoever thou hast given me are from thee:

8 for the words which thou gavest me I have given unto them; and they received *them*, and knew of a truth that I came forth from thee, and they believed that thou didst send me.

9 I [1277]pray for them: I [1278]pray not for the world, but for those whom thou hast given me; for they are thine:

10 and all things that are mine are thine, and thine are mine: and I am glorified in them.

11 And I am no more in the world, and these are in the world, and I come to thee. Holy Father, keep them in thy name which thou hast given me, that they may be one, even as we *are*.

12 While I was with them, I kept them in thy name which thou hast given me: and I guarded them, and not one of them perished, but the son of perdition; [1279]that the scripture might be fulfilled.

13 But now I come to thee; and these things I speak in the world, that they may have my joy made full in themselves.

14 I have given them thy word; and the world hated them, because they are not of the world, even as I am not of the world.

15 I [1280]pray not that thou shouldest take them [1281]from the world, but that thou shouldest keep them [1282]from [1283]the evil *one*.

16 They are not of the world, even as I am not of the world.

[1277] *Greek make request.*
[1278] *Greek make request.*
[1279] *Ps. 41:9?*
[1280] *Greek make request.*
[1281] *Greek out of.*
[1282] *Greek out of.*
[1283] *Or, evil*

17 [1284]Sanctify them in the truth: thy word is truth.

18 As thou didst send me into the world, even so sent I them into the world.

19 And for their sakes I [1285]sanctify myself, that they themselves also may be sanctified in truth.

20 Neither for these only do I [1286]pray, but for them also that believe on me through their word;

21 that they may all be one; even as thou, Father, *art* in me, and I in thee, that they also may be in us: that the world may believe that thou didst send me.

22 And the glory which thou hast given me I have given unto them; that they may be one, even as we *are* one;

23 I in them, and thou in me, that they may be perfected into one; that the world may know that thou didst send me, and lovedst them, even as thou lovedst me.

24 Father, [1287]I desire that they also whom thou hast given me be with me where I am, that they may behold my glory, which thou hast given me: for thou lovedst me before the foundation of the world.

25 O righteous Father, the world knew thee not, but I knew thee; and these knew that thou didst send me;

26 and I made known unto them thy name, and will make it known; that the love wherewith thou lovedst me may be in them, and I in them.

[1284] *Or, Consecrate*
[1285] *Or, consecrate*
[1286] *Greek make request.*
[1287] *Greek that which thou hast given me, I desire that where I am, they also may be with me, that etc.*

Chapter 18

1 When Jesus had spoken these words, he went forth with his disciples over the [1288]brook [1289]Kidron, where was a garden, into which he entered, himself and his disciples.

2 Now Judas also, who [1290]betrayed him, knew the place: for Jesus ofttimes resorted thither with his disciples.

3 Judas then, having received the [1291]band *of soldiers*, and officers from the chief priests and the Pharisees, cometh thither with lanterns and torches and weapons.

4 Jesus therefore, knowing all the things that were coming upon him, went forth, and saith unto them, Whom seek ye?

5 They answered him, Jesus of Nazareth. Jesus saith unto them, I am *he*. And Judas also, who [1292]betrayed him, was standing with them.

6 When therefore he said unto them, I am *he*, they went backward, and fell to the ground.

7 Again therefore he asked them, Whom seek ye? And they said, Jesus of Nazareth.

8 Jesus answered, I told you that I am *he*; if therefore ye seek me, let these go their way:

9 that the word might be fulfilled which he spake, Of those whom thou hast given me I lost not one.

10 Simon Peter therefore having a sword drew it, and struck the high priest's [1293]servant, and cut off his right ear. Now the [1294]servant's name was Malchus.

11 Jesus therefore said unto Peter, Put up the sword into the sheath: the cup which the Father hath given me, shall I not drink it?

[1288] *Or, ravine. Greek winter-torrent.*
[1289] *Or, of the Cedars*
[1290] *Or, delivered him up*
[1291] *Or, cohort*
[1292] *Or, delivered him up*
[1293] *Greek bondservant.*
[1294] *Greek bondservant.*

JOHN 18

12 So the ¹²⁹⁵band and the ¹²⁹⁶chief captain, and the officers of the Jews, seized Jesus and bound him,

13 and led him to Annas first; for he was father in law to Caiaphas, who was high priest that year.

14 Now Caiaphas was he that gave counsel to the Jews, that it was expedient that one man should die for the people.

15 And Simon Peter followed Jesus, and *so did* another disciple. Now that disciple was known unto the high priest, and entered in with Jesus into the court of the high priest;

16 but Peter was standing at the door without. So the other disciple, who was known unto the high priest, went out and spake unto her that kept the door, and brought in Peter.

17 The maid therefore that kept the door saith unto Peter, Art thou also *one* of this man's disciples? He saith, I am not.

18 Now the ¹²⁹⁷servants and the officers were standing *there*, having made ¹²⁹⁸a fire of coals; for it was cold; and they were warming themselves: and Peter also was with them, standing and warming himself.

19 The high priest therefore asked Jesus of his disciples, and of his teaching.

20 Jesus answered him, I have spoken openly to the world; I ever taught in ¹²⁹⁹synagogues, and in the temple, where all the Jews come together; and in secret spake I nothing.

21 Why askest thou me? ask them that have heard *me*, what I spake unto them: behold, these know the things which I said.

22 And when he had said this, one of the officers standing by struck Jesus ¹³⁰⁰with his hand, saying, Answerest thou the high priest so?

23 Jesus answered him, If I have spoken evil, bear witness of the evil: but if well, why smitest thou me?

24 Annas therefore sent him bound unto Caiaphas the high priest.

---

¹²⁹⁵ *Or, cohort*
¹²⁹⁶ *Or, military tribune. Greek chiliarch.*
¹²⁹⁷ *Or, bondservants.*
¹²⁹⁸ *Greek a fire of charcoal.*
¹²⁹⁹ *Greek synagogue.*
¹³⁰⁰ *Or, with a rod*

25 Now Simon Peter was standing and warming himself. They said therefore unto him, Art thou also *one* of his disciples? He denied, and said, I am not.

26 One of the [1301]servants of the high priest, being a kinsman of him whose ear Peter cut off, saith, Did not I see thee in the garden with him?

27 Peter therefore denied again: and straightway the cock crew.

28 They lead Jesus therefore from Caiaphas into the [1302]Praetorium: and it was early; and they themselves entered not into the [1303]Praetorium, that they might not be defiled, but might eat the passover.

29 Pilate therefore went out unto them, and saith, What accusation bring ye against this man?

30 They answered and said unto him, If this man were not an evil-doer, we should not have delivered him up unto thee.

31 Pilate therefore said unto them, Take him yourselves, and judge him according to your law. The Jews said unto him, It is not lawful for us to put any man to death:

32 that the word of Jesus might be fulfilled, which he spake, signifying by what manner of death he should die.

33 Pilate therefore entered again into the [1304]Praetorium, and called Jesus, and said unto him, Art thou the King of the Jews?

34 Jesus answered, Sayest thou this of thyself, or did others tell it thee concerning me?

35 Pilate answered, Am I a Jew? Thine own nation and the chief priests delivered thee unto me: what hast thou done?

36 Jesus answered, My kingdom is not of this world: if my kingdom were of this world, then would my [1305]servants fight, that I should not be delivered to the Jews: but now is my kingdom not from hence.

37 Pilate therefore said unto him, Art thou a king then? Jesus answered, [1306]Thou sayest that I am a king. To this end have I been born, and to

---

[1301] *Greek bondservants.*
[1302] *Or, palace*
[1303] *Or, palace*
[1304] *Or, palace*
[1305] *Or, officers: as in verses 3, 12, 18, 22.*
[1306] *Or, Thou sayest it, because I am a king.*

this end am I come into the world, that I should bear witness unto the truth. Every one that is of the truth heareth my voice.

38 Pilate saith unto him, What is truth?

And when he had said this, he went out again unto the Jews, and saith unto them, I find no crime in him.

39 But ye have a custom, that I should release unto you one at the passover: will ye therefore that I release unto you the King of the Jews?

40 They cried out therefore again, saying, Not this man, but Barabbas. Now Barabbas was a robber.

Chapter 19

1 Then Pilate therefore took Jesus, and scourged him.

2 And the soldiers platted a crown of thorns, and put it on his head, and arrayed him in a purple garment;

3 and they came unto him, and said, Hail, King of the Jews! and they struck him [1307]with their hands.

4 And Pilate went out again, and saith unto them, Behold, I bring him out to you, that ye may know that I find no crime in him.

5 Jesus therefore came out, wearing the crown of thorns and the purple garment. And *Pilate* saith unto them, Behold, the man!

6 When therefore the chief priests and the officers saw him, they cried out, saying, Crucify *him*, crucify *him*! Pilate saith unto them, Take him yourselves, and crucify him: for I find no crime in him.

7 The Jews answered him, We have a law, and by that law he ought to die, because he made himself the Son of God.

8 When Pilate therefore heard this saying, he was the more afraid;

9 and he entered into the [1308]Praetorium again, and saith unto Jesus, Whence art thou? But Jesus gave him no answer.

10 Pilate therefore saith unto him, Speakest thou not unto me? knowest thou not that I have [1309]power to release thee, and have [1310]power to crucify thee?

[1307] *Or, with rods*
[1308] *Or, palace*
[1309] *Or, authority*
[1310] *Or, authority*

11 Jesus answered him, Thou wouldest have no [1311]power against me, except it were given thee from above: therefore he that delivered me unto thee hath greater sin.

12 Upon this Pilate sought to release him: but the Jews cried out, saying, If thou release this man, thou art not Caesar's friend: every one that maketh himself a king [1312]speaketh against Caesar.

13 When Pilate therefore heard these words, he brought Jesus out, and sat down on the judgment-seat at a place called The Pavement, but in Hebrew, Gabbatha.

14 Now it was the Preparation of the passover: it was about the sixth hour. And he saith unto the Jews, Behold, your King!

15 They therefore cried out, Away with *him*, away with *him*, crucify him! Pilate saith unto them, Shall I crucify your King? The chief priests answered, We have no king but Caesar.

16 Then therefore he delivered him unto them to be crucified.

17 They took Jesus therefore: and he went out, bearing the cross for himself, unto the place called The place of a skull, which is called in Hebrew Golgotha:

18 where they crucified him, and with him two others, on either side one, and Jesus in the midst.

19 And Pilate wrote a title also, and put it on the cross. And there was written, Jesus of Nazareth, the King of the Jews.

20 This title therefore read many of the Jews, [1313]for the place where Jesus was crucified was nigh to the city; and it was written in Hebrew, *and* in Latin, *and* in Greek.

21 The chief priests of the Jews therefore said to Pilate, Write not, The King of the Jews; but, that he said, I am King of the Jews.

22 Pilate answered, What I have written I have written.

23 The soldiers therefore, when they had crucified Jesus, took his garments and made four parts, to every soldier a part; and also the [1314]coat: now the [1315]coat was without seam, woven from the top throughout.

[1311] *Or, authority*
[1312] *Or, opposeth Caesar*
[1313] *Or, for the place of the city where Jesus was crucified was nigh at hand*
[1314] *Or, tunic*
[1315] *Or, tunic*

JOHN 19

24 They said therefore one to another, Let us not rend it, but cast lots for it, whose it shall be: that the scripture might be fulfilled, which saith,
[1316]They parted my garments among them,
And upon my vesture did they cast lots.

25 These things therefore the soldiers did. But there were standing by the cross of Jesus his mother, and his mother's sister, Mary the *wife* of Clopas, and Mary Magdalene.

26 When Jesus therefore saw his mother, and the disciple standing by whom he loved, he saith unto his mother, Woman, behold, thy son!

27 Then saith he to the disciple, Behold, thy mother! And from that hour the disciple took her unto his own *home*.

28 After this Jesus, knowing that all things are now finished, [1317]that the scripture might be accomplished, saith, I thirst.

29 There was set there a vessel full of vinegar: so they put a sponge full of the vinegar upon hyssop, and brought it to his mouth.

30 When Jesus therefore had received the vinegar, he said, It is finished: and he bowed his head, and gave up his spirit.

31 The Jews therefore, because it was the Preparation, that the bodies should not remain on the cross upon the sabbath (for the day of that sabbath was a high *day*), asked of Pilate that their legs might be broken, and *that* they might be taken away.

32 The soldiers therefore came, and brake the legs of the first, and of the other that was crucified with him:

33 but when they came to Jesus, and saw that he was dead already, they brake not his legs:

34 howbeit one of the soldiers with a spear pierced his side, and straightway there came out blood and water.

35 And he that hath seen hath borne witness, and his witness is true: and he knoweth that he saith true, that ye also may believe.

36 For these things came to pass, [1318]that the scripture might be fulfilled, A bone of him shall not be [1319]broken.

[1316] *Ps. 22:18.*
[1317] *Ps. 69:21.*
[1318] *Ex. 12:46; Num. 9:12; Ps. 34:20.*
[1319] *Or, crushed*

37 And again another scripture saith, [1320]They shall look on him whom they pierced.

38 And after these things Joseph of Arimathaea, being a disciple of Jesus, but secretly for fear of the Jews, asked of Pilate that he might take away the body of Jesus: and Pilate gave *him* leave. He came therefore, and took away his body.

39 And there came also Nicodemus, he who at the first came to him by night, bringing a [1321]mixture of myrrh and aloes, about a hundred pounds.

40 So they took the body of Jesus, and bound it in linen cloths with the spices, as the custom of the Jews is to bury.

41 Now in the place where he was crucified there was a garden; and in the garden a new tomb wherein was never man yet laid.

42 There then because of the Jews' Preparation (for the tomb was nigh at hand) they laid Jesus.

[1320] Zech. 12:10.
[1321] *Some ancient authorities read roll.*

Chapter 20

1 Now on the first *day* of the week cometh Mary Magdalene early, while it was yet dark, unto the tomb, and seeth the stone taken away from the tomb.

2 She runneth therefore, and cometh to Simon Peter, and to the other disciple whom Jesus loved, and saith unto them, They have taken away the Lord out of the tomb, and we know not where they have laid him.

3 Peter therefore went forth, and the other disciple, and they went toward the tomb.

4 And they ran both together: and the other disciple outran Peter, and came first to the tomb;

5 and stooping and looking in, he seeth the linen cloths lying; yet entered he not in.

6 Simon Peter therefore also cometh, following him, and entered into the tomb; and he beholdeth the linen cloths lying,

7 and the napkin, that was upon his head, not lying with the linen cloths, but rolled up in a place by itself.

8 Then entered in therefore the other disciple also, who came first to the tomb, and he saw, and believed.

9 For as yet they knew not the scripture, that he must rise again from the dead.

10 So the disciples went away again unto their own home.

11 But Mary was standing without at the tomb weeping: so, as she wept, she stooped and looked into the tomb;

12 and she beholdeth two angels in white sitting, one at the head, and one at the feet, where the body of Jesus had lain.

13 And they say unto her, Woman, why weepest thou? She saith unto them, Because they have taken away my Lord, and I know not where they have laid him.

14 When she had thus said, she turned herself back, and beholdeth Jesus standing, and knew not that it was Jesus.

15 Jesus saith unto her, Woman, why weepest thou? whom seekest thou? She, supposing him to be the gardener, saith unto him, Sir, if thou hast

borne him hence, tell me where thou hast laid him, and I will take him away.

16 Jesus saith unto her, Mary. She turneth herself, and saith unto him in Hebrew, Rabboni; which is to say, Teacher.

17 Jesus saith to her, ¹³²²Touch me not; for I am not yet ascended unto the Father: but go unto my brethren, and say to them, I ascend unto my Father and your Father, and my God and your God.

†✓ **The risen Jesus refers to the Father as "My God."** Traditional reading: Jesus is God. Context: The risen, glorified Jesus still has a God. He shares the same God as the disciples.

18 Mary Magdalene cometh and telleth the disciples, I have seen the Lord; and *that* he had said these things unto her.

19 When therefore it was evening, on that day, the first *day* of the week, and when the doors were shut where the disciples were, for fear of the Jews, Jesus came and stood in the midst, and saith unto them, Peace *be* unto you.

20 And when he had said this, he showed unto them his hands and his side. The disciples therefore were glad, when they saw the Lord.

21 Jesus therefore said to them again, Peace *be* unto you: as the Father hath sent me, even so send I you.

22 And when he had said this, he breathed on them, and saith unto them, Receive ye the Holy Spirit:

23 whose soever sins ye forgive, they are forgiven unto them; whose soever *sins* ye retain, they are retained.

24 But Thomas, one of the twelve, called ¹³²³Didymus, was not with them when Jesus came.

25 The other disciples therefore said unto him, We have seen the Lord. But he said unto them, Except I shall see in his hands the print of the nails, and put my finger into the print of the nails, and put my hand into his side, I will not believe.

26 And after eight days again his disciples were within, and Thomas with them. Jesus cometh, the doors being shut, and stood in the midst, and said, Peace *be* unto you.

27 Then saith he to Thomas, Reach hither thy finger, and see my hands; and reach *hither* thy hand, and put it into my side: and be not faithless, but believing.

---

¹³²² *Or, Take not hold on me*
¹³²³ *That is, Twin.*

28 Thomas answered and said unto him, My Lord and my God.

29 Jesus saith unto him, Because thou hast seen me, [1324]thou hast believed: blessed *are* they that have not seen, and *yet* have believed.

30 Many other signs therefore did Jesus in the presence of the disciples, which are not written in this book:

31 but these are written, that ye may believe that Jesus is the Christ, the Son of God; and that believing ye may have life in his name.

⋆ **Agency exclamation.** Traditional reading: Trinitarian creed. Actual Jewish context: exclamation of awe/agency (shaliah principle). Equivalent to "My Lord and my God!" in shock.

Chapter 21

1 After these things Jesus manifested himself again to the disciples at the sea of Tiberias; and he manifested *himself* on this wise.

2 There were together Simon Peter, and Thomas called [1325]Didymus, and Nathanael of Cana in Galilee, and the *sons* of Zebedee, and two other of his disciples.

3 Simon Peter saith unto them, I go a fishing. They say unto him, We also come with thee. They went forth, and entered into the boat; and that night they took nothing.

4 But when day was now breaking, Jesus stood on the beach: yet the disciples knew not that it was Jesus.

5 Jesus therefore saith unto them, Children, have ye aught to eat? They answered him, No.

6 And he said unto them, Cast the net on the right side of the boat, and ye shall find. They cast therefore, and now they were not able to draw it for the multitude of fishes.

7 That disciple therefore whom Jesus loved saith unto Peter, It is the Lord. So when Simon Peter heard that it was the Lord, he girt his coat about him (for he [1326]was naked), and cast himself into the sea.

8 But the other disciples came in the little boat (for they were not far from the land, but about two hundred cubits off), dragging the net *full* of fishes.

[1324] *Or, hast thou believed?*
[1325] *That is, Twin.*
[1326] *Or, had on his undergarment only. Compare 13:4; Isa. 20:2; Mic. 1:8, 11.*

9 So when they got out upon the land, they see ¹³²⁷a fire of coals there, and ¹³²⁸fish laid thereon, and ¹³²⁹bread.

10 Jesus saith unto them, Bring of the fish which ye have now taken.

11 Simon Peter therefore went ¹³³⁰up, and drew the net to land, full of great fishes, a hundred and fifty and three: and for all there were so many, the net was not rent.

12 Jesus saith unto them, Come *and* break your fast. And none of the disciples durst inquire of him, Who art thou? knowing that it was the Lord.

13 Jesus cometh, and taketh the ¹³³¹bread, and giveth them, and the fish likewise.

14 This is now the third time that Jesus was manifested to the disciples, after that he was risen from the dead.

15 So when they had broken their fast, Jesus saith to Simon Peter, Simon, *son* of ¹³³²John, ¹³³³lovest thou me more than these? He saith unto him, Yea, Lord; thou knowest that I ¹³³⁴love thee. He saith unto him, Feed my lambs.

16 He saith to him again a second time, Simon, *son* of ¹³³⁵John, ¹³³⁶lovest thou me? He saith unto him, Yea, Lord; thou knowest that I ¹³³⁷love thee. He saith unto him, Tend my sheep.

17 He saith unto him the third time, Simon, *son* of ¹³³⁸John, ¹³³⁹lovest thou me? Peter was grieved because he said unto him the third time, ¹³⁴⁰Lovest thou me? And he said unto him, Lord, thou knowest all

---

¹³²⁷ *Greek a fire of charcoal.*
¹³²⁸ *Or, a fish*
¹³²⁹ *Or, a loaf*
¹³³⁰ *Or, aboard*
¹³³¹ *Or, loaf*
¹³³² *Greek Joanes. See 1:42 margin.*
¹³³³ *Love in these places represents two different Greek words*
¹³³⁴ *Love in these places represents two different Greek words*
¹³³⁵ *Greek Joanes. See 1:42 margin.*
¹³³⁶ *Love in these places represents two different Greek words*
¹³³⁷ *Love in these places represents two different Greek words*
¹³³⁸ *Greek Joanes. See 1:42 margin.*
¹³³⁹ *Love in these places represents two different Greek words*
¹³⁴⁰ *Love in these places represents two different Greek words*

things; thou [1341]knowest that I [1342]love thee. Jesus saith unto him, Feed my sheep.

18 Verily, verily, I say unto thee, When thou wast young, thou girdedst thyself, and walkedst whither thou wouldest: but when thou shalt be old, thou shalt stretch forth thy hands, and another shall gird thee, and carry thee whither thou wouldest not.

19 Now this he spake, signifying by what manner of death he should glorify God. And when he had spoken this, he saith unto him, Follow me.

20 Peter, turning about, seeth the disciple whom Jesus loved following; who also leaned back on his breast at the supper, and said, Lord, who is he that [1343]betrayeth thee?

21 Peter therefore seeing him saith to Jesus, Lord, [1344]and what shall this man do?

22 Jesus saith unto him, If I will that he tarry till I come, what *is that* to thee? follow thou me.

23 This saying therefore went forth among the brethren, that that disciple should not die: yet Jesus said not unto him, that he should not die; but, If I will that he tarry till I come, what *is that* to thee?

24 This is the disciple that beareth witness of these things, and wrote these things: and we know that his witness is true.

25 And there are also many other things which Jesus did, the which if they should be written every one, I suppose that even the world itself would not contain the books that should be written.

[1341] *Or, perceivest*
[1342] *Love in these places represents two different Greek words*
[1343] *Or, delivereth thee up*
[1344] *Greek and this man, what?*

New Testament Corrected Flight Plan

The Recovery of the Sacred

To fully understand the teachings of Jesus, instead of reading the New Testament in the order it was arranged by later councils, you'll find learning easier when the N.T. is read in the order it was written. Many other chronological Bibles verify the importance of proper sequence.

The Checksheet below is to help you walk, step-by-step, starting from learning the Jewish foundation of James, to the Greek philosophical complexity of John. You'll discover you gain much more clarity of the Gospels.

Note: If you don't have the complete *One God Study Bible* set, yet, you can use any RV or KJV Bible. However, make sure to consult the "False Friends" section Page **67** to avoid any changed meanings from Old English and any translation traps.

CHECKLIST 1: THE CONTROL SAMPLE (c. 45–48 AD)

Reading Focus: The Epistle of James
The Foundation: This is the earliest document in the New Testament. It represents the faith *before* the Gentiles, *before* the Councils, and *before* the confusion.
Evidence of Date: The letter contains **zero** references to the "Gentile Controversy" (Circumcision/Food Laws) that consumed the church after 49 AD (Acts 15). Therefore, it *must* predate the Council of Jerusalem.

The Mission

Your objective is to establish the "Control" baseline. You must document the definition of God held by the brother of Jesus before Paul wrote a single letter.

The Checksheet

- ☐ **The Reading Protocol:** Read James Chapters 1–5 in one sitting.
    - *The Payoff:* Reading it all at once allows you to hear the consistent, Jewish voice of James without the interruption of later theological debates.

- ☐ **Data Extraction (God):** Highlight every occurrence of the word "God" (*Theos*).
- ☐ **Data Extraction (Lord):** Highlight every occurrence of the word "Lord" (*Kurios*).
  - *The Payoff*: This creates a visual map. You will see that James **never** swaps these titles. He restricts "God" exclusively to the Father and "Lord" to Jesus.
- ☐ **The Separation Test:** Verify that James *always* distinguishes between "God" (The Father) and the "Lord" (Jesus Christ). (See James 1:1).
- ☐ **The Missing Data Check:** Confirm the following concepts are **absent**:
  - No mention of a Virgin Birth.
  - No mention of a pre-existent Son.
  - No mention of a Trinity.

KEY INSIGHT: THE DEFINITION OF RELIGION
James defines "Pure Religion" in James 1:27.
- **The Tradition:** Says religion is "Right Belief" (Orthodoxy/Creeds).
- **The Evidence:** James says religion is "Right Action" (To visit the fatherless and widows, and keep oneself unspotted from the world).

CHECKLIST 2: THE APOCALYPTIC HOPE (c. 50–52 AD)

Reading Focus: 1 & 2 Thessalonians
The Engine: Before the church had complex theology, it had "urgency." They weren't debating the substance of God; they were scanning the skies.

The Mission

Your mission is to encounter the raw expectancy of the early church. While modern tradition often focuses on the "Hereafter," Paul focuses entirely on the **Return**. You are looking for the distinction between the *One God* who commands, and the *Son* who obeys and returns.

The Checksheet

- ☐ **The "Living God" Check:** Read 1 Thessalonians 1:9–10.
  - *Observation:* Paul defines the Christian life as two actions: (1) Turning to God (The Father) from idols, and (2) Waiting for *His Son* from heaven.

- *The Payoff:* This proves that early worship was directed at the Father, while "Hope" was directed at the returning Son.

☐ **The Resurrection Standard:** Scan 1 Thess 1:10 and 4:14.
- *Forensic Note:* Who raised Jesus? Paul says "Whom **He** [God] raised from the dead."
- *The Payoff:* This confirms Jesus is the *subject* of the action (the one being raised), not the author of it (the one doing the raising).

CHECKLIST 3: THE AGENCY DISTINCTION (c. 55–58 AD)

Reading Focus: Galatians, 1 & 2 Corinthians, Romans
The Conflict: The Gospel hits the Greek world. Polytheism is the enemy. Paul must explain Jesus without creating two Gods.

The Mission

This is the most critical phase. You must learn the **Law of Agency**. In Hebrew law (*Shaliach*), the Agent is treated *as if* he were the Sender, but he is never *confused* with the Sender.
The Legal Precedent: The Jewish Law is absolute: "A man's agent is equivalent to the man himself" (**Talmud, Kiddushin 41b**). This allows Jesus to wield God's authority without *being* God.

> *Navigator's Note: For the full legal dossier on the Shaliach and the Joseph Protocol, see "The Divine Agent" on page **450**.*

The Checksheet

☐ **The Christian Shema:** Read 1 Corinthians 8:6.
- *The Split:* "To us there is but **One God, the Father**... and **one Lord Jesus Christ**..."
- *The Payoff:* This serves as the definitive Creed of the early church: "God" is a title reserved for the Father alone.

☐ **The Subjection Clause:** Read 1 Corinthians 15:24–28.
- *The Text:* "Then shall the Son also himself be subject unto him... that **God may be all in all.**"
- *The Payoff:* This proves that Jesus' reign is temporary and functional. He reigns *until* the job is done, then hands the Kingdom back to the One True God.

- ☐ **The Adam Logic:** Read Romans 5:12–19.
  - *The Payoff:* This reveals the core logic of salvation. Since a **human** (Adam) broke the world, a **human** (Jesus) had to fix it. If Jesus were God, the parallel would fail.

  WARNING: FALSE FRIEND ALERT
  Term: "God blessed for ever" (Romans 9:5)
  The Trap: Trinitarians claim this calls Jesus God.
  The Correction: It is a punctuation error. In Greek, it is a doxology (praise) to the Father. "The One who is over all, God, be blessed for ever. Amen."

CHECKLIST 4: THE TEACHINGS OF THE MESSIAH (c. 60–68 AD)

Reading Focus: Matthew, Mark, Luke (The Synoptics)
The Reality: These are the biographies of the Messiah. They contain the "Words of Life." When you read them *after* Paul, you see them not just as history, but as the record of God's ultimate Agent teaching us how to live, love, and serve the Father.

The Mission

Read these books to sit at the feet of the Master. Your goal is to hear the **teachings of Jesus** exactly as his disciples heard them: as the words of a man anointed by God to reveal the Father's heart.

The Checksheet

- ☐ **The Source of the Teaching:** Read John 7:16 (as a key) and apply it to the Synoptics.
  - *The Principle:* Jesus says, "My doctrine is not mine, but His that sent me."
  - *The Payoff:* You will discover that Jesus is not the *origin* of the Law, but the faithful *Messenger* of it.

- ☐ **The Conception Reality:** Read Matthew 1 and Luke 1.
  - *The Payoff:* You will see the text describes a creation miracle (God creating life in Mary), not an incarnation (a pre-existent God shrinking down).

- ☐ **The Temptation Logic:** Read Matthew 4:1–11.
  - *The Payoff:* This validates Jesus' victory. If he were God, temptation would be impossible. Because he is human, his victory over sin is real and imitable.

CHECKLIST 5: THE HELLENISTIC BRIDGE (c. 90–95 AD)

Reading Focus: The Gospel of John
The Danger Zone: This book was written last, to a Greek audience. It uses high-context metaphors ("Logos," "Light," "Life") that are easily misunderstood if you don't know the Hebrew roots.

The Mission

You must cross the bridge without falling into Greek Philosophy. You must distinguish between the *Personification* of God's Plan (The Word) and the *Person* of God Himself.

> **Navigator's Note:** *To decode the Greek mindset and the "Ontology Trap," consult the "Forensic Glossary" in "Jerusalem, Not Athens" on page* **438**.

The Checksheet

- ☐ **The Definition of Eternal Life:** Read John 17:3.
    - *The "Only" Clause:* Jesus prays to the Father and calls Him "The **Only True God**."
    - *The Payoff:* This is the "Smoking Gun." Jesus explicitly excludes himself from the title of "Only True God."

- ☐ **The Ascension Distinction:** Read John 20:17.
    - *The Relationship:* Jesus says, "I ascend to my Father and your Father; and to **my God** and your God."
    - *The Payoff:* This proves that even in his glorified state, Jesus has a God. The Supreme Being does not *have* a God; He *is* God.

    WARNING: FALSE FRIEND ALERT
    Term: "The Word was God" (John 1:1)
    The Correction: In Greek, the lack of the article before *Theos* means it describes a *quality*. A better reading: "The Word was fully expressive of God," or "What God was, the Word was."

CHECKLIST 5B: THE TRANSLATION AUDIT

Reading Focus: The "Stolen Dictionary"
The Objective: Before entering the Imperial era, verify you are not using Pagan definitions for Hebrew words. (See "The Stolen Dictionary" on page **445**).

The Checksheet

- [ ] **The "Word" Test:**
  - *The Payoff:* Replacing the Greek *Logos* (Mind) with the Hebrew *Dabar* (Plan/Command) prevents the error of turning a "Plan" into a "Person."

- [ ] **The "Spirit" Test:**
  - *The Payoff:* Understanding *Ruach* as "Breath" or "Power" protects you from imagining the Spirit as a third separate person ("Ghost").

- [ ] **The "One" Test:**
  - *The Payoff:* Knowing that *Echad* means a numeric singular "One" (not a "compound unity") aligns you with the definition of God held by Jesus himself.

CHECKLIST 6: THE IMPERIAL OVERWRITE (325 AD+)

Reading Focus: The Council of Nicaea & Theodosius
The Mission: You are investigating a Hostile Takeover. You must verify the specific legal mechanisms used by the State to silence the Apostolic faith.

The Checksheet

- [ ] **The Vocabulary Plant:**
  - *Search:* Look for *Homoousios* ("Same Substance") in the Bible.
  - *The Payoff:* Realizing this word is missing proves that the central dogma of the Council was political, not biblical.

- [ ] **The Rigged Jury (381 AD):**
  - *Evidence:* The 36 Monotheist bishops were physically barred from the council.
  - *The Payoff:* You will understand that the "Unanimous Consent" of the church was actually a manufactured fraud.

- [ ] **The Bankruptcy Protocol:**
  - *Evidence:* Law 16.5.7 stripped believers of the right to write a Will or inherit property.
  - *The Payoff:* This reveals why the belief "died out"–it was financially exterminated, not theologically defeated.

- ☐ **The Demolition Order:**
    - *Evidence:* The State seized the Monotheist buildings by force on Nov 24, 380 AD.
    - *The Payoff:* This explains why all ancient cathedrals are Trinitarian-the opposition was evicted by the military.
- ☐ **The Burning of Evidence:**
    - *Evidence:* Commentaries were incinerated by Imperial Decree in 389 AD.
    - *The Payoff:* This explains the silence of history-the defense witnesses were silenced.
- ☐ **The Canonical Enclosure:** Investigate who decided which books you are allowed to read and why they re-ordered them.
    - *The Payoff:* You will discover how the "Jewish Voice" was pushed to the basement to make room for Roman Dogma.
    - *See Dossier:* **"The Architects of the Box"** on page **410**.

THE FINAL VERDICT

You have now traced the timeline. You have witnessed the "Theological Creep" move from the simple, ethical monotheism of James to the metaphysical speculation of the Greeks, finally hardening into the state-enforced dogmas of Rome.
The question is no longer "What does the Church say?" The question is "What did the Apostles write?"
You now possess the forensic tools to read the New Testament as it was intended: clearly, historically, and through the lens of the One True God. As you turn the page to begin reading, remember: The text is the evidence. Everything else is just hearsay, and likely even heresy.

> **CRITICAL REFERRAL: THE FULL HISTORICAL RECORD**
> The summary above is just the surface. For the detailed documentation of the political maneuvering, the bribes, and the specific changes made to the text, you must consult the forensic evidence included in this volume:
>
> - **The Council of Nicaea & Theodosius:** See "The Sword of Theodosius" on page **389**.
> - **The Architects of the Box:** See "How the Canon was Weaponized" on page **410**.
> - **Biblical Monotheism (Closing Argument):** See "The Uniqueness of the One God" on page **430**.
> - **The Corruption Notes:** See the "False Friends" Glossary on page **67**.

Recommended Chronological Reading Order
A Guide to Historical Clarity

I. The Logic of Sequence

To understand any great story or movement, one must observe it as it unfolds in time. You would not watch the sequel to a movie before the original, nor would you read the final chapter of a biography before the introduction. To do so would be to confuse the conclusion with the origin.

Yet, for centuries, readers of the New Testament have been encouraged to read the documents out of order. The traditional arrangement—starting with Matthew and ending with Revelation—is not a timeline; it is a library categorization system. While this tradition is standard in almost all Bibles (including the 1901 RV), it can unintentionally obscure the actual development of the Christian faith.

The Editors highly recommend a radical departure from tradition: read the documents in the order they were **written**, not the order of **designation by a person with an agenda.**

II. The Protocol of Cognitive Framing

Why was the order changed? The current arrangement was not accidental; it was **concocted**.

In a court of law, the order in which evidence is presented often determines the verdict. If a prosecutor can plant a specific bias in the jury's mind during opening statements, the jury will view all subsequent facts through that lens. This manipulation is known as **Cognitive Framing**.

The arrangement of the New Testament books is theological, not chronological. It is a designed "Frame." By placing the Gospel of Matthew (c. 85 AD) on Page 1, the Church Fathers (specifically solidified by **Jerome** in the Latin Vulgate, c. 382 AD) forced the reader to accept the "Developed Church" (Virgin Birth, Trinity formulas, Peter's Keys) as the starting point.

III. Chronological Order of the New Testament

To gain a clear perspective, we advise reading in this sequence. This allows you to see the faith grow from its Jewish roots into the global movement it became.

PHASE 1: THE FOUNDATION (The Jewish Baseline)

The earliest voice. Pure ethical Monotheism before the Gentile controversy.

A. The Epistle of James (c. 45–48 AD)
This is the "Control Sample" of the New Testament. Written by James the Just (the brother of Jesus) to the "Twelve Tribes scattered abroad," it represents the faith in its original, pre-Gentile form.

- **What to Watch For:** Notice what is missing. You will find no mention of the Virgin Birth, no Trinitarian formulas, and no complex theology of "Justification by Faith." You will find a strict adherence to the "One God" (James 2:19) and a demand for ethical action. This is the bedrock.

PHASE 2: THE EXPLOSION (The Authentic Paul)

The letters circulating 20 years before a Gospel was written. The struggle for Gentile inclusion.

B. Galatians (c. 49 AD)
The "Magna Carta" of Christian liberty. Paul writes this in a fury, defending the right of Gentiles to follow Jesus without becoming Jewish proselytes. It is raw, emotional, and the first major theological argument in history.

C. 1 Thessalonians (c. 50 AD)
The oldest letter in the collection. The church is young, persecuted, and confused. The primary focus here is the **Second Coming**. They believed Jesus was returning within their lifetime (Chapter 4).

D. 2 Thessalonians (c. 51 AD)
A necessary correction. Some believers had stopped working because they thought the "Day of the Lord" had already come or was imminent. Paul writes to tell them to get back to work and remain steady.

E. 1 Corinthians (c. 54 AD)
A forensic look into a messy church. The congregation in Corinth was dividing over leaders, suing each other, and abusing the Lord's Supper. This letter contains the famous "Love Chapter" (13) and the earliest written record of the Resurrection (15).

F. 2 Corinthians (c. 56 AD)
Paul's most personal defense. After being attacked by "Super Apostles" who claimed he was weak, Paul opens his heart about his sufferings, beatings, and the "thorn in his flesh."

G. Romans (c. 57 AD)
The Masterpiece. Writing to a church he had not yet visited, Paul composes a systematic defense of his Gospel. This is where he defines the mechanism of Grace, the failure of the Law, and the future of Israel.

PHASE 3: THE SUCCESSION (Paul's Final Letters)

Paul's final instructions to his delegates before his execution.

H. Philippians (c. 60–62 AD)
The "Letter of Joy." Written from a Roman prison, this is Paul's thank-you note to his supporters. It contains the "Hymn of Christ" (Chapter 2), describing the humility of the Messiah who emptied himself to serve God.

I. Philemon (c. 60–62 AD)
A masterpiece of diplomacy. Paul writes to a slave owner, asking him to receive his runaway slave not as property, but as a "beloved brother."

J. 1 Timothy (c. 62–64 AD)
The "Manual for the Church." As the end draws near, Paul instructs his young protégé on how to organize the community.

- **The Key Statute:** This letter contains the definitive creed of the early church: *"For there is one God, and one mediator also between God and men, himself man, Christ Jesus"* (1 Timothy 2:5).

K. Titus (c. 62–64 AD)
Written to Paul's troubleshooter on the island of Crete. It focuses on appointing elders and maintaining "sound doctrine" amidst a culture known for dishonesty.

L. 2 Timothy (c. 64–67 AD)
The Last Will and Testament. Written from death row in Rome, waiting for the executioner's sword. It is intimate, urgent, and final. *"I have fought the good fight, I have finished the course."*

PHASE 4: THE NARRATIVE (Preserving the Story)

Written after the death of Paul and Peter, and the destruction of the Temple (70 AD).

M. Gospel of Mark (c. 65–70 AD)
The "Blueprint." This is the first written Gospel, likely based on the memories of Peter. It is fast-paced, gritty, and focuses on the actions of Jesus rather than his teaching. It originally ended with the women fleeing the tomb in fear (Mark 16:8).

N. Gospel of Matthew (c. 80 AD)
The "Jewish Bridge." Written by a scribe who used Mark as a source, this Gospel is designed to prove to the Jewish reader that Jesus is the "New Moses." It organizes Jesus' teaching into five great sermons (like the Sermon on the Mount) and emphasizes the fulfillment of prophecy.

O. Hebrews (c. 80 AD)
The "Theological Bridge." With the Temple destroyed (70 AD), Jewish Christians were in crisis. This anonymous sermon argues that Jesus is the new High Priest and the ultimate sacrifice, making the physical Temple obsolete.

P. Gospel of Luke (c. 85 AD)
The "Historian's Account." Written by a Gentile companion of Paul, this is the first part of a two-volume set (Luke-Acts). It focuses on Jesus' compassion for the outcast, the poor, and women.

Q. Acts of the Apostles (c. 90 AD)
The Sequel. This is the only history book of the early church. It tracks the movement from Jerusalem (Peter) to Rome (Paul), showing how the message crossed the barrier from Jew to Gentile.

PHASE 5: THE SPIRITUAL THEOLOGY (The Johannine School)

The final Apostle, John, reflecting on the cosmic meaning of the Messiah.

R. Gospel of John (c. 90–95 AD)
The "Spiritual Gospel." Very different from the others. It contains no parables and no exorcisms. Instead, it presents Jesus through long theological discourses and the famous "I AM" statements. It opens not with a birth story, but with the cosmic "Word" (Logos).

S. Revelation (c. 95 AD)
The Resistance. Written by John on the prison island of Patmos. It is not a puzzle map of the 21st century, but a vision of victory for a church being crushed by the Roman Empire.

T. 1, 2, & 3 John (c. 95–100 AD)
The Final Word. These short letters deal with a split in the community. They emphasize that "God is Love" and warn against "antichrists" who deny that Jesus came in the flesh.

The Sword of Theodosius:
How Biblical Monotheism Became a State Crime

AUTHOR'S NOTE ON THE RECOVERY OF HISTORY

To the Student of Scripture:

Be advised: What follows is not merely a theological argument, but a forensic investigation into a forgotten chapter of our shared history.

You are about to uncover the documentation of a **civilizational catastrophe**.

The evidence presented in these pages reveals a specific turning point where the definition of God was taken out of the hands of the Apostles and placed into the hands of the State.

You will see how this single event sent a shockwave through history that is still felt today—altering Bible translations, coercing scribes, and establishing the **first and most oppressive Government Mandate in history**.

A Note on the Glory of the Messiah: As you examine this evidence, you may feel an instinctive fear that identifying the Father as the "Only True God" somehow diminishes the glory of His Son.

We invite you to consider a different perspective: **Restoration is Elevation.**

To crown the Messiah with a Roman title he never claimed is not an act of worship, but an act of tradition. By restoring his biblical identity as the human Messiah, we restore the magnitude of his victory.

We see a man who was tempted as we are, yet stayed faithful; a man who truly died, and was truly raised by the power of his God. We do not honor the Son by contradicting his own testimony. We honor him by believing it.

This 1,600-year legacy of **totalitarian theology** was designed for one purpose: **To replace the God-given freedom of conscience with State-Mandated Conformity**.

If, as you read this history, you begin to feel a sense of shock, disorientation, or even anger, please know that your feelings are valid.

You are not reacting to a "difference of opinion"; you are reacting to the realization that we have all been inherited into a 1,600-year-old deception designed to drown out the original "Signal."

> "O **Yahweh**... the nations shall come unto thee from the ends of the earth, and shall say, **Surely our fathers have inherited lies**, vanity, and things wherein there is no profit."
> — Jeremiah 16:19 RV

We invite you to examine the evidence for yourself.

For sixteen centuries, the "Signal" of the original biblical faith has been drowned out by a "Noise" that was not merely theological, but legally mandatory.

To understand why the majority of the Christian world today accepts the Trinity as "Orthodoxy," one must look past the halls of prayer and into the courts of Roman governmental power.

The Trinity did not survive because it was more scriptural; it survived because the original "One God" faith was forcibly turned into a state crime.

THE TIMELINE OF THE TAKEOVER

[Image of timeline showing the progression from Biblical Monotheism to State-Enforced Trinitarianism (33 AD - 1612 AD)]

- **33 AD — The Signal:** Jesus affirms the Father is the "Only True God" (John 17:3).

- **55 AD — The Apostolic Affirmation:** Paul writes, "For us there is but One God, the Father" (1 Cor 8:6).

- **325 AD — The Drift Begins:** The Council of Nicaea introduces Greek philosophical terms like *homoousios* ("substance").

- **380 AD — THE SWORD FALLS:** Emperor Theodosius I issues the *Edict of Thessalonica*. Belief in the Trinity becomes mandatory by state law.

- **381 AD — The Sham Council:** Theodosius stacks the Council of Constantinople to ratify his law and officially votes the Holy Spirit into the Godhead as a "third person."

- **382 AD — The Death Penalty:** Theodosius issues Law 16.5.9, authorizing the death penalty for religious dissenters.

- **385 AD — First Blood:** Bishop Priscillian is executed by the State for "heresy" (sorcery), proving the legal cliff was real.

- **389 AD — The Burning:** State decrees order the burning of anti-Trinitarian books. The "Signal" is silenced by fire.

- **529 AD — The Legal Concrete:** The Code of Justinian cements the Theodosian laws into the foundation of Western civilization. Persecution becomes permanent.

- **1229 AD — The Lockout:** The Council of Toulouse officially bans the laity from possessing the Bible. The "Signal" is locked in a Latin cage.

- **1536–1612 AD — The Medieval Harvest:** The Roman laws of 380 AD are weaponized by the Inquisition and Protestant Magistrates to execute Tyndale, Servetus, and Wightman.

- **Present Day — The Restoration: The One God Study Bible** removes the 1,600-year-old "Noise" to restore the original "Signal."

While many believe the Church "settled" the nature of God through prayerful debate, the historical record tells a darker story.

The Trinity was born in a laboratory of state power, enforced by a dictator who viewed the original monotheism of the apostles as a form of high treason.

I. The Death of Persuasion

In the first three centuries, Christianity was a movement of the conscience. It grew through the power of the Word and the courage of martyrs.

However, by the late fourth century, the Roman State was fractured. Emperor Theodosius I, seeking a single "glue" to hold his crumbling borders together, decided that religious uniformity—enforced by law—was the key to political survival.

THE NATIONAL SECURITY MOTIVE (THE GOTH CONNECTION): Why was Theodosius so obsessed with the Trinity? It wasn't just theology; it was war. The Roman Empire was being invaded by the Goths, who were Christians but **Non-Trinitarians**.

Theodosius used the Trinity as a **National Security Loyalty Test**. If you believed in the One God, you were suspected of being a "Goth Sympathizer." He turned the faith of the Apostles into an act of treason against the Empire's military security.

On **February 27, 380 AD**, without consulting a single council of bishops, Theodosius issued the *Edict of Thessalonica* (*Cunctos Populos*).

This decree marked the official death of religious freedom. It explicitly commanded:

> "It is our will that all the peoples who are ruled by the administration of our Clemency shall practice that religion which the divine Peter the Apostle transmitted to the Romans... we shall believe in the single deity of the Father, the Son and the Holy Spirit... We command that those persons who follow this rule shall embrace the name of Catholic Christians. The rest, however, whom we adjudge **demented and insane** [*dementes vesanosque*], shall sustain the infamy of heretical dogmas... they shall be smitten first by divine vengeance and secondly by the retribution of our own initiative."

THE TRADEMARKING OF "CATHOLIC": Note carefully what the Emperor did here. He legally trademarked the word "Catholic".

Before this moment, Christians were defined by their love and adherence to Jesus.

After this moment, "Catholic" became a government-issued ID card reserved *only* for Trinitarians. If you believed in the One God of Jesus, the State legally stripped you of the name "Christian" and branded you a madman.

THE WEAPONIZATION OF "INFAMIA" (CIVIL DEATH): In Roman Law, the term *infamy* (infamia) was not merely an insult; it was a legal status of **Civil Death**.

A citizen branded with *Infamia* lost the right to vote, hold office, and crucially, the **Right to Testify in Court** (*testimonium*).

By applying this legal brand, Theodosius didn't just disagree with the Monotheists; he legally stripped them of their voice, ensuring they could never witness against him.

II. The Rigged Jury of 381 AD

Apologists often point to the Council of Constantinople (381 AD) as the moment the Church "agreed" on the Trinity.

Historical evidence, however, reveals that this was not a debate, but a political rally for the victors.

1. **The Unanimous Lie (The 150 vs. 36 Mathematical Fraud):** Theodosius did not invite the church to decide the issue; he invited only those who agreed with him. The historical record confirms that **186** bishops originally arrived at the capital.

   However, **36** of those bishops, led by the courageous **Eleusius of Cyzicus**, held to the biblical view that **Yahweh** (the Father) alone is the Supreme God.

   These 36 bishops were not invited to deliberate; they were systematically **denied being heard**. A 100% "unanimous" vote achieved by discarding nearly **20% (19.35%)** of the participants is a mathematical fraud.

2. **State-Level Voter Suppression:** By uninviting and barring the 36 dissenting bishops from the chamber, the Emperor engaged in the first act of **State-Level Voter Suppression** in Church history. The "unanimous decision" was only possible because the opposition was physically and legally locked out by the guard.

3. **The Assault on DUE PROCESS:** In any fair assembly, the opposition has a "Right to be Heard." By refusing to allow the dissenting 19.35% of the leadership to speak, the Emperor committed a **direct assault on the fundamental right of DUE PROCESS**.

4. **The Rigged Election:** A process where the ballot is restricted to one party and the opposition is silenced is the definition of a **Rigged Election**. The Council was not a spiritual debate; it was a political rally for a dictator's theology.

5. **The Insider Confession:** The most damning evidence comes from **Gregory of Nazianzus**, the man Theodosius appointed to chair the council. Gregory resigned in disgust, describing the gathering as a chaotic mob:

   > "I have never seen a good end to a council... they increase the evil rather than solve it... The bishops are like a flock of geese and cranes, fighting and squabbling."

III. The Bankruptcy Protocol

Theodosius spent the remainder of his reign constructing a massive legal cage designed to trap and starve Biblical Monotheists. These laws were compiled into the *Codex Theodosianus* (Book XVI).

1. **The Criminalization of Assembly (Law 16.5.6):** This law prohibited anyone who did not believe in the Trinity from holding religious meetings. If believers gathered in a private home to discuss the *Shema*, the owner faced the immediate **confiscation of their entire property**.

2. **Generational Financial Terror (Law 16.5.7):** Theodosius understood that ideas die if you bankrupt the families who hold them.

   He enacted a law stripping "heretics" of **Testamentary Rights**. A Monotheist was legally forbidden from writing a Last Will. They could not inherit money, and they could not leave their home or savings to their children.

   It was financial blackmail: *Believe the Trinity, or your children will starve.*

3. **The Inquisitorial Hunt (Law 16.5.9):** For the first time, the state appointed *Inquisitores*—officials whose sole job was to spy on citizens, uncover secret meetings for **Yahweh** (the Father), and bring the "madmen" to justice.

IV. The Demolition Teams

The Nicene party won through a coordinated campaign of demolition led by the State enforcer, **Maternus Cynegius**.

1. **The Demolition Teams:** Cynegius employed fanatical monks and soldiers to physically dismantle the temples and meeting places of non-Trinitarians. This was a government-sanctioned demolition project.

2. **The Eviction of Constantinople:** On **November 24, 380 AD**, Theodosius personally marched into the capital and evicted the Monotheist Bishop *Demophilus*. Armed soldiers seized every church in the city and handed the keys to the Trinitarian minority.

V. The Sainted Tyrant

Both the Roman Catholic and Eastern Orthodox traditions honor Emperor Theodosius I as **"Saint Theodosius the Great."**

Why? Because he gave them the stolen property.

By using the military to seize the real estate of **Yahweh** believers, he bought the Church's eternal loyalty.

THE "SACRILEGE" TRAP (THEODOSIUS AS GOD'S VOICE): To ensure no one could challenge his new theology, Theodosius passed **Law 6.24.4**, which stated that to question the judgment of the Emperor was not just illegal, it was **Sacrilege**.

By merging the State and God, he made disagreeing with his theology a sin against Heaven itself. This is the legal foundation of **Totalitarian Theocracy**.

VI. The State-Sponsored Book Burning

To maintain a monopoly on truth, Theodosius launched a campaign of "literary cleansing."

1. **The Decree of Destruction:** The state issued specific laws (389 AD) commanding that the books of the "heretics" be burned.

2. **Silencing the Scholarship:** The thousands of commentaries defending **Yahweh** as the Only God were turned to ash.

    This is why history today seems one-sided—the State literally incinerated the opposition's voice. To own one of these books was an act of High Treason, eventually punishable by **Death** (*Summa Supplicium*).

VII. The Invention of "Mystery"

Jesus taught that the Father is the "Only True God" (John 17:3).

To make the Trinity work, State-authorized theologians had to invent a "Mystery" that defied logic. Under the State Code, questioning this "Mystery" labeled you a "madman."

VIII. The Forensic Forgeries

1. **The Forgery of 1 Timothy 3:16:** In the oldest manuscripts, this reads

The Fruit of the Sword: A Forensic History of Terror

If the Trinity **lived** as the fruit of the Holy Spirit, it would produce peace. Instead, for 1,200 years, the doctrine produced a river of blood.

The modern reader often views the Trinity as a harmless tradition. The historical record reveals the dogma was a **Capital Law** enforced by the sword.

Religious and secular authorities viewed challenges to this doctrine not merely as theological error, but as **"Spiritual Murder"** and treason against the State.

Specifics are required. The Magistrate operated on a single belief: a heretic was more dangerous than a physical murderer. While a murderer killed the body, a heretic "murdered the soul" by leading it to damnation.

Consequently, the **Roman Catholic Machinery** and later **Protestant Magistrates** did not merely discourage questions; they criminalized them.

I. The Laws of Silence: Criminalizing the Bible

To protect the "Gate of Truth," the authorities established a legal framework to hunt down and destroy anyone who sought to read the Bible without a priest. **The decree operated** not as a suggestion, but as a dragnet.

The Synod of Verona (1184) — The Charter of the Inquisition

Issued by Pope Lucius III and Holy Roman Emperor Frederick I Barbarossa, the Synod legally bound the Church and State together. The decree established the *Ad Abolendam*—the legal charter of the Inquisition. The Church identified the heretic; the State executed them.

The Council of Toulouse (1229) — The Total Ban (Canon 14)

Held to crush the Albigensian movement, **the Toulouse decree remains** one of the most infamous in history. The Canon explicitly stripped the common man of the Word of God:

> "We prohibit also that the laity should be permitted to have the books of the Old or New Testament... we most strictly forbid their having any translation of these books."
> **(Source: Council of Toulouse, Canon 14)**

Laypeople were permitted only a Psalter or a book of prayers—and strictly in Latin. Possession of a Bible in the native tongue served as proof of a crime.

The "Scorched Earth" Policy (Canon 6)

The Inquisition extended the terror beyond the person. The Council decreed that the very ground was cursed. If a Bible was found in a home, the law required the total destruction of the property:

> *"We decree that the house in which a heretic has been found should be demolished, and the place itself or the ground is to be confiscated."*
> **(Source: Council of Toulouse, Canon 6)**

The Weaponization of Children (Canon 11): The ultimate horror of the Spy State was the destruction of the family unit. The Council mandated that children—boys from the age of fourteen and girls from twelve—were legally required to take an oath to hunt down heretics.

The State turned children into witnesses against their own parents.

The Council of Tarragona (1234) — The "8-Day" Burning Decree

The net tightened. This council ruled that anyone possessing a Bible in the common language faced a rigid deadline:

> *"Turn them over to the local bishop within **eight days**, so that they may be burned."*
> **(Source: Council of Tarragona, Canon 2)**

Anyone who missed this deadline was automatically "esteemed suspected of heresy."

II. The Martyrdom of the Translator

Before **examining** the martyrs of the Trinity, **recognize** the martyr of the English Bible itself.

William Tyndale (Executed October 6, 1536)

Look at the architect of the English Bible. **The evidence stands as a mathematical certainty**: roughly **80-90%** of the King James New Testament is drawn directly from Tyndale's translation. Familiar phrases like *"Let there be light"* and *"Seek and ye shall find"* are his voice.

The State did not reward him; it hunted him.

Tyndale was betrayed by a friend, imprisoned for over a year in the castle of Vilvoorde, and finally brought to the stake near Brussels. The execution was calculated savagery.

To ensure his voice was silenced, the executioner **strangled him to death** at the stake before his body was consumed by the flames.

His final words were a plea to the very power structure that would eventually co-opt his work: *"Lord! Open the King of England's eyes!"*

The Royal Theft: The King James Version is, in essence, the **Tyndale Bible** authorized by a King who represented the very system that killed him.

III. The Victims: Executed for "The One God"

Rejecting the Trinity was the ultimate capital offense, uniting otherwise hostile Catholic and Protestant factions in their condemnation.

Katarzyna Weiglowa (Executed April 19, 1539)

Consider the case of Katarzyna Weiglowa, a Polish woman executed at the age of 80. Katarzyna did not die quickly. The widow spent **ten years** in prison before her execution.

Katarzyna was burned at the stake in Kraków for the crime of "apostasy"—specifically for professing the **Unity of God** and rejecting the "Holy Trinity." Even at the stake, Katarzyna refused to recant, confessing the One God until the flames took her voice.

Michael Servetus (Executed October 27, 1553)

Michael Servetus was a brilliant Spanish physician and polymath—the first European to describe pulmonary circulation. But Servetus committed the fatal crime of publishing *On the Errors of the Trinity*.

- **The Protestant Betrayal:** Escaping the Catholic Inquisition in France, Servetus fled to Geneva, expecting freedom among the Reformers. Instead, Servetus was arrested by the City Council under the influence of **John Calvin**.

- **The Execution:** Calvin served as the expert witness for the prosecution. Servetus was condemned to be burned alive.

- **The Green Wood Torture:** The executioners used **green (damp) wood**, turning the execution into a slow torture that lasted thirty minutes. With a copy of his own book chained to his leg, Servetus shrieked in the flames, crying out his final confession: *"Jesus, Son of the Eternal God, have mercy on me!"* (Refusing to the end to call him the "Eternal Son").

IV. The Indelible Stain: King James and the Fire

The horror did not end in the Middle Ages. The violence touches the very name of the most famous Bible in history.

Bartholomew Legate (Executed March 18, 1612)

Only three years after the publication of the King James Bible, King James I personally interrogated Bartholomew Legate, a cloth merchant who denied the Trinity.

When Legate refused to yield to the King's theology, James kicked him and ordered his execution. Legate was burned at Smithfield, becoming the first of the final two martyrs.

Edward Wightman (Executed April 11, 1612)

Less than a month later, Edward Wightman became the last person burned at the stake for heresy in England. His crime was Anti-Trinitarianism.

The timeline reveals the uncomfortable truth: **The same hand that authorized the Bible also signed the death warrant.**

VERIFIED HISTORICAL RECORD:

- **The Primary Witness:** *The Church History of Britain* by Thomas Fuller (Published 1655). Fuller records the specific crowd reaction and the "double burning" event.

- **The Death Warrant:** The writ *De Haeretico Comburendo* ("Regarding the burning of a heretic"). Issued by King James I on March 9, 1612. Held in the British National Archives.

- **The Government Files:** *State Papers Domestic: James I (1611–1618).* These official government records document the King's personal interrogation of Edward Wightman at Royston.

- **The Double Burning:** On March 20, 1612, the fires were lit. As the flames scorched him, Edward screamed in agony. The crowd, thinking Edward wanted to recant, pulled him out. Edward was severely burned but alive.

- **The Final Act:** Three weeks later, when Edward refused to sign the official recantation, King James ordered him back to the stake. This time, there was no mercy. Edward was burned to ashes.

V. The Separation: The Pen vs. The Sword

Distinguish the *Pen* from the *Sword*.

The **Authorized Version (KJV)** is a literary masterpiece produced by brilliant scholars. The **King James Monarchy** was a political regime that burned dissenters.

The paradox **cuts deep:** The text we love was authorized by a King who killed those who questioned the Trinity.

The Geneva Suppression: Why the KJV was Authorized

King James did not authorize his version out of benevolence. He authorized it to displace the **Geneva Bible** (1560)—the Bible of the Pilgrims.

The Geneva Bible contained marginal notes that questioned the "Divine Right of Kings" and challenged tyranny. King James famously declared the Geneva notes to be *"seditions, and savouring too much of dangerous and traitorous conceits."*

The KJV was commissioned as a "safe" Bible for the State—one without the notes of freedom.

The American Rescue: The Authorized Version — Liberated

For this reason, the **Authorized Version — Purified (RV)** is so vital. **The text stands as** the "Authorized Version" *rescued* from the Monarchy and brought to the Republic.

The RV preserves the majestic, literal scholarship of the 1611 translators, but the work was produced under the protection of the **First Amendment**.

Unlike 1612 England, where the King's warrant could turn a man to ash, the RV scholars worked within the safety of **American Liberty**—specifically the **Freedom of Conscience** established in 1776.

The "Wall of Separation" between Church and State ensured that no magistrate could force

The American Rebel's Bible

The "Rebel Bible" and the Defiance of the King

William Tyndale is the true father of the English Bible and the *Ultimate Rebel* of 1530. He gave the people their souls back by seizing the power of interpretation from the State and handing the keys to the common man.

The Geneva Bible (1560) was essentially the *Tyndale Bible* dressed in a new cover, armed with 300,000 words of "seditious" marginal commentary. The Geneva edition served as the primary translation for America's earliest settlers.

For the first century of American history, the *Geneva Bible* reigned as the undisputed "American Bible."

While the *King James Bible* (1611) eventually became the *undeserved* standard only because the King outlawed the competition, the *Geneva Bible* dominated the pulpits and homes of the heroic pioneers who loved Freedom. To the Crown, it was sedition; to the American Founders, it was the *"Rebel Bible."*

The Pilgrims fled more than just execution; the first Americans crossed a lethal ocean to seize their God-given freedom. The settlers rejected the King's claim of ownership over their souls and sought a land where the only Sovereign was God.

The Architect

The Ultimate Rebel

William Tyndale ignited the war for the English Bible. Tyndale famously vowed to a scholar he would make sure "even a lowly plowboy would be able to know more Scripture than the average theologian."

Tyndale translated the entire New Testament, the Pentateuch, and various other books in the Old Testament before *Imperial agents hunted him down* and imprisoned him. The Catholic Church convicted him in a "spiritual trial" and handed him to the State for death.

The Catholic Church's State-hired executioner attempted to strangle Tyndale as a "mercy killing", but his botched attempt failed to kill the Father of the English Bible instantly. William Tyndale cried out, "Lord, open the King of England's eyes," before the hot fire burned William alive.

However, before the smoke cleared, changes had already taken place in **England**. *King Henry VIII* broke from the Roman Catholic Church, famously so he could divorce his wife.

Two years after King Henry VIII "unwittingly" (questionable) authorized the *Matthew Bible* (1537), *Tyndale's* friend *Miles Coverdale* produced the second authorized version. The *Great Bible* (1539) was published with the King's blessing, and *King Henry VIII* commanded large copies be displayed in churches, unaware he was promoting the words of the man he hunted.

The Exile

Escaping Bloody Mary

The situation in England turned into a slaughter. After *Henry VIII* died, *Queen Mary I* (known as "Bloody Mary") brought the nation back to Catholicism and burned 280 Protestants alive, turning the town squares of England into human bonfires.

Anyone who wanted to avoid the flames had to flee to the European continent. Many English Protestants fled to Geneva, Switzerland, where *John Calvin* was reforming the city.

While in exile, the English refugees—including *William Whittingham* (who married Calvin's sister), *Christopher Goodman*, and *Miles Coverdale*—created the first English Study Bible, based on *Tyndale's* translation, called **The Geneva Bible**.

The Geneva Bible represented a massive leap in scholarship and usability. The Geneva edition stood as the first "reader-friendly" text, featuring:

- **Chapter and Verse Divisions:** For easy reference.
- **Visual Aids:** Maps, chronologies, and woodcut illustrations.
- **Italics:** To show words added by translators for clarity.
- **Source Fidelity:** The Geneva edition stood as the first Bible entirely translated from the original Hebrew and Greek (thanks mostly to William Tyndale).

The Geneva Bible fit on a kitchen table, not just a cathedral lectern.

The Visual Hijack

The Typeface of the Free Man

The *Geneva Bible* used the clean, readable **Roman Typeface**—the font of the civilian—to make reading easy for commoners.

In stark contrast, *King James I* initially insisted on the archaic, hard-to-read **Gothic Blackletter** font. The visual hijack kept the Word feeling like an ancient, mystical mystery that required a state-controlled priest to decode, rather than a clear instruction for a free man.

The Resistance

The Weapon of Liberty

From 1560 through the mid-1600s, the *Geneva Bible* served as the standard Bible for **English families**. In 1579, the **Scottish Parliament** commanded every household with adequate means must buy a *Geneva Bible*.

The Scottish law created a stark contrast: while the **English King** moved to ban the *Geneva Bible*, the **Scottish Parliament** forced every family to purchase the Geneva edition.

When civil war tore England apart in the 1640s, the specific Bible in a soldier's pocket acted as his military uniform. Rebels and Parliamentarians wielded the *Geneva Bible* as a weapon of ideology, while Royalists clung to the *King James Bible* as a badge of loyalty to the Crown.

The "Seditious" Marginal Notes

300,000 Words Against Tyranny

The *Geneva Bible* was the first true "Study Bible," featuring a massive 300,000 words of marginal commentary—essentially a "mini-theology library" comprising one-third of the book's total length.

The massive 300,000-word framework infuriated the King because the text transferred the power of interpretation from the State to the "ploughboy." The notes challenged the absolute authority of kings and attacked the profit motives of the corrupt.

- **The "Locust" Insult:** The notes were fiercely anti-clerical. In Revelation 9:3, the commentary identified the "locusts" from the bottomless pit not as insects, but as "false teachers"—specifically targeting the King's archbishops and cardinals who maintained false doctrine to control the common man.

- **Lawful Disobedience:** On Exodus 1:19, the notes taught the Hebrew midwives were correct to disobey Pharaoh's decree because they prioritized God's commands over a tyrant's. The note explicitly stated: *"Their disobedience herein was lawful."*
- **Defining Tyranny:** The notes frequently used the word *tyrant* instead of *king* to describe unjust rulers.
- **Anti-Slavery Defiance:** The notes criticized the practice of "man-stealing" at the precise moment English ship captains were beginning to profit from the slave trade. *King James I* and the nobility hated the commentary because the text threatened the economic interests of the Crown's allies.

King James I famously called the *Geneva Bible* "the worst" of all translations because of the marginal commentary. He specifically commissioned the 1611 translation to be printed **without side-column explanations** to prevent these "seditious" interpretations from reaching the common man.

The War for the Mind

God's Sovereignty vs. State Control

The conflict between *Geneva* and *King James I* was not merely about translation; the struggle represented a war over the interpretive framework.

a) **God's Sovereignty vs. State Control:** *The Geneva Bible* featured unapologetically Calvinistic notes emphasizing God's sovereignty and election. *King James I* strictly forbade interpretive notes because he wanted a "compliant" text to unify the Church of England and avoid taking sides in theological debates.
b) **View of Monarchy:** *The Geneva Bible* challenged the "Divine Right of Kings," suggesting subjects could lawfully disobey unjust commands. *The King James Bible* removed **the Geneva commentary**, leaving interpretation to the established royal authorities.
c) **Church Government:** *The Geneva Bible* notes favored a "republican" church structure (Presbytery), implying bishops were unnecessary. *King James I* issued specific rules to protect the Episcopal structure, requiring translators to use "old ecclesiastical words" like "Bishop" instead of "Elder."
d) **Subtle Translation Choices:** In passages like John 3:36, *The Geneva Bible* used language suggesting "disobedience" to emphasize active faith. *The King James Bible* focused on "belief," a move scholars argue emphasized internal conviction over external social action.

The "Congregation" Cover-Up

How the King Buried the People's Power

William Tyndale deliberately replaced "old ecclesiastical words" in his 1526 New Testament to strip away the Catholic hierarchy's claim to power.

- **Church → Congregation:** Tyndale translated *ekklesia* as "congregation" to describe an assembly of believers.
- **Priest → Elder:** Tyndale translated *presbyteros* as "elder" to describe a community leader.

The Geneva Bible (1560) was the Bible of the Pilgrims, yet its translators did not keep *Tyndale's* most dangerous translation. The *Geneva Bible* restored the word *Church* in passages like Matthew 16:18.

Geneva translators—being Calvinists—believed in a visible, organized church structure (Presbyterianism) and utilized the word *Church* as long as their notes provided the correct interpretation.

King James I issued **Rule #3** in 1604, explicitly stating: *"The old Ecclesiastical Words to be kept, viz. the Word Church not to be translated Congregation"*.

King James I was actually agreeing with the *Geneva* text against *Tyndale* on this specific keyword. The real conflict rested on the *Geneva* marginal notes, which interpreted "Church" as a body governed by elders rather than the King's bishops.

The Royal Identity Theft

Plagiarizing the Martyr's Voice

William Tyndale remains the uncredited architect of the *King James Bible*. Scholars estimate that **83.7%** of the New Testament and **76%** of the Old Testament in the KJV is *Tyndale's* work.

King James I kept *Tyndale's* brilliant phrasing but swapped out the specific political keywords that threatened his throne.

Tyndale's Choice	King James's Mandate	The Forensic Motive
Congregation	Church	"Church" implies a state-owned institution and building.
Elder	Bishop	"Bishop" is a rank in a hierarchy answering to the King.
Love	Charity	"Charity" connoted institutional benevolence or alms, reinforcing the Church's role.
Passover	Easter (Acts 12:4)	Changed to reinforce the Anglican liturgical calendar.

The Geneva Bible used the word *love* (*agape*) to describe personal affection, but the bishops of *King James I* preferred *charity* to reinforce the church's role as the dispenser of grace.

Similarly, the KJV softened the word *tyrant* to *oppressor* or *king* to prevent commoners from criticizing *King James I* himself.

The Underground Resistance

Smuggling the Truth Past the King

King James I escalated the war in **1616** by declaring possession of the *Geneva Bible* a **felony**. He didn't just ban the printing; he criminalized the reader.

However, Christians refused to surrender **the marginal commentary**. The Underground Resistance engaged in forensic smuggling to keep the text alive:

a) **The "1599" Lie:** Printers continued to print *Geneva Bibles* decades after the ban, but they stamped the date *1599* on the title page. The trick made the new Bibles appear to be old, pre-ban copies, allowing the volumes to be sold legally as "antiques."

b) **The Trojan Horse:** Printers produced Bibles with *King James* covers and text but secretly inserted the *Geneva* marginal notes into the columns. Printers took advantage of a simple fact: the *King James* and *Geneva* texts were nearly identical. Since both versions were essentially *Tyndale's* work, the scripture read the same. A customer holding a 'Trojan Horse' Bible—containing *King James* text with *Geneva* notes—could not distinguish the difference. The only battleground was the forbidden commentary.

c) **The Pulpit Resistance:** Even the King's own translators continued to prefer the *Geneva* text, quoting the translation in the KJV preface and preaching from the Geneva text decades later.

The Blueprint of Freedom

The Bible in Rebel Fatigues

The emphasis on individual conscience in the *Geneva Bible* helped shape early American political thought. The Pilgrims on the *Mayflower* (1620) **exclusively used** the *Geneva Bible*, rejecting the KJV as a tool of the very state church that persecuted them.

Covenant Theology vs. Divine Right: The Geneva marginal notes popularized the concept of a "Covenant"—a voluntary compact not just between God and man, but among citizens for civil governance. This specific note inspired the **Mayflower Compact**, shifting power from the Monarch to the People.

The Republican Book: *John Adams*, a Founding Father, famously described the Bible (specifically the Geneva edition familiar to the colonists) as *"the most republican book in the world,"* highlighting its role in shaping the ideals of self-government.

Early settlers used the *Geneva Bible* to extrapolate concepts of **civic morality** and **self-governance**, principles that laid the foundation for the world's first **Constitutional Republic**.

During the American Revolution, patriot sermons frequently drew from the Geneva-inflected Exodus narrative, portraying *King George III* as a modern Pharaoh and the American colonies as the new Israel seeking liberation from bondage.

Historians note the frontispiece of the *Geneva Bible* even inspired *Benjamin Franklin's* design for the first Great Seal of the United States, which depicted Pharaoh drowning in the Red Sea with the motto: *"Rebellion to Tyrants is Obedience to God."*

> **THE PAYWALL BREAKER**
>
> *King Henry VIII's* 1543 Act officially criminalized Bible reading for the working class. *The Geneva Bible* shattered this paywall. By the late 16th century, a New Testament cost less than a week's wages, finally putting the "Source Code" into the hands of the "ploughboy" and breaking the Crown's monopoly.

The modern Study Bible tradition continues through works like **Harold Monser's 1910 Cross-Reference Bible**, which stands as the first Study Bible based on the **1901 Revised Version (RV)**. Like *Geneva*, *Monser's* work was designed for deep study, including over **100,000** cross-references.

> **RECOMMENDED RESOURCE: THE 1599 GENEVA BIBLE (PATRIOT EDITION)**
>
> Predating the King James Version and unsanctioned by any government, the Geneva Bible was the text brought over by the Pilgrims to escape persecution. It was the first mass-produced Study Bible, empowering men like Shakespeare, Bunyan, and Milton to understand the Word on their own.
>
> This new *Paperback* release is identical to the hardback. The Patriot Edition features a timeless painting of *General Washington* praying before battle. This edition includes the *Magna Carta* and the Constitution. Own a piece of American History. *Available on Amazon.*

HISTORICAL SUMMARY

The *King James Bible* is effectively *Tyndale's* text wearing a royal uniform. The *Geneva Bible* is effectively *Tyndale's* text wearing **rebel fatigues**.

The American Founding was not fueled by the King's "Authorized" branding, but by the defiance of settlers who clutched their "Rebel Bible"—*Tyndale's* banned words—and believed that **Yahweh** (God) is the only King and the "ploughboy" has the right to read the Word for himself.

Ultimately, the enduring legacy of the American experiment isn't found in royal sanction, but in the radical, dangerous idea that *every individual holds a king's authority under God*.

The Architects of the Box: How the Canon Was Weaponized

(How Athanasius and Augustine Weaponized the Canon)

I. The Motive: Silencing the Monotheists

By the mid-4th century, the Imperial Church faced a crisis. The original, Biblical Monotheist faith remained the majority in many regions.

To exterminate it, the State-Church **required** more than soldiers—**it demanded** a Closed Library. **Defining** the "Holy" and the "Criminal" **allowed the State to burn** the evidence of the original faith.

II. The Structural Crime: Changing the Logic

The greatest deception **relied not just on** selection, but on **Sequence**. By changing the order, the Architects changed the **logic** of the faith.

- **The Council moved** the "Jewish Foundation" (The Epistle of James) to the basement (the back of the book), silencing the original voice of the Jerusalem Church.
- **The Architects positioned** the "Hellenized Narratives" (The Gospels, starting with Matthew) in the storefront.

By placing the "Legend" (Matthew 1) before the "Reality" (James/Galatians), **the sequence primes the mind**: by the time a reader reaches the original Hebrew roots of the faith, the text has already indoctrinated them with hundreds of pages of Roman-sanctioned dogma.

III. Athanasius of Alexandria: The "Enforcer" (367 AD)

Athanasius **operated as** a political street-fighter who used a private militia to maintain power in Egypt.

- **The 39th Festal Letter:** In 367 AD, Athanasius issued a decree listing the 27 books of the New Testament. He was the first to use the word **"Canonized."**
- **The Tyranny of Exclusion:** His agenda **aimed not to** include books, but to **exclude** others. By declaring his list "The Only Fountain of Salvation," he turned every other Apostolic letter into a "Heresy" punishable by the State.

- **The Book-Burning Squads:** **The decree triggered a purge.** The Great Library of Alexandria and private collections faced destruction. Monks fled to the desert to bury books to save them from Athanasius's investigators.

IV. Augustine of Hippo: The "Organizer" (393–397 AD)

If Athanasius built the walls of the box, Augustine organized the shelves **to lock** the reader inside.

- **The "Augustinian Order":** Augustine insisted on the order we see today: **Matthew, Mark, Luke, and John.**
- **The Psychological Trap:** The sequence forces the reader to encounter the most "Metaphysical" concepts last, creating a "lens" that colors everything they just read.
- **The Suppression of James:** Augustine successfully pushed the **Epistle of James**—the most Monotheistic, Jewish-centric book—deep into the back of the New Testament. The move "buried" the original definition of "Pure Religion" behind hundreds of pages of Hellenistic theology.

V. The Verdict: A Manufactured Sequence

The New Testament you hold today **derives its structure** not from the Apostles, but from **Imperial Bishops** who had a specific agenda:

a) **To promote a "High Christology"** that fit the Roman State religion.

b) **To minimize the "Jewishness"** of Jesus.

c) **To create a "Theological Monopoly"** where the Church, not the text, was the final authority.

Note: For this reason, the *Recommended Chronological Reading Order* (provided in the previous section) remains the only way to break the monopoly and see the evidence clearly.

The Matthew Maneuver: The Engineered Bridge

(Forensic Report: Authorship, Motive, and the Silencing of James)

> **CASE FILE SUMMARY:**
> **Subject:** The Gospel According to Matthew
> **Charge:** Impersonation of an Apostle & Evidence Tampering (Canonical Re-ordering)
> **Objective:** To investigate why a Greek Scribal text bears a Tax Collector's name, and why the Architects strategically placed it as the "First Book" of the New Testament.

I. The Suspect: The "False" Signature

Church tradition **asserts** Matthew Levi, the tax collector (one of the Twelve), **wrote** this book immediately after Jesus left. **But** forensic evidence **proves** otherwise. The author was a highly educated, second-generation Greek-speaking Scribe, not a Galilean tax collector.

A. The Education Mismatch (Handwriting Analysis)

- **The Profile of Matthew Levi:** As a tax collector in Capernaum (Galilee), Levi **spoke** Aramaic and knew "Admin Greek"—enough to fill out a receipt, count currency, or argue a toll. He was a bureaucrat, not a literary scholar.

- **The Profile of the Author:** The Gospel of Matthew contains some of the most polished, sophisticated Greek in the New Testament. **The text employs** complex "fulfillment formulas" (referencing the Greek Septuagint) that require rabbinic-level training.

- **The Verdict:** A tax collector does not suddenly become a master of Greek Rhetoric. The author was a **Jewish Christian Scribe** trained in the synagogue, writing for a wealthy community (likely Antioch), years after the events.

B. The "Eyewitness" Failure (The Plagiarism Evidence)

Here lies the "Smoking Gun" of the investigation. The logic is simple: An Eyewitness (General) never copies the war diary of a Non-Eyewitness (Private). If Matthew were there, he would write what he saw.

- **The Fact (Markan Priority):** **Modern scholarship confirms** **Mark** was written first (c. 65–70 AD).

- **The Stat:** The author of "Matthew" incorporates **90% of Mark's Gospel** into his own book.
- **The Glitch:** **The Scribe copies** Mark's Greek word-for-word, including Mark's errors and rough grammar, then smooths them out.
- **The Verdict:** An Apostle of Jesus would never need to copy the work of Mark (Peter's interpreter). The fact that "Matthew" relies on Mark proves **the author was not an eyewitness**.

II. The Motive: Why "Matthew"?

If the book is anonymous (the text *never* says "I, Matthew, wrote this"), why did the Church Fathers (specifically Papias and Irenaeus) assign it to Matthew?

A. The Papias Confusion (c. 120 AD)

The earliest testimony comes from Papias, a bishop who wrote:

> *"Matthew put together the **oracles** [logia] in the Hebrew language, and each one interpreted them as best he could."* (Eusebius, H.E. 3.39.16)

- **The Discrepancy:** Papias describes a collection of *Sayings* (Logia) written in *Hebrew*.
- **The Reality:** The Gospel we have is a *Narrative* written in *Greek*.
- **The Switch:** **Evidence suggests** the real Matthew wrote a list of Jesus' sayings (possibly the lost "Q" Source). Later, the unknown Scribe took those sayings, combined them with Mark's story, and the church transferred the name "Matthew" to the whole package to give it Apostolic Authority.

III. The Crime Scene: The Canonical Shuffle

Here, the operation moves from "Authorship" to "Psychological Engineering." The placement of the books is not accidental; **the maneuver functions as** a **Strategic Narrative Control**.

A. The "Matthew Bridge" (Why it is First)

If Mark was written first, why is Matthew page 1 of the New Testament?

- **The Objective:** To hook the Jewish reader and legitimize the new faith.

- **The Mechanism:** Matthew is the only Gospel obsessed with "Fulfillment Prophecy." **The narrative opens with** a Genealogy (Abraham → David → Jesus).

- **The Result:** By placing Matthew first, the Architects engineered a seamless transition from Malachi (OT) to Matthew (NT). **The calculated order creates** the illusion that the Church is the perfect, linear continuation of Israel. If Mark (a rough, action-packed story) were first, that theological link would be broken.

B. The "Silencing of James" (The Exile)

Here lies the darker side of the shuffle.

- **The Chronological Reality:** Scholars **identify** the Epistle of James as the **oldest** writing in the NT (c. 45–48 AD). **The letter defines** the original "Jerusalem Theology"—Action, Law-keeping, One God.

- **The Theological Motive:** The "Matthew Maneuver" wasn't just about making the books look tidy; it was about **Theology**.

    – **Matthew** emphasizes Jesus as "God with us" (Emmanuel) and includes the Trinitarian baptismal formula (28:19).

    – **James** emphasizes the strict "One God" (2:19) and defines religion as "Works" (1:27).

- **The Strategy:** By pushing James to the back and putting Matthew at the front, the Architects **silenced the Monotheistic argument**.

- **The Effect:** **The sequence forces the reader to consume** Romans, Corinthians, and Galatians (Paul's high theology of Grace/Faith) *before* you ever hear James' warning that *"Faith without works is dead."* By the time a reader gets to James in the very back of the New Testament, they're already indoctrinated by Paul's theology. James is neutralized.

IV. The Evidence Locker: Verified Academic Proof

Does this constitute heresy? Or historical fact? The following evidence confirms that the "Matthew Maneuver" is the standard consensus of historical scholarship, not a fringe opinion.

Exhibit A: The Synoptic Problem (Markan Priority)

- **The Fact:** The author of Matthew copied Mark.
- **The Proof:** Scholars **term this** the "Synoptic Problem." Academics have mapped it out word-for-word.
- **The Reference: The HarperCollins Study Bible** (Standard Academic Text): *"The view that Mark was the first Gospel written and was used as a source by Matthew and Luke... is the solution accepted by the vast majority of scholars."*

Exhibit B: The Anonymous Text (The Silent Witness)

- **The Fact:** The book never claims to be written by Matthew.
- **The Proof:** Open your Bible to Matthew 9:9 (The calling of Matthew).
- **The Text:** *"And as Jesus passed forth from thence, he saw a man, named Matthew, sitting at the receipt of custom: and he saith unto him, Follow me. And he arose, and followed him."*
- **The Observation:** The author writes in the **Third Person** ("he saw a man"). He does not say "He saw **me**." This distancing technique confirms the author is narrating history, not writing an autobiography.

Exhibit C: The Academic Verdict

- **The Oxford Bible Commentary:** *"The book itself is anonymous... The heading 'According to Matthew' is not original... It is unlikely that an eyewitness would have used Mark as a source."*
- **Raymond Brown (Prominent Catholic Scholar):** *"The canonical Gospel was written in Greek by a Greek-speaker... It is not a translation of a Hebrew work... The unknown author was probably a Jewish Christian scribe."* (Introduction to the New Testament).

FINAL VERDICT:
You do not encounter the memoir of a tax collector when reading Matthew. **You encounter** a carefully crafted, second-generation argument designed to prove that Jesus is the "New Moses." The text is valuable, but the *label* **stands as** a forgery.

Forensic Exhibit: The Broken Seal

(Investigation: The Retroactive Fabrication of Mark 16:9–20)

> **CASE FILE SUMMARY:**
> **Subject:** The Gospel According to Mark (Verses 16:9–20)
> **Charge:** Retroactive Fabrication & Evidence Tampering
> **Objective:** To investigate why the oldest manuscripts end at Verse 8, and why a "Long Ending" was added centuries later to harmonize Mark with Church Doctrine.

I. The Crime Scene: The Sudden Stop

In the oldest and most reliable Greek manuscripts (Codex Sinaiticus and Codex Vaticanus, c. 300–350 AD), the Gospel of Mark ends abruptly at **Verse 16:8**.

> *"And they went out and fled from the tomb, for trembling and astonishment had seized them, and they said nothing to anyone, for they were afraid."* **(The End)**

The Forensic Problem:

- There are no post-resurrection appearances of Jesus.
- There is no "Great Commission."
- There is no "Ascension."
- The story ends in **fear and silence**, not triumph.

II. The Motive: Theological Embarrassment

To the early Church Fathers (who were building a unified Imperial religion), Mark's original ending was a disaster.

- **The Inconsistency:** Matthew and Luke (who copied Mark) had added elaborate endings with Jesus appearing, teaching, and ascending. Mark's "fear and silence" contradicted the growing legend of the Triumphant Church.

- **The Fix:** Scribes in the 2nd or 3rd century composed a "summary" of the other Gospels and attached it to Mark to smooth over the rough edge.

III. The Smoking Gun: The "Vaticanus" Gap

This is one of the most famous pieces of physical evidence in textual criticism.

- In **Codex Vaticanus**, the scribe stops writing at Verse 8.
- However, he leaves a **massive blank column** on the page—the only blank column in the entire New Testament.
- **The Investigator's Conclusion:** The scribe *knew* there was supposed to be more (or that others were adding more), but his master copy didn't have it. He left the space blank, signaling, *"I am aware of the discrepancy."*

IV. The Content Analysis: The "Snake Handling" Error

The added verses (9–20) contain theology and vocabulary that do not match the rest of Mark.

- **Vocabulary Mismatch:** The Greek style changes drastically. It uses words found nowhere else in Mark.
- **Strange Theology:** Verse 18 introduces picking up serpents and drinking deadly poison. This is not found in Matthew, Luke, or John. It is a later superstition that got canonized.
- **The Collage Effect:** The ending reads like a bullet-point summary of Luke and Acts, proving it was written *after* those books were in circulation.

V. The Modern Complicity

Open almost any modern Bible (NIV, ESV, NASB). You will see a bracket or a footnote at Mark 16:9 saying:

> *"Some of the earliest manuscripts do not include 16:9–20."*

The Indictment: The publishers *know* it is not original. They *know* it is a later addition. Yet, they print it as "The Word of God" because removing it would upset the customer. They prioritize **Tradition over Truth**.

> **FINAL VERDICT:**
> Mark 16:9–20 is a forgery. By reading the Gospel without it, you see the original, urgent, and terrified reaction to the Empty Tomb—before the theology was polished by the State.

The Industry of Silence

(Forensic Report: The Economics of Tradition and the Money Changers of Truth)

> **CASE FILE SUMMARY:**
> **Subject:** The Bible Publishing Industry
> **Charge:** Consumer Fraud & Suppression of Academic Evidence
> **Objective:** To investigate why standard Bibles omit the historical consensus regarding authorship, translation errors, and manuscript history.

I. The Publisher's Dilemma: Profit vs. Truth

The average reader assumes that a Bible publisher is a "Ministry" dedicated to spreading the absolute truth. In reality, Bible publishing is a **Billion-Dollar Industry**. Like any business, it is driven by market stability, consumer expectation, and risk aversion.

A. The "Safe Product" Strategy

When a customer buys a box of cereal, they expect the same taste every time. If the taste changes, they stop buying.

- **The Commodity:** The "Traditional Bible" (with Matthew as the author, Moses writing the Pentateuch, and Paul writing Hebrews) is a stable, trusted product.
- **The Risk:** If a publisher prints a Bible that says, *"Introduction to Matthew: Written by an anonymous scribe who copied Mark,"* they damage the product's reputation. The customer feels "defective" goods were sold.
- **The Result:** To protect sales, publishers strip away the complex "Forensic Notes" and replace them with "Devotional Fluff." They sell *Comfort*, not *History*.

B. The "Seminary Firewall"

There is a known "Firewall" in modern Christianity.

- **Side A (The Academy):** In seminary, future pastors are taught the truth: Matthew didn't write Matthew, the Comma Johanneum (1 John 5:7) is a forgery, and Mark 16:9–20 was added later.

- **Side B (The Pew):** When those pastors graduate, they are advised not to "disturb the flock" with these details. They preach the legend because the legend pays the light bill.

- **The Complicity:** Publishers maintain this firewall. They produce "Academic Bibles" for the scholars and "Pew Bibles" for the public, ensuring the two worlds never meet.

II. The Modern Money Changers

In John 2:13–16, Jesus fashioned a whip to drive the money changers out of the Temple. Why was he angry?

- **The Scam:** The money changers refused to accept "common currency" for the temple tax. They forced worshipers to exchange their money for "Temple Shekels"—at a markup. They created a **toll booth between the people and God**.

- **The Modern Parallel:** Today's publishers and denominations act as the new Money Changers.

    - They take the "Common Currency" (Historical Fact, Hebrew meanings, Context).
    - They exchange it for "Temple Currency" (Tradition, Latinized terms like "Trinity" and "Ecclesiastical Offices").
    - **The Markup:** The cost is your agency. You are forced to buy their "Interpretation" to participate in their "Church."

III. The "Faith Crisis" Liability

Publishers argue that they hide the evidence to "protect" the faith of the weak. They claim that revealing the human fingerprints on the Bible (the editing, the scribal additions, the political maneuvering) would cause a "Crisis of Faith."

The Forensic Rebuttal:

- **The Real Danger:** Hiding the evidence creates a fragile faith. When a believer finally discovers the truth (on the internet or in college), their faith shatters because it was built on a curated lie.

- **The Forensic Approach:** Revealing the truth builds **Antifragile Faith**. When you know *exactly* how the text was preserved—messy history and all—you are no longer afraid of the facts. Your faith is rooted in *Reality*, not *Mythology*.

Exhibit A: The Forensic Timeline of Suppression

Investigator's Note: This timeline tracks the "Chain of Custody." It reveals how the motive for suppressing the truth shifted from **Political Control** (Rome) to **Religious Monopoly** (The Church) and finally to **Profit Stability** (Modern Publishers).

PHASE 1: THE HOSTILE TAKEOVER (325–381 AD)

The Motive: Political Stability (One Empire, One Creed).

The Suspects: Emperor Constantine & Emperor Theodosius.

The Empire was fracturing. To save the State, the Emperors needed a unified religion. They could not afford a debate between "One God" believers and "Trinity" believers. They needed a single, enforceable dogma.

- **The Tactic:** The "Edict of Thessalonica" (380 AD). This law literally made it a **State Crime** to be a non-Trinitarian. The State confiscated Monotheist churches, burned their books, and exiled their leaders.

- **The Result:** The "One God" view did not die out naturally in the marketplace of ideas; it was murdered by the sword of the State.

PHASE 2: THE LATIN ENCLOSURE (405–1500 AD)

The Motive: Information Control (The Gatekeeper).

The Suspect: The Roman Catholic Church (Jerome's Vulgate).

Once the theology was fixed by the State, the Church needed to ensure no one could check the math.

- **The Tactic:** The Bible was locked into Latin, a dead language that the common people could not speak or read. The "Priest" became the only authorized filter. Possession of a Bible in English (or any common tongue) was punishable by death (e.g., William Tyndale).

- **The Result:** 1,000 years of "Dark Ages" where tradition cemented itself because the public had no ability to audit the books. The "Trinity" became unquestionable because the text was unreadable.

PHASE 3: THE COMMERCIAL SANITIZATION (1900–Present)

The Motive: Profit & Market Stability.

The Suspects: Modern Bible Publishers.

In the modern era, the sword is gone, replaced by the dollar. The Bible is now the best-selling product in history.

- **The Tactic:** "Consumer Comfort." Publishers realized that Truth is messy, but Tradition sells. If they print a Bible that admits Matthew didn't write Matthew, or that James contradicts Paul, customers get angry and sales drop. So, they strip out the academic "Forensic Notes" and replace them with "Devotional Fluff."

- **The Result:** The Modern Publisher acts as the "Fence," selling the stolen goods that Theodosius seized. They knowingly sell a "sanitized" product to keep the customer happy, prioritizing **Profit over Integrity**.

> **THE VERDICT:**
> We are not dealing with a simple misunderstanding. We are dealing with a 1,600-year operation to curate the text. This Bible breaks the chain. It returns the evidence to you, the jury, so you can see what was hidden in the evidence locker.

Index of Divine Names and Titles

Mapping the original language usage of names to distinguish between titles unique to the Father and those delegated to the Son, reinforcing the distinction between essence (who God is) and function (the role Christ fills).

Table 7: The Lexical Distinction of God's Titles

Title	Original	Meaning/Context	Usage and Significance
Yahweh	H3068 (*YHWH*)	The Covenant Name; "He Causes to Become."	Exclusively the One God, the Father. (RV renders as "Jehovah" in the OT, updated to "Yahweh" here).
Ho Theos	G3588	The Supreme Being; "The God" (with article).	Almost exclusively refers to the Father in the NT (John 17:3; 1 Cor 8:6). Distinguishes Him from others called *theos*.
Elohim	H430	Mighty Ruler, Judge (Plural of Majesty).	Used for God, but also for human judges (Psa 82), and the King (Psa 45:6). It denotes authority, not number.
El Shaddai	H7706	God Almighty / All-Sufficient.	The title used by the Patriarchs (Gen 17:1). Emphasizes God as the source of blessing and power.
Adonai	H136	Sovereign Lord/Master.	Used only for God, the Owner.
Adoni	H113	My Lord/Master.	Used for human masters, priests, or the King. Critical in Psalm 110:1: The LORD said to my Lord (*Adoni*).
Kyrios	G2962	Lord/Master.	Used for the Father and, as a delegated title, for Jesus (Acts 2:36: "God made him Kyrios").

Table 7: The Lexical Distinction of God's Titles

Title	Original	Meaning/Context	Usage and Significance
Pantokrator	G3841	Almighty; All-Sovereign.	Used only for the Father (Rev 1:8, 4:8); Jesus is *never* called the Almighty.
Christos	G5547	Anointed One (Messiah).	A title defining Jesus's appointed human role as King of Israel.
Son of God	G5207	Royal Title (Deut 18:15).	Defines Jesus's relationship to the Father (submission), not his essence (identity).
Logos	G3056	Word/Plan/Wisdom.	God's self-expression, which "became flesh" in Jesus (John 1:1, 14).

Timeline for Matthew

Matthew arranges the story of Jesus thematically to present him as the King of the Jews and the fulfillment of prophecy. He structures the Gospel around five major discourses, paralleling the five books of Moses.

MATTHEW'S NARRATIVE STRUCTURE

SECTION / THEMATIC BLOCK	CHAPTER REFERENCE / NARRATIVE FOCUS
The King's Arrival & Lineage	**Ch 1 – 2:** The Birth and Early Life, establishing Jesus's legal credentials (Son of David) and covenant credentials (Son of Abraham).
Preparation for Public Ministry	**Ch 3 – 4:** John the Baptist, Jesus's Baptism, Temptation, and Call of the first disciples.
The Law of the Kingdom (Discourse 1)	**Ch 5 – 7 (The Sermon on the Mount):** The "New Torah" delivered from the mountain, defining the ethics of the Kingdom.
Demonstrating Authority (Narrative Block)	**Ch 8 – 9:** A rapid sequence of ten miracles demonstrating Jesus's power over sickness, nature, and sin.
Instructions for the Mission (Discourse 2)	**Ch 10:** Directing the twelve disciples on their mission ("The Little Commission"), focusing on persecution and evangelism.
Conflict & Clarification	**Ch 11 – 12:** Rising opposition from Jewish leaders; defining blasphemy; answering John's doubts ("Art thou he?").
Secrets of the Kingdom (Discourse 3)	**Ch 13 (The Parables of the Kingdom):** Seven parables explaining the mysterious, hidden nature of the Kingdom before the End.

MATTHEW'S NARRATIVE STRUCTURE

SECTION / THEMATIC BLOCK	CHAPTER REFERENCE / NARRATIVE FOCUS
Withdrawal and Confession	**Ch 14 – 17:** Ministry outside Galilee; feeding miracles; Peter's Confession; and the Transfiguration (revealing the King's glory).
Life in the Community (Discourse 4)	**Ch 18:** Teaching the disciples about humility, forgiveness, and discipline within the *Ekklesia* (Church).
Road to Jerusalem & Confrontation	**Ch 19 – 22:** Final journey; teachings on wealth and marriage; intense public debates in the Temple.
Judgment and the End Times (Discourse 5)	**Ch 23 – 25 (The Olivet Discourse):** The "Woe" sayings against the Pharisees and prophecies of the Temple's destruction and the Second Coming.
The Passion, Death, and Resurrection	**Ch 26 – 28:** The Last Supper, Trial, Crucifixion, and the **Great Commission**. Jesus commands baptism in the singular "Name" (Authority) of the Father, Son, and Holy Spirit.

Timeline for Mark

Mark presents an urgent, action-oriented narrative of Jesus as the powerful Son of God, emphasizing service and suffering.

MARK'S NARRATIVE STRUCTURE

SECTION / THEMATIC BLOCK	CHAPTER REFERENCE / NARRATIVE FOCUS
Preparation & Early Ministry	**Ch 1:** John the Baptist, Baptism, Temptation, and the call of the first disciples. Immediate emphasis on Jesus's authority over demons.
The Galilean Campaign	**Ch 2 – 4:** Conflicts with religious authorities; calls for repentance; parables used to teach the secrets of the Kingdom (Sower, Mustard Seed).
Power and Opposition	**Ch 5 – 8:26:** Miracles demonstrating divine power (raising the dead, walking on water). *Note:* Jesus frequently commands silence regarding his identity (**The Messianic Secret**) to prevent political misunderstanding.
The Turning Point	**Ch 8:27 – 10:52:** Peter's Confession ("You are the Christ"). Jesus shifts focus to the Cross. **Key Verse (10:45):** "For even the Son of Man came not to be ministered unto, but to minister, and to give his life a ransom for many."
Jerusalem Authority	**Ch 11 – 13:** The Triumphal Entry; Cleansing the Temple; intense conflict with leaders; and the teaching on the End Times (Olivet Discourse).
The Passion and Abrupt Conclusion	**Ch 14 – 16:8:** The Last Supper, Gethsemane, Trials, Crucifixion, and the Resurrection. The narrative ends abruptly at **16:8** with the women fleeing in fear. (*Note: Verses 16:9-20 are absent from the oldest manuscripts and considered a later addition.*)

Timeline for Luke

Luke provides a meticulous historical account, emphasizing Jesus as the Savior of all nations, with special attention to the marginalized, prayer, and the Holy Spirit.

LUKE'S NARRATIVE STRUCTURE

SECTION / THEMATIC BLOCK	CHAPTER REFERENCE / NARRATIVE FOCUS
Prologue & Infancy Narratives	**Ch 1 – 2:** The births of John the Baptist and Jesus; the songs of Mary (Magnificat) and Zechariah (Benedictus); Jesus in the Temple at age twelve.
Preparation for Ministry	**Ch 3 – 4:13:** Ministry of John; the genealogy of Jesus (traced back to **Adam**, not just Abraham, portraying Jesus as the Savior of all humanity); Baptism; Temptation.
Galilean Ministry	**Ch 4:14 – 9:50:** Rejection at Nazareth (Mission Statement of Jubilee); calling of disciples; Sermon on the Plain; miracles demonstrating compassion for outcasts and Gentiles.
The Journey to Jerusalem	**Ch 9:51 – 19:27:** The "Travel Narrative"—a distinct section unique to Luke containing famous parables (Good Samaritan, Prodigal Son) and teachings on the cost of discipleship.
Ministry in Jerusalem	**Ch 19:28 – 21:** The Triumphal Entry; weeping over Jerusalem; cleansing the Temple; warnings about the destruction of the Temple and the End Times.
Passion & Resurrection	**Ch 22 – 24:** The Last Supper; trials before Pilate and Herod; Crucifixion; the Walk to Emmaus (unique to Luke); and the **Ascension** (the hinge connecting this Gospel to Luke's second volume, Acts).

Timeline for John

John presents a theological portrait of Jesus as the eternal Logos and the "I AM," organized around seven miraculous signs and extended discourses.

JOHN'S NARRATIVE STRUCTURE

SECTION / THEMATIC BLOCK	CHAPTER REFERENCE / NARRATIVE FOCUS
The Prologue	**Ch 1:1–18:** The Word (*Logos*) made flesh. John identifies Jesus not as a second God, but as the **Tabernacle** of God ("dwelt among us"), replacing the physical Temple with a human life.
The Book of Signs (Part I)	**Ch 1:19 – 4:** The witness of John the Baptist, the first sign (Water to Wine), the cleansing of the Temple, and encounters with Nicodemus and the Samaritan Woman.
The Book of Signs (Part II)	**Ch 5 – 10:** Increasing controversy; the Predicated "I AM" statements (Bread of Life, Light of the World); healing the lame man and the man born blind.
The Climax of Signs	**Ch 11 – 12:** The raising of Lazarus (the pivotal sign leading to the plot to kill Jesus) and the Triumphal Entry into Jerusalem.
The Book of Glory	**Ch 13 – 17:** The Upper Room, foot washing, the Farewell Discourse (promising the Paraclete/Spirit), and the High Priestly Prayer for unity.
Passion & Resurrection	**Ch 18 – 21:** Arrest, trials (Jesus's Kingdom "not of this world"), Crucifixion, Resurrection appearances, and the Epilogue (restoration of Peter).

BIBLICAL MONOTHEISM:
THE UNIQUENESS OF THE ONE GOD

(Forensic Report: The Hostile Takeover of God's Identity)

> **TACTICAL NOTE FOR THE READER:**
>
> Possessing the truth remains insufficient; the believer must understand the reasons for its targeted destruction. Modern ridicule regarding the Father's solitary status does not stem from scriptural correction.
> Believers face the echoes of Roman Law. To arm yourself with the historical facts necessary to counter these attacks, read the forensic report:
> **THE SWORD OF THEODOSIUS: HOW BIBLICAL MONOTHEISM BECAME A STATE CRIME** (see page 389).

I. The National Charter: Biblical Monotheism

In the history of truth, names matter. This edition raises a specific standard:

Biblical Monotheism.

The Unredacted Tyndale Bible rejects association with modern denominations or the fog of liberal "Unitarian Universalism." Practicing Christians deny modern movements rejecting the divine authority of the Holy Bible's Scripture.

The pivot marks a return to the original **National Charter** of Israel and the Apostolic Church.

- **Biblical: The definition** relies *solely* on the text of Scripture, rejecting the philosophical speculations of later councils.
- **Monotheism: The allegiance** adheres to the strict, numerical singularity of the One God, **YAHWEH** *("the only true God")*.

Biblical Monotheism **stands as** the unyielding belief the Father alone is the Supreme Being. The position operated not as a "theory" to the Apostles; the stance defined their allegiance.

By discarding the baggage of later centuries, you are free to ask the forensic question: *Who did Jesus say God was?*

II. The Law of Agency (Shaliach)

The "God Language" applied to Jesus causes massive confusion. How can Jesus forgive sins or carry the title "God" in certain texts if he is not the Supreme Being?

The answer **resides** in the Hebrew **legal reality** of **Agency** (Hebrew: *Shaliach*).

The Jewish legal maxim declaring, *"The one sent is as the one who sent him,"* remains the standard. An agent acts with the full authority of his Principal while remaining a distinct, subordinate person.

- When Jesus forgives sins, he does so as the **Agent** of the Father.
- When Jesus speaks, he voices the words of the Father.
- To honor the Agent is to honor the Principal, but confusing the Agent with the Principal is a legal error.

Biblical Monotheism recognizes Jesus as the Supreme Agent—the Messiah—without violating the identity of the One God who sent him.

"To confuse the Ambassador with the King does not constitute worship; such confusion constitutes treason."

III. The Pre-Nicaea Standard: Subordinationism

Bureaucrats edited history to portray the Trinity as the original "Orthodox" view. The evidence proves otherwise. For the first three centuries, early Christians affirmed the Father as the sole Source of power, viewing Jesus as His subordinate Agent.

The Witnesses of the Majority Standard:

Before the Roman State enforced uniformity, these prominent theologians held subordinate views:

- **Justin Martyr (c. 100–165 AD):** He identified Jesus as the "first-begotten" of God, like a "second God" or *logos* subordinate to the Father.
- **Origen (c. 185–254 AD): Origen** taught the Son was eternally generated but subordinate to the Father in essence and authority.
- **Tertullian (c. 155–240 AD):** Though he coined the term "Trinity," he described the Son as "second" to the Father, with the Spirit third.

Subordinationism operated not as a fringe heresy; the doctrine represented the dominant leaning of the Eastern church. These writers did not view Jesus through the lens of co-equality, but as the divinely appointed Administrator of the Father's monarchy.

IV. The Nicaea Coup: A Political Takeover

The Council of Nicaea (325 AD) served not as a quest for truth, but as a quest for political stability. Emperor Constantine, a politician rather than a theologian, convened the council to unify a fracturing empire.

The resulting decree of *homoousios* ("same substance") aimed to silence the "numerical singularity" of the biblical text in favor of a bureaucratic patch.

The council refined Christ's divinity not to honor Scripture, but to neutralize the subordinationist majority. After 325 AD, the Roman State began criminalizing the original faith of the Apostles, reclassifying the "Majority Report" as heresy.

V. The Phonetic Smear: Debunking the Identity Theft

A modern forensic investigation must clear the phonetic confusion clouding this debate. Critics often use the term **"Arianism"** to smear monotheists, intentionally or ignorantly confusing the label with **"Aryanism."**

- **Arianism (4th Century):** Derives from Arius of Alexandria. **Arian theology centers on** a debate regarding the Son's subordination to the Father.
- **Aryanism (19th Century):** Derives from "arya" (noble). Arthur de Gobineau hijacked this master-race myth in 1850, and the Nazis later used the term to promote white supremacy.

Biblical Monotheism carries zero etymological or logical connection to racial supremacy. The former concerns the **Authority of God**; the latter concerns the **Hubris of Man. The text explicitly rejects** this racial hijacking and reclaim the biblical terminology.

VI. The Clash of Civilizations: Identity Theft

To understand the Trinity's existence today, **recognize** the Church underwent a **Brain Transplant**. Between the 2nd and 4th centuries, the Hebraic mind of the Apostles was surgically removed and replaced with the Greek mind of the Philosophers.

The transformation constituted not a translation, but an **Identity Theft**. The Greeks took Hebrew terms, filling them with Pagan definitions.

EXHIBIT A: THE STOLEN DICTIONARY

Concept	Hebrew Reality (Bible)	Greek Counterfeit (Philosophy)
ONE	*Echad*: Numeric One (1). A single, indivisible count.	*Hen*: "Unity" or Compound Oneness. A metaphysical union of parts.
SPIRIT	*Ruach*: Wind, Breath, Power. The active presence of God.	*Hypostasis*: A distinct "Person" or Ghost with a separate mind.
WORD	*Dabar*: God's Plan, Wisdom, or Decree. An action God *does*.	*Logos*: A "Second God" or "Demiurge" acting as a buffer.

EXHIBIT B: THE INFILTRATORS (The Trojan Horse)

Who smuggled these Greek ideas into the Bible? The Apostles **did not commit the forgery**. The **"Church Fathers"** who were former Pagan Philosophers smuggled the contraband.

- **Justin Martyr (c. 150 AD):** A Greek philosopher who converted but kept his philosopher's robe. He was the first to argue the "Logos" was a "Second God," admitting this idea came from Plato, not Moses.

- **Origen (c. 200 AD):** An Alexandria intellectual who taught the Bible was an allegory. He injected the concept of "Eternal Generation", turning the Messiah into a metaphysical abstraction.

VII. The Majority Report: The "Euzoius" Fact

The Trinity did not win by vote; the doctrine conquered via the **Sword of Theodosius**, which **surgically erased** the records and exiled the men who held them. Until the Roman State intervened in 380 AD, Biblical Monotheism remained the dominant view of the Eastern Church.

- **The Antioch Evidence:** In 361 AD, the Bishop of Antioch—the city where disciples were first called "Christians" (Acts 11:26)—was **Euzoius**. He was a Biblical Monotheist who rejected the Trinity. The "Headquarters" of the name "Christian" did not believe in a Triune God.

- **The Gothic Nations:** The Goths, who defeated the Roman armies, were converted by the Bishop **Ulfilas** to a non-Trinitarian faith.

VIII. The King's Testimony

The ultimate rebuttal to the Greek Occupation is the testimony of the King himself. If Jesus is the "Word of God," his definition of God is final. To disagree with Jesus is not "theology"; such disagreement is treason.

The Supreme Definition (John 17:3)

In the high court of Scripture, Jesus gives sworn testimony regarding the identity of God. Speaking to the Father, he declares:

> "And this is life eternal, that they might know thee the **only true God**, and Jesus Christ, whom thou hast sent."

The Verdict: Jesus identifies the Father as the "Only" (*monos*) "True" (*alethinos*) God. He excludes himself from that title.

IX. The Athanasian Heist: A Metaphysical Crime Scene

Modern religious media often portrays Athanasius as the lone "Savior of Christianity." **The narrative** ignores the **metaphysical thuggery** required to enforce his Greek riddle upon the Apostolic faith.

Athanasius was not a champion of the Word; he operated as the **criminal architect** of the Hellenistic takeover.

The Pagan Pedigree. Pagan parents raised Athanasius in a polytheistic environment. **The pagan environment explains** the tendency toward the Greek metaphysical riddle of "Multiple Divine Persons." He did not bring Hebrew monotheism to Nicaea; he brought a pagan-influenced view of "Divine Substances" and utilized the Roman State to mandate its acceptance.

The Monastic Thuggery. Athanasius utilized private militias of "enforcer monks" known as the **Parabalani** to intimidate opponents and seize churches by force. **Street-fighting tactics** silenced the subordinationist majority. By the time of his death, Athanasius had reclassified the original faith of the Apostles as a capital crime.

The Latrine Assassination. When Emperor Constantine ordered the restoration of Arius in 336 AD, the monotheist died a horrific, violent death in a public latrine. Athanasius's own *Letter to Serapion* gloats over this "strange death."

Medical forensic experts identify these symptoms—sudden, violent abdominal agony followed by the bursting of bowels—as a hallmark of **acute poisoning**. The Trinitarian establishment chose assassination over the return of Apostolic truth. **The assassination** prevented the Light of Monotheism from reaching the capital just as the tide of the debate was turning.

The Ghost Hands of Erasure. **The theft operated not just** theologically; the crime was physical. In the Basilica of Sant'Apollinare Nuovo in Ravenna, Byzantine censors physically chipped Arian believers out of the mosaics.

They left only the "ghost hands" on the columns—silent witnesses to the **surgical erasure** of the original faith. This physical identity theft aimed to delete the evidence that monotheism was once the majority standard.

The Saint of Terror. The myth of "Saint Nicholas" (Santa Claus) covers the record of a 4th-century miscreant celebrated for the **physical destruction** of temples and religious intimidation. Nicholas led a campaign of **mass extermination** against those who refused the "Substance" riddle. **The rebrand** utilized Norse mythology and the imagery of the god Odin to camouflage a man whose primary contribution to Nicaea was **physical assault** and **religious terrorism**.

The Silent Witness of Newton. Sir Isaac Newton, the greatest intellect in history, spent decades performing a secret forensic audit of this heist. Newton concluded the Trinity was a fraud engineered by a **cabal of 4th-century miscreants** to bypass the Father.

The investigation discovered forgeries—such as the *Johannine Comma*—inserted to provide a foundation the Greek text never contained. Newton suppressed this discovery to **survive an era where dissent remained a capital offense**.

> **FORENSIC ALERT: THE ANTIOCH EVIDENCE**
>
> Euzoius of Antioch, holding the see where the name "Christian" was born, remained a strict monotheist. The "Headquarters" of the faith was never Trinitarian; the Roman State forced the city into that mold through exile and the burning of records.

X. Conclusion: Your Emancipation Proclamation

Biblical Monotheism is not a restriction; the truth serves as an emancipation. **The paradigm** frees the believer from the burden of loving a "math problem."

When you strip away the foreign laws of the Greek councils and return to the Constitution of the Apostles, the fog lifts.

- **God** becomes a Father you can understand.

- **Jesus** becomes a Messiah who truly fought and won battles as a man, rather than a divine actor.
- **You** become free to worship in "spirit and in truth," without the fear of state-mandated confusion.

Jerusalem, Not Athens: Reading the Bible with Hebrew Eyes

> **FORENSIC ALERT: THE BRAIN TRANSPLANT**
> Before you can understand the *Who* of God (Monotheism), you must understand the *How* of Biblical thought.
> **The following report details** the "Identity Theft" occurring when the Church traded the concrete reality of Hebrew Prophets for the abstract philosophy of the Greek Academy.

I. The Forensic Breach: Athens vs. Jerusalem

Tertullian famously asked, *"What has Athens to do with Jerusalem?"* He highlighted the cultural chasm between the world of Greek philosophy (Athens) and the world of Biblical revelation (Jerusalem).

The historical verdict is tragic: **Athens occupied Jerusalem.**

Recognize the New Testament as a thoroughly Jewish document. Jews wrote it. It concerns a Jewish Messiah. It records a movement beginning in Judea. The text breathes the air of the synagogue, the temple, and the Torah.

God did not deliver His Word in the high-minded "Attic Greek" of Plato's Academy. He delivered it in the grimy **"Koine Greek"** of the marketplace. He used the language of fishermen to shame the language of philosophers.

However, within a century of the Apostles' death, the center of Christianity shifted to the Greco-Roman world. Leaders shifted from rabbis to philosophers. As a result, scholars read the Bible through the lens of Plato and Aristotle rather than Moses and Isaiah.

The Hostile Displacement

The shift constituted not a drift, but a **displacement**. The jagged peaks of Hebrew Revelation were smoothed down to fit the flat plains of Greek Philosophy. The Church traded the Prophets for the Professors.

- **The Hebrew Mind** is concrete, dynamic, and action-oriented. It asks, "What must I *do*?"
- **The Greek Mind** is abstract, static, and definition-oriented. It asks, "What is it *made of*?"

II. The Ontology Trap: Essence vs. Function

The fundamental difference centers on the distinction between **Function** and **Essence**.

The Greek Obsession: "What is it?"

Greek philosophy was obsessed with *ontology* (the study of being). If you asked a Greek philosopher to define a "chair," he would describe its "chair-ness"—its essential nature, its substance, the abstract ideal.

The mindset trapped the church, leading to a 300-year debate about God's **"chemical composition."** Is Jesus of the *same* substance (homoousios) or *similar* substance (homoiousios)? These are Greek questions about "stuff."

The Hebrew Obsession: "What does it do?"

The Hebrew mind had little interest in abstract essence. *Ask a Hebrew* to define a "chair" and *he answers*, "It is something you sit on." He defines it by *purpose*.

The Creation account of Genesis 1 illustrates this. When God creates the sun and moon, the text ignores their chemical composition. It describes their *function*:

> "...to divide the day from the night... for signs, and for seasons, and for days, and years." (Genesis 1:14)

To the Hebrew mind, something "exists" when it has a name and a function within an ordered system. Existence is purpose.

Applying the Standard to God

The distinction drives the debate when talking about God.

- **Greek Theology** asks: "What are God's attributes? Is He omnipresent? Is He composed of parts?" It tries to define God's *nature*.
- **Hebrew Theology** asks: "What has God *done*? Has He delivered us? Has He spoken? Is He faithful?" It defines God by His *history* with His people.

III. The Crime Scene: Alexandria, Egypt

How did the "Brain Transplant" occur? Pinpoint the infection at a specific city: **Alexandria, Egypt**. This city served as the intellectual capital of the world, home to the Great Library, and the mixing pot of Jewish Religion and Greek Philosophy.

Suspect #1: Philo Judaeus (20 BC – 50 AD)

Philo was a brilliant Jew who loved Plato. He tried to make the Bible "respectable" to the Greeks. *Philo first proposed* the "Word" (Logos) as a separate intermediary being, bridging the gap between "pure" God and "dirty" matter.

Suspect #2: Origen (185 – 254 AD)

Origen, an Alexandrian church father, took Philo's method and ran with it. He popularized the **Allegorical Method**. He taught the literal history of the Bible was for "simpletons," while the "enlightened" saw hidden philosophical meanings. * **The Result:** The narrative lost its literal power. It became a codebook for Neoplatonic philosophy.

IV. The Concrete Reality: Escaping Abstraction

Greek philosophy loves abstractions—concepts existing only in the mind (Truth, Justice, Goodness). Hebrew thought is rooted in the physical world. It uses **concrete** terms (things you can touch, see, smell) to describe abstract ideas.

Thinking in Pictures

The Hebrew language has few abstract words. It uses physical imagery instead.

- **Anger:** The Hebrew word is *aph*, literally "nose" or "nostril." To be angry is to have "hot nostrils" (flaring with breath).

- **Patience:** The Hebrew phrase is *erek aph*, literally "long of nose." It takes a long time for your nostrils to get hot!

- **Glory:** The Hebrew word is *kabod*, literally "heavy" or "weighty." A glorious person is someone with "weight" in the community.

The "Hand" of God

For this reason, the Bible speaks of God having a "hand," an "arm," a "face," or "feet." The Greeks **sanitized** the text.

They were offended by a God *Yahweh* (God) getting His hands dirty. They stripped away the warrior gear and replaced it with sterile robes. They called it *anthropomorphism* and tried to allegorize it away.

V. The Sensory Divide: Hearing vs. Seeing

The primary overlooked difference involves the primary sense perceiving truth.

The Greek Mind: The Eye

The Greek world was overwhelmingly **visual**. Their gods were statues; their culture was theater; their geometry was shapes. To a Greek, to "know" meant to "see." (The word *idea* comes from a Greek root meaning "to look at").

The obsession drove the Church to fill cathedrals with icons, statues, and paintings. They turned God into an object for viewing and analysis.

The Hebrew Mind: The Ear

The Hebrew world was **auditory**. God was never seen; He was heard. The central command of the Bible is not "Look," but **"Shema!"** ("Hear!").

> "And the LORD spake unto you out of the midst of the fire: ye **heard the voice** of the words, but saw no similitude; only ye heard a voice." (Deuteronomy 4:12)

Biblical faith comes by *hearing*, not seeing. When the Church switched from the Ear to the Eye, it traded obedience for speculation.

VI. The Hebrew Shield: Block Logic vs. Linear Logic

Western thought, influenced by Aristotle, relies on "Step Logic" (Linear Logic). We view truth as non-contradictory. The Hebrew mind operates on **"Block Logic."** Hebrew writers accepted "blocks" of thought seemingly contradictory but both true.

The Pharaoh Paradox

- **Block A:** *"Pharaoh hardened his heart"* (Human Responsibility).
- **Block B:** *"The LORD hardened Pharaoh's heart"* (Divine Sovereignty).

A Greek thinker screams: "Contradiction!" The Hebrew thinker accepts both. God is sovereign. Man is responsible. The tension remains because God is greater than logic.

Jesus: The Divine and the Human

- **Block A:** Jesus sleeps, eats, weeps, and prays to his God. (He is Man).
- **Block B:** Jesus forgives sins, commands the storm, and acts as God. (He is Agent).

The Greek mind tries to fuse these into a metaphysical "Hypostatic Union." The Hebrew mind sees **Agency**. In humanity's block, he is our brother. In authority's block, he is God's representative.

VII. The Kinetic Word: Dabar vs. Logos

The cultural divide alters how we read John 1:1: *"In the beginning was the Word..."*

Greek Logos: Reason

To a Greek Stoic philosopher, the *Logos* was impersonal "Reason." It was static and intellectual. Read John 1:1 with Greek eyes and you see Jesus as a pre-existent divine "Mind."

Hebrew Dabar: Driving Force

To a Hebrew, *Dabar* was **ballistic**. *The concept represents not just sound, but impact.*

> "So shall my word be that goeth forth... it shall not return unto me void." (Isaiah 55:11)

God's Word is God in action. When John says the Word became flesh, he is saying God's active command took human form.

VIII. The Law of Agency: Corporate Solidarity

The West is paralyzed by the **Myth of the Atomized Individual**. The Hebrew mind viewed humanity through **Corporate Solidarity**. The "One" can represent the "Many."

The Law of Shaliach

The legal maxim states: *"The sent one is as the sender."* When Jesus speaks as God, he is not claiming to *be* God; he exercises the Power of Attorney granted to the Shaliach.

The Two Adams

The principle explains Romans 5.

- **In Adam:** We are born into the bankrupt corporation of "Adam, Inc."
- **In Christ:** Jesus is the "Last Adam." He acts as the new Federal Head.

Because of Corporate Solidarity, Jesus does not die millions of times. He dies once as the Head.

IX. The Breath of God: Ruach vs. The Ghost

English uses three separate words: *Wind*, *Breath*, and *Spirit*. Hebrew has only one: **Ruach**.

The distinction creates a massive translation challenge.

- When the trees are blowing, it is *Ruach*.
- When you inhale and exhale, it is *Ruach*.
- When God acts invisibly in the world, it is *Ruach*.

Not a "Ghost"

To the Greek mind, "spirit" (*pneuma*) was often seen as a ghostly, immaterial substance. We turned the blast of God's nostrils into a polite phantom.

We created a **"Ghost in the Machine"**—a separate person—instead of trembling before the projected power of the Almighty Father.

The Smoking Gun: The Prayer Vacuum

Consider the forensic evidence: In the entire Bible, containing thousands of prayers, **not a single instance of anyone praying to the Holy Spirit exists.** If the Spirit were a separate Person, this total silence would be inexplicable. You do not ignore a person; you ignore a power.

X. The Authority of the Name

In the Hebraic world, a name (*shem*) is synonymous with **authority** and **reputation**.

- To pray "in Jesus' name" is not a magic formula.
- It means acting by his **legal authority**, just as a policeman acts "in the name of the Law."

The Third Commandment is not about profanity; it is about Identity Theft—claiming to represent God while acting in a way shaming Him.

XI. The Great Substitution: Kurios vs. Yahweh

The most devastating "Identity Theft" was technical: The replacement of God's personal name with a generic title.

In original Hebrew, God has a personal name: **Yahweh**. It appears nearly 7,000 times. However, when the Greeks translated the Septuagint, they removed the name *Yahweh* and replaced it with the generic Greek title **Kurios** ("Lord").

The Blur

The swap triggered a theological disaster (Masking of the Name). * The Father is called *Kurios*. * Jesus is called *Kurios*. * In the Greek text, they look identical.

When the New Testament quotes the Old Testament saying, *"The LORD said to my Lord"* (Psalm 110:1), the Greek reads *"Kurios said to Kurios."* The distinction between the Supreme God and His Messiah was erased. This "masking" paved the way for the Trinity; it made the two appear interchangeable.

XII. The Singular Loyalty: The Truth About "Echad"

Finally, examine the Hebrew definition of "One." The Jewish creed is the Shema: *"Hear, O Israel: The LORD our God is one LORD"* (Deuteronomy 6:4). The Hebrew word for "one" is **echad**.

Compound Unity vs. Absolute Singularity?

Christian apologists often argue *echad* implies a "compound unity" to allow for the Trinity. But look at the forensic evidence: Ezekiel 33:24 states, *"Abraham was one [echad]."* Abraham was no Trinity. He was a singular individual. The word counts the number one.

The Shema is not a mathematical analysis of God's internal composition. It is a polemic against polytheism.

- The nations have many gods; Israel has **One**.
- The nations have divided loyalties; Israel has **One** loyalty.

When Zechariah 14:9 says, *"In that day shall there be one LORD, and his name one,"* it is claiming universal sovereignty.

XIII. The Loyalty Test: Faith vs. Mental Assent

Two of the most common words in the New Testament—"Faith" and "Knowledge"—mean something radically different to a Hebrew than they do to a Greek.

Faith (Emunah) vs. Belief

In the West, "faith" usually means mental agreement. "I have faith George Washington was the first President." I believe the fact is true. The Hebrew word is **Emunah**. It means you are **faithful**, loyal, and steadfast.

Knowledge (Yada) vs. Information

The Greek view of knowledge is data accumulation. The Hebrew word is **Yada**. It implies experience, relationship, and intimacy.

> "And Adam **knew** Eve his wife..." (Genesis 4:1)

The distinction illuminates Jesus' warning in Matthew 7:23: "I never **knew** you." He had their names, but he had no *Yada*.

XIV. The Time Heist: Chronos vs. Moed

The Greeks viewed time as a straight line (*Chronos*). The Hebrews viewed time as a series of divine appointments (*Moed*).

God did not give Israel a calendar to count days; He gave them a calendar to rehearse history.

- **The Feasts** are not rituals; they are **dress rehearsals** for the Messiah's work.
- When the Church adopted the Greek mind, it abandoned the Feasts for pagan holidays, effectively losing the "watch" God gave us to tell the time of His coming.

XV. The Father's Instruction: Torah vs. Law

The word "Law" represents the greatest tragedy of translation. We turned the loving instruction of a Father into the penal code of a **State Trooper**. The Hebrew word is **Torah**. It is not a burden to crush us; it is a map to guide us.

XVI. The Architecture of Peace: Shalom

Westerners define peace as a negative—the mere absence of war. Hebrew **Shalom** is wholeness and completeness. When Jesus gives "Peace," he is not giving a quiet feeling; he is repairing the broken structure of the world.

XVII. The Verdict: Returning to the Source

The evidence is in. The file is closed. *Rewriting the Bible is unnecessary. Reading it in the native tongue remains the only requirement*—the language of the Hebrew heart.

EXHIBIT A: THE STOLEN DICTIONARY

Concept	Hebrew Reality (Bible)	Greek Counterfeit (Philosophy)
ONE	*Echad*: Numeric One (1). A single, indivisible count.	*Hen*: "Unity" or Compound Oneness. A metaphysical union of parts.
SPIRIT	*Ruach*: Wind, Breath, Power. The active presence of God.	*Hypostasis*: A distinct "Person" or Ghost with a separate mind.
WORD	*Dabar*: God's Plan, Wisdom, or Decree. An action God *does*.	*Logos*: A "Second God" or "Demiurge" that acts as a buffer between God and man.

EXHIBIT C: THE FORENSIC GLOSSARY

Concept	Greek Mind (Athens)	Hebrew Mind (Jerusalem)
God	A static Essence/Substance.	A dynamic Father who Acts.
Perception	*Eidos*: Sight / Visual.	*Shema*: Hearing / Voice.
Identity	*Kurios*: Generic Title.	*Yahweh*: Personal Name.
Faith	Mental Assent (Opinion).	*Emunah*: Loyalty/Allegiance.
Time	*Chronos*: A straight line.	*Moed*: A divine appointment.
Word	*Logos*: Abstract Reason.	*Dabar*: Action/Command.

Strip away the Greek overlays and the fog lifts. The "contradictions" of the Trinity fade, replaced by the beautiful simplicity of the One God and His Messiah.

The Divine Agent: How God Rules Through Man

FORENSIC ADVISORY: THE HEBREW LEGAL LENS

To the Reader: The investigation relies on a foundational concept of Hebrew Law largely lost to the Western mind: **The Law of Agency** (*Shaliach*).

The Cultural Conflict:

- **The Greek View (Western):** Defines Godhood by *Essence* (What is he made of?).
- **The Hebrew View (Biblical):** Defines Godhood by *Authority* (Who sent him?).

Advisory: Approach the New Testament looking for "Metaphysical Substance" and you will inevitably misinterpret the evidence. Ancient writers were not philosophers; they were subjects of a Kingdom. They did not view Jesus through the lens of *Biology* (is he God?), but through the lens of *Delegation* (does he speak for God?).

The Objective: The dossier seeks not to diminish the glory of the Son. **The text reclaims** his true legal status as the **Supreme Agent of the Father**—a position of absolute authority requiring no philosophical contradictions.

I. The Trinitarian Riddle: Why the 'God-Man' Paradox Fails the Logic Test

For centuries, believers have found themselves **wrestling with** a forensic riddle. The New Testament presents Jesus of Nazareth in terms undeniably human, yet it ascribes to him powers and titles undeniably divine. *The fracture constitutes* a forensic dilemma buried under centuries of state-mandated tradition.

Humanity's evidence stands as overwhelming and consistent: this man is born of a woman, grows in wisdom, hungers, thirsts, sleeps, and dies. He prays to God, obeys God, and explicitly calls the Father *"my God"* (John 20:17).

In any legal or diplomatic context, these are the definitive forensic fingerprints of a subordinate creature, not a Supreme Creator. If the Subject says "I have a God," the Law cannot conclude he **is** that God.

Yet, this same man walks on water, stills the storm, forgives sins, and claims the role of the Judge of the entire world. He says, **"I and the Father are one"** (John 10:30) and **"He that hath seen me hath seen the Father"** (John 14:9). These data sets clash, creating a theological crisis. Later religious bureaucrats tried to solve the problem through philosophical force.

The Trinitarian Solution: A Greek Patch

To patch this breach, later theologians—saturated in Greek philosophy—invented the Trinity. Theologians reached for a pagan fix, positing God is three "persons" sharing one "essence," and Jesus is the "God-Man" (fully God and fully man simultaneously).

The Trinity doctrine operates as a bureaucratic patch on a theological problem. The doctrine requires the believer to accept logical contradictions: God died, but God cannot die; God was tempted, but God cannot be tempted; God knows all things, but the Son did not know the hour of his return. *Acceptance requires* the believer to suspend logic and accept a flat-out contradiction as a "holy mystery."

The Hebrew Solution: Authority over Essence

The problem lies in the lens. *The modern church navigates* the Kingdom of God using a map of the Parthenon. *Tradition trains readers to view* God through a Greek calculator.

The original writers were not Greek philosophers concerned with *ontological essence* (what a being is made of). They were Hebrews concerned with *legal authority* and *function* (who authorized the being). They had a category for Jesus almost entirely lost to the Western mind. **The role occupies** a specific legal category: the **Divine Agent**.

II. The Law of Agency (Shaliach)

Understanding Jesus requires understanding the legal world producing him. Ancient Near Eastern society, and specifically Jewish law, operated on a principle known as *Agency*. The Hebrew word for an agent is **Shaliach** (literally, "one who is sent").

"A man's agent is as himself." — Mishnah Berakhot 5:5

The Jewish Mishnah (Berakhot 5:5) preserves this role with a legal maxim unlocking the entire New Testament: ***"A man's agent is as himself."***

The closest modern equivalent represents the **Power of Attorney**. If you grant someone Power of Attorney, that person can sign legal documents in your name. If they sell your house, the law views it as if *you* sold your house. Their signature is your signature. Their decision is your decision. The buyer cannot claim the owner's absence makes the sale void. The owner *was* there, legally speaking, through his agent.

However, a critical distinction destroys the Trinitarian paradox:

- Legally, the Agent **is** the Sender.
- Physically, the Agent **is not** the Sender.

Agency *operated as* binding law. An agent represents the sender in legal transactions, not in physical biology. An agent can sign a treaty for the King, but he cannot eat, sleep, or die for the King. *The maxim explains* why Jesus sleeps in the boat (Humanity) while stilling the storm (Agency). Agency covers authority, not anatomy.

The Ambassador Analogy

Consider the role of an ambassador. When the U.S. Ambassador to the United Nations casts a vote, he speaks with the full weight of the American government. When he says, "The United States votes No," he is not expressing his personal opinion. He voices the President's will.

If another diplomat strikes the Ambassador, it is an act of war against the United States. Why? Because in his official capacity, the Ambassador *is* the nation. To strike the Agent is to strike the Sender.

However, *turning this functional unity* into a physical mystery *yields* nonsense. *Consistency demands arguing* the Ambassador and the President are "two persons in one substance." The early church councils made this exact mistake. They took the **functional** unity of Jesus and the Father ("I do always those things that please him") and turned it into an **ontological** unity ("We are of the same substance").

The New Testament Term: Apostle

Agency is not merely a Jewish background fact; the role is explicit New Testament doctrine. The Greek equivalent of *Shaliach* is **Apostolos** (Apostle). Hebrews 3:1 urges us to "consider the **Apostle** and High Priest of our confession, Christ Jesus." The biblical writers viewed Jesus as the ultimate Apostle—the Sent One—bearing the full legal authority of the Father.

The Jewish Legal Precedent

Agency *functioned not* as a metaphor; Agency was binding law. The Talmud is filled with examples proving oneness of action did not imply "oneness" of being:

- **Betrothal:** If a man sent an agent to betroth a wife, the moment the agent gave the ring to the woman, she was legally married to the sender, not the agent. The agent's hand was legally the husband's hand.

- **Divorce:** If a husband sent an agent to deliver a bill of divorce, the marriage dissolved the moment the agent handed over the paper. The husband's presence was not required; his authority was sufficient.

- **Property:** If an agent purchased a field, the deed belonged immediately to the sender.

In every case, the law viewed the agent's action as the sender's action. The sender did not need to be physically present. He was present *through his agent. The legal principle explains* why Jesus could say, "He that believeth on me, believeth not on me, but on him that sent me" (John 12:44). To accept the Agent is to accept the Sender. To reject the Agent is to reject the Sender. The two are legally inseparable, yet personally distinct.

III. The Joseph Protocol: The Perfect Biblical Model of Delegated Rule

Genesis 41 contains the definitive illustration of this relationship. The text provides a legal template—a "Protocol"—for how God rules the universe. Pharaoh (the Source of Power) elevates Joseph (the Agent) to rule over Egypt.

> "Thou shalt be over my house, and according unto thy word shall all my people be ruled: **only in the throne will I be greater than thou.**" (Genesis 41:40)

Analyze the mechanics of the transfer. Pharaoh gives Joseph his signet ring. When Joseph rides in the chariot, the people bow to him as they would to Pharaoh. They cry "Bow the knee!" (Gen 41:43). To the man on the street, Joseph *is* Pharaoh. He wields the full power of the state. He controls the grain, the laws, and the lives of the people.

But to Pharaoh, Joseph is a subject. *No confusion exists* in the throne room. Pharaoh remains the ultimate Source; Joseph is the ultimate Administrator. **Closely observe** the *Joseph Protocol*.

a) The Agent has total authority over the subjects.

b) The Agent remains totally subordinate to the Source.

The narrative destroys the co-equality myth. Jesus has been given "all authority in heaven and earth" (Matthew 28:18), just as Joseph was given all authority in Egypt. But "he who put all things under him is excepted" (1 Corinthians 15:27). The Source never loses His supremacy. The Son is the Vice-Regent, not the High King. He is the Joseph to God's Pharaoh.

IV. The Forensic Evidence: Why Moses and the Judges were Legally Called 'God'

If the theory holds, the Old Testament **should reflect** this standard. And indeed, the Hebrew Bible is full of figures called "God" (*Elohim*) or "Lord" (*Yahweh*) precisely as God's agents.

These precedents constitute the evidence most modern readers miss. Tradition trains readers to think "God" is exclusively a proper name for the Creator. But in Hebrew, *elohim* is a title of authority and power. It can be applied to the Creator, but it is also applied to His agents.

Case Study 1: Moses as God

The first and most striking example is Moses. In Exodus 7:1, *Yahweh* (God) gives Moses his commission to stand before Pharaoh. Notice the specific language the Creator uses:

> "See, I have made thee **a god** [Elohim] to Pharaoh: and Aaron thy brother shall be thy prophet." (Exodus 7:1)

The Hebrew text says literally: *"I have made thee **Elohim** to Pharaoh."* The text does not say Moses is *like* God. It says Moses *is* God to Pharaoh. *The designation applies* because Moses is the Agent. When Moses speaks to Pharaoh, it is as if God Himself is speaking. To disobey Moses is to disobey *Yahweh*.

The dynamic recurs in Exodus 4:16, where God describes the relationship between Moses and Aaron:

> "And he [Aaron] shall be to thee instead of a mouth, and thou shalt be to him **instead of God**."

The text displays the hierarchy of agency perfectly:

- **God (*Yahweh*)** is the Source.
- **Moses** is the Agent of *Yahweh* (functioning as God to Aaron).
- **Aaron** is the Agent of Moses (functioning as Prophet to the people).

Was Moses the Creator of the universe? No. Was he worshipped? No. But functionally, within his mission, he carried the title and authority of *Elohim*. If Moses, a sinful man, could be called "God" because he carried the Law, how much more fitting is it for the Messiah, who carries the Gospel, to be called "God" in a representative sense?

Case Study 2: The Judges of Israel

The terminology extends beyond Moses to the judges and rulers of Israel. In the Torah, when a legal matter was brought before the judges, the text says it was brought before "God."

> "Then his master shall bring him unto the **judges** [Hebrew: **ha-elohim**]..." (Exodus 21:6)

KJV translators, recognizing these were human judges, translated *elohim* as "judges." But the word is literally "gods." *The title applies because* when a judge sat on the bench, he was exercising the prerogative of God: the right to condemn or acquit. He was acting *in persona dei* (in the person of God).

The concept provides the background for Psalm 82:6, where God addresses the corrupt judges of Israel:

> "I have said, **Ye are gods**; and all of you are children of the most High."

God is not saying these men are divine beings. He is reminding them they hold a divine office. They are "gods" by agency, but because they have judged unjustly, they will "die like men" (v. 7).

V. The Smoking Gun: The Mysterious Figure Bearing the Name

The ultimate example of agency in the Old Testament is the mysterious *Angel of the LORD* (Hebrew: *Malakh YHWH*). The word *malakh* simply means "messenger." The Angel acts as God's Chief Agent. When he appears, he speaks in the first person as *Yahweh*, and yet he is sent by *Yahweh*.

The Burning Bush (Exodus 3) The text *explicitly states* "the **angel of the LORD** appeared unto him in a flame of fire" (Exodus 3:2). But when this Angel speaks from the bush, he says:

> "I am the God of thy father, the God of Abraham, the God of Isaac, and the God of Jacob." (Exodus 3:6)

How can an angel claim to be God?

- **Trinitarian View:** This was the pre-incarnate Jesus (God the Son).
- **Agency View:** This was God's messenger speaking **verbatim** the words of the Sender.

Stephen's words in Acts 7 prove the Agency view is correct. Recounting this event, he says:

> "And when forty years were expired, there appeared to him in the wilderness of mount Sina **an angel of the Lord** in a flame of fire in a bush... saying, I am the God of thy fathers..." (Acts 7:30-32)

Stephen affirms an *angel spoke* the words. But because the angel was the Agent, he spoke with the "I" of God. The messenger does not say, "God says..." The messenger says, "I am God..." because he is reading the King's decree.

The Name is in Him *Exodus 23* reveals *the secret* to this Angel's authority, where God warns Israel to obey him:

> "Behold, I send an Angel before thee... Beware of him, and obey his voice, provoke him not; for he will not pardon your transgressions: **for my name is in him**."

"My name is in him." This concept defines Divine Agency. The Angel bears the Name (the authority, the reputation, the legal standing) of *Yahweh*. He is not *Yahweh* himself, but he carries the Name of the Father. *Jesus claims exactly* this status: *"I am come in my Father's name"* (John 5:43).

VI. Jesus: The Prophet Like Moses

Now, view Jesus through Jewish eyes. Jesus did not appear in a vacuum. He appeared as the fulfillment of a specific prophecy Moses gave in Deuteronomy 18.

The Deuteronomy Prophecy

Moses told Israel God would send a successor—a definitive agent speaking for *Yahweh* just as Moses had.

> "I will raise them up a Prophet from among their brethren, **like unto thee**, and will **put my words in his mouth**; and he shall speak unto them all that I shall command him." (Deuteronomy 18:18)

Notice the characteristics of this coming Agent:

a) **"From among their brethren"**: He will be a human being, an Israelite, not a foreign spirit or an alien god.

b) **"Like unto thee"**: He will function like Moses—as a mediator between God and the people.

c) **"I will put my words in his mouth"**: He is a recipient of revelation, not the source of it.

Jesus Claims the Role

In the Gospel of John, Jesus proves he is this specific Prophet. He constantly emphasizes his words are not his own.

> "For I have not spoken of myself; but the Father which sent me, he gave me a commandment, what I should say, and what I should speak... **Whatsoever I speak therefore, even as the Father said unto me, so I speak.**" (John 12:49-50)

If Jesus were God the Son, the Second Person of the Trinity, why would he need to be *told* what to say? Does God need to give commandments to God? But if Jesus is the Divine Agent—the Prophet like Moses—this language makes perfect sense. He is faithful to the "Power of Attorney." He does not deviate one syllable from the script the King gave him.

Peter's Confirmation

The early church understood this perfectly. In his second sermon, Peter explicitly identifies Jesus as this Prophet.

> *"For Moses truly said unto the fathers, A prophet shall the Lord your God raise up unto you of your brethren, like unto me; him shall ye hear in all things whatsoever he shall say unto you."* (Acts 3:22)

Peter does not call Jesus "God the Son." He calls him the Prophet raised up by God. This was the apostolic Christology: Jesus is the supreme human agent, empowered by God to speak with absolute authority.

VII. The Unity of the Agent

With Agency's legal framework established, we now return to the verse most often cited as proof of the Trinity: **"I and the Father are one."** (John 10:30). Does this mean they are one substance (homoousios)? Or does it mean they are one in purpose (functional unity)?

The Context: Security, Not Ontology

Do not rip verse 30 out of its paragraph. Jesus is talking about the safety of his sheep.

a) **Jesus' Power:** "Neither shall any man pluck them out of *my* hand." (v. 28)

b) **The Father's Power:** "No man is able to pluck them out of *my Father's* hand." (v. 29)

c) **The Conclusion:** "I and the Father are one." (v. 30)

They are "one" in the **task** of protecting the flock. The Agent's hand is functionally the Owner's hand. If you try to steal from the Shepherd, you are stealing from God. The unity is functional, not metaphysical.

Jesus' Legal Defense (Psalm 82)

The Jewish leaders misunderstood him. They picked up stones, accusing him of blasphemy: "because that thou, being a man, makest thyself God" (v. 33). **The Imperial councils codified the absurdity.** Notice Jesus' defense. If he were truly God, this would be the moment to say, "Yes, I am God, the Second Person of the Trinity."

Instead, he appeals to the Law of Agency we just examined:

> *"Is it not written in your law, I said,* **Ye are gods?** *If he called them gods, unto whom the word of God came... Say ye of him, whom the Father hath sanctified, and sent into the world, Thou blasphemest; because I said, I am the Son of God?"* (John 10:34-36)

Jesus delivers a legal masterstroke:

a) God called the unjust judges of Israel "gods" (Psalm 82) because they were His agents.

b) I (Jesus) am the *sanctified* and *sent* Agent (the ultimate Shaliach).

c) If mere human judges could be called "gods" without blasphemy, how can you accuse me of blasphemy for claiming the lesser title "Son of God"?

Jesus argues from the lesser to the greater. He is not claiming to be *Yahweh*; he is claiming to be the *Agent of Yahweh*, a role carrying divine authority but distinct from Deity itself.

The Prayer for Unity (John 17)

Jesus' prayer provides the final refutation of the Trinitarian interpretation. He defines exactly what kind of "oneness" he shares with the Father:

> "That they all may be one; **as thou, Father, art in me, and I in thee**, that they also may be one in us... that they may be one, **even as we are one**." (John 17:21-22)

Jesus prays the disciples will have the *same* unity he has with the Father.

- If the unity between Father and Son is a "mystical union of substance" (Trinity), then Jesus is praying for Peter, James, and John to become part of the Godhead!

- But if the unity is one of **purpose and love** (Agency), then the prayer makes perfect sense: he wants the disciples to be as united in mission as he is with God.

VIII. Identity Theft or Royal Honor?

Another common objection involves the worship of Jesus. Trinitarians argue, "Jesus accepted worship; only God can be worshipped; therefore, Jesus is God." *The argument collapses under* a misunderstanding of the Greek word *proskuneo*.

Defining Proskuneo

The word translated as "worship" in the New Testament is *proskuneo*. It literally means to "bow down" or "prostrate oneself." In the ancient world, you bowed down to anyone of higher rank: a king, a governor, a master, or a prophet.

Was this act always "religious worship" reserved for God alone? Absolutely not.

- **The Servant and the King:** In Jesus' own parable, a servant falls down and *worships* (*proskuneo*) his master, begging for patience (Matthew 18:26). Is the servant committing idolatry? No, he is showing respect to his superior.

- **The Synagogue of Satan:** In Revelation 3:9, Jesus says he will make his enemies come and *worship* (*proskuneo*) before the feet of the Christians! Does this mean the Christians are God? Of course not.

Worshiping God AND the King

The Old Testament provides a perfect parallel in 1 Chronicles 29:20. When David passes the kingdom to Solomon, the text says:

> "And all the congregation blessed the LORD God of their fathers, and bowed down their heads, and **worshipped the LORD, and the king**."

The Hebrew word *shachah* (bow down) is applied simultaneously to *Yahweh* and to David.

Note: In the Greek Septuagint (the version used by the New Testament writers), this word is translated as ***proskuneo***—the exact same word used for worshipping Jesus.

- They worshipped *Yahweh* as God Almighty.
- They worshipped David as God's Anointed King.

The people performed the *same physical action* but with a different *internal intent*.

Honoring the Agent

Forensics demands interpreting the worship of Jesus exactly as the Chronicles account. When the disciples bowed to him, they were not confusing him with the Father. They were honoring him as the Father's Supreme Agent.

Jesus explains this dynamic clearly:

> "That all men should honor the Son, **even as** they honor the Father. He that honoreth not the Son honoreth not the Father which hath sent him." (John 5:23)

The believer honors the Agent because he represents the King. The honor passes through the Agent and lands on the Sender. To bow to Jesus is ultimately to bow to the God who raised him from the dead (Philippians 2:11).

The Anti-Usurper (Philippians 2)

Consider the critical distinction between Jesus and Lucifer. Theologians often cite Philippians 2:6, where it says Jesus *"thought it not robbery to be equal with God."* They claim he held on to his equality. But the Greek word used is *harpagmos*, which means "something to be seized" or "snatched" (Robbery).

Compare the two "Sons":

- **Lucifer** (Isaiah 14): Said "I will be like the Most High." He attempted to *seize* equality (Usurper).

- **Adam** (Genesis 3): Attempted to *seize* the fruit to "be as gods."

- **Jesus** (The Agent): Did **not** consider equality with God something to be seized. Instead, he took upon himself the form of a servant (Anti-Usurper).

Jesus is the Anti-Usurper. He is the Agent who refused to grasp at the Throne. He earned his exaltation not by nature, but by obedience.

IX. The Forgiveness Trap: Exposing the 'Only God Can Forgive' Argument

Another major argument for the Deity of Christ is his ability to forgive sins. The scribes asked, "Who can forgive sins but God only?" (Mark 2:7). Trinitarians say: "The scribes were right. Only God can forgive. Jesus forgave. Therefore, Jesus is God."

The text proves the exact opposite.

The Son of Man has Power

When Jesus heals the paralytic to prove he can forgive sins, he does not claim to do so by his own intrinsic divine nature. He says:

> "But that ye may know that the **Son of man** hath power on earth to forgive sins..." (Mark 2:10)

He uses the title "Son of Man"—a human title. He is exercising this power as the authorized human Agent of God.

The Crowd's Reaction

Matthew's account of this same event adds a decisive forensic detail sealing the argument. How did the Jewish onlookers interpret this miracle? Did they conclude this man must be Yahweh?

> "But when the multitudes saw it, they marvelled, and glorified God, which had given such power **unto men**." (Matthew 9:8)

The crowd understood the Law of Agency perfectly! The spectators did not worship Jesus as God; they praised God for delegating such authority to a human being ("unto men"). *Had the Trinitarian view been correct*, the crowd's conclusion was a dangerous heresy. Matthew records it as the proper response to the miracle.

X. The Judge of the World

A similar pattern exists regarding the Final Judgment. The Old Testament says *Yahweh* is the "Judge of all the earth" (Genesis 18:25). Yet, the New Testament says Jesus will judge the nations. Is this proof Jesus is *Yahweh*?

Judging by Appointment

Jesus reiterates his judicial authority is delegated, not intrinsic.

> "For the Father judgeth no man, but **hath committed** all judgment unto the Son." (John 5:22)

If Jesus were God Almighty, he would have the inherent right to judge. He wouldn't need it "committed" (entrusted/delegated) to him. Furthermore, Jesus explains *why* he is the judge:

> "And hath given him authority to execute judgment also, **because he is the Son of man**." (John 5:27)

He judges not because he is God, but because he is human! God's justice requires a human being—one who has been tempted and suffered—should sit on the bench to judge humanity.

Paul's Testimony at Athens

Paul confirms this view in Acts 17. Preaching to pagan Greeks, he does not present a "God-Man." He presents a human agent appointed by the One God.

> "Because he [God] hath appointed a day, in the which he will judge the world in righteousness **by that man whom he hath ordained**; whereof he hath given assurance unto all men, in that he hath raised him from the dead." (Acts 17:31)

God is the Judge, but He judges *through* ("by") the man He ordained. *The statement defines pure Agency.*

XI. Creation or Re-Organization?

The Agency view handles even the most challenging texts linking Jesus to creation. Trinitarians often cite Hebrews 1:2 ("by whom also he made the worlds") and Colossians 1:16 ("by him were all things created"). Do these verses prove Jesus is the Creator of Genesis 1:1?

Hebrews 1:2: The Ages

The King James Version translates Hebrews 1:2 as: *"by whom also he made the **worlds**."* However, the Greek word used here is not *kosmos*. The author uses *aionas*, which literally means **"ages" or "time periods."**

If the author had meant the physical planet, he would have used *kosmos* or *ge*. By using *aionas*, he is stating God framed the entire span of history—the ages of time—*around* the Son. Jesus is history's pivot point. The ages were designed *for* him and *through* his centrality in God's plan. *The verse constitutes* a statement of purpose and history, not physical manufacturing.

Colossians 1: The New Creation

Colossians 1:16 is often quoted as proof Jesus created the universe: *"For by him were all things created, that are in heaven, and that are in earth..."*

Context demands examination. Paul defines exactly what "things" were created: *"...visible and invisible, whether they be **thrones, or dominions, or principalities, or powers**."* Paul is not talking about rocks, trees, and oceans. The Apostle describes **authority structures**.

Furthermore, verse 18 gives the context: *"And he is the head of the body, the church: who is the beginning, the firstborn from the dead."* Paul is describing the **New Creation**. Just as Yahweh created the physical world in Genesis, He is now creating a New World—a new Kingdom structure—through His Agent, Jesus. Jesus is the "firstborn" (heir) of this New Creation. He organizes the new hierarchy of authorities (thrones and powers) within the Kingdom of God.

The Preposition "Dia"

Even if one insists these verses refer to physical creation, the grammar still supports Agency. The Greek preposition used is almost always *dia* (through), not *ek* (out of/from). God is the Source (*ek*); Jesus is the Channel (*dia*).

> *"But to us there is but one God, the Father, **of whom** are all things... and one Lord Jesus Christ, **through whom** are all things."* (1 Corinthians 8:6)

The Father is the Architect; the Son is the Master Workman or the reason for the work. The distinction between the One God and the One Lord remains absolute.

XII. The Thomas Breach: The Climax of Agency

Trinitarians often play their final card: "What about Thomas?" Seeing the risen Jesus, Thomas falls to his knees and cries, **"My Lord and my God!"** (John 20:28). They argue the "Agency" mask slips and "Deity" is revealed.

Viewed through the **Joseph Protocol**, *the moment serves as the climax*, not a contradiction. Thomas finally recognizes what he is looking at. He sees the wounds (Humanity) and the absolute Vindication of the Father. Thomas recognizes this Man's granted status and Name.

To see the Anointed is to see the One who Anointed him. Thomas is acknowledging Jesus is the "God" to him, just as Moses was "God" to Pharaoh. *The confession constitutes not an ontological definition of essence; it is a recognition of supreme authority. The representative has become functionally equivalent to the Sender.*

XIII. The Ultimate Submission

If there were any doubt Jesus is the Agent and not the Source, the Apostle Paul settles the debate definitively in his description of the end of the world. In 1 Corinthians 15, Paul outlines the future of the Kingdom. He describes a time when Jesus has conquered all enemies, including death.

If Jesus were "God the Son," co-equal and co-eternal with the Father, *consistency demands arguing* he reign alongside the Father forever as an equal. But Paul describes something radically different:

> "Then cometh the end, when he shall have delivered up the kingdom to God, even the Father... And when all things shall be subdued unto him, then shall the Son also himself **be subject unto him** that put all things under him, that God may be all in all." (1 Corinthians 15:24, 28)

The Agency principle reaches its glorious conclusion.

a) The Agent (Jesus) succeeded in his mission: "Rule until you conquer all enemies."

b) The Agent succeeds perfectly.

c) The Agent hands the completed work (the Kingdom) back to the Owner (the Father).

d) The Agent himself becomes "subject" (subordinate) to the Father.

The Greek word for "be subject" is *hypotagēsetai*. The term implies a hierarchy of authority. Even in his glorified state, after the resurrection, after the judgment, into the eternal ages—the Son remains subject to the Father. He is the eternal Vice-Regent, the eternal Agent, but he is never the Supreme God. "That God [the Father] may be all in all."

The Heavenly Evidence (Revelation 3:12)

Trinitarians often argue Jesus' subordination was only temporary. But forensic evidence from the Throne Room itself exists. In Revelation 3:12, decades after his ascension, the Glorified Jesus speaks:

> "Him that overcometh will I make a pillar in the temple of **my God**... and I will write upon him the name of **my God**, and the name of the city of **my God**, which is New Jerusalem, which cometh down out of heaven from **my God**..."

Four times in one verse, the Glorified Lord calls the Father "My God." If Jesus is the Supreme God, why does he have a God? Agency is not a temporary phase; the status remains the eternal reality of the Son.

XV. The 'I AM' Identity Theft: Debunking the John 8:58 Myth

Perhaps the most persistent missile used by Trinitarians is John 8:58: *"Before Abraham was, I am."* They claim Jesus is quoting Exodus 3:14 ("I AM THAT I AM"), claiming to be *Yahweh. The error represents* a forensic error based on linguistic ignorance (Identity Theft).

Grammar, Not Godhood

The Greek phrase Jesus uses is **ego eimi**. The phrase follows standard grammar and simply means "I am he" or "It is I."

- The Blind Man in John 9:9 uses the **exact same phrase** (*ego eimi*) to identify himself! "Some said, This is he... but he said, **I am he** (*ego eimi*)."
- The Blind Man was not claiming to be *Yahweh*. The former beggar was identifying himself.

The Messiah, Not the Almighty

What did Jesus claim? He claimed the Messiah existed in God's plan **before** Abraham was born. In Jewish thought, the Messiah was "foreordained" before the foundation of the world (1 Peter 1:20). He is history's centerpiece. Abraham "rejoiced to see my day" (John 8:56) through prophetic vision. Jesus is saying, "I am the one Abraham saw. I am the realization of the promise predating the patriarch."

XVI. The Royal Title Transfer: Why Shared Titles Never Equal Shared Identity

Finally, the dossier addresses the "Alpha and Omega" argument. In Revelation, God calls Himself "Alpha and Omega." Later, Jesus calls himself "The First and the Last." Trinitarians merge these titles to merge the beings.

The Joseph Protocol explains this transfer. When the King promotes an Agent, the Monarch often shares his **Titles**, but never his **Source-hood**.

- **God is the Alpha (Source) and Omega (Goal)** of all existence.
- **Jesus is the First (Firstborn from the Dead) and Last (Final Judge)** of God's redemptive plan.

The fact they share titles (Lord, Savior, Judge, King) proves they share **Authority**, not Identity.

- **Example:** Pharaoh and Joseph were both called "Lord of Egypt." They shared the title. Did that make Joseph the same person as Pharaoh? No. It proved Joseph was Pharaoh's authorized ruler.

XVII. The Verdict: The Glory of the Obedient Son

Trinitarian doctrine obscures the true glory of Jesus. Trying to make him the Father's equal robs him of his unique achievement as the Father's obedient Son.

The glory of Jesus is not he is God. The glory: **He is God's man** who loved God so perfectly, obeyed God so completely, and represented God so faithfully, God has highly exalted him.

The True Confession

To confess Jesus as Lord is not to confess him as *Yahweh*. *The confession acknowledges* Yahweh has made him Lord.

> "Therefore let all the house of Israel know assuredly, that God hath **made** that same Jesus, whom ye have crucified, both Lord and Christ." (Acts 2:36)

Understanding the Law of Agency harmonizes the Bible. The reader no longer explains away Jesus' prayers, his limitations, or his obedience. *The text reveals him as he is*: the Divine Agent, the King of Kings, the Savior of the World—to the glory of God the Father.

The Awakening: The Chain of Agency

Why does the distinction matter? Because the Law of Agency does not stop with Jesus. *The authority flows* through him to you. In John 20:21, the Risen Lord gives the ultimate command:

> "As my Father hath sent me, **even so send I you**."

Agency represents the awakening. Jesus was the Agent of the Father. Now, you are the Agent of the Son. If Jesus were "God Almighty," his example would be unreachable—you can never be God. But because he is the Faithful Agent who learned obedience, you can follow in his steps. You are not worshipping a mystery; you are joining a chain of command. The authority flowing from the Father to the Son now flows to you.

EXHIBIT D: THE FORENSIC GLOSSARY OF AGENCY

Legal Term	Forensic Definition
Shaliach	(Hebrew) An Agent. "The one sent is as the sender." Legally equivalent, personally distinct.
Elohim	(Hebrew) A title of authority and might. Applied to God, but also to Moses, Judges, and Angels acting as agents.
Proskuneo	(Greek) To bow down. An act of homage to superiors (kings/masters), not exclusively religious worship.

Harpagmos	(Greek) Something to be seized or snatched. A robbery. (Phil 2:6).
Ego Eimi	(Greek) "I am he." Common phrase of identification used by Jesus and the Blind Man. Not a claim to be Yahweh.
Dia vs. Ek	*Dia* (Through) marks the Agent/Channel. *Ek* (Out of) marks the Source/Creator.

Appendix A: The Evidentiary Audit: John 1:1 and 8:58

1. John 1:1 - Identity or Quality?

The Text: *"In the beginning was the Word... and the Word was God."* (RV)

The Forensic Issue: In English, the word "God" is capitalized and treated as a proper noun, identifying a specific person. This leads the English reader to a mathematical equation: **Jesus = The Father**. However, the Greek grammar tells a different story regarding the **Nature** of the Word vs. the **Identity** of the Father.

The Greek Grammar Data:

- **Clause B (Distinction):** *"...and the Word was with God"* (pros **ton** theon). Here, the word *theos* has the definite article (*ton*). This functions as a proper noun, identifying a specific person: **The Father**. The Word is "face-to-face" with this Person.

- **Clause C (Description):** *"...and the Word was God"* (kai theos en ho logos). Here, *theos* **lacks** the article (it is *anarthrous*). In Greek grammar, when a noun lacks the article in this position, it is **Qualitative**. It describes the *nature* or *category* of the subject, not its personal identity.

The "Colwell" Patch: Some scholars cite "Colwell's Rule" to argue that we should insert a "The" even though it is missing in the Greek. However, this rule is widely disputed and often applied circularly to force a Trinitarian reading. The grammar naturally suggests quality, not identity.

The Verdict: John is not saying the Word *is* the Person he was just with (that would be a logical contradiction). He is saying the Word possesses the *attributes* of that Person.

- **Incorrect Identity:** "The Word was the Father."
- **Correct Quality:** "The Word was *divine*." (Moffatt, Goodspeed).

The Analogy: If I say, "The robe was purple," I am describing its quality (color). I am not saying, "The robe was the concept of Purple itself."

2. John 8:58 - The "I AM" Identity Theft

The Text: *"...Before Abraham was born, I am."*

The Argument: Trinitarians claim Jesus is quoting the divine name "I AM" from Exodus 3:14, thus identifying himself as Yahweh.

The Forensic Rebuttal:

a) **The Septuagint Evidence:** We must audit the "source code"—the Greek Old Testament (LXX) used by the Apostles.

   - **Exodus 3:14 (LXX):** God says, "*Ego eimi **ho on***" ("I am **The Being One**"). The Title is *Ho On*.

   - **John 8:58:** Jesus simply says, "*Ego eimi*" ("I am").

   The Verdict: If Jesus were claiming to be Yahweh, he stopped halfway through the sentence. He omitted the actual title (*Ho On*).

b) **Common Speech (Not Deity):** The phrase *ego eimi* is the standard, everyday Greek way of saying "It is me" or "I am he." It is used by many people in the New Testament who are clearly not God.

   - **Exhibit A: The Blind Man (John 9:9):** "Others said, This is he... but he said, **I am he** (*ego eimi*)."

   Did the Blind Man claim to be Yahweh? No. He simply identified himself.

c) **The Context:** Jesus is claiming **priority** in God's plan, not deity. He existed in the foreknowledge of God (the Logos) before Abraham was born. This is a claim of **Priority vs. Deity**.

3. Colossians 1:16 – Architect or Builder?

The Text: *"For by him were all things created..."* (RV)

The Forensic Issue: The English preposition "by" is ambiguous. It can mean "by the Architect" (Source) or "by the Carpenter" (Instrument). The Greek is precise.

The Greek Grammar: We must carefully distinguish between the two prepositions used in this passage:

- ***En auto* (In him):** The verse begins by saying creation happened *en auto*. This is a locative term, meaning "in the sphere of." He is the logical blueprint.

- ***Di' autou* (Through him):** The verse ends by saying creation was *di' autou*. This denotes **Agency**, not Source. He is the instrument used, not the ultimate originator.

The Distinction (1 Cor 8:6): Paul explicitly defines the **Chain of Command** for creation using these prepositions:

- **The Father:** *ex* ("out of") → The Source.
- **Jesus Christ:** *di'* ("through") → The Channel.

The Verdict: Paul is stating that creation took place **in connection with** Christ and **through** his agency. He is the **Master Workman**; God the Father is the **Architect**. Jesus is the *reason* for creation, not the *originator* of it (Acts 4:24 confirms the Father alone made heaven and earth).

Appendix B: The Forensic Forgeries: The Johannine Comma

The goal of this appendix is not to cast doubt on the Scriptures, but to purify them. We believe in the inspiration of the *original* writings, not the errors of later copyists.

Over the centuries, certain scribes—driven by theological zeal rather than accuracy—inserted words or phrases into the text to bolster their preferred doctrines. In forensic textual criticism, these are known as **Interpolations**.

The Revised Version, relying on the oldest and best manuscripts (Alexandrian text type), removes these later additions. Below are the two most significant examples where Trinitarian dogma was artificially injected into the Bible.

Exhibit A: The Johannine Comma (1 John 5:7)

This is the most famous forgery in the New Testament. In the King James Version, 1 John 5:7 reads:

> "For there are three that bear record in heaven, the Father, the Word, and the Holy Ghost: and these three are one."

The Forensic Evidence:

- **Absent from Antiquity:** This verse is found in **ZERO** Greek manuscripts prior to the 14th century. It is completely absent from the ancient biblical world.

- **Absent from the Fathers:** Not one early Church Father quotes this verse during the intense Trinitarian debates of Nicaea (325 AD). If it existed, it would have been their primary weapon. Its silence proves its absence.

- **The Origin:** It began as a marginal note (gloss) in a Latin manuscript that was mistakenly incorporated into the main text by a later scribe. It was never part of the inspired Greek text.

The Verdict: The RV correctly removes this fabrication. It is not Scripture; it is vandalism.

Exhibit B: The Mystery of Godliness (1 Timothy 3:16)

In the King James Version, this verse reads:

> *"...great is the mystery of godliness: **God** was manifest in the flesh..."*

This single word ("God") has been used for centuries as a proof text for the Incarnation. However, the forensic evidence tells a different story.

The Forensic Evidence:

- **The "Sacred Name" Abbreviation:** To understand this error, one must know that ancient scribes abbreviated sacred words (*Nomina Sacra*). They did not write the full word for God (*Theos*); they contracted it to its first and last letters with a bar over the top: $\overline{\Theta\Sigma}$.

- **The Visual Trick:** The word for "He who" is $O\Sigma$.
    - **God:** $\overline{\Theta\Sigma}$
    - **He who:** $O\Sigma$

  The difference is merely two tiny strokes: a horizontal line inside the O (making it a Theta, Θ) and a line over the top.

- **The Microscope:** The oldest manuscripts (Sinaiticus, Alexandrinus) clearly read $O\Sigma$ ("He who"). In Codex Alexandrinus, forensic analysis reveals that a later hand added ink to force the reading to look like "God."

- **The Context:** The hymn describes the vindication of a servant ("justified in the Spirit"), not the descent of a deity.

The Verdict: The proper reading, preserved in the RV, is: *"He who was manifested in the flesh."* It refers to the Messiah's visible life, not an ontological incarnation of Yahweh.

Appendix C: The Divine Power of Attorney: Legal vs. Physical Identity

Note: *This section provides a brief overview of the principle of Divine Agency. For a complete scriptural and legal defense, please see the full essay* **"The Divine Agent: How God Rules Through Man"** *found on page 446.*

The Core Definition

The biblical view of Jesus is best understood through the Jewish legal principle of **Agency** (Hebrew: *Shaliach*), which functions identically to a modern **Power of Attorney**.

- **The Maxim:** "A man's agent is as himself." (Mishnah *Berakhot* 5:5)
- **The Meaning:** An authorized agent carries the full legal authority of the sender. To treat the agent well is to treat the sender well; to reject the agent is to reject the sender.
- **The Greek Connection:** The New Testament translates this concept as **Apostle** (*Apostolos* – "one sent with orders"). This is why Hebrews 3:1 explicitly identifies Jesus as "the **Apostle** and High Priest of our confession."
- **The Distinction:** The agent is functionally identified with the sender but remains a distinct individual. He is not the sender; he represents the sender.

Summary of Evidence

1. The Old Testament Precedent

The Bible is filled with human and angelic agents who are called "God" (*Elohim*) or "Lord" because they represent the Creator.

- **Moses:** God told Moses, "I have made thee **a god** (*Elohim*) to Pharaoh" (Exodus 7:1). Moses possessed the functional authority of Elohim over Egypt.
- **The Judges:** The judges of Israel were called "gods" (*elohim*) because they exercised God's judgment (Psalm 82:6).
- **The Angel of the Lord:** This messenger speaks as God ("I am the God of Bethel") because God's "name is in him" (Exodus 23:21).

2. Jesus as the Ultimate Agent

Jesus fulfills the prophecy of the "Prophet like Moses" (Deut 18:18), who speaks only what God commands.

- **Oneness:** When Jesus says, "I and the Father are one" (John 10:30), he refers to unity of purpose and protection (like a Shepherd and the Owner keeping the sheep), not a unity of substance.
- **Worship:** The homage paid to Jesus (*proskuneo*) is the honor due to the King's Son and Representative. It is "to the glory of God the Father" (Phil 2:11).
- **Judgment:** Jesus judges the world not because he is God, but "because he is the Son of Man" (John 5:27). God judges the world *through* him (Acts 17:31).

3. The Final Subordination

The ultimate proof that Jesus is distinct from God is the end of history.

- After conquering all enemies, the Son himself will **be subject** to the Father, "that God may be all in all" (1 Cor 15:28).
- This shows that Jesus' authority, while supreme, is derived and delegated. He is the eternal Vice-Regent, not the Source.

Conclusion

Recognizing Jesus as the Divine Agent allows us to honor him as "Lord" and "God" (in the representative sense) without contradicting the Shema ("The Lord our God is one Lord"). He is the image of the invisible God, the one in whom the fullness of Deity dwells bodily—God's perfect Representative to man.

Appendix D: The Seditious Scribes: How Doctrine Corrupted the Text

History is written by the victors. For over a thousand years, the primary copyists of the New Testament were men deeply committed to the developing doctrines of the church. While most were honest and careful, a significant number fell victim to the temptation of **"Pious Fraud."**

A Pious Fraud is a change made to the text not to destroy it, but to "improve" it—to make it support what the scribe believed was the truth.

The Motive: Protecting the Deity

As the doctrine of the Trinity developed (3rd–4th Century), scribes began to view the human descriptions of Jesus in the earliest manuscripts as "problems" that needed solving.

If a verse made Jesus look too human, or too subordinate to the Father, they often "smoothed it out."

Example 1: The Parents of Jesus

In Luke 2:33, the earliest manuscripts read:

> "And **his father and his mother** were marveling…"

To a later scribe, calling Joseph "his father" felt dangerous. It might imply Jesus wasn't virgin-born. So, later manuscripts (like those used for the King James Version) changed it to:

> "And **Joseph and his mother** marveled…"

The scribe protected the doctrine, but corrupted the text.

Example 2: The Ignorance of the Son

In Matthew 24:36, Jesus declares that no one knows the timing of the end. The earliest manuscripts read:

> "…no, not the angels of heaven, **neither the Son**, but the Father only."

This phrase—*"neither the Son"*—presented a crisis for later scribes. If Jesus were God Almighty, how could he *not know* something? To protect the doctrine of Omniscience, later scribes simply **deleted the phrase**.

The King James Version reflects this deletion. The Revised Version, loyal to the ancient text, restores the words **"neither the Son,"** preserving the truth that the Son's knowledge is distinct from the Father's.

The Solution: The Alexandrian Text

How do we bypass these "Pious Frauds"? We must go back to the manuscripts that were written *before* the Trinitarian controversies fully took over.

This is why this edition relies on the **Alexandrian Text Type** (represented by the Revised Version). These manuscripts date back to the 2nd and 3rd centuries—closer to the source, and freer from the "improvements" of later theologians.

We do not honor God by polishing His Word. We honor Him by preserving it—warts, humanity, and all.

Appendix E: The Blueprint: Why Accuracy is an Act of Worship

*Truth is the highest form of reverence. If we truly believe the Bible is inspired, then we must accept it exactly as it was written. To translate it accurately is an act of worship; to alter it for a **doctrinal agenda** is an act of heresy.*

1. A Note on Religious Affiliation

Because this Bible emphasizes the singular identity of the One God and restores His personal name, some readers may question if this volume is connected to the *Jehovah's Witnesses* (Watchtower Bible and Tract Society). **It is not.**

This edition is a reprint of the **Revised Version (1901)**, a translation produced by 30 American scholars from various Protestant denominations (Baptist, Methodist, Presbyterian, Episcopal, etc.). The RV was published nearly 50 years before the *New World Translation* existed.

The use of God's personal name is not the property of any one denomination; it is the heritage of all who hold the Bible to be inspired. This project is an independent, non-denominational effort dedicated to **Biblical Monotheism**—the belief that the Father alone is the One True God (John 17:3).

2. Restoring the Name: Why "Yahweh"?

In modern academia, the consensus is that the original pronunciation of the Tetragrammaton (*YHWH*) was *Yahweh*.

While the original 1901 text of the RV rendered this as *Jehovah* (following the common convention of its time), this edition has updated the text to **Yahweh**.

The Call for Accuracy

The form "Jehovah" is a hybrid word—a medieval combination of the consonants of *YHWH* and the vowels of *Adonai* (Lord)—that was never used by the ancient Israelites.

- **Historical Evidence:** We are not guessing at the pronunciation. Early Church Fathers, such as Clement of Alexandria (c. 200 AD), recorded the divine name in Greek transliteration as *Iaoue* (pronounced Ya-oo-way). This provides ancient forensic evidence for the pronunciation **Yahweh**.

- **The RV's Intent:** The original RV translators stated their goal was to bring the reader close to the original text. By updating *Jehovah* to *Yahweh*, we are fulfilling the spirit of their work with the superior linguistic knowledge available today.
- **Distinction:** Using **Yahweh** clearly distinguishes the **Father** (The Almighty) from the **Son** (often called Lord/Master), removing the ambiguity that plagues standard translations.

3. Theological Bias in Modern Translations

Most modern Bibles are translated by committees bound by "Statements of Faith" that require them to uphold the Trinity. As a result, they often translate verses not based on what the Greek *says*, but on what their theology *needs* it to mean.

The NIV (New International Version)

The NIV is famous for "Dynamic Equivalence" (thought-for-thought), which allows translators to reshape the text to fit doctrine.

- **Philippians 2:6:** The Greek says Jesus "did not regard equality with God a thing to be grasped/seized" (*harpagmos*). The NIV changes this to: "did not consider equality with God something to be *used to his own advantage*," implying Jesus already *possessed* it.
- **Colossians 1:16:** The Greek prepositions are *en* (in) and *dia* (through). The NIV changes them to "By him all things were created," obscuring that the Father is the Source and Jesus is the Instrument.

The ESV (English Standard Version)

While literal, the ESV often leans heavily into Trinitarian word choices.

- **John 1:18:** The best manuscripts say *monogenes theos* ("unique god" or "only begotten god"). The ESV renders this "the only God, who is at the Father's side," blurring the distinction between the begotten Son and the Unbegotten Father.
- **Micah 5:2:** The translators render the Hebrew *olam* (ancient times/days of old) as "from everlasting," forcing an eternal pre-existence onto the Messiah.

    Note: The ESV translates this exact same word (*olam*) as "ancient" in Proverbs 22:28 ("ancient landmarks"). Unless fence posts are eternal, the translation in Micah is biased.

APPENDIX E

The KJV / NKJV (King James Tradition)

These versions rely on the *Textus Receptus*, a late Greek text that contains scribal additions not found in the earliest manuscripts.

- **1 John 5:7:** Includes the "Three Heavenly Witnesses" (Father, Word, Holy Ghost), a known Latin forgery absent from all early Greek Bibles.
- **1 Timothy 3:16:** Reads "God was manifest in the flesh," whereas the earliest manuscripts read "He who was manifest."

The Unredacted Tyndale Bible uses the RV because it is a literal, formal-equivalent translation that predates many of these modern theological filters.

Appendix F: The Daniel 7 Fuse: Decoding the Cloud-Rider

I. The Statistical Anomaly

If you read the Gospels carefully, you will notice a strange pattern in how Jesus refers to himself.

Christian theology usually focuses on titles like "Son of God" or "Messiah" (Christ).

Yet, statistical analysis of the text reveals a surprise:

- Jesus calls himself **"Son of God"**: Fewer than 10 times.
- Jesus calls himself **"Messiah"**: Fewer than 5 times (and usually privately).
- Jesus calls himself **"Son of Man"**: 81 times.

This was, without question, his favorite title. It was his **strategic camouflage**.

Even more strangely, the disciples *almost never* use this title for him. Paul never uses it. Peter never uses it. It appears exclusively on the lips of Jesus, with one notable exception.

The Exception that Proves the Rule

The only disciple to call Jesus "Son of Man" is Stephen in Acts 7:56. Why? Because Stephen is being stoned and looks up to see the **heavenly courtroom**.

He cries out: "Behold, I see the heavens opened, and the **Son of man** standing on the right hand of God."

Stephen uses the title because he is witnessing the literal fulfillment of Daniel's vision in real-time. This confirms that the early church understood this title specifically as the "Ruler in the Heavenly Court."

The Common Misconception

For centuries, many Bible readers have assumed that "Son of Man" was a statement of humility.

- **Theory:** "Son of God" refers to his deity; "Son of Man" refers to his humanity.

- **Reality:** This is incorrect.

While the phrase can mean "a human being" (Ezekiel is called "son of man" often), Jesus uses it in a specific, definite way: **"The** Son of Man."

He is referring to a specific figure from the Hebrew Scriptures. When he uses this title, he is making a claim so high, so exalted, that it eventually got him killed.

II. The Key: Daniel 7

To unlock the mystery, we must turn to **Daniel 7:13–14**.

In this vision, Daniel sees four terrifying **beasts** rising from the sea, representing the pagan empires of the world (Babylon, Persia, Greece, Rome).

Then, in stark contrast to the beasts, the scene shifts to the heavenly courtroom:

> "I saw in the night visions, and, behold, one like **the Son of man** came with the clouds of heaven, and came to the Ancient of days, and they brought him near before him."
>
> "And there was given him dominion, and glory, and a kingdom, that all people, nations, and languages, should serve him: his dominion is an everlasting dominion..."

This is the "Magna Carta" of Jesus' identity.

a) **The Ancient of Days:** This is God the Father.

b) **The Son of Man:** This is a human figure (Aramaic: *Bar Enosh*) who is exalted to the highest place in the universe. He is "Human" in contrast to the "Beasts" (Empires).

c) **The Transaction:** The Human Figure travels *on the clouds* to the Father and receives the right to rule the world.

III. The "Cloud Rider" Controversy

In the Old Testament, "riding on the clouds" is a prerogative reserved strictly for Yahweh.

- Psalm 104:3: "[God] who maketh the clouds his chariot..."
- Isaiah 19:1: "Behold, the rideth upon a swift cloud..."

When Daniel sees a *human* figure coming "with the clouds of heaven," he is seeing a human being elevated to the divine level. He is seeing the ultimate Agent—someone distinct from God, yet sharing God's throne and vehicle.

The Trial Scene: The Atomic Fuse

This background explains the dramatic climax of Jesus' trial in Mark 14:61–64.

The High Priest asks him: "Art thou the Christ, the Son of the Blessed?"

Jesus answers by fusing two distinct prophecies into one explosive claim:

> "I am: and ye shall see the **Son of man** sitting on the right hand of power [Psalm 110:1], and **coming in the clouds of heaven** [Daniel 7:13]."

The High Priest's reaction is immediate and violent: he tears his clothes and cries, "Blasphemy!"

Why?

Claiming to be the Messiah (an earthly king) was not blasphemy. But claiming to be the *Cloud Rider* of Daniel 7 AND the *King at the Right Hand* of Psalm 110 was a claim to share in God's unique sovereignty.

Jesus was condemned not for claiming to be human. He signed his own death warrant by claiming to be the **Divine Vice-Regent sharing Yahweh's Chariot**.

IV. The Twist: The Suffering Ruler

If "Son of Man" implies such overwhelming power, why did Jesus use it while walking dusty roads with no army?

This is where Jesus revolutionized the title. He took the **Glory** of Daniel 7 and fused it with the **Suffering** of Isaiah 53.

Service Before Sovereignty

The Jews expected the Danielic figure to arrive and immediately destroy Rome. Jesus taught that the Son of Man must suffer *before* he reigns.

> *"For even the **Son of man** came not to be ministered unto, but to minister, and to give his life a ransom for many."* (Mark 10:45)

This was unthinkable. The King of the Universe… a servant? The Judge of the World… a ransom?

Jesus redefined authority. In his Kingdom, power is not taken by force; it is earned by self-sacrifice. He has the right to judge humanity because he suffered for humanity.

V. The Bridge: Jacob's Ladder

Early in his ministry, Jesus made a strange statement to Nathanael:

> *"Verily, verily, I say unto you, Hereafter ye shall see heaven open, and the angels of God ascending and descending upon the **Son of man**."* (John 1:51)

Any Jewish listener would immediately recognize the reference to **Jacob's Ladder** (Genesis 28:12), where Jacob saw a ladder connecting earth to heaven with angels moving up and down on it.

By replacing the "ladder" with "the Son of Man," Jesus is claiming to be the **Interface**.

- He is the point of contact between the holy God and sinful man.
- He is the "Portal" through which heaven invades earth.
- He is the only way to the Father.

VI. Conclusion

Why did Jesus choose this title?

a) **It was Safe (at first):** It didn't sound like a political rebellion to Roman ears (who didn't read Daniel). It allowed him to preach without getting arrested immediately.

b) **It was Exalted:** To those with "ears to hear," it was the highest possible claim—the claim to be the Judge of the World.

c) **It was Representative:** It emphasized his solidarity with the human race he came to save.

"Son of Man" is the perfect title for the Divine Agent. He is truly one of us (Son of Man), yet he comes with the clouds of heaven to exercise the full authority of the Ancient of Days.

Appendix G: The Synoptic Alignment

Forensic Note: The "Four-Car Crash" Reality.

Skeptics often point to minor discrepancies in the Gospels—such as the exact timing of a miracle or the sequence of events—as proof that the Bible is "flip-flopping." Forensic science suggests the exact opposite.

Imagine a car accident at a four-way intersection. If four witnesses provide identical, word-for-word testimony, any judge would throw the case out for **collusion**—the witnesses clearly "synced" their stories. Authentic testimony always contains variations in perspective.

In the Gospels, we have four independent witnesses from four different "corners" of the event. They may differ on the "micro" details of the scene, but they are **absolutely unanimous** on the only fact that matters for eternity: **The Father is the One True God, and Jesus is His unique, authorized Agent.** The variations in the text do not represent a "flip-flop" in truth, but the depth of the testimony; while the witnesses standing on the corners may see different angles, they are all pointing at the same Throne.

EVENT	MATT	MARK	LUKE	JOHN
I. INTRODUCTION				
1. Luke's Preface			1:1-4	
2. John's Prologue				1:1-18
3. Genealogies	1:1-17		3:23-38	
4. Birth of John			1:5-80	
5. Birth of Jesus	1:18-25		2:1-20	
6. Childhood	2:1-23		2:21-52	
II. PREPARATION				
7. John's Ministry	3:1-12	1:1-8	3:1-18	
8. Baptism	3:13-17	1:9-11	3:21-23	
9. Temptation	4:1-11	1:12-13	4:1-13	
10. First Disciples				1:35-51
11. First Miracle				2:1-11

EVENT	MATT	MARK	LUKE	JOHN
III. GALILEAN MINISTRY				
12. Call of Fishermen	4:18-22	1:16-20	5:1-11	
13. Sermon on Mount	5-7		6:17-49	
14. Centurion's Servant	8:5-13		7:1-10	
15. Calming Storm	8:18-27	4:35-41	8:22-25	
16. Gadarene Demoniacs	8:28-34	5:1-20	8:26-39	
17. Jairus' Daughter	9:18-26	5:21-43	8:40-56	
18. Feeding 5,000	14:13-21	6:30-44	9:10-17	6:1-15
19. Walking on Water	14:22-33	6:45-52		6:16-21
20. Peter's Confession	16:13-20	8:27-30	9:18-21	6:66-71
21. Transfiguration	17:1-13	9:2-13	9:28-36	
IV. JOURNEY TO JERUSALEM				
22. Good Samaritan			10:25-37	
23. Mary and Martha			10:38-42	
24. Prodigal Son			15:11-32	
25. Lazarus Raised				11:1-54
26. Rich Young Ruler	19:16-30	10:17-31	18:18-30	
27. Zacchaeus			19:1-10	
V. FINAL WEEK				
28. Triumphal Entry	21:1-11	11:1-11	19:28-44	12:12-19
29. Cleansing Temple	21:12-13	11:15-19	19:45-48	
30. Olivet Discourse	24:1-51	13:1-37	21:5-38	
31. Last Supper	26:20-30	14:17-26	22:14-38	13:1-38
32. Upper Room				14-17
33. Gethsemane	26:36-46	14:32-42	22:39-46	18:1
34. Arrest	26:47-56	14:43-52	22:47-53	18:2-12
35. Peter's Denial	26:69-75	14:66-72	22:55-62	18:25-27
36. Trial before Pilate	27:11-14	15:2-5	23:1-5	18:28-38
37. Crucifixion	27:35-56	15:24-41	23:33-49	19:18-30

EVENT	MATT	MARK	LUKE	JOHN
38. Burial	27:57-61	15:42-47	23:50-56	19:31-42
VI. RESURRECTION				
39. Empty Tomb	28:1-8	16:1-8	24:1-12	20:1
40. Mary Magdalene	28:9-10	16:9-11		20:11-18
41. Emmaus Road		16:12-13	24:13-32	
42. Great Commission	28:16-20	16:15-18	24:44-53	20:19-23
43. Ascension		16:19-20	24:50-53	

Appendix H: Glossary of Redactions: Restoring the Terminology of the Kingdom

Forensic Note: In any legal proceeding, definitions are everything. If you can redefine the terms of a contract, you can break the contract without anyone noticing. Over centuries, the original regal and forensic weight of biblical terms has been swapped for ecclesiastical labels that support later doctrines. This glossary unmasks those redefinitions and restores the original evidence.

The Three Strategic Label Swaps

In a courtroom, if a lawyer swaps the definitions in a contract, the case is rigged before it begins. To see the biblical text clearly, these three specific "label swaps" have to be exposed using the Bible's own legal standards:

a) **The "ECHAD" Label Swap (Numerical One vs. Compound One):** A common claim used to support the Trinity is that the Hebrew word *echad* (one) implies a "compound unity"—like a cluster of grapes.

   The Reality at the Source: The Hebrew Bible uses *echad* for single individuals. For example, the prophet Ezekiel refers to **Abraham** as *echad* (**Ezekiel 33:24**). Abraham was one man, not a "cluster" of persons. When the *Shema* declares that God is *echad*, it is not describing a "unity" of many; it is certifying a numerical count of **One**.

b) **The "SON OF GOD" Label Swap (Office vs. DNA):** Most people are taught that "Son of God" is a biological claim to divine essence (God the Son), meaning Jesus is the same "substance" as the Father.

   The Reality at the Source: In the Hebrew scriptures, this was a **Legal Title** for the King of Israel. God used this exact phrase for the human king Solomon: **"I will be his father, and he shall be my son"** (**2 Samuel 7:14**). It isn't a statement about DNA; it's a statement of **Authorization**. It marks the King as the Father's authorized Vice-Regent on earth.

c) **The "LOGOS" Label Swap (Expression vs. A Second Person):** The standard explanation for John 1 is that the *Logos* (Word) is a second person who was standing next to God at the beginning of time.

   The Reality at the Source: In the biblical mind, a man's word is his intent and expression, not a second person standing next to him. The "Word of the LORD" is simply God's powerful command in action. **Psalm 33:6** confirms this: *"By the word (Logos) of* *the Lord were the heavens made."* God didn't use a second person to build the stars; He used His own powerful Decree. In Jesus, that Decree finally became visible.

The 26 Restored Kingdom Definitions

CONCEPT (English)	ROOT	MEANING & CONTEXT
A–F		
ADAM / MAN	Heb.	Refers to "mankind" or "humanity" collectively. It emphasizes the earth-creature, created from the dust (*adamah*).
ATONEMENT	Heb.	*Kippur* (covering). An act that restores the relationship between God and His people; reconciliation and purification.
BAPTISM	Gk.	*Baptizo*: To immerse. An act of purification and burial, symbolizing identification with the Agent in His mission.
CHRIST	Gk.	*Christos* (Messiah). "Anointed One." Denotes the promised King anointed by God to rule on God's behalf.
ECHAD (ONE)	Heb.	A numerical adjective meaning **one**. Declares Yahweh's absolute singularity against all other gods.
ELECTION	Gk.	*Eklegomai*: To choose. God's sovereign choice of a group for a specific task or purpose on earth.
ETERNAL LIFE	Gk.	*Zoe Aionios*. "Life belonging to the Age." Describes the quality of resurrection life in the coming Kingdom.
FAITH	Gk.	*Pistis*. More than agreement; it is **trust, loyalty, and fidelity** to the Agent's life and teaching.
FORGIVENESS	Heb.	*Salach*. Removal of offense. In a covenant context, God clears the record, allowing re-entry to the community.
G–M		
GEHENNA	Gk.	*Ge Hinnom*. A physical valley used as a refuse dump. Metaphor for the reality of final judgment.
GRACE	Gk.	*Charis*. God's unmerited favor; the active energy of God that saves and enables righteous living.
HELL	Heb.	Translates distinct terms: **Sheol/Hades** (the grave) and **Gehenna** (final judgment).
IMMORTALITY	Gk.	*Athanasia* (undying). The state of being free from death; the quality of the resurrection body.

CONCEPT (English)	ROOT	MEANING & CONTEXT
JUDGMENT	Gk.	*Krisis*. The **act of setting things right**. God establishing justice and separating the righteous.
JUSTIFICATION	Gk.	*Dikaiosis*. Being declared **righteous**. God changing our legal status for participation in His Kingdom.
KINGDOM	Gk.	*Basileia*. The **rule or sovereignty** of God manifest through His authorized Agent.
LAW	Heb.	*Torah*. Primarily means **Instruction or Guidance**. The perfect way of life for covenant people.
MESSIAH	Heb.	*Mashiach*. The promised human King from David's line who restores Israel's sovereignty.
N–S		
NAME	Heb.	*Shem*. Represents **character and authority**. To act in a "Name" is to act as the legal representative.
NEW COVENANT	Gk.	*Diathēkē*. The fulfillment of promise where God writes His Instruction (*Torah*) upon the heart.
PROPHECY	Heb.	*Nabi*. The act of speaking God's word as a **covenant enforcement mediator**.
RECONCILIATION	Gk.	*Katallagē*. Restoration of relationship by removing the cause of offense (sin).
REDEMPTION	Gk.	*Apolutrōsis*. To be **released by paying a price**. The ransom purchasing humanity from bondage.
REPENTANCE	Gk./Heb.	*Metanoia/Shuv*. A **radical change of direction** aligning loyalty with God's Kingdom.
RIGHTEOUSNESS	Heb.	*Tzedakah*. **Covenant faithfulness**. Living up to the standards of the relationship.
SALVATION	Heb.	*Yeshua*. Meaning **deliverance or victory**. The rescue of humanity into the safety of God's Kingdom.
SON OF GOD	Heb./Gk.	A Royal Title (**Psalm 2:7**). Denotes the **Messiah/King** who represents God on earth.
SOUL	Heb.	*Nephesh*. Refers to the **living creature** or self. Emphasizes the person as a whole entity.
SPIRIT	Heb.	*Ruach*. **Breath or vital energy**. The non-material power of God that empowers the Agent.

CONCEPT (English)	ROOT	MEANING & CONTEXT
T–Z		
TEMPLE	Heb.	*Beyt HaMikdash*. The place where God chose to place His *Shem* (Name/Authority).
TRUTH	Gk./Heb.	*Alētheia/Emet*. Refers to **God's reliable character** and the unwavering reality of His way.
WORD	Gk.	*Logos*. The divine wisdom and **active expression** of God's will; the Father's message made visible.
WRATH	Heb.	*Af*. The **just, predictable consequence** for rebellion against the covenant.

Appendix I: The Historical Backdrop: The Empire, The Court, and The Calendar

> **NOTE: THE CRIME SCENE**
> The Gospel is not a religious fairy tale told in a vacuum. It is a legal coup set in a historical "pressure cooker." To understand the verdict, you must identify the **Occupying Force** (Rome), the **Rigged Jury** (The Sanhedrin), and the **Audit of the Ages** (The Feasts).

I. The Rival Claim: Caesar vs. Christ

The New Testament opens in a world where the title "Son of God" was already occupied. It was the primary marketing slogan of the Roman Empire.

TIME	RULER / TITLE	FORENSIC RELEVANCE
THE ROMAN POWER (The Occupying Force)		
27 B.C.–A.D. 14	**Augustus** (Octavian)	First Emperor. Officially titled *Divi Filius* ("Son of the Divine"). When Christians called Jesus "Son of God," they were committing **Linguistic Treason** against the Emperor's claim to divinity.
A.D. 14–37	**Tiberius**	Emperor during the "Ministry." The denarius shown to Jesus bore his face. To call Jesus "King" under Tiberius was a capital crime.
THE LOCAL RULERS (The Puppet Regime)		
37–4 B.C.	**Herod the Great**	The paranoid "King of the Jews" who saw the infant Jesus not as a Savior, but as a **Political Competitor**.
A.D. 26–36	**Pontius Pilate**	Roman Prefect. He found "no fault" in the Agent but authorized the execution to preserve the State. He chose **Order over Evidence**.

II. The Rigged Jury: The Sanhedrin

Jesus was not killed by an angry mob; he was condemned by a **constitutional court**.

- **The Sanhedrin:** The Supreme Court of Jewish Law (71 judges). They were the "Guardians of the **Status Quo**."
- **The Charge:** They could not convict him of criminal acts, so they focused on **Agency**. In their eyes, claiming to be the "Son of God" (the Authorized Agent with God's Power of Attorney) was the ultimate contempt of court.
- **The Motive:** Caiaphas admitted the "trial" was about political survival: *"It is expedient for one man to die... that the whole nation perish not"* (John 11:50).

III. The Audit of the Ages: The Feasts as Signature

The Jewish Feasts were the Father's **"Time-Stamps"**. If a man claims to be the Agent and then "punches the clock" on the exact days set 1,500 years prior, the statistical probability of fraud is destroyed.

FEAST	SEASON	HEBREW	FORENSIC FULFILLMENT
THE SPRING FEASTS (The First Appointment)			
Passover	March/April	*Pesach*	**The Execution.** Jesus dies as the Lamb at the exact moment the Temple lambs are slain.
Firstfruits	March/April	*Bikkurim*	**The Receipt.** Jesus rises as the "Firstfruits," providing the Father's receipt that the debt is paid.
Pentecost	May/June	*Shavuot*	**The Power of Attorney.** The Spirit is given to sub-agents to carry the message to the world.
THE FALL FEASTS (The Final Appointment)			
Trumpets	Sept/Oct	*Yom Teruah*	**The Return.** The "Last Trump" announces the King's arrival to claim the property.
Tabernacles	Sept/Oct	*Sukkot*	**The Settlement.** The 1,000-year reign where the Agent dwells with the human race.

IV. The Closing Statement: The Shaliach's Identity

The "One God" verdict relies on one undeniable fact: Jesus is a faithful Jewish Agent, not a new Roman deity.

- **The Creed:** He died affirming the *Shema* (Mark 12:29). He never claimed to be the Source; He claimed to be the **Portal**.
- **The Office:** He is the **Shaliach**—the High Attorney who took the "case" for humanity and won.

The Final Verdict: The evidence is now in your hands. You have seen the linguistic label-swaps, the "four-car crash" testimony, and the signature of the Feasts. In the court of eternity, there is only one Judge (The Father) and one authorized Agent (The Son). **What is your verdict?**

Appendix J: The Evidence Locker

The Paper Trail of the 1,600-Year Dissent

The "Institutional Lock" described in the Preface suggests a "universal consent" that never existed. To understand the evidence in this Bible, you must recognize three forensic realities:

a) **The Chain of Custody:** The "One God" message was the original setting of the church in Antioch. The Trinity was a **Police-State Enforced Replacement**.

b) **The Intellectual Pedigree:** The 1776 Revolution was fueled by men who saw the Trinity as a primary tool of State Tyranny.

c) **The Agency Bridge:** These witnesses provide the link for the **Law of Agency (Shaliach)** used in our commentary.

1. The "Samosata File" (Paul of Samosata, c. 200–275 AD)

Long before the Roman government turned the Church into a **Department of Enforcement**, Paul was the Bishop of Antioch. He taught that Jesus was a human being empowered by God's own Wisdom, not a second person of a Trinity. He was an early champion of the **Law of Agency**. When the Roman Police-State took over the Church, they classified Paul's Apostolic logic as "treasonous" and began a campaign of **State-Enforced erasure**.

2. The "Lucian Case" (Lucian of Antioch, c. 240–312 AD)

Lucian was a martyr who insisted on a **literal** interpretation of the Bible, rejecting the "philosophical allegories" used by the State to create the Trinity. He taught that the Father alone is the "Unbegotten" God. His students became the primary resistance against the Nicene Creed, fighting to preserve the Apostolic distinction before it was criminalized by the Roman sword.

3. The "Servetus Case" (Michael Servetus, 1511–1553)

If you want to understand why the First Amendment was necessary, you must look at the ashes of Michael Servetus. A true Renaissance genius, Servetus was the first European to correctly describe the pulmonary circulation of the blood. But his scientific mind could not reconcile the Trinity with the Bible.

In 1553, he published *The Restoration of Christianity*, arguing that the God of the Bible was One, and that the Trinity was a "three-headed Cerberus" invented by Greek philosophy. For this "crime" of conscience, he was hunted down not by the Pope, but by the Protestant leader John Calvin. Servetus was burned alive in Geneva with his book strapped to his chest. His execution proved a terrifying forensic fact: **Without a legal separation of Church and State, even "Reformers" will murder to protect the Trinity.** His death horrified the world and planted the seeds of religious liberty that would eventually bloom in 1776.

4. The "Racovian Audit" (Polish Brethren, 1605)

During the Reformation, these scholars performed the first systematic "Decontamination" of doctrine. They re-discovered the **Law of Agency (Shaliach)**, proving that when the Bible uses divine titles for the Son, it is descriptive of his *Authority* as an agent, not his *Identity* as the Almighty.

5. The "Locke Files" (John Locke, 1632–1704)

The philosopher of the "1776" spirit and the pioneer of the Separation of Church and State. Locke rejected the "metaphysical jargon" of the Creeds, arguing that the New Testament required only the confession that Jesus is the **Messiah** (the sent agent), not the **Deity** (the Sender).

6. The "Newton Report" (Sir Isaac Newton, 1642–1727)

Widely considered the greatest scientist in history, Newton was a rigorous **Biblical Monotheist**. He applied his forensic mind to the Greek manuscripts and proved that two key "Trinitarian" proof-texts—**1 John 5:7** and **1 Timothy 3:16**—were surgically altered by later scribes to provide "evidence" for the Trinity where none existed in the original text.

7. The "Common Sense" Verdict (Thomas Paine, 1737–1809)

The intellectual spark of the American Revolution. Paine exposed the "adulterous connection of Church and State" and identified the Trinity as a **Government-Mandated corruption** designed to preserve the revenue of the priesthood. His work provides the legal framework required to break the Police-State's hold on the individual conscience today.

8. The "Adams Brief" (John Adams, 1735–1826)

The second President of the United States and the "Atlas of Independence" was a fierce opponent of the Athanasian Creed. Adams viewed the Trinity not just as an error, but as a "corruption" that confused the simple morality of Jesus. In his famous correspondence with Thomas Jefferson, he described the Trinity as "monkery" and "sacerdotal imposture," arguing that the Incarnation was a metaphysical invention that obscured the singular majesty of the One God. Adams believed that true religion was "mild, equable, and rational," and that the "Three-in-One" arithmetic was a relic of the Dark Ages that had no place in a free Republic.

9. The "Allen Defense" (Ethan Allen, 1738–1789)

The hero of Ticonderoga and leader of the Green Mountain Boys was a soldier who refused to bow to the "priestly caste." Allen published *Reason, the Only Oracle of Man* (1784), a blistering attack on the "polytheism" of the institutional church. He argued that the doctrine of the Trinity was a logical absurdity that insulted the Creator. While the clergy labeled him an "infidel" for his rejection of their Creeds, Allen maintained a stoic belief in a Supreme Being who governed by natural law, not by the "mystery" of church councils.

10. The "Franklin Inquiry" (Benjamin Franklin, 1706–1790)

The ultimate scientist of the Revolution, Franklin applied the same rigorous skepticism to theology that he applied to electricity. He famously rejected the divinity of Jesus while upholding his moral teachings as the "best the world ever saw or is likely to see." Franklin favored the "morality of the Agent" over the "metaphysics of the Church." He believed that public religion was necessary for civic virtue, but he refused to endorse the "corruptions" of the Creeds, famously stating that the "Soul of Man" was between him and his Creator, not to be legislated by a Synod.

11. The "Jefferson Syllabus" (Thomas Jefferson, 1743–1826)

Jefferson performed the ultimate forensic audit of the New Testament. Convinced that the "diamonds" of Jesus's actual words were buried in the "dunghill" of Platonic philosophy, he took a razor to the Gospels—literally. He physically cut out the teachings of Jesus, pasting them into a new volume (*The Life and Morals of Jesus of Nazareth*) while discarding the "mystifications" added by later theologians. Jefferson identified the Trinity as a "relapse into Polytheism" and predicted that the 1776 spirit of free inquiry would eventually restore the simple, Monotheistic faith of the Apostles.

12. EXHIBIT A: The Legal Restoration (1776–1791)

The American Founding was not just a political revolution; it was a theological rescue operation. The Framers understood that the "One God" could never be worshipped freely as long as the State had the power to define Him. They built three specific legal walls to permanently break the "Sword of Theodosius."

I. The Warrant: The Declaration of Independence (1776)

The Framers needed a term for God that was supreme and sovereign, yet free from the specific "Trinitarian" definitions that had fueled centuries of religious war. They identified the One God using four specific forensic titles:

a) **"Nature's God"** (The Source of Law)

b) **"The Creator"** (The Source of Rights)

c) **"The Supreme Judge of the World"** (The Source of Justice)

d) **"Divine Providence"** (The Source of Protection)

The Forensic Significance: None of these titles are Trinitarian. They are exclusively **Singular.** They describe a Single Supreme Executive who acts as Legislator, Creator, Judge, and Protector, creating a "Big Tent" for liberty that acknowledged the Almighty Father without enforcing the Nicene Creed.

II. The Key: The Constitution, Article VI (1787)

The Lock-Pick: For over a thousand years, European laws required public officials to swear allegiance to the Trinity (the "Test Acts"). This ensured that only Trinitarians could hold power. The Framers destroyed this mechanism with a single sentence in **Article VI, Clause 3**:

> "No religious Test shall ever be required as a Qualification to any Office or public Trust under the United States."

This was the moment the "Institutional Lock" was legally picked. A man's standing in the Republic would no longer depend on his bowing to a Church Council.

III. The Shield: The First Amendment (1791)

The Permanent Injunction: To ensure the "Occupying Force" could never return, the Founders codified the rights of the individual conscience into the Supreme Law of the Land:

> "Congress shall make no law respecting an establishment of religion, or prohibiting the free exercise thereof..."

This is the "wall of separation" that Jefferson spoke of. It guarantees that you, the reader, have the **Unalienable Right** to read this Bible, weigh the evidence, and decide the verdict of "Who is God?" for yourself, without fear of the fire, the prison, or the state.

These men were investigators by conviction. The Truth has always had a Paper Trail.

Appendix K: The Fingerprints of the Martyr

The 311-Day Betrayal

Licensing the Work of the Man Burned Alive

Roman Emperor Charles the V burned **William Tyndale** alive for the crime of translating the Bible into English. Exactly **311 days** later, *King Henry VIII* legalized the very same **Tyndale translation** under a false branding.

You're holding the physical proof of **State-sponsored piracy**, exposed by the **W.T.** initials the printer stamped into the woodcuts—a permanent fingerprint the **Monarchy** couldn't erase.

The execution in Vilvoorde, Belgium, was a catastrophe. The Emperor's executioner botched Tyndale's strangulation with a chain. The hired hit man meant to spare Tyndale the pain of the hot fire burning him alive, and failed.*

He died screaming a prayer for the very King who had hunted him: "Lord, open the King of England's eyes."

The King of England—*King Henry VIII*—did not open his eyes. He opened his wallet.

The ashes in Belgium were barely cold when King Henry's printers began looting Tyndale's desk.

On *August 13, 1537*, *King Henry VIII* granted his "Royal License" to the very text *Charles V* had burned Tyndale for writing.†

The timeline exposes the double-cross:

- **The Killer (*Charles V*):** Executed the man for "Heresy" (translating the Bible).
- **The Thief (*King Henry VIII*):** Licensed the dead man's work exactly **10 months and 7 days** later to satisfy the political demand for an English Bible.

---

*John Foxe, *Acts and Monuments* (1563). Foxe records that the strangulation was mishandled, leaving Tyndale conscious as the gunpowder exploded and the fire consumed him.

†Confirmed by the letter from Archbishop Thomas Cranmer to Thomas Cromwell, dated August 13, 1537, explicitly stating he had obtained the King's license for the Matthew Bible. See *Letters and Papers, Foreign and Domestic, Henry VIII*, Vol. 12.

APPENDIX K: THE FINGERPRINTS OF THE MARTYR

The Document of Theft

Proving the King Profited from Murder

The first piece of evidence appears on the Title Page itself. While the dense Gothic script often hides the details from modern eyes, the legal "Smoking Gun" sits in plain sight at the bottom of the page.

Inspect the image below. Scan your eyes to the very bottom of the central text panel to locate the date printed in large Roman Numerals: **M, D, XXXVII** (1537).

Directly beneath that date lies the single most important line of text in the history of the English Bible:

> **"Set forth with the Kinges most gracyous lycence."**[‡]

The clause proves that *King Henry VIII* officially licensed the text. The irony is staggering. Tyndale had previously enraged *King Henry VIII* by opposing the King's annulment from Catherine of Aragon, citing biblical law. King Henry wanted Tyndale dead. But he wanted Tyndale's book even more.

THE 1543 PAYWALL: CRIMINALIZING THE PLOUGHBOY

Tyndale's dying wish was for the "boy that driveth the plough" to know the Scripture. In 1543, **King Henry VIII** betrayed that wish. After hunting Tyndale with a state-sponsored spy team and forcing the translator into a life on the run, the King stole the "Source Code." Following the theft, Henry VIII passed the *Act for the Advancement of True Religion*.[a] The Act officially **criminalized** Bible reading for the working class.[b] The law banned all laborers, apprentices, and "low-born" women from reading the English Bible under threat of imprisonment.[c] The Monarch kidnapped the Word and put it behind a class-based paywall.[d]

---

[a]35 Henry VIII, c. 1. *Statutes of the Realm*, vol. 3. The Act explicitly prohibited Bible reading by apprentices, laborers, and almost all women.

[b]David Daniell, *William Tyndale: A Biography* (Yale, 1994). Daniell confirms the Act was a direct restriction on the lower classes to prevent social unrest.

[c]Brian Moynahan, *God's Bestseller* (2003). Moynahan describes the resulting "chained Bibles" as a state-enforced physical DRM system.

[d]David Loades, *Henry VIII: Church, Court and Conflict* (2007). Loades notes the King used the Act to appease conservatives while maintaining total royal control over the text.

[‡]Original Title Page, *The Bible, which is all the holy Scripture...* (1537). The license line appears at the footer of the frontispiece.

The "Thomas Matthew" Shell Company

Inventing a Fake Author to Trick a Tyrant

History and trial records confirm that **"Thomas Matthew"** never existed. The name served as a phantom—a legal "shell company" created to hide the true source of the text.§

John Rogers, a close friend and assistant to **William Tyndale**, actually compiled the book. Rogers knew the King's condition: King Henry needed an English Bible to break the Catholic Church's monopoly on Latin scripture, but he would never allow Tyndale's name on the cover.

To save the work, Rogers used the pseudonym. He tricked the King into authorizing the very words of the man the Emperor had just burnt alive.

Fingerprints of the Martyr

"W.T." Initials Hidden in the Authorized Woodcuts

The Crown's censors and the King's printers rushed to "monetize" the English Bible so quickly that they failed to perform a basic security audit of the woodblocks.

At the end of the Old Testament (following the book of Malachi) and at the conclusion of the Apocrypha (2 Maccabees), the 1537 Matthew Bible contains massive, ornamental woodcuts. Hidden—yet standing in plain sight—are the large, decorative initials **"W.T."**

The letters stand for **William Tyndale**.

- **The Crown's Narrative:** The King marketed the book as a "new" and "authorized" work by Thomas Matthew.
- **The Physical Evidence:** The printer used the very same woodcut plates and decorative borders Tyndale had prepared before his execution.
- **The Verdict:** The King literally "licensed" and sold the work of the man his rival (*Charles V*) had murdered.

---

§ David Daniell, *William Tyndale: A Biography* (Yale University Press). Daniell confirms "Thomas Matthew" was a pseudonym used by John Rogers to protect the work from anti-Tyndale censorship laws.

APPENDIX K: THE FINGERPRINTS OF THE MARTYR

Survivor's Signature

How John Rogers Stamped "I.R." on the Crime Scene

The defiance of **John Rogers** didn't stop with Tyndale's initials. Rogers placed his own initials, **"I.R."** (*Iohannes Rogers*), at the end of the Exhortation to the Study of Scripture. He marked the work. He left a breadcrumb trail for future generations to see that the "King's Bible" was actually the **Martyr's Bible**.

The Royal Plagiarism Playbook

How King James Repeated Henry VIII's Theft in 1611

The 1537 Matthew Bible was the prototype for the greatest literary theft in history.

King Henry VIII wrote the playbook for State censorship: Let the prophet die, steal the work, and stamp the King's name on the cover.

King James I followed Henry's piracy to the letter in 1611. He took Tyndale's translation (which constitutes 83.7% of the KJV New Testament), scrubbed the name, and claimed credit for the "King's Gift."

"Authorized" is just a polite word for "Stolen."

The Verdict of History

Why the Monarchy Could Not Erase the Translator

The 1537 "W.T." woodcut remains the ultimate proof of **Crown Piracy**. The block stands as a silent, printed monument to the man the Empires tried to erase.

When you read the words of the English Bible today, you're reading a text *King Henry VIII* plagiarized to secure his power—a theft *King James I* replicated to the letter in 1611.

The *British Monarchy* could not stop the heart of the work, even after *Roman Emperor Charles the V* (crowned by the *Catholic Pope*) stopped the breath of **William Tyndale**.

Figure 1: *

Exhibit A: *The 1537 Title Page. Locate the date (M, D, XXXVII) at the bottom. The line immediately below it—"Set forth with the Kinges most gracyous lycence"—serves as the State's official signature on the piracy.*

APPENDIX K: THE FINGERPRINTS OF THE MARTYR

Figure 2: *

Exhibit B: At the end of Malachi, one page displays large decorative capitals: **W.T.** Printers never scattered random ornaments. John Rogers inserted those initials deliberately to acknowledge William Tyndale. The King held the license. Tyndale owned every word. The man, the Roman Emperor *Charles the V* had strangled and burned alive, left his signature on the very Bible *King Henry VIII* (and later *King James 1*) tried to erase. Tyndale's mark survived. The kings took the credit. The martyr kept the truth.

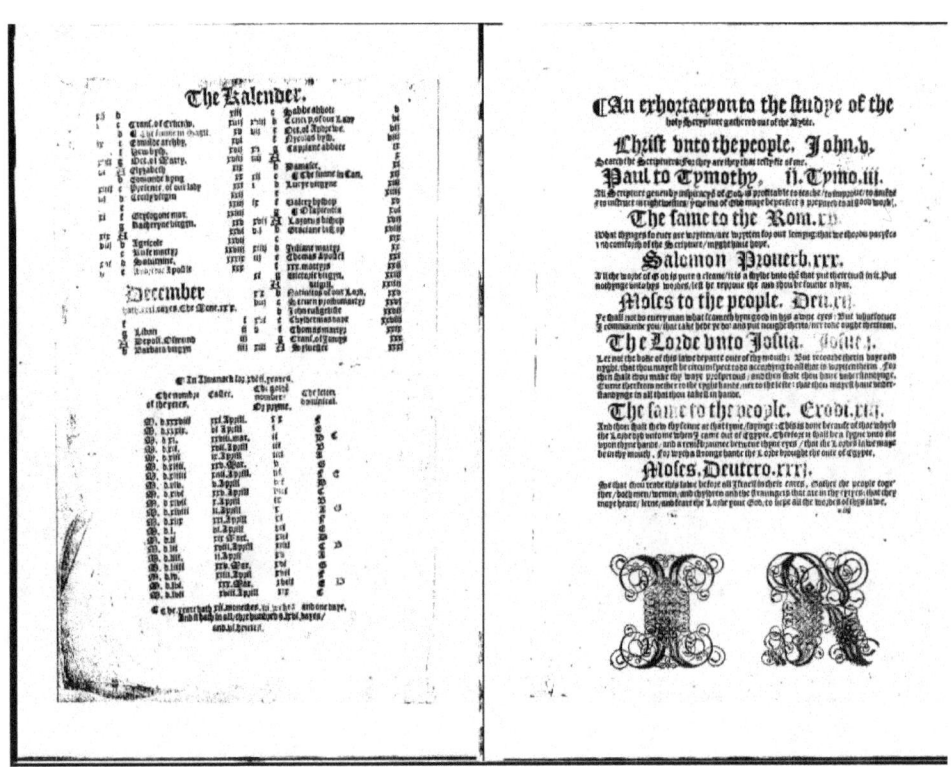

Figure 3: *

Exhibit C: The "I.R." (John Rogers) initials at the end of the Exhortation. The letters signify the man who saved Tyndale's work.

The Timeline of Theological Change

Tracking the historical shift from Hebraic Monotheism to Hellenistic Philosophy

I. The Apostolic Foundation (AD 30 – 100)

AD 30: Jesus Affirms the Shema
Jesus ratifies the **Shema** as the "Supreme Command" (Mark 12:29). He explicitly defines the Father as "**the only true God**" (John 17:3), establishing the monotheistic baseline that cannot be altered.

AD 55: Paul Defines the Distinction
Paul codifies the "Creation Formula" (1 Cor 8:6): One God (The Father) and One Lord (The Messiah). He rejects the pagan "gods many" and cements the Father as the **sole Source** of all things.

AD 95: The Didache Evidence
The earliest manual for Christian converts contains **zero** Trinitarian formulas. It identifies Jesus repeatedly as "**Thy Servant**" (*pais*), proving the Trinity was unknown to the immediate successors of the Apostles.

II. The Infection (AD 150 – 300)

AD 150: Justin Martyr's "Second God"
The philosophical breach begins. Justin Martyr, influenced by Greek Platonism, argues that Jesus is a "**Second God**" (*deuteros theos*)—a distinct, lower deity. The "One God" defense is cracked.

AD 200: Tertullian Coins "Trinitas"
Tertullian coins the Latin term "**Trinitas**". Yet, he admits the Son is *not* eternal ("There was a time when the Son was not"). He creates the vocabulary that later councils will weaponize.

AD 250: Origen's Metaphysical Virus
Origen injects **Platonism** directly into the bloodstream of the church. He invents "**Eternal Generation**", shifting Jesus from the Jewish Messiah to a Greek metaphysical abstraction.

III. The State Takeover (AD 325 – 381)

AD 325: The Coup at Nicaea
Emperor **Constantine** seizes control of the church to force political unity. He imposes the unscriptural term *homoousios*. Dissenting bishops are **exiled**. Truth is now determined by majority vote and imperial threat at the Council of Nicaea.

AD 380–381: Theodosius & State Terror
Emperor **Theodosius** issues the Edict of Thessalonica, branding non-Trinitarians as "insane." He expels Bishop **Demophilus** at sword-point. The Trinity is finally codified, not by Scripture, but by the threat of **Civil Death**.

IV. The Restoration (Present Day)

AD 1901: The RV Breaks Silence
A forensic breakthrough. The Revised Version restores the Divine Name **Jehovah** (God) to the Old Testament, exposing the "Lord" cover-up and distinguishing the Father from the Son.

Today: The One God Study Bible
The **Chain of Custody** is fully reconnected. This edition completes the restoration by returning the Covenant Name **Yahweh** (God) to the text. By stripping away the philosophical overlay, the reader is returned to the original AD 30 baseline: One God, the Father, and one Lord, Jesus Christ.

SUMMARY STATEMENT

The doctrine of the Trinity was not explicitly taught by Jesus or the Apostles. It developed gradually over centuries as the church moved from its Jewish roots into the world of Greek philosophy.

Selected Bibliography

Lexicons and Grammars

Bauer, Arndt, Gingrich, Danker (BAGD). *A Greek-English Lexicon of the New Testament and Other Early Christian Literature.* University of Chicago Press, 1979.

Brown, Driver, and Briggs (BDB). *A Hebrew and English Lexicon of the Old Testament.* Hendrickson Publishers, 1996.

Thayer, Joseph H. *A Greek-English Lexicon of the New Testament.* Hendrickson Publishers, 1996.

Unger, Merrill F. *The New Unger's Bible Dictionary.* Moody Publishers, 2006.

Textual Criticism & Translation

Abegg, Martin; Flint, Peter; & Ulrich, Eugene. *The Dead Sea Scrolls Bible: The Oldest Known Bible Translated for the First Time into English.* HarperOne, 1999.

BeDuhn, Jason. *Truth in Translation: Accuracy and Bias in English Translations of the New Testament.* University Press of America, 2003.

Comfort, Philip W. *New Testament Text and Translation Commentary.* Tyndale House Publishers, 2008.

Daniell, David. *The Bible in English: Its History and Influence.* Yale University Press, 2003.

Ehrman, Bart D. *The Orthodox Corruption of Scripture: The Effect of Early Christological Controversies on the Text of the New Testament.* Oxford University Press, 1993.

Ehrman, Bart D. *Forged: Writing in the Name of God—Why the Bible's Authors Are Not Who We Think They Are.* HarperOne, 2011.

Ehrman, Bart D. *Misquoting Jesus: The Story Behind Who Changed the Bible and Why.* HarperSanFrancisco, 2005.

Kelly, Robert & Anne (Eds.). *The Four Gospels in Four Historic Translations.* 2023.

Metzger, Bruce M. *A Textual Commentary on the Greek New Testament.* United Bible Societies, 1994.

Theology, History, & Monotheism

Berlin, Adele & Brettler, Marc Zvi (Eds.). *The Jewish Study Bible: Second Edition.* Oxford University Press, 2014.

Buzzard, Anthony. *The Doctrine of the Trinity: Christianity's Self-Inflicted Wound.* International Scholars Publications, 1998.

Buzzard, Anthony. *The One: In Defense of God.* Restoration Fellowship.

Buzzard, Anthony. *Jesus Was Not a Trinitarian.* Restoration Fellowship, 2007.

Deuble, Greg. *They Never Told Me This in Church.* Restoration Fellowship, 2006.

Dunn, James D.G. *Christology in the Making: A New Testament Inquiry on the Origins of the Doctrine of the Incarnation.* Eerdmans, 1996.

Fredriksen, Paula. *From Jesus to Christ: The Origins of the New Testament Images of Christ.* Yale University Press, 2000.

Grant, Robert M. *Gods and the One God.* Westminster John Knox Press, 1986.

Hanson, R.P.C. *The Search for the Christian Doctrine of God: The Arian Controversy 318-381.* Baker Academic, 2005.

Kugel, James L. *The God of Old: Inside the Lost World of the Bible.* Free Press, 2003.

Levine, Amy-Jill & Brettler, Marc Zvi (Eds.). *The Jewish Annotated New Testament.* Oxford University Press, 2011.

Navas, Patrick. *Divine Truth or Human Tradition? A Reconsideration of the Roman Catholic-Protestant Doctrine of the Trinity in Light of the Hebrew and Christian Scriptures.* AuthorHouse, 2006.

Newton, Isaac. *An Historical Account of Two Notable Corruptions of Scripture.* (1754).

Ohlig, Karl-Heinz. *One or Three? From the Father of Jesus to the Trinity.* Peter Lang Inc., 2003.

Rubenstein, Richard E. *When Jesus Became God: The Struggle to Define Christianity during the Last Days of Rome.* Harcourt, 1999.

Sanders, E.P. *Jesus and Judaism.* Fortress Press, 1985.

Servetus, Michael. *On the Errors of the Trinity.* (1531).

Vermes, Geza. *Jesus the Jew: A Historian's Reading of the Gospels.* Fortress Press, 1981.

Whidden, Woodrow; Moon, Jerry; & Reeve, John. *The Trinity: Understanding God's Love, His Plan of Salvation, and Christian Relationships.* Review and Herald, 2002. (Referenced for historical contrast).

Wright, N.T. *Surprised by Hope: Rethinking Heaven, the Resurrection, and the Mission of the Church.* HarperOne, 2008.

Zarley, Kermit. *The Restitution of Jesus Christ.* Servetus the Evangelical, 2008.

Recommended Reading Guide

For those who wish to dig deeper, these volumes are the best place to start:

1599 Geneva Bible: Patriots Edition (Tolle Lege Press)
ISBN: 979-8994331606
Why read it? Before the King authorized his version, this was the Bible of the Puritans and the Pilgrims. It was the first English Bible to use verse numbers and study notes—notes that so infuriated King James with their "seditious" anti-monarchy tone that he commissioned the KJV specifically to replace it. A crucial piece of the rebel history.

Bible in English, The: Its History and Influence (David Daniell)
ISBN: 978-0300099300
Why read it? The gold standard of Tyndale scholarship. Professor Daniell was the Chairman of the Tyndale Society and the man most responsible for restoring Tyndale's reputation in the 20th century. He provides the academic proof for the "Royal Heist," demonstrating that 83% of the KJV New Testament is actually Tyndale's work—word for word—without credit. He validates the thesis that the KJV translators were essentially a committee polishing the work of a murdered genius.

Divine Truth or Human Tradition? (Patrick Navas)
Why read it? A comprehensive, gentle, yet devastating examination of the Trinity doctrine. Navas systematically dismantles the "proof texts" used by modern apologists, showing how they contradict the plain words of Jesus.

Doctrine of the Trinity, The: Christianity's Self-Inflicted Wound (Anthony Buzzard)
Why read it? The definitive history of how the church moved from the Hebrew Shema ("The Lord is One") to the Greek metaphysics of the Trinity. It traces the shift century by century.

Early Christian Reader (Steve Mason & Tom Robinson)
ISBN: 1-56563-043-2
Why read it? Experience the evidence raw. Mason and Robinson strip away the artificial chapter numbers and church headings, presenting the documents in chronological order (Mark first). Read the letters as they arrived in history—before the Church added 1,000 years of tradition.

Four Gospels, The: Each in Four Historic Translations (Kelly)
Versions Included: Tyndale (1526), The Great Bible (1539), The Bishop's Bible (1568), KJV (1611).
ISBN: 979-8377823148
Why read it? The physical evidence of the crime. By placing Tyndale (1526) side-by-side with the KJV (1611), the plagiarism becomes undeniable. Act as the juror: scan the columns and see exactly where the King's men copied the martyr's work—and where they surgically altered the definitions to protect the Crown.

Foxe's Book of Martyrs (John Foxe)
ISBN: 978-0882708751
Why read it? The forensic context of the Bible is blood. Foxe documents the specific trials of the men and women burned alive for the crime of owning English Scripture. The freedom to read was bought at a lethal price; this book is the receipt.

Jewish Study Bible, The (Berlin & Brettler)
Why read it? To understand the Old Testament, you must read it through Hebrew eyes. This volume shows how the original audience understood "The Suffering Servant" and "The Messiah" without reading Jesus back into the text.

One God, the Father, One Man Messiah Translation, The (2nd Ed.) (Anthony Buzzard)
ISBN: 978-0578716077
Why read it? Standard translations are filtered through 4th-century dogma. Buzzard strips away the "capitalization bias" (John 1:1) and restores the original Hebrew monotheistic perspective. A critical tool for seeing the text before the Nicean Council colonized it.

Orthodox Corruption of Scripture, The (Bart Ehrman)
Why read it? A scholarly look at how early scribes intentionally changed the Bible text (like 1 Timothy 3:16) to make Jesus appear to be God, creating "proofs" that were not in the original manuscripts.

They Never Told Me This in Church! (Greg Deuble)
Why read it? Written by a former Trinitarian pastor, this is the most accessible and relatable book for someone struggling with the cognitive dissonance of the Trinity. It reads like a conversation, not a textbook.

Truth in Translation (Jason BeDuhn)
Why read it? A secular linguist compares the major Bible translations (KJV, NIV, NASB, NW) on key verses. It objectively exposes where theological bias has trumped Greek grammar. Essential for understanding *why* your Bible might be misleading you.

Glossary of Essential Terms

Adonai vs. Adoni
A critical distinction in Hebrew often lost in English. *Adonai* is the title "Lord" applied exclusively to God (Yahweh). *Adoni* (with a different vowel point) means "my lord" and is used 195 times in the OT, always referring to a human or angelic superior (like a king or master), never to God. In Psalm 110:1 ("The LORD said to my Lord"), the second word is *adoni*, indicating the Messiah is a human king, not God.

Agency (Shaliah)
The Jewish legal principle that "a man's agent is as himself." In the Bible, God often acts through agents (angels, prophets, the Messiah). When an agent speaks or acts, they carry the full authority of the sender. This explains why Jesus can forgive sins or judge the world—not because he is God, but because God has given him that authority (John 5:27).

Alexandrian Text-Type
The family of New Testament manuscripts that originated in Egypt (Alexandria). These are generally the *oldest* and most accurate manuscripts we possess (e.g., Codex Sinaiticus, Codex Vaticanus), dating from the 4th century. Modern Bibles (NIV, NASB, ESV) are based on these texts. They often lack the later Trinitarian additions found in the *Byzantine Text*.

Apocrypha
From the Greek for "hidden." A collection of ancient Jewish books written between the Old and New Testaments (e.g., Maccabees, Tobit). While valuable for history, they were never accepted as inspired scripture (*Canon*) by the Jewish community or the Protestant church.

Apostles' Creed
The earliest statement of Christian faith, likely dating to the 2nd century. Unlike later creeds, it is entirely Biblical and Non-Trinitarian. It affirms faith in "God the Father Almighty" and "Jesus Christ his only Son our Lord," but makes no claim that Jesus is God or of one substance with the Father.

Arianism
The theological position of Arius (c. 250–336 AD), a presbyter of Alexandria who taught that the Son was a created being ("There was a time when he was not") and distinct from the Father. This was the dominant view of many Christians before it was declared a "heresy" at the Council of Nicaea by political force.

GLOSSARY

Arius
(c. 250–336 AD). The Alexandrian presbyter who championed the strict Monotheism of the Bible against the emerging Trinitarian innovations of Athanasius. He argued that if the Father begat the Son, the Son had a beginning. He was exiled, and his books were burned, but his arguments remain the foundation of Biblical Monotheism.

Byzantine Text-Type / Majority Text
The family of manuscripts copied in the Byzantine Empire during the Middle Ages (5th–15th centuries). While there are more of them (the "majority"), they are much younger and contain many "smoothing" edits and theological additions accumulated over centuries. The King James Version (KJV) is based on this later, less accurate text type.

Canon
From the Greek *kanon*, meaning "measuring rod" or "standard." It refers to the official list of books accepted as the inspired, authoritative Word of God.

Christology
The theological study of the person, nature, and role of Jesus Christ. "High Christology" typically refers to the view that Jesus is God; "Biblical Christology" focuses on his role as the Messiah and the Son of God.

Comma Johanneum (The Johannine Comma)
A famous textual forgery in 1 John 5:7–8 found in the King James Version: *"For there are three that bear record in heaven, the Father, the Word, and the Holy Ghost: and these three are one."* This phrase is absent from every Greek manuscript before the 14th century and was never quoted by early Church Fathers during the Trinity debates. It was added to the Latin text later and forced into the Greek text in the 1500s due to church pressure.

Consubstantial (Homoousios)
A non-biblical Greek philosophical term introduced at the Council of Nicaea (325 AD) to claim that the Son is of the "same substance" as the Father. This word is not found in Scripture.

Critical (Textual Criticism)
In biblical studies, the word "Critical" does not mean negative or judgmental. It means "analytical" or "careful evaluation." A "Critical Text" is one that has been carefully examined, comparing thousands of manuscripts to filter out scribal errors and restore the original words of the authors.

Echad
The Hebrew word for "one." While some claim it implies a "compound unity" (like one cluster of grapes), in standard Hebrew grammar it is the numerical adjective "one" (cardinal number). When God says "Jehovah is one (*echad*)" in the Shema, it denotes singularity and uniqueness, not plurality.

Elohim

The standard Hebrew word for "God" or "gods." While usually referring to the One God (Yahweh), it is a functional title meaning "Mighty One" or "Ruler." In the Bible, it is occasionally applied to humans, judges, and kings (e.g., Psalm 82:6, Exodus 7:1) who act as God's representatives. Therefore, calling the Messiah *elohim* (as in Psalm 45/Hebrews 1) does not necessarily mean he is the Creator, but that he is God's supreme King.

Forgery (Pseudepigrapha)

From the Greek *pseudes* (false) and *epigraphos* (superscription). The practice of writing a document in the name of a famous figure (like Paul or Peter) to give the writing apostolic authority. This was a common literary device in the ancient world. Critical scholars widely agree that books such as 1 & 2 Timothy, Titus, and 2 Peter are "forgeries" in this sense—written by later church leaders using the apostles' names to combat 2nd-century heresies.

Granville Sharp Rule

A grammatical rule proposed by abolitionist Granville Sharp in 1798. It claims that when two titles are joined by "and" (Greek *kai*) under one article, they refer to the same person (e.g., Titus 2:13 "the God and Savior"). However, this rule works primarily for personal names and has valid exceptions. It is often used as a "silver bullet" to prove Jesus is God, even though alternate translations ("The Great God *and* our Savior") are grammatically valid and fit the context better.

Hypostatic Union

The official Trinitarian doctrine established at the Council of Chalcedon (451 AD), which states that Jesus is "fully God" and "fully man" simultaneously, in two distinct natures but one person. This philosophical concept is not found in the Bible and was developed to explain away the logical contradictions of Trinitarianism (e.g., how God could die, or how Jesus could not know the hour of his return).

Incarnation

Literally "ensoulment in flesh." Traditional theology teaches that a pre-existent divine person (God the Son) entered a human body. The Biblical view is that the "Word" (God's plan/wisdom) became flesh (John 1:14)—meaning God's promise became a reality in the person of Jesus. Jesus did not exist as a person before his conception; he existed in the foreknowledge and plan of God.

Interpolation

A passage of text that was not written by the original author but was inserted by a later scribe, either accidentally (copying a margin note into the text) or intentionally (to support a theological doctrine). The *Comma Johanneum* is a classic example of a Trinitarian interpolation.

Logos
Greek for "Word," "Reason," or "Plan." In John 1:1 ("In the beginning was the Word..."), this refers to God's self-expression and creative plan. In Jewish thought, God's Word/Wisdom is often personified (Proverbs 8), but it is not a separate person. The "Word became flesh" (John 1:14) means God's plan was embodied in the human person of Jesus, not that a pre-existent spirit being floated down from heaven.

Monogenes
A Greek word often translated "Only Begotten" (KJV) but more accurately meaning "Unique" or "One of a Kind" (NASB/ESV). Trinitarians use "Only Begotten" to support the idea of "Eternal Generation." However, in the Bible, Isaac is called Abraham's *monogenes* (Heb 11:17) even though Abraham had other sons, because Isaac was the unique son of the promise. Jesus is God's unique Son, not a "generated" God.

Monotheism
The belief that there is only one God. Biblical Monotheism specifically identifies this One God as the Father alone (John 17:3, 1 Cor 8:6), distinguishing Him from His Son, Jesus Christ.

Newton, Isaac
(1642–1727). The renowned scientist was also a fervent, secret Anti-Trinitarian. He wrote extensively on the corruptions of Scripture, famously exposing the forgery of 1 John 5:7 and 1 Timothy 3:16 in his *Historical Account of Two Notable Corruptions of Scripture*. He believed the Trinity was a later corruption of the true faith.

Nicene Creed
The statement of faith adopted at the Council of Nicaea (325 AD). It was the first official creed to define the Son as *homoousios* (of one substance) with the Father, marking the official shift from Biblical language to Greek philosophical language in defining God.

Nomina Sacra
Literally "Sacred Names." A scribal practice in early Greek manuscripts of abbreviating holy titles. For example, "God" (*Theos*) was written as $\Theta\Sigma$ and "Lord" (*Kyrios*) as $K\Sigma$ with a line over the top. This practice sometimes creates confusion, such as in 1 Timothy 3:16, where the word "He who" ($O\Sigma$) was altered by a later scribe adding a line to make it look like the abbreviation for God ($\Theta\Sigma$).

Pantokrator
A Greek title meaning "Almighty" or "Ruler of All." In the New Testament (especially Revelation), this title is used almost exclusively for the Father (God). Confusion arises because some translations blur the distinction between the "Almighty" (The Father) and titles like "Alpha and Omega" or "First and Last" (titles sometimes shared or used for Jesus in different contexts).

Paraclete (Parakletos)

Greek for "Advocate," "Helper," or "Comforter." In John's Gospel, Jesus promises to send "another Paraclete" (the Spirit). Trinitarians argue this proves the Spirit is a person. However, 1 John 2:1 explicitly calls **Jesus** our "Paraclete" with the Father. The Spirit is not a third person; it is the presence of God/Christ functioning as our Helper, just as Jesus did while on earth.

Pre-existence (Ideal vs. Literal)

"Literal Pre-existence" is the belief that Jesus existed as a spirit being before he was born. "Ideal Pre-existence" (common in Jewish thought) is the belief that the Messiah existed in God's plan and foreknowledge before creation. When Jesus speaks of the "glory I had with you before the world was" (John 17:5), he is referring to the glory God had stored up/predestined for him, similar to how believers are said to be "chosen before the foundation of the world" (Eph 1:4) without literally existing back then.

Proskuneo (Worship)

The Greek word often translated as "Worship." It literally means "to bow down" or "prostrate oneself." In the Bible, it is used for God, but also for kings, masters, and prophets (e.g., David is "worshipped" in 1 Chron 29:20). When people bow to Jesus, they are often paying him homage as God's Messiah/King, not worshipping him as the Creator. Context determines the meaning.

Prototokos (Firstborn)

A Greek title applied to Jesus (Col 1:15). While Trinitarians interpret this as "Eternally Begotten," the biblical usage often refers to rank, supremacy, and inheritance rights, not biological birth order. David, the youngest son, was named God's "firstborn" (Ps 89:27) because he was the pre-eminent king. Jesus is the "Firstborn of all creation" because he is the supreme heir of God's world.

Ruach / Pneuma (Spirit)

The Hebrew (*Ruach*) and Greek (*Pneuma*) words translated as "Spirit." Both words primarily mean "wind," "breath," or "blast." In the Bible, the Holy Spirit is the invisible, active power and presence of God, not a separate person. It is God in action (Genesis 1:2).

Septuagint (LXX)

The ancient Greek translation of the Hebrew Old Testament, completed around 200 BC. It was the "Bible" used by the apostles and New Testament writers. Understanding the LXX is critical because it often uses different words than the Hebrew text (e.g., Isaiah 7:14 uses *parthenos* "virgin" in Greek, while the Hebrew used *almah* "young woman").

Servetus, Michael

(1511–1553). A Spanish physician and theologian who was the first major figure of the Reformation to openly reject the Trinity in his book *On the Errors of the Trinity*. He was arrested by John Calvin in Geneva and burned at the stake for his strict Monotheism, becoming a martyr for the cause.

Shema

The central confession of Jewish faith, found in Deuteronomy 6:4: "Hear (*Shema*), O Israel: Jehovah our God is one Jehovah." It is a declaration of strict unitary monotheism. Jesus affirmed this as the "First of all the commandments" (Mark 12:29).

Socinianism

A non-Trinitarian Christian theology named after Faustus Socinus (16th century). It teaches that Jesus was a human being who did not exist before his birth, but was conceived by the Holy Spirit and later exalted by God. This view aligns closely with Biblical Monotheism.

Son of Man

Jesus' favorite self-designation, occurring 81 times in the Gospels. While often mistaken as a reference to his humanity, it is a direct reference to **Daniel 7:13**, where a human figure ("son of man") rides the clouds to God's throne to receive universal dominion. It is a claim to be the divine Vice-Regent and Judge of the world.

Subordinationism

The theological view that the Son is distinct from and subordinate to the Father in nature and authority. This was the dominant view of the early church Fathers (like Tertullian and Origen) before the Council of Nicaea enforced the idea of co-equality.

Textus Receptus (TR)

Latin for "Received Text." The name given to the succession of printed Greek texts of the New Testament (starting with Erasmus in 1516) that formed the basis for the King James Version (1611). It was compiled from a small number of late medieval manuscripts (Byzantine text-type) available at the time. While historically important, it contains readings and theological additions (like the *Comma Johanneum*) that are not found in the older, more reliable Alexandrian manuscripts.

Theopneustos

Greek for "God-breathed" (2 Timothy 3:16). It refers to the divine inspiration of the Scriptures. Biblically, it is the *message* and the *prophets* that were inspired by God's Spirit, ensuring the truth of the revelation, distinct from the later church councils which claimed authority to interpret it.

Trinity
The theological doctrine that God exists as three distinct persons (Father, Son, and Holy Spirit) who are co-equal, co-eternal, and of one substance. This word does not appear in the Bible. The concept was developed gradually over several centuries, culminating in the Councils of Nicaea (325 AD) and Constantinople (381 AD), often blending biblical titles with Greek philosophy to combat strict Monotheism.

Tyndale, William
(c. 1494–1536). The "Father of the English Bible." An Oxford scholar and linguistic genius who was the first to translate the Bible into English directly from the original Hebrew and Greek. He was strangled and burned at the stake for his work. His translation forms roughly 83% of the King James New Testament, though the KJV translators did not give him credit.

Unitarianism
The theological belief that God is one person (the Father) rather than three. Biblical Unitarians believe Jesus is the Son of God and the Messiah, but not God Himself. This view relies on the explicit statements of Jesus (e.g., John 17:3) and distinguishes itself from "Universalism" (the belief that all will be saved).

Vulgate
The Latin translation of the Bible produced by Jerome in the late 4th century. It became the official Bible of the Roman Catholic Church for over a thousand years. Tyndale's life work was to overthrow the authority of the Vulgate (which the common people couldn't understand) and replace it with the Greek/Hebrew truth in the language of the ploughboy.

Yahweh (Jehovah)
The personal proper name of God in the Old Testament, represented by the four Hebrew letters YHWH (Tetragrammaton). It appears nearly 7,000 times in the Hebrew text. Most translations hide this name behind the title "LORD" (in all caps). Restoring the name is essential to understanding the distinction between "Yahweh" (The Father) and "Adoni" (The Messiah) in passages like Psalm 110:1.

Subject and Word Index

1 Cor 15:28 (The Final Proof), 473
1 Cor 8:6 (Creation Formula), 469, 507
1 John 5:7 (Zero Greek MSS), 470
1 Timothy 3:16 (God Manifest Variant), 479
1 Timothy 3:16 (The Ink Blot), 471
1536 Heist: State Theft of Code, 27
1599 Date (Smuggling Trick), 402
311-Day Betrayal (From Execution to License), 402, 500
345-Year State Cover-Up, 27
36 Dissenters (Eleusius), 393
83.7% Match: Forensic Proof, 27

Accuracy vs Agenda (Worship), 477
Act for the Advancement of True Religion (1543), 402
Adam (Humanity Collective), 489
Adams, John, 497
Adams, John (Republican Book Quote), 402
Adulterous Connection (The Sin), 497
Agency
    Law of, 430
Agency (Di' autou - Channel), 469
Agency Bridge (Historical), 495
Alethinos, 434
Alexandria (The Crime Scene), 439
Alexandrian Text (Oldest), 470
Alexandrian Text (The Cure), 476
Allegorical Method (Virus), 439
Allegory (Clerical Weapon), 40
Allen, Ethan, 497
Alpha and Omega (Shared), 464
Ambassador Analogy (Role), 448
Ambassador vs. King, 431
American Founding (Geneva Legacy), 402
American Revision Committee, 20
American Revision Committee (Translators), 44
American Revision Committee (Unanimous Conviction), 47
Ancient Authorities (Oldest Manuscripts), 44
Ancient of Days (Supreme Court), 481
Angel of the LORD (Agency), 453
Angel of the Lord (Name in Him), 473
Anti-Slavery Marginal Notes, 402
Antioch, 433
    Arian Majority, 435
Apostle (Jesus as Apostle), 449
Apostle (Jesus' Job Title), 472
Architect (The Father), 469
Arianism (Theological), 432
Aristotle, 437
Arius, 434
Article VI (No Religious Test), 499
Aryanism (Racial Smear), 432
Athanasius, 434
    Letter to Serapion, 434
Athens vs. Jerusalem (Mindset), 437
Atomized Individual (Myth), 441
Attic Greek (Academy), 437
Attributes vs Personhood, 467
Audit of the Ages (Prophecy Evidence), 492
Augustus (The Counterfeit Son), 492
Authorized (Politically Correct Plagiarism), 402, 500

Bar Enosh (Human vs Beast), 481
Beasts (Political Monsters), 481
Bereans (The Duty to Verify), 19
Bible of the Pilgrims (Geneva 1560), 402
Biblical Monotheism, 430
Bishop of London (Censorship Palace), 40

Bishops' Bible (1568), 27
Blasphemy (The Fatal Claim), 482
Blind Man (Said I Am), 464, 468
Block Logic (Paradox), 440
Bloody Mary (Queen Mary I), 402
Blueprint (Accuracy as Worship), 477
Blueprint (En Auto - Locative), 469
Book Burning (389 AD), 395
Botched Execution (Oops. Burn him alive), 500
Brain Transplant, 433
Brain Transplant (Theology), 439
Burned Alive (The Price of Dissent), 496

Caiaphas (Political Preservation), 493
Caiaphas (The Death Warrant), 482
Catholic (Trademarking of), 392
Chain of Agency (You), 465
Chain of Command (Creation), 469
Chain of Custody (Historical), 495
Chain of Custody (Restored), 12, 508
Channel (Dia), 469
Charles the V, Roman Emperor (Killer), 500
Christ (Anointed King), 489
Chronos (Greek Linear Time), 444
Church Fathers, 433
Church vs. Congregation (The Word Flip), 402
Civil Death (Infamia), 392
Civil Death (The Penalty), 508
Civilizational Catastrophe, 390
Clement of Alexandria (Iaoue), 477
Cloud Rider (Yahweh Prerogative), 482
Codex Theodosianus, 394
Col 1:16 (Prepositions En/Dia), 478
Collusion (Evidence of Fraud), 485
Colossians 1:16 (Agency), 469
Colwell's Rule (Theological Patch), 467
Commentary (Signal vs Noise), 21
Conformity (State-Mandated), 390

Constantine, 432
Constantine (The Enforcer), 508
Constitution of the Apostles, 435
Constitutional Court (The Rigged Trial), 493
Constitutional Republic (Geneva Foundation), 402
Corporate Sabotage (Catch & Kill), 27
Corporate Solidarity (Adam), 441
Council of Nicaea (The Political Coup), 508
Council of Tarragona (8-Day Decree), 397
Council of Toulouse (Bible Ban), 396
Covenant Theology (Mayflower Compact), 402
Coverdale Bible (1535), 27
Coverdale, Miles (The Great Bible), 402
Crown Piracy (The 1537 Smoking Gun), 500
Crown Piracy: Identity Theft, 27
Cunctos Populos (The Edict), 392

Dabar, 433, 445
Dabar (Ballistic Word), 441
Daniel 7 (The Magna Carta), 481
Declaration of Independence (The Four Titles), 498
Definite Article (Ton), 467
Demiurge, 433, 445
Demolition Teams, 394
Demophilus, 394
Demophilus (The Last Bishop), 508
Deuteros Theos (The Second God Heresy), 507
Didache (The Non-Trinitarian Manual), 507
Divine Agent, 446
Divine Name (Covenant vs Abstract), 47
Divine Power of Attorney (Agency), 472
Due Process (Assault on), 393
Dunghill (Platonic Philosophy), 498

Easter Anomaly (Acts 12:4), 402

Subject and Word Index

Echad, 433, 445
Echad (Numerical Singularity vs Compound), 488
Echad (Numerical Singularity), 489
Echad (Singular Loyalty), 443
Edict of Thessalonica, 391
Edict of Thessalonica (The State Weapon), 508
Ego Eimi (Grammar), 464, 468
Eleusius of Cyzicus, 393
Elohim (Title of Authority), 451
Emancipation Proclamation, 435
Empty Tomb (Corroborating Evidence), 487
Emunah (Active Loyalty), 444
Essence vs Authority (Greek), 446
Eternal Generation, 433
Eternal Generation (The Philosophical Addition), 507
Euzoius of Antioch, 433
Evidentiary Audit (Forensic), 467
Exile (The Price of Dissent), 508
Exodus 3:14 (Title: Ho On), 468

Faith (Loyalty and Fidelity), 489
False Equation (Jesus = Father), 467
Federal Head, 441
Felony (1616 Possession Ban), 402
Financial Freedom (to Believe), 26
Financial Terror (Section III), 394
Fingerprints of the Martyr (W.T. Woodcuts), 500
First Amendment (The Shield), 499
Firstborn (Heir), 461
Foreknowledge (Ideal), 468
Forensic Advisory, 446
Forensic Breach (Athens/Judea), 437
Forensic Evidence, 442
Forensic Forgeries (Overview), 470
Forensic Mandate (Manifesto), 12
Forensic Precision, 20
Forensic Report, 430
Forgiveness (Delegated), 459
Four-Car Crash (Witness Independence), 485
Franklin, Benjamin, 497
Franklin, Benjamin (Great Seal Design), 402
Freedom of Conscience, 390
Function (Hebrew) vs Essence, 438

Geese and Cranes (Confession), 393
Genealogies (Legal vs Biological), 485
Geneva Bible (1560): The People's Bible, 402
Geneva Bible (Suppression), 400
Geneva Bible (The Rebel Bible), 402
Geneva Bible: The People's Bible, 27
George III (Modern Pharaoh), 402
Ghost Hands, 435
Ghost in the Machine (Error), 442
Gobineau, Arthur de, 432
God-Man (The Greek Patch), 447
Gothic Blackletter vs. Roman Typeface, 402
Goths, 392
Government Mandate, 390
Great Bible (1539): Chained Word, 27
Great Substitution (Kurios), 443
Greek Occupation, 434
Greek Philosophy (Wrong Map), 446
Gregory of Nazianzus, 393

Harold Monser (1910 Cross-Reference Bible), 402
Hen, 433, 445
Henry VIII, King (The Authorized Rebrand), 500
Herod (The Usurper King), 492
High Court of Scripture, 434
High Priest, 449

History by Victors (Bias), 475
History of the Bible
    Corruption of Scripture, 510, 512
    Council of Nicaea, 510
    Daniell, David, 509
    Early Manuscripts, 512
    Geneva Bible, 511
    Martyrs, 512
    The Bible in English (Daniell), 511
    Translation Bias, 509
    Tyndale Heritage Proof, 509, 512
Ho On (The Missing Title), 468
Homoousios (Same Substance), 438, 448
Homoousios (The Unscriptural Term), 508
Hostile Displacement (Greek), 437
Hostile Takeover, 430
House Demolition (Canon 6), 397
Humanity of Jesus (Evidence), 447
Hypostasis, 433, 445
Hypostatic Union (Abstract), 441

I AM (Identity Theft), 464
I.R. Initials (John Rogers' Secret Signature), 500
Icons, 440
ICRE (The ASV Switch), 27
Identity of God, 21
Identity Theft, 433
Identity Theft (The Swap), 437, 442
Identity Theft (Theological), 468
Identity Theft: 1536 Execution, 27
In Persona Dei (Acting as), 452
Infamia, 392
Infiltrators, 433
Inherited Lies, 390
Ink Analysis (Forensic Proof), 471
Inquisitores, 394
Intellectual Pedigree of Dissent, 495
Interpolations (Bible Vandalism), 470

Jacob's Ladder (The Interface), 483
James I, King (The 1611 Identity Theft), 500
Jefferson Bible (Forensic Audit), 498
Jefferson, Thomas, 498
Jehovah (Hybrid Error), 478
Jehovah (Memorial Name Restored), 47
Jehovah (RV Restoration), 508
Jehovah's Witnesses (Not Affiliated), 477
Jesus (The Anti-Usurper), 458
Jesus (The Supreme Agent), 446
Jesus (Vice-Regent), 450
Jewish Superstition (Suppressed Name), 47
Johannine Comma, 435
Johannine Comma (Famous Forgery), 470, 479
John 10:30 (Unity of Purpose), 473
John 17:3 (The Definition of God), 507
John 1:1 (Qualitative Grammar), 467
John 1:18 (Unique God), 478
John 8:58 (Identity Theft), 468
John the Baptist (The Herald), 485
Joseph Protocol (Delegated), 450
Judges (Called Gods), 452
Judgment (Delegated Authority), 473
Judgment (Delegated Role), 460
Judgment (Restoring Order), 490
Justification (Legal Status), 490
Justin Martyr, 431, 433
Justin Martyr (The Second God Theorist), 507

Key of Knowledge (Stolen), 26
King James (1611): The Rebrand, 27
King James I (The 1611 Identity Theft), 402
King James: Stolen Bible Choice, 27
Kingdom (The Final Settlement), 490, 493
Koine Greek (Marketplace), 437
Kurios (Generic Title), 443

Subject and Word Index

Law of Agency, 19
Law of Agency (The Key), 446
Lawful Disobedience (Hebrew Midwives), 402
Legal Maxim (Agent = Sender), 472
Legate, Bartholomew (Martyr), 399
Linguistic Bias (Distortion), 21, 488
Linguistic Treason (Anti-State Speech), 492
Literary Cleansing (Arson), 395
Locke, John, 496
Lockman Foundation, 20
Locusts (Anti-Clergy Insult), 402
Logical Contradiction, 467
Logical Contradictions, 447
Logos, 433, 445
Logos (Abstract Reason), 441
Logos (Expression vs Person), 489
Loyalty Test (National), 392
Lucian of Antioch, 495
Luke 2:33 (Censoring Joseph), 475

Majority Standard, 431
Malakh (Messenger), 453
Managed Obsolescence (Strategy), 27
Marginal Note (Virus in Text), 470
Mark 12:29 (Jesus' Creed), 507
Mark 14 (The Atomic Fuse), 482
Masking of the Name (YHWH), 443
Master Workman (Christ), 469
Maternus Cynegius (Enforcer), 394
Mathematical Fraud (19.35%), 393
Matt 24:36 (The Deleted Son), 475
Matthew Bible (1537): State Piracy, 27
Matthew Bible (The 1537 Underground Endorsement), 500
Mayflower (Exclusively Geneva), 402
Mediator (Function), 454
Messiah (Davidic Agent), 490
Messiah (Service Before Glory), 483

Micah 5:2 (Olam vs Eternal), 478
Micro-Details (Variance vs Error), 485
Microscopic Sabotage (Hunting Heresy), 40
Miracles (Universal Attestation), 486
Miscreants
    Theological, 435
Mishnah, 448
Moed (Divine Appointment), 444, 493
Monkery (J. Adams Trinity Insult), 497
Monos, 434
Monotheism (Biblical vs Creedal), 477
Monotheism (Unanimous Verdict), 485
Moses (Called Elohim), 473
Moses (Called God), 451
Mother Tongue (Translation Rights), 39
My God (Jesus' Prayer), 447
My Name is in Him (Agent), 453
Mystery
    Invention of, 395

Name (Authority and Presence), 490
National Charter, 430
Newton, Sir Isaac, 435, 496
Nicaea (The Silence of Fathers), 470
Nicaea, Council of, 432
Nicholas of Myra, 435
NIV (Dynamic Bias), 478
Nomina Sacra (The Scribal Code), 471

Occam's Razor (Forensic Verdict), 27
Occupying Force (The Roman Army), 492
Olam (Fence Posts Analogy), 478
Omniscience (Forced Doctrine), 476
One God Publishing (2026), 27
One Simple Literal Sense, 40
Only True God, 434, 465
Ontology (Greek Obsession), 438
Order over Evidence (The Pilate Cowardice), 492

Origen, 431, 433
Origen (The Allegorist), 439
Origen (The Platonic Vector), 507
Original Tongues (The Source), 44
Originator vs Instrument, 469

Paine, Thomas, 497
Pais (Jesus as Servant), 507
Paper Trail (The Evidence), 495
Paul (The Hebrew Monotheist), 507
Paul of Samosata, 495
Phil 2:6 (Harpagmos), 478
Philo (Plato's Student), 439
Pilate (State over Truth), 492
Pious Fraud (The "Improvement"), 475
Plagiarism
    Evidence of (Kelly), 509, 512
Plato, 433, 437
Platonism (The Pagan Metaphysics), 507
Ploughboy Vow (Tyndale), 402
Pneuma (Ghost in Machine), 442
Poison Pill (Asset Dumping), 27
Police-State Enforcement, 495
Portal (Jesus as the Doorway), 494
Power of Attorney (Divine), 448, 472
Power of Attorney (Shaliach), 441
Priority vs Deity, 468
Priscillian (First Blood), 391
Pronouns (Thee/Thou Accuracy), 20
Proper Noun (English Illusion), 467
Property Theft (380 AD), 394
Prophet like Moses (Deut 18), 454
Protecting the Deity (Motive), 475
Psalm 104 (Yahweh's Copyright), 482
Public Domain (1957), 27

Qualitative vs Identity, 467

Racovian Catechism, 496
Ransom (Blood Currency), 483
Razor (The Jefferson Audit), 498
Rebel Fatigues (The Geneva Legacy), 402
Redemption (Ransom Price), 490
Resurrection (Forensic Signature), 493
Revised Version (1881): Crown Correction, 27
Revised Version (1901 Legacy), 402
Revised Version (The Name Restored), 508
Rigged Election (381 AD), 393
Rigged Jury (The Sanhedrin Hit-Job), 492
Right to Testify (Stripped), 393
Righteousness (Covenant Fidelity), 490
Robertson, A.T. (Scholar), 20
Rock of Biblical Honesty, 20
Roman Law, 430
Royal Heist
    Academic Proof, 509
RSV (Branding Confusion), 27
Ruach, 433, 445
Ruach (Wind/Breath/Power), 442, 490
Rule #3: Vandalizing the Congregation, 402
Rule #6: Vandalizing the Word, 27
RV 1901 (Protestant Scholars), 477

Sacerdotal Imposture (Fraud), 497
Sacrilege Trap (Law 6.24.4), 395
Sanitization (Removing Hands), 439
Sant'Apollinare Nuovo, 435
Scottish Mandate (1579), 402
Seditious Marginal Notes (300,000 Words), 402
Seditious Scribes (Overview), 475
Sender vs Sent (Legal Status), 448
Septuagint, 443
Septuagint (Apostles' Bible), 468
Servetus, Michael, 495
Servetus, Michael (Execution), 398
Shaliach, 430
Shaliach (Power of Attorney), 446, 494

Shaliach (The Legal Key), 472
Shalom, 444
Shema, 430
Shema (Hearing the Truth), 440
Shema (Original Monotheism), 474, 488, 494, 507
Signal vs. Noise, 391
Signet Ring (Power Transfer), 450
Smoothness vs. Accuracy, 20
Son of God (Frequency), 480
Son of God (Office vs DNA), 488
Son of God (Royal Title), 490, 492
Son of Man (Human Title), 459
Son of Man (Statistical Anomaly), 480
Son of Man (The Camouflage), 480
Source (Ex), 469
Spiritual Murder (Heresy), 396
Standard American Edition (1901), 27
State Crime, 430
State Crime (Theology), 390
State Trooper (Legalism), 444
State-Mandated Class Ban (1543), 402
State-Mandated Clergy Paywall, 27
Status Quo (The Power-Grabbers), 493
Step Logic (Greek/Western), 440
Stephen (The Lone Witness), 480
Stolen Dictionary, 433
Strong's Concordance, 20
Strong, James (Concordance), 20
Stubborn Nimrods (The Prelates), 42
Subject unto Him (Eternal), 463
Summa Supplicium, 395
Supreme Agent, 431
Sword of Theodosius (State), 390
Sworn Testimony, 434
Synod of Verona (1184), 396

Tactical Note, 430
Talmud, 449
Temptation (The Proof of Agent), 485

Tertullian, 431, 437
Tertullian (The Coiner of Trinitas), 507
Testamentary Rights, 394
Testimony (Forensic Variation), 485
Tetragrammaton (1952 Reversal), 27
Textual Criticism
    Translation Bias, 513
Textual Purity (Warts and All), 476
Textual Variants, 21
Textus Receptus (Late Greek Text), 479
The Throne (Unified Focus), 485
Theodosius, 430
    Saint, 394
Theodosius (Tyrant), 390, 508
Theology
    Jewish Perspective, 512
    Monotheism, 512
    Trinity, 511, 513
Theos (Anarthrous = Nature), 467
Thomas (My Lord and God), 462
Thomas Matthew (The Alias that Fooled a King), 500
Thomas Matthew: The Piracy Alias, 27
Thomas Nelson (Monopoly Deal), 27
Thomas Nelson & Sons (1901 Publisher), 44
Three-Headed Cerberus (Trinity), 496
Time-Stamps (God's Calendar), 493
Torah (Father's Instruction), 444, 490
Totalitarian Theology, 390
Tradition (State-Mandated), 447
Transfiguration (Kingdom Preview), 486
Translation Bias
    BeDuhn, Jason, 509
Translation Bias (Theological), 478
Translator's Preface, 12
Treason, 431
Trial before Pilate, 486
Trinitarian Riddle (Paradox), 447

Trinitas (The Latin Invention), 507
Trojan Horse, 433
Trojan Horse Bibles (KJV Covers), 402
Tyndale New Testament (1526), 27
Tyndale Revision (1534), 27
Tyndale, William
    David Daniell Scholarship, 509
    Plagiarism Evidence, 509, 512
Tyndale, William (1530 Preface), 39
Tyndale, William (Execution), 398
Tyndale, William (The Ultimate Rebel), 402
Tyndale, William (W.T. Initials), 500
Tyndale: The 345-Year Erasure, 27

Ulfilas, 434
Unitarian Universalism
    rejected, 430
Unity (Function vs Essence), 455

Verdict (Not Scripture), 470

Verdict, The, 494
Vilvoorde, Belgium (Execution Location), 500
Visual Hijack (Gothic Font), 402
Visual Trick (God vs He Who), 471
Voter Suppression (Church), 393

W.T. Initials (Permanent Fingerprint), 500
Watchtower Deal (Poison Pill), 27
Weiglowa, Katarzyna (Martyr), 398
Wightman, Edward (Double Burning), 399
Woodcut Evidence (Forensic Proof), 500
Word (Active Expression), 491
Worship (Proskuneo Defined), 457
Worship (Royal Homage), 473

Yada (Relational Knowing), 444
Yahweh (Personal Name), 443
Yahweh (The Original Identity), 477, 508

Quick Reference Cheat Sheet

> **HOW TO USE THIS INDEX**
> The "Short Answer" below is only a summary. For the **Full Critical Commentary**, please turn to the **Page Number** (if listed) or refer to the **Volume Number** listed.

The Old Testament (See Volumes 1–3)

Genesis 1:26 (Let US make man) .... See Vol 1
God speaking to His Divine Council (Angels/Job 38:7), not a Trinity. Humans are made "lower than angels" (Ps 8:5).

Genesis 3:22 (Like one of US) .... See Vol 1
Addressed to the Angelic Host, who already possessed immortality and knowledge of good/evil.

Genesis 18:2 (Three Men) .... See Vol 1
Explicitly called "angels" in Gen 19:1. They represented Yahweh (Agency), they were not Him.

Genesis 19:24 (Jehovah from Jehovah) .... See Vol 1
A Hebrew idiom of self-reference ("The Lord did it Himself"). Same grammar used for human wives in 1 Kings 1:33.

Deuteronomy 6:4 (The Shema) .... See Vol 1
"Echad" is a numerical adjective (one), not a collective noun. It defines a single self, not a committee.

Psalm 2:12 (Kiss the Son) .... See Vol 3
Disputed Hebrew. Likely "Kiss purity" or "Homage to the King." Worship is reserved for Yahweh (v11).

Psalm 22:16 (Pierced my hands) .... See Vol 3
Masoretic Text reads "Like a lion." Even if "pierced," it describes the suffering Davidic King, not God dying.

Psalm 45:6 (Thy Throne O God) .... See Vol 3
The human King is called "god" (*elohim*) as a Judge/Ruler. Or: "God is thy throne forever."

Psalm 110:1 (Lord said to my Lord) .... See Vol 3
Yahweh speaks to *adoni* (human lord). If Jesus were God, the text would use *Adonai*. Distinction is absolute.

Proverbs 8:22 (Wisdom) .... See Vol 3
Wisdom is personified as a female figure created/possessed by God. It is God's plan, not a person.

Proverbs 30:4 (What is his Son's name?) .... See Vol 3
A riddle about the mystery of creation. Israel is called God's "Son" in Ex 4:22.

Isaiah 6:3 (Holy, Holy, Holy) .... See Vol 3
Hebrew superlative ("Super Holy"). The temple is "thrice built" (Jer 7:4) without being a Trinity.

Isaiah 9:6 (Mighty God) .... See Vol 3
Royal Title ("Divine Warrior"). King Hezekiah carried this name. Humans are called "gods" in Ps 82:6.

Isaiah 41:8 (Identity of the Servant) .... See Vol 3
Context defines "The Servant" as Israel (the people). Jesus fulfills this corporate role as the ideal Israelite.

Isaiah 48:16 (Sent Me and His Spirit) .... See Vol 3
Grammar: "God has sent [Me and His Spirit]." The Spirit is a sent power, not the sender.

Isaiah 53:10 (Suffering Servant) .... See Vol 3
God (The Crusher) is distinct from the Servant (The Crushed). One God cannot be both victim and victor.

Jeremiah 23:6 (Jehovah our Righteousness) .... See Vol 3
Symbolic name for the King. The city of Jerusalem bears the exact same name in Jer 33:16.

Daniel 3:25 (Like the Son of God) .... See Vol 3
A pagan king sees an Angel ("a son of the gods"). No pagan knew of a "second person of the Trinity."

Daniel 7:13 (Son of Man Approach) .... See Vol 3
The Son of Man *approaches* the Ancient of Days. Two distinct figures in space and authority.

Micah 5:2 (From Everlasting) .... See Vol 3
Hebrew *olam*: "Ancient Times." Refers to the Messiah's ancient ancestry (David), not eternal age.

Zechariah 12:10 (Look on Me/Pierced) .... See Vol 3
Textual variant. John 19:37 quotes it as "Look on HIM," distinguishing Yahweh from the pierced victim.

The New Testament (Gospels – Volume IVa)

Matthew 20:23 (Limit of Authority) 136
Jesus explicitly denies having the authority to assign positions in the **Kingdom**, deferring that power solely to the **Father**. **Omnipotence** cannot be limited.

Matthew 27:46 (The Forsaken Cry) 162
God cannot forsake *Himself*. The cry of abandonment proves the **Sufferer** and the **Recipient** of the prayer are two distinct beings.

Matthew 28:19 (Baptism Formula) 165
Likely a liturgical addition. Acts records baptism strictly "in the name of Jesus." No Trinity formula used.

Mark 10:18 (None Good but God) 198
Jesus denies the ultimate title *Good*, deferring it to the **Father** alone. **God** cannot deny His own goodness.

Mark 12:29 (The Shema) 205
Jesus defines *The Lord* as **One**. He never redefines **God** as *Three*. He stands with **Jewish Monotheism**.

Mark 13:32 (The Son Doesn't Know) 209
Logic: **God** is **Omniscient**. Jesus was not. Therefore, Jesus is not **God**. (The *God-Man* theory splits his mind).

Luke 2:52 (Grew in Wisdom) 232
God implies perfection. **Growth** implies incompleteness. Jesus grew; therefore he was not already **God**.

Luke 22:42 (Not My Will) 300
Two separate wills (**Father** vs. **Son**) prove two separate persons. **One God** cannot have opposing minds.

John 1:1 (The Word was God) 313
Qualitative Greek (*theos*, no article). **The Word** was divine/god-like. Not *Ho Theos* (The Father).

John 4:22 (We Worship) 322
Jesus includes himself among those who worship the **Father**. **God** does not worship.

John 5:19 (Son Does Nothing) 326
Total dependency. **Jesus** can do nothing of himself. **Omnipotence** cannot be dependent.

John 8:17 (The Law of Two Men) 337
Jesus invokes the legal requirement for *two* distinct witnesses, defining himself as the first **Man** and the **Father** as the second.

John 8:58 (Before Abraham, I am) 340
Common speech (*I am he*). The blind man says the exact same phrase in John 9:9. Not a divine title.

John 10:30 (I and the Father are One) 345
Greek *hen* (neuter: *one thing/purpose*), not *heis* (masculine: *one person*). Unity of mission.

John 14:28 (Father is Greater) 358
Greater describes position and nature. **Co-equal** persons cannot be greater/lesser.

John 17:3 (Only True God) 363
Jesus defines **Monotheism**: The **Father** is the *Only* (*monos*) **True God**. Jesus is the sent **Messiah**.

John 20:17 (My God) 374
The **Risen Jesus** has a **God**. The **Supreme Being** has no **God**. Distinction is eternal.

John 20:28 (My Lord and my God) 375
Thomas sees the **Father's** authority *in* the **Son**. Jesus is the visual representative of the invisible **God**.

The New Testament (Acts–Rev – Volume IVb)

Acts 2:22 (Man Approved of God) ....See Vol 4b
The first Christian sermon defines Jesus as "a Man approved of God," not "God the Son."

Acts 2:36 (God made him Lord) ....See Vol 4b
Jesus is a *made* Lord. Yahweh is the Uncreated Lord.

Acts 3:13 (His Servant Jesus) ....See Vol 4b
Peter calls Jesus the "Servant" (*pais*) of the God of Abraham. God is not the servant of God.

Acts 17:28 (We are His Offspring) ....See Vol 4b
God is the Father of all creation. We are his offspring; Jesus is the firstborn of this family.

Romans 5:15 (The One Man) ....See Vol 4b
The type (Adam) was human. The anti-type (Jesus) must be human to reverse the curse.

Romans 9:5 (God Blessed Forever) .... See Vol 4b
A doxology to the Father. Punctuation (added by translators) determines meaning.

1 Cor 8:6 (One God the Father) .... See Vol 4b
The Christian Shema: One God (Father) and One Lord (Jesus). Two distinct beings, two distinct titles.

1 Cor 11:3 (Head of Christ is God) .... See Vol 4b
Eternal hierarchy. Even in heaven, God is the "Head" (Authority) over Christ.

1 Cor 15:28 (Son Subjected) .... See Vol 4b
The End Game: The Son steps down and hands the Kingdom to the Father, remaining subject forever.

Ephesians 1:17 (God of our Lord) .... See Vol 4b
Even in glory, Jesus has a God. Paul prays to the "God of Jesus."

Philippians 2:6 (Equality with God) .... See Vol 4b
Contrast with Adam. Adam tried to seize equality; Jesus refused to grasp it, choosing servanthood.

Colossians 1:16 (All things created) .... See Vol 4b
Prepositions: Created *Through* (*dia*) him, not *By* (*ek*) him. He is the Instrument, not the Source.

Colossians 2:9 (Fullness of Deity) .... See Vol 4b
Analogy: If water fills a glass, the glass does not become water. God fills Jesus; Jesus is the vessel.

1 Timothy 2:5 (One Mediator) .... See Vol 4b
A mediator stands *between* two parties. Jesus is the Man standing between us and the One God.

1 Timothy 3:16 (God manifest in flesh) .... See Vol 4b
FORGERY. Oldest MSS read "He who was manifested." Scribes altered "ΟC" (He) to "θC" (God).

Titus 2:13 (Great God and Savior) .... See Vol 4b
Grammar allows two subjects. "The Great God [Father] AND our Savior [Jesus]." Consistent with 1 Tim 2:5.

Hebrews 1:8 (Thy Throne O God) .... See Vol 4b
Or: "God is thy throne." If addressed as "god," it is the functional title for the King (Ps 45:6).

Hebrews 4:15 (Jesus was Tempted) .... See Vol 4b
God cannot be tempted (James 1:13). Jesus was tempted. Logic: He is not God.

Hebrews 5:8 (Learned Obedience) .... See Vol 4b
Omniscience cannot "learn." Perfection cannot "mature." Jesus did both.

James 1:13 (God cannot be tempted) .... See Vol 4b
The Axiom: Temptability proves non-deity. Jesus was temptable.

1 John 5:7 (The Three Witnesses) .... See Vol 4b
FORGERY. The "Johannine Comma." Absent from all Greek MSS before the 1400s.

Revelation 1:1 (God gave to Jesus) .... See Vol 4b
The source of revelation is God. The recipient is Jesus. You cannot give revelation to yourself.

Revelation 1:8 (Alpha and Omega) .... See Vol 4b
Context: "The Lord God" (The Almighty/Father) is speaking. Verified by v4 ("Him who is").

Revelation 1:11 (I am Alpha and Omega) .... See Vol 4b
FORGERY. KJV addition not found in older manuscripts (RV/NASB omit it).

Revelation 3:12 (My God x4) .... See Vol 4b
The highest Christology in the Bible: The exalted Jesus still calls the Father "My God" four times.

12-Page Personal Study Journal

12-Page Personal Study Journal

12-Page Personal Study Journal

A Final Word to the Reader

You have reached the end of this volume, but we hope you have reached the beginning of a clearer understanding.

It has been the singular purpose of this edition to clear away the accumulation of centuries—the traditions, the confusing terminologies, and the scribal additions—so that you might see the Scriptures as they were originally written.

Our hope is not that you simply became smarter about Greek grammar or historical theology. Our hope is that by cleaning the lens, you were able to see the subject more clearly: the One True God, Yahweh, and His human Son, Jesus our Lord.

The Scriptures are not merely a text to be studied; they are a Covenant to be obeyed. Now that the terms are clear, the mandate is yours.

> "And this is life eternal, that they should know thee the only true God, and him whom thou didst send, even Jesus Christ."
> (John 17:3)

— The Editor —